100 Essential
Silent Film Comedies

100 Essential
Silent Film Comedies

James Roots

ROWMAN & LITTLEFIELD
Lanham • Boulder • New York • London

Published by Rowman & Littlefield
A wholly owned subsidary of The Rowman & Littlefield Publishing Group, Inc.
4501 Forbes Boulevard, Suite 200, Lanham, Maryland 20706
www.rowman.com

Unit A, Whitacre Mews, 26-34 Stannary Street, London SE11 4AB

British Library Cataloguing in Publication Information Available

Library of Congress Cataloging-in-Publication Data

Names: Roots, James, 1955– author.
Title: 100 essential silent film comedies / James Roots.
Other titles: One hundred essential silent film comedies
Description: Lanham : Rowman & Littlefield, 2017. | Includes bibliographical
  references and index.
Identifiers: LCCN 2016052684 (print) | LCCN 2017008440 (ebook) | ISBN
  9781442278240 (hardcover : alk. paper) | ISBN 9781442278257 (electronic)
Subjects: LCSH: Comedy films—Catalogs. | Comedy films—Evaluation. | Silent
  films—Catalogs. | Silent films—Evaluation.
Classification: LCC PN1995.9.C55 R66 2017 (print) | LCC PN1995.9.C55 (ebook)
  | DDC 016.79143/617—dc23
LC record available at https://lccn.loc.gov/2016052684

♾™ The paper used in this publication meets the minimum requirements of
American National Standard for Information Sciences—Permanence of Paper
for Printed Library Materials, ANSI/NISO Z39.48-1992.

Printed in the United States of America

Contents

Acknowledgments

This is my opportunity to profusely apologize to Steve Rydzewski for failing to credit him as the supplier of two photographs in *The 100 Greatest Silent Film Comedians*—one of Al St. John (page 263) and another of Paddy McGuire, Ben Turpin, and "unknown" (page 379). These were both generously provided by Steve, and I am grateful to him for his support and his cheerful patience in awaiting proper credit.

As with my earlier book, I had confidently relied upon Robert S. Birchard to supply me with the vast majority of photos for this book. Only ten weeks before my deadline, unthinkably, Bob died. His collection has been tied up as a consequence, and I was unable to acquire anywhere close to the 100 photos I wanted. Bob was one of the greatest keepers of the flame of silent films; he is keenly missed now, and he will be profoundly missed for many years to come.

I would like to thank those who were able to help with photos from their own collections: Bruce Calvert, Derek Boothroyd, Ben Model (Undercrank Productions), Claudia Sassen, Steve Massa, and once again, Steve Rydzewski.

Information about casts, crews, and histories of the films discussed in this book was collected from the best sources; that is to say, not from the IMDb or Wikipedia, but from Brent Walker's *Mack Sennett's Fun Factory* (2010), Robert Klepper's *Silent Films 1877–1996* (1999), Robert Connelly's *The Silents: Silent Feature Films 1910–1936* (1998), Ephraim Katz's *The Film Encyclopedia* (various editions), Leonard Maltin's various movie guides and his books on Our Gang and movie comedy teams, Glenn Mitchell's various encyclopedias, Kalton Lahue's books, and many other publications by the likes of David Robinson, Anthony Slide, Tom Dardis, Jeffrey Vance, Richard M. Roberts, and so on, not to mention the American Film Institute (AFI) catalogue compiled largely by Bob Birchard. I verified listings and credits from these publications against the evidence of my own eyes in watching my copies of the films; I have at least one copy of every film listed herein except three, which I watched on YouTube: *Fireman, Save My Gal!* (1919, George Ovey), *Jerry's Mother-in-Law* (1913, Sidney Drew), and *Madame Behave!* (1925, Julian Eltinge).

Introduction

My previous book was all about ranking the greatest silent film comedians on a scale of 1 to 100 in descending order. To provide some semi-objective legitimacy to the rankings that would hopefully take them beyond the level of mere personal opinion, I devised a scorecard that rated each comedian on the basis of funniness, creativity, teamwork, timelessness, appeal, and intangibles. This provided a quasi-scientific structure to justify calling Charlie Chaplin and Buster Keaton joint numbers 1, and Cliff Bowes sole number 100. It justified some rankings that boggled a few readers, those who thought I was nuts to crown Phyllis Haver number 12—actually tied for number 11—while denigrating the revered Ben Turpin as number 29, Snub Pollard as number 49, and Lloyd Hamilton as number 31.

The resultant book, pointedly titled *The 100 Greatest Silent Film Comedians*, fairly compared apples with apples and could therefore use the superlative "greatest" to decide among them.

For the book you are now reading, I intend to compare apples with oranges, bananas, and raspberries. (I leave it to you to figure out which film matches up with which fruit.) That is, all of the films in this book would be comedies, but they would be of various lengths, various styles, various epochs, and even various countries.

When you do this, you cannot really build a fair structure of comparison. What structure could reasonably evaluate a 70-second practical joke such as *The Biter Bit* (1900) against a 70-minute complex slapstick feature such as *The Gold Rush* (1925), let alone a 90-minute swashbuckling adventure such as *The Mark of Zorro* (1920)? On what grounds can you force a Méliès magician comedy from 1898 to stack up against a 1932 Japanese social-reality comedy like *I Was Born, But . . .* ?

Since it is impossible to devise a rational chart of comparison, I couldn't in all conscience call this book *The 100 Greatest Silent Film Comedies*. It would have made sense to call it *100 Great Silent Film Comedies*, but that feels too nondescript. Compromise led to the title of *100 Essential Silent Film Comedies*.

Not all of the films included herein rank among the "greatest." I think all of them are terrific in at least one way or another, if not entirely "great" all the way through. If the goal is to provide you with guidance as to which silent comedies you really ought to see—a bucket list, if you will—then "essential" is closest to being the right word to use.

I confess, though, that even "essential" is a term that troubles me. And I will point to the one movie that exemplifies the difficulty: *Tillie's Punctured Romance*

(1914). This is supposedly the first feature-length comedy film ever made (the more cautious historians add the qualifier: "in Hollywood"), and as such, it has always been classified as an "essential" inclusion in any kind of film history. You can no more leave it out of the silent movie narrative than you can leave out *The Birth of a Nation* (1915).

Well, I've left it out.

And not just to prove the rebel in me isn't dead yet.

This is a book about comedy films, and I'm a purist about comedy: it's got to make me *laugh*, dammit! A comedy film that doesn't make me laugh is a lousy comedy film, and a lousy comedy film by its very nature cannot be an "essential" comedy film.

Tillie's Punctured Romance is one of the worst films ever made, comedy or otherwise. It stars about a million silent clowns, nearly every one of whom I love and enjoy, and was made by Mack Sennett, whom I proudly claim as a countryman. It's the film that made Charlie Chaplin a star—or, rather, it elevated him from star status to megastar status. And it doesn't give me one solid laugh.

I get about three half-smiles out of it. One is the sight of ten liveried servants in the house of "Millionaire Banks" trying to look busy by repeatedly dusting the edge of one picture frame and making the tiniest adjustment to the position of a sofa cushion (there were actually five servants, but Sennett filmed them in two rooms to make it look double the number). The second half-smile is when Chaplin, desperate to get married to "Tillie" as fast as possible, grabs the first available "holy book" and shoves it into the hands of the minister: it's a tattered phone book.

The third half-smile comes from Chaplin falling backward off a bench at the social party; that half-smile, though, gets acid thrown on it by Chaplin and Chester Conklin repeating the fall seven times between them—which raises another of the reasons I find *Tillie's Punctured Romance* unworthy of inclusion in this book: its appalling repetitiveness. In a two-reeler or a one-reeler, you don't have enough time to repeat a gag more than once, maybe twice if you put a different comic spin on the third go-round. Mack Sennett made *Tillie* as six self-contained one-reelers, or at best, three two-reelers. He filled the extra time by running the same gags over and over again. Don't believe me? Okay, I actually counted the number of times someone got kicked in the butt, either by another person or by a swinging door (in the scene where "Tillie" is a restaurant waitress). It happens ten times in the first reel alone, sixteen times in the first two reels, *thirty-five* times in the entire movie.

There are movies I have included in this book for historical reasons; they all had to pass the laugh test, though. *The Biter Bit* (1900) wasn't exactly fresh and original even for its own era (it was a remake of a remake), but it still gets one laugh, and since it's a one-minute film built entirely around getting that one laugh, it's a winner. *Tillie* simply doesn't pass the laugh test.

There are other no-shows in this book—or rather, *not* in this book—that will surprise a lot of people: *The Kid* (1921), *The Gold Rush* (1925), *Big Business* (1929), *Hands Up!* (1926), and so on. In most cases, I have written explanations for leaving out these great films and choosing other great films instead.

Look, it could have been very simple: 15 films by Chaplin, 15 films by Keaton, 10 films by Laurel and Hardy, 10 films by Lloyd, and *bang!* we're halfway through the book already and I've only covered four artists (counting Laurel and Hardy as one). Where does that leave room to present you with a real palette of silent comedy films?

What I've given you instead are 70 or more starring comedians, from George Ovey to Mary Pickford. Wait a minute, that's only one letter apart; let's say, rather, from Frank Alexander to Harry Watson Jr. There are others who would have been included in a comprehensive encyclopedia of silent comedians but who couldn't cut the mustard here, people like "Ham and Bud," Wallace Beery (he's here only in a bit role in *A Clever Dummy*), André Deed, Joe Rock, Alice Day, Glenn Tryon, Billy Dooley, several other guys named either Billy or Johnny, Clyde Cook, and maybe even my personal sleep-inducer, Billy West.

Even after eliminating these clowns, I still had to set other limits on what to include. There is no animation here; that is not one of my strong areas. There are no avant-garde experimental films: mostly they aren't funny, at least in the silent era, and while I own a couple of hundred of them, it's not a field of intensive study for me. I included a few foreign films; they are more of a representative selection than a comprehensive one.

If you count the films for which I've given mini-reviews or references, you'll find I've actually recommended more than 400 movies for your viewing pleasure.

And so I repeat: this is not a book of the "greatest" silent comedies, nor does it attempt to rank them. It's a book of films that made me laugh and that ought to make you laugh, too. And laughter is *essential* to life.

Lastly, a word—okay, a paragraph—about the sequencing. I would have preferred to have listed the 100 films in chronological order; it would have been interesting to observe the growth in sophistication and stylishness (not just style) of silent comedy from the turn of the century to the onslaught of the talkies. Alphabetical order was visited upon me instead. This has created a bit of a concern for me in the case of comedians who have more than one starring vehicle in this book. I have provided background information for each film in order to put it in a historical context; alphabetical sequencing of the films means that the biographies of Chaplin, Fairbanks, even Reginald Denny, spread out over more than one entry, are not recited in chronological order. I hope this will prove to be only a minor inconvenience.

Silent comedies have kept us laughing joyfully for 90-odd years since their official demise. My hope is that this book will inspire you to seek out as many as possible and to enjoy them as much as I have.

Some Notes
about the Entries

I seem to have a bit of a phobia about filmographies (filmographobia?): I can never bring myself to do a complete listing of cast and crew for any film, in any of my books. In this tome, I have included nearly all of the credited cast members for each movie, and in several cases I spotted uncredited actors whom most filmographies don't even credit for their uncredited performance (usually it was Dick Sutherland!). When it came to the crew, however, I limited myself to the directors, writers, camera operators, and editors. This is not to deny the importance of other crew members. The fact is that in the silent era, lighting directors and set designers and makeup artists did not receive credits, even in feature films, at least until the 1920s. I felt it would be more consistent to identify only the four positions that were most often credited. If an entry does not cite a camera operator or an editor, that means I couldn't establish that information.

Sometimes I have listed the number of reels to indicate the length of a film; sometimes I have listed the minutes in length; sometimes I have listed both. The objective here is to give the reader a pretty solid idea of how long a film runs. Since the cameras of the time were hand cranked and the projection speed was at the whim of the exhibitor, actual running times vary. Also impacting on length is the current condition of available elements; there are countless silent movies that were originally edited to 24 minutes but less than 24 minutes survive today. This is why a film listed at six reels might run only 47 minutes in available versions.

Silent films were produced and distributed by a bewildering variety of companies, some of which changed names frequently, or flipped from producing to distributing and vice versa, or merged with other companies and issued films under their combined names. There are researchers who specialize in tracing the convulsions of these companies; I leave the field to them with great respect, and I endeavor only to indicate at least one company that was involved in the production and/or distribution of each film in this book.

In the synopses, I have put quote marks around the names of the characters in the film. This is to distinguish the character from the performer. Most of the silent comedians used their real first name in their films; without utilizing quote marks, it can be awkward for a writer to make a point about the character "Harry" or "Charlie" and not have the reader assume he is referring to the actor Harry Langdon or Charlie Murray, as the case may be. You can call me overcautious, but I like clarity.

The availability of a film or short on DVD or VHS (if not available on DVD) will be indicated. Bear in mind that films go out of print without notice, but once a title has been produced on DVD or VHS, it can be obtained through some means, whether purchased directly through a vendor or available for rental from a library or some other resource. Amazon has many titles available on Instant Video and they are likely to continue adding scarce titles that might not make it to a DVD, but I have not indicated these. Most, if not all, titles listed as VHS are only available through vendors selling used copies. On the other hand, many companies (Warner Archive Collection, MGM Limited Edition Collection, Universal Archives, for example) are now producing DVDs on demand, making many more titles available than they might have otherwise. I have indicated the most common—and in most cases, only—manufacturer of each title in parentheses after the format. If "no availability" is indicated, don't be discouraged, since it's possible that the film or short title may be released in the future.

A

ALL NIGHT

(1918, Universal)

Director: Paul Powell
Writer: Fred Myton (Edgar Franklin)
Cast: Carmel Myers, Rudolph Valentino, Charles Dorian, Mary Warren, William
   Dyer, Wadsworth Harris, Jack Hull
Running Time (Length): 57 minutes (approximately five reels) in surviving print
Availability: DVD (Grapevine Video)

Background: In 1918 Rudolph Valentino was still essentially an unknown quality; his breakout role in *The Four Horsemen of the Apocalypse* was six years in the future, and it was not yet certain how to fit him into one of the crystalized types that Hollywood preferred to assign its performers. The obvious Italianness of his name didn't necessary identify him as a Latin lover or a Mediterranean villain, although both of those stereotypes were tested. He was attractive enough in an oily way (or maybe it was just his hair that seemed excessively greased) to put him in matinee idol contention, but as a fairly novice actor he first had to pay his dues in supporting roles before he could get a chance to challenge Francis X. Bushman in the romantic-leading-man sweepstakes. His pinched features and serious, wary default facial expression did not instantly suggest comedy might be a natural fit for his screen presentation.

In *All Night*, his role is uncharacteristic of what we have come to typecast as a Valentino role. He's apparently an all-American "boy" (he was 23 years old at the time), with no suggestion of foreignness or exoticism. Far from being the suave, worldly wise sophisticate who was comfortable in any situation, he's agonizingly shy, a handsome yet pallid wallflower easily pushed aside by the more self-assured playboys of society in the pursuit of available females. The future aggressive seducer of swooning womenfolk is here a prude who covers his pajamaed body in outraged (virginal?) horror when inadvertently exposed to the girl for whom he yearns. He plays the comedy completely straight-faced and wholeheartedly, not displaying the toothy leer that turns *The Son of the Sheik* into unintentional comic farce at its most scandalous moments. It is one of the most accomplished performances of an actor whose genuine talent became a bloated feedbag for wild-eyed exaggeration in his future peak.

Synopsis: Trading places was a Hollywood staple long, long, *long* before the 1983 film with Dan Aykroyd and Eddie Murphy. With servant roles involved, it was a reliable plot twist in probably hundreds of silent comedies; Laurel and Hardy alone used it in at least four films made later than *All Night*. What makes *All Night* a little different is that the switch is not simply the masters in place of the servants; it is the additional switch of the friends in place of the masters.

Timid wallflower Valentino (probably the only time those three words have been used together without irony) asks his friends (Dorian and Warren) to invite Myers, the apple of his eye, to a dinner at their house, so that he can casually drop in and grab the chance to corner her into agreeing to a date with him. Dorian is depending upon a windfall investment from a rich client that will make his newly acquired copper mine glow with success. His eavesdropping servants interpret this to mean they won't be getting their wages because Dorian is on the verge of bankruptcy; they demand to be paid and are peremptorily fired as a non-cash bonus.

Unluckily for Dorian, his would-be sugar daddy chooses that evening to drop in for a visit, on the grounds that seeing how a potential partner conducts his household affairs is a mirror for how he conducts his business affairs. On the only mildly convincing theory that Dorian and Warren know their own house better than Valentino and Myers do, the masters replace the departed servants while the guests replace the masters in order to fool the magnate.

That same magnate wastes no time in displaying his personal boorishness, bossiness, and nosiness, bragging about his interference in other people's private lives as a tool of micromanagement for which he refuses to apologize. What this entails is his forcibly undressing Valentino and dumping him into the bed that Myers must share with him as his alleged wife. While those two circle squeamishly about each other in *déshabillé*—remember, they haven't even had a date together yet, let alone been legally married—Dyer lavishes hypocrisy by ordering manservant Dorian to give up *his* wife to Dyer's carnal appetites without hesitation.

Spicing up the mixture is Myers's father, who has every intention of enforcing his paterfamilias dictate that she must be home by 11:00 p.m. Barging into Dorian's house to extract her forcibly therefrom, he gets played-off Dyer by the desperate conniving of the two young couples, resulting in a rumble between two angry old coots that is sure to end up in financial disaster and reputational Armageddon. Until, of course, it doesn't.

Comment: Valentino and Carmel Myers work together well and fluidly without actually displaying chemistry. They more or less played a similar team in *A Society Sensation* (also 1918), but any thoughts of building them up into the new Mr. and Mrs. Sidney Drew dissipated within the same year. Myers is attractive but uncharismatic; in this film, it is only when supporting actress Mary Warren dons a maid's uniform that the viewer can tell the two actresses apart, and in no scene does Myers's presence leap off the screen. She went on to have a long career, much of it incongruously playing sexy vamps; after that archetype became a thing of derision, she played mostly in small or supporting roles with the occasional showy sashay in big-ticket items such as *Ben-Hur* (1925), *Beau Brummel* (1924), and Lon Chaney's *Tell It to the Marines* (1926).

One would expect a lot of "cute" bits in a social comedy about trading places; it is quite a pleasant surprise to find instead a more adult sheen overriding the nonsense. Dorian is terrific and believable as the flailing young would-be millionaire in the sequence in which his anxiety about his financial situation gets ignited into a hysterical explosion of immature rage and he fires his staff on the spot. Myers and Warren are both levelheaded women trying to think for their menfolk as well as for the preservation of their own sexual morality; they are very far from being airhead bimbos fluttering helplessly in expectation that their men will obligingly pull their feet out of the fire.

In showing *All Night* to a modern audience, it is important to make that audience cognizant (in advance) of the morality of the first half of the twentieth century. Unless they understand that even a married woman couldn't be expected to glimpse her own husband in his underwear without fainting from outraged virtue, let alone that an unmarried couple should share the same bed (even fully clothed), the film's key comedy thread of Valentino and Myers being forced to go and sleep together loses its entire premise; the audience, if it laughs at all, will laugh merely at the "stupidity" of the situation and wonder aloud why Valentino and Myers don't just jump in and go at it like rabbits.

On the other hand, if the audience is primed to understand the old morals, *All Night* will give them a lot of laughs. It's a fun picture.

Bonus: William Dyer's performance as the uncouth, bullying financier from the lawless Midwest (Hollywood appeared to think Montana was a small town somewhere in either Texas or Nevada) is quite a tour de force. He takes a one-dimensional caricature of the rowdy, loudmouthed, power-grasping tycoon and makes him a consistent, credible, and still comic buffoon bent on controlling every aspect of the lives of those under and beside him. He can't help himself: it's the way he makes certain of coining profits instead of losing his shirt on his high-risk mining ventures. True, he is overbearing at times and you wish he would get off the screen more frequently so the four youngsters can advance the plot; and at just that moment, he will flip to his other, slimier side and make us laugh uncomfortably at his pursuit of illicit lust with Warren. He keeps us in unbalanced amusement.

ALL NIGHT LONG

(1924, Mack Sennett)

Director: Harry Edwards
Writers: Vernon Smith, Hal Conklin
Camera: Billy Williams, Leland Davis
Editor: William Hornbeck
Cast: Harry Langdon, Vernon Dent, Natalie Kingston, Billy Gilbert, Fanny Kelly, Leo Sulky, Andy Clyde, Vance Veith
Running Time (Length): Two reels
Availability: DVD (Facets: *Lost and Found: The Harry Langdon Collection*)

Background: Few silent comedians are as divisive as Harry Langdon. There are no opinions between the two extremes of "boring, too slow, too stupid, creepiest comic in film history" and "absolutely hilarious, brilliantly constructed, unforgettable character." Probably 80 percent of silent comedy lovers, and at least 98 percent of all other film fans, fall into the first camp. Yet even his haters routinely rank Langdon the fourth-, or at worst, fifth-greatest silent film comedian of all time. I love the guy, but I ranked him sixth in my book *The 100 Greatest Silent Film Comedians*, and not just as a concession to the deeply rooted repulsion with which so many viewers regard him. He's a comedian with some quite serious drawbacks.

He squandered an unbelievable 20 years performing only two acts in vaudeville, and didn't make the move into films until he was forty years old. After a trio of D.O.A. films for Sol Lesser that have all disappeared except for four minutes of mediocrity, Mack Sennett signed him and had no idea what to do with him. That was standard operating procedure for Sennett: he also hadn't known what to do with Charlie Chaplin, Sydney Chaplin, Mabel Normand, Harold Lloyd, Charley Chase, and practically all other comedians he had signed up other than Roscoe Arbuckle and Ford Sterling. He recognized great talent, that's all, and left it to his underlings to figure out what might work for Langdon.

The myth created by Frank Capra and perpetuated by everybody else (including Sennett) was that Langdon only found his way when the self-sainted Capra took charge of him. But that didn't happen until 1925 (*Plain Clothes*); Langdon made 15 shorts for Sennett before that happened, and almost every one of those 15 (two or three are lost) contains at least some moments of excellence, and a handful of them are among the best and funniest films "the Little Elf" ever made, which means they are among the best and funniest films ever made in the silent era. *All Night Long* is one of these.

Synopsis: In an interestingly odd prelude—a modern viewer might trace its lineage down to *The Simpsons*'s modern-era conceit of approaching its storyline from an out-of-left-field introductory sequence—Langdon wakes up in an emptied movie theater, attempts to find his way out in the dark, bumbles upon a robbery in progress, and discovers the head thief is none other than his old army buddy, Vernon Dent. They settle down (in the middle of the theft!) to reminisce, and the film becomes a flashback to the Great War.

Humble Private Langdon falls for Sergeant Dent's ooh-la-la French village girlfriend, Natalie Kingston. Who wouldn't? Dent's efforts to eliminate Langdon as his rival-in-love end up getting the latter promoted above him to the rank of lieutenant, while Dent himself ends up in the stockade. This humiliation, presumably, ignited the spiral that ended up with Dent's current occupation of civilian thief. Remembering that they are indeed currently in the midst of a robbery, the two old pals manage to blow themselves up in camaraderie, and find they will be nursed back to health by Harry's wife, the delectable Ms. Kingston, now Mrs. Harry and the mother of children named in honor of the brave soldiers.

Comment: Langdon has so many beautiful bits of comedy in this film, it would take pages to rhapsodize about all of them. He peels a mountain of potatoes, consoled by a letter in which his boneheaded stateside girlfriend tells him she is proud of his "promotion to KP." He does everything he can think of (which isn't much) to wangle the extremely reluctant Dent's invitation to dinner with Kingston. He tries to confiscate the best parts of the chicken dinner. He gets a kiss from her that knocks him out of a window and inspires him to rip up the photograph of the American girlfriend. He tries to avoid getting killed when Dent maliciously assigns him to a battlefield suicide post. And so many others. . . . It's a wonderful performance and foreshadows the best of the feature comedies to which he would soon be graduating. And for those who find him revolting, *All Night Long* displays him at his least creepy.

Bonus: This was only the second film in which Langdon was paired with Vernon Dent; the previous teaming, quite fleeting, was in his first film, *Picking Peaches* (1924). Their chemistry was so beautiful and seamless and obvious, they were put together in eight of the next eleven shorts Langdon made, and again in one feature film, *His First Flame* (1927, but filmed two years earlier) and in his last silent short, *Fiddlesticks* (likewise filmed in 1925 but released in 1927).

Teaming a fat straight man or supporting man with a thin lead comic was nothing new. Oliver Hardy made a career of it beginning in 1913 in a series with the telltale tagline of "Plump and Runt." Roscoe Arbuckle, who entered films in 1908, graduated to stardom in the same year as Hardy when he started being paired with the petite Mabel Normand. "Ham and Bud" films featured tall, husky Lloyd Hamilton with Bud Duncan, who was the same size as Danny DeVito. The *Mutt and Jeff* comic strip was animated in many films. Short, slim Buster Keaton had burly Joe Roberts; short, slim Charlie Chaplin had mammoth Eric Campbell; short, slim Larry Semon had the balloon-like Frank Alexander; and every skinny comic had portly Bud Jamison.

Yet Langdon and Dent were arguably the first big-and-small pairing in silent comedy films to be a true *team*. Dent had to have been one of the smartest men in movies: he learned from everything he undertook, and used those lessons to instantly fit his performance to that of his costars. He started in 1919 with Hank Mann and Larry Semon, soaked up valuable understanding of comedy performance from his own failed attempt at stardom, and then smoothly flowed his skills into the comic styles of everybody from Ben Turpin to Billy Bevan to Monty Collins, and on into the talkies where he supported a random list of stars from Judy Garland to Bob Hope to the Three Stooges—a testimony to his limitless versatility. In the end, he made more than four hundred films, and the best partner he ever had was Harry Langdon.

Aside from real affection—they became lifelong friends offscreen—there are two factors that made them so good together. One was Dent's brilliance at providing a setting through which Langdon's comedy could shine all the brighter; he wasn't just supporting Langdon, he was providing a black-velvet spread that enabled the latter to really glitter. They weren't equal comedians the way Laurel and Hardy (and *only* Laurel and Hardy) were because Langdon was clearly the lead funnyman; but Dent was not just his partner, he was Langdon's onscreen *director*, too.

The other factor was the way their moral natures shook hands and hugged one another. Langdon's character was a tabula rasa infant without moral distinctions or compass: he was pre-moral. Dent's character was likewise neither moral nor immoral: he was amoral. In *His Marriage Wow* (1925), his dark machinations were the work of insanity, not immorality; in *Lucky Stars* (1925), his cons were a desperate man's attempts to earn a living, not evil principles; in *Saturday Afternoon* (1926), he's just a working stiff determined to have a good time—morals never enter the equation for him. In each case, Dent's flexible motivations and principles cozy up neatly to Langdon's clueless plasticity: there's no good versus bad, as there always is with Abbott and Costello, no straight arrow versus bend-all-the-rules as there always is with every more-recent matchup in buddy comedies (e.g., straight-arrow Dan Aykroyd with Eddie Murphy, or with Tom Hanks, or with almost anyone else in any buddy movie Aykroyd ever made). Pre-morality and amorality make a natural couple. Langdon and Dent were the only team to take this route, and that makes them as unique as Laurel and Hardy.

B

THE BATTLE OF THE CENTURY

(1927, Roach)

Director: Clyde Bruckman
Writer: Hal Roach
Titles: H. M. Walker
Camera: George Stevens
Editor: Richard Currier
Cast: Stan Laurel, Oliver Hardy, Noah Young, Sam Lufkin, Charlie Hall, Dick
   Gilbert, Dick Sutherland, George French, Eugene Pallette, Lyle Tayo, Anita Garvin,
   Dorothy Coburn, Charlie Young, Ellinor Van Der Veer
Running Time (Length): Two reels
Availability: VHS (Image Entertainment)

Background: Laurel and Hardy's fifteenth film together, although only their fifth as the team of the century (excluding their bit roles in *Call of the Cuckoo* a couple of months earlier), *The Battle of the Century* attained instant legendary status for the massive pie fight that takes up most of the second reel. An entire day's baking, totaling 3,000 pies, was demolished, practically every one of them hilariously.

Synopsis: Laurel is perhaps the most unprepossessing prizefighter in history, and the awesomely muscled Noah Young proves why. Depressed by vanishing visions of lucrative title fights, manager Oliver Hardy, not exactly the Don King of the Twenties, resorts to insurance fraud in an attempt to extract at least some profit out of his slack-armed slugger. Signing on for a policy that will pay him nicely if Laurel gets hurt outside the ring, Hardy immediately begins scattering banana peels on the sidewalk as if they were rose petals on a bridal aisle. Evidently, he has seen a slapstick comedy or two. After the requisite accidental slip-up by a cop, the last victim of peeling is pie vendor Charlie Hall. Hall's effort at revenge for losing his tray ignites the pie fight to end all pie fights. It culminates with the exquisitely sexy Anita Garvin slipping and dumping her delicious derriere into an equally delicious pie on the sidewalk, gingerly getting to her feet, and slowly stepping away, with a subtle shake of the leg in a futile attempt to dislodge a bit of mischievously located custard.

Comment: In 1965, director Blake Edwards made an epic-scale comedy called *The Great Race*, which he opened with a dedication to Laurel and Hardy and ended with a brazen attempt to outdo their famous pie fight. Whatever one thinks of the rest of the film, virtually everyone panned the pie fight, and not just out of reverence for "The Boys." Edwards did everything wrong that Laurel and Hardy (and supervisor Leo McCarey) did right. He let it run on and on and on; Laurel and Hardy's fight takes up a fair chunk of their film, but they kept it brisk so that it seems short and you're left wanting much more. Edwards showed nearly all of his isolated tosses in the same brain-dead throw-and-catch-with-the-face manner; Laurel and Hardy set nearly every isolated toss in unique, imaginative settings—a dental office, a dowager's sedan, a mailbox, a would-be peacemaker in the middle of the chaos—so that the variety and creativity kept everything lively and each new toss was fresh. Edwards had no idea how to pace or end the fight; Laurel and Hardy audaciously brought everything to a dead stop at one point (the peacemaker's intervention) and came up with the wonderful ending focusing on Anita Garvin.

Garvin claimed she did her little walk-on on her lunch break, and later in life was bemused that this simple (but perfectly, skilfully executed) ten-second bit, in which she is only seen from behind, made her immortal among comedy legends. Regardless of what she thinks, she earned it.

Bonus: For decades, only the pie fight survived of this film, and even that scene survived only in a slightly truncated form spliced together by Robert Youngson for his compilation *The Golden Age of Comedy* (1958). Bits and pieces were recovered starting around 1979, and by 2015 nearly all of it had been found again. About 90 percent of it now survives, with, unfortunately, the pivotal insurance scene being most of the still-unfound 10 percent. The general feeling among those who have seen the restored version is that the pie fight is by far the highlight, but you didn't need to be a classic film maven to have figured that out even without seeing the first reel.

The boxing sequence was intended to satirize the Jack Dempsey–Gene Tunney "long count" championship bout of 1927. However tame it might appear to us in the 21st century, it surely hit the perfect funny bone among audiences for whom the bout was still only three months old, fresh and burning in the memory.

The pie fight was likewise preconceived as a deliberate satire, this time on the public perception of slapstick as consisting of nothing *but* pie fights. William K. Everson, the revered historian and collector who wrote the seminal *The Films of Laurel and Hardy* (1967), pointed out that in fact only *one* pie fight had ever been made—Chaplin's *Behind the Screen* (1916); all the other incidents of pie throwing had been the pitching of a *single* pie, and always as the trigger for some other kind of action rather than a custard-flinging war—which is another reason why Blake Edwards got it all wrong.

THE BETTER 'OLE

(1926, Warner Bros.)

Director: Chuck Reisner
Writers: Darryl Zanuck and Chuck Reisner
Titles: Robert Hopkins, from Bruce Bairnsfather and Arthur Eliot

Camera: Edwin Dunbar
Editor: Ray Enright
Cast: Sydney Chaplin, Jack Ackroyd, Edgar Kennedy, Harold Goodwin, Charles
  Gerard, Hank Mann, Tom Kennedy, Doris Hill, Arthur Clayton, Tom McGuire,
  Kewpie Morgan, Theodore Lorch
Running Time: 95 minutes
Availability: DVD (Warner Archive Collection)

Background: Any way you want to define it, Sydney Chaplin was the epitome
of the survivor. Born to an unknown father and a schizophrenic mother living in
abject poverty in Victorian England, he and his kid half-brother Charles endured
childhoods that veered from close-knit marginality to isolation, the poorhouse,
rejection, starvation, and illness, and then to premature independence, escape,
and return. In and out of school, in and out of orphanages and poorhouses, in
and out of adolescent theater jobs, yet always close to his brother and mother,
Sydney finally got old enough to sign up for the merchant marine and try to get
some stability into their codependent lives—his pay kept Charlie and Hannah
alive back in London.

Out of the merchant marine, Sydney enrolled in Fred Karno's comedy troupe;
as soon as he could, he talked Karno into hiring Charlie as well (Hannah by now
was in a mental hospital and Syd was completely responsible for Charlie). The
rest, almost, is history: Syd talked Charlie into accepting the invitation to go to
America with one of Karno's companies, Syd negotiated Charlie's movie contracts, Syd handled Charlie's lucrative investments and business arrangements,
Syd probably even still made sure Charlie washed behind his ears every night.

And he did all this while following Charlie's trail-breaking footsteps into silent
slapstick comedy films. That may have been the hardest thing to survive: knowing your baby brother (and not even your full brother, at that) was a genius clown
and that any comedy you essayed would be compared unfavorably to his, yet going ahead and punching your way through a quite decent career of your own in
defiance of the fates, the audiences, and the critics.

And Syd did have a good career. He did it the way a survivor does it: by
reinventing himself repeatedly as time and circumstances required. He started
out at Sennett as "Gussle," a huge and hugely violent comedian in dozens of
one-reelers, practically a one-man "Ham and Bud" brutality-and-laffs machine.
When this character lost its appeal, he retreated into supporting roles, mostly in
Charlie's vastly superior films: *A Dog's Life, Shoulder Arms, The Bond, Pay Day,* and
The Pilgrim. Then, when Charlie was ready to graduate to feature films, so did
Syd, although not into Charlie's products; instead, Syd completely reversed his
dead-and-buried "Gussle" character by becoming a light social comedian, notably
in *The Man on the Box* (1925) and *Charley's Aunt* (1925), the latter being probably
his biggest-ever hit. Oddly, both of those films put him in drag. Their success led
to him being cast as "Old Bill" in the film version of the legendarily popular and
long-running comic sketches about a phlegmatic English infantryman in World
War I, *The Better 'Ole.*

Synopsis: "Old Bill" and his slightly younger, or at least more callow, sidekick "Alfie" have survived trench warfare mostly by staying in a shell hole and in their dugout, practicing their singing; their reward is two weeks' leave in a little village "somewhere in France." At the promptings of a traitor in the British command, the German Army is secretly targeting this innocuous village as the place to start a major offensive. The attack is launched in the middle of an evening's entertainment for the British troops. Unintentional stars of the play are our two heroes, sewn inside a realistic horse costume. Unable to shed the rawhide, they find themselves herded with real horses by a couple of worn-out German sentries. After a fitful night of shenanigans among this foursome of accomplished slapstick performers, "Old Bill" and "Alfie" finally get free of both the costume and the sentries, and strive to save their army pals from the destruction that the Germans and the traitorous British officer have planned for them.

Comment: It helps immensely to know something about both film history and social history before watching any film (comic or serious) made in the silent era. In the case of *The Better 'Ole*, it also helps immensely to know something about the Great War and, in particular, the common Englishman's take on the British Army during that period. This book isn't the place to offer that much information, even in encapsulated form; I can only suggest here that the typical attitude of class cynicism felt by the English soldier toward his officers—incompetents to a man because their commissions were all purchased rather than earned through war experience and intelligence—was aptly expressed in their unofficial anthem, "We're Fred Karno's Army."

Bairnsfather and Eliot's "Old Bill" and "Alfie" duo were born of this attitude. Working-class dumbbells, they were lazy, slow of mind, and slow of foot, both passively and actively resistant (yet submissive) to authority whose ineptitude they knew to the bottom of their horsewhipped bums, loyal and brave cowards, affable idiots who muddled through to victory in spite of themselves and especially in spite of their treacherous and idiotic leaders.

Unlike post–World War II novels and films, such as *Catch-22*, *Slaughterhouse Five*, etc., the "Old Bill" comics were gentle satire, even bucolic in tone. A modern viewer of *The Better 'Ole* will be disappointed if the film is not approached in a relaxed frame of mind, and a willingness to enjoy the leisurely pace and the sometimes corny wit. Pretty much the entire first half of the film is about a lifestyle lost forever: French villages where cellars are filled with barrels of wine, chickens and geese and ducks are raised in backyards, and there are even haystacks and hay wagons behind a couple of houses, and soldiers have plenty of off time to sit around smoking pipes and pretending to be sages.

Abruptly, the stage show then lights a fire under the film. "Old Bill" and "Alfie" are ensconced in a horse's costume, and it is a wonderful, convincing costume. They prance about the stage as Tom Kennedy and a couple of other actors mess up a playlet intended to entertain the troops; all hell breaks loose internally and externally, and the film becomes hilarious. It stays hilarious as long as Chaplin and Jack Ackroyd remain sewn into the horse costume; once they get out, the laughs become more spotty (although Syd's work in pretending a semiconscious German soldier's legs are his own is wonderful). That middle section makes *The Better 'Ole* a worthy inclusion among 100 great silent comedies.

Bonus: The Chaplins discovered they shared another half brother, a man named Wheeler Dryden. They brought Wheeler to America and helped him break into the movies as well, though mostly in behind-the-scenes capacities. His son, Spencer Dryden, was the drummer for the Jefferson Airplane rock group during their great years (i.e., before they morphed into the regrettable Jefferson Starship). Considering Charlie Chaplin's attitude toward rock music as demonstrated in *A King in New York* (1957), it's a lovely irony that his half nephew ended up playing in one of the most drug-loving acid-rock bands of all time.

A BUSY NIGHT

(1916, Eagle Films)

Creator: Marcel Perez
Cast: Marcel Perez, Nilde Baracchi, Tom Murray
Running Time (Length): 17 minutes of the original two reels survived
Availability: DVD (Undercrank Productions: *The Marcel Perez Collection*)

Background: Although his comic career in Europe was a big hit and he was in demand as a "national comedian" in at least three countries (France, Italy, and Spain), Marcel Perez had had enough of that scene by the time the Great War broke out in 1914. He seized upon the war as a good reason to punt across the pond to America.

Perez was not well known on this side of the Atlantic Ocean, possibly because he had used too many aliases and *noms du cinema* to have carved out a recognizable, consistent image in a country that liked its performers to remain the same, decade after decade. His talent and his self-marketing aggressiveness, however, meant he didn't have to wait long to find jobs once he got through the Ellis Island immigration station. Unfortunately for his immediate legacy, he proceeded to whip off comedies at his accustomed breakneck pace under a dizzying variety of pseudonyms: Tweedledum, Twede-Dan, Tweedy, Bungles, and probably several more. In other words, he perpetrated the same problem as with his European output: too many different names to make himself familiar to American audiences.

Some of his early American films toned down the cataclysm quotient; others kept it up but strove to provide somewhat stronger motivations and story development. He explored elements that seemed popular in American slapstick; you can find "Ham and Bud" references almost as prolific as Keystone references in these films, and Roscoe Arbuckle thoughtfulness as much as Ford Sterling hamminess. Perez didn't really find his niche in American film during the war years.

Synopsis: One of the earliest comedies in which the star played all the roles—Georges Méliès did it many times—*A Busy Night* is also one of the best, particularly in the pre-computer-generated-imagery (CGI) era. A drunken "Tweedledum" gets kicked out of his club for demolishing the pool table, throwing food, fighting, and otherwise disturbing the peace. Despite tumbling (expertly and amusingly) out of the taxi that was taking him home, he does get to his destination eventually, not noticeably any the more sober, and falls asleep after mumbling misanthropically, "If everyone were like me . . . ."

The earth literally explodes and is refashioned into the home of "Tweedledum" and his clones: 16 of them. He proceeds to fall in love with himself as a woman, whose husband is himself, and then he two-times himself with . . . himself, of course. The husband goes off hunting and shoots a lobster out of the sky (that's not a typo); he returns home and fights with the lover as the wife hides; the cops—all "Tweedledums" in various permutations—are called and give chase, and it all ends very strangely with a cop throwing the lover off a pier into the ocean.

Comment: Not particularly funny, *A Busy Night* rates inclusion in this book as a showcase for Perez's assiduous efforts to meld into the silent comedy vanguard in American film and for his extremely impressive technical achievement. The editing cuts that allow him to play against himself in scene after scene are very, very subtle, and his transitions from one character in a scene to the other character are dazzling. For example, he could be dressed as the wife, turn his back to the camera and bend over slightly, then transition to the lover in the other half of the screen, and the actor who is now doubling as the wife is not a smidgeon out of position: indeed, her dress has the exact same creasing in her bent position as when Perez was playing her.

Bonus: Perez worked with something like eight different studios during the American leg of his career (at least six studios as the performer). It's yet another reason why it was so difficult for historians and enthusiasts alike to pin down his oeuvre and to find his surviving films. Some of those studios don't have great survival rates for their products. Many of the studios also had limited theatrical circuits, usually due to being distributed on a state's rights basis. They shipped their films around third-rate runs to play in fourth-rate movie houses that were not inclined to either save the films for posterity or treat them with white kid gloves. We owe a serious debt to those like Ben Model and Steve Massa, who did the spadework to recover this curious, ingenious comic and his fascinating movies.

C

CALL OF THE CUCKOO

(1927, Roach)

Director: Clyde Bruckman
Writers: Uncredited, probably Bruckman, Charley Chase, and Stan Laurel
Titles: H. M. Walker
Camera: Floyd Jackman
Editor: Richard Currier
Cast: Max Davidson, Spec O'Donnell, Lillian Elliott, Leo Willis, Lyle Tayo, Fay Holderness, Edgar Dearing, Stan Laurel, Oliver Hardy, Charley Chase, James Finlayson, Frank Brownlee, Charlie Hall, Charles Meakin, Otto Fries
Running Time (Length): Two reels
Availability: DVD (Image Entertainment: *The Lost Films of Laurel & Hardy: The Complete Collection*, vol. 1)

Background: Their tenth film together, *The Second Hundred Years* (1927), was the first official Laurel and Hardy film. Because they played convicts in it, their heads had been shaved. The tremendous popularity of *The Second Hundred Years* finally got it through the heads of Hal Roach and his studio brainiacs that they had a fantastic comedy team on their hands; consequently, they couldn't wait for the boys' hair to grow back in before putting them before the cameras again. They also wanted hair on their heads so audiences would be able to recognize them and would flock to their next official film, which was going to be *Hats Off* (1927). Since *Hats Off* is now the only lost Laurel and Hardy silent, there is huge irony here. At any rate, to keep the "new" team in front of the public eye, even while unrecognizable (these are comedy masters thinking, remember), Roach tossed Laurel and Hardy into a vehicle for Max Davidson, *Call of the Cuckoo*. For good measure, they also tossed in Laurel and Hardy's usual nemesis, James Finlayson. It's not entirely clear why the superlative Charley Chase was added, other than that Chase seems to have had his hand in every comedy the Roach studio produced. This quartet of comedians-for-the-ages bolstered Davidson with brief appearances as fixtures in a lunatic asylum.

Synopsis: Davidson has had enough of the legally certified nuts next door; just imagine how they must have lowered the property values! He pulls up stakes and moves into a new house. Unfortunately, this new house was constructed by workers who deserved places of honor in the asylum. Everything breaks, leaks, washes away, or rolls down the sloping floors, including the bathtub just as Davidson is inconveniently taking a wash, resulting in probably the cinema's first fully naked shot of a middle-aged Jewish comedian. The topper comes when the asylum inmates, lonely for Max, move in next door again.

Comment: The four window-dressing comedians are not really needed: they are little more than a publicity gag, or stunt casting. The film is so strong and so funny, the quartet of nuts are actually the weakest thing about it.

Bonus: One of the many, many, many great supporting comedians of the silent era and thereafter was Spec O'Donnell. Like Mickey Daniels (of Our Gang), he was one of those fellows born with red hair and more "speckles" (hence his nickname) than a Georges Seurat painting. One interesting side effect of these freckles and hair is that O'Donnell (and Daniels, too) looks exactly the same at age fifty as he did at age twelve. Compare him at age twelve in *Paging Money* (1924) and at age sixteen in *Call of the Cuckoo,* and the only difference is that he has shot up about ten inches in height; then compare him at age fifty in his recurring role in *The Andy Griffith Show* (1961) and all that's changed in a lifetime is his hairline.

O'Donnell could play a range of personalities. In the silent era, he was usually cast as exasperating offspring ("Love's Greatest Mistake," as he is identified in *Call of the Cuckoo*), but he could spin that role into overgrown malicious brat (*A Pair of Tights,* 1929), obstinate yet affectionate accomplice (*Don't Tell Everything,* 1927), or just plain stupid doofus (*Call of the Cuckoo*). When he outgrew the "son of" roles, O'Donnell kept himself busy with a couple of hundred minor and bit parts, often uncredited, in mostly unspectacular bottom-of-the-bill movies. Every time he pops up for a couple of seconds, even if he doesn't get the chance to do or say anything, lovers of classic comedy erupt in huge grins and exclaim, "There's Spec!"

CHASING CHOO-CHOOS

(1927, Monty Banks Enterprises)

Director: Joseph Henebery
Writers: Monty Banks, Charles Horan, Harry Sweet
Camera: Blake Wagner
Cast: Monty Banks, Virginia Lee Corbin, Charles Mailes, Charles Gerard, Bud
   Jamison
Running Time (Length): 21 minutes (two reels)

Background: The late and much lamented aficionado, collector, preservationist, historian, Cinefest organizer, and just incidentally Oscar-winning movie editor Robert Birchard told a great story about how Mario Bianchi became Monty Banks, and it may even have been true. According to Birchard, when Bianchi was working with Roscoe Arbuckle at Comique in 1918–1919, Arbuckle told him he had to Americanize his name if he wanted to get anywhere in films. Bianchi objected that he had just had all his underwear embroidered with the initials "MB."

Arbuckle's response was, "With all the mountebanks you've been playing, you should change your name to Monty Banks, then you won't have to change the monograms."

Banks was recognized early as someone with above-average gag sense. He was eternally cursed with bad distribution deals, production studios that sabotaged or screwed up his output, and just generally a continuous run of bad luck that prevented his achieving to the best of his potential. But just what *was* that potential? He comes up with fine gag ideas and situations, but seems incapable of realizing them to their fullest extent. He was good enough, and popular enough, to work steadily throughout the silent era. But his American silent film career ended ingloriously, and the rest of his life is best described as awkward: resurgence as a director overseas, marriage to the legendary Gracie Fields in England, deportation as an Italian (enemy) national during World War II, return to America to direct one of films that sent Laurel and Hardy inexorably on their descent into the hell of unfunniness, and sudden death in 1950 while back on his native Italian soil.

In short, Banks was a very minor but not totally insignificant silent comedian with a potential greater than what he was ever able to realize . . . except for ten minutes of some of the greatest filmmaking ever recorded. That ten minutes is now half of what is known as *Chasing Choo-Choos*, which in turn is (less than) half of a five-reel feature film that bombed, *Play Safe* (1927).

Synopsis: The first three reels of *Play Safe*, which were unsuccessful anyway, are neatly condensed into a very brief prologue to establish that heiress Virginia Lee Corbin wants to marry a "mere workman" (Banks) in defiance of her father, his crony, and the son-of-a-crony who wants to marry her himself so he can get his hands on her fortune. "Big Bill," thug-for-hire, loads up about twelve of his henchmen to waylay Banks. There's a long one-on-one fight in a locked office before Banks is able to flee to the train station. Another tussle with the thugs causes the train to start running away. Banks escapes the train, but then spots Corbin in it, so he has to chase after it. He commandeers a horse-driven buggy; half of it is sheared off by a race car inexplicably running down a city street, then the remaining half of the cart is jammed into a fence and Banks finds himself riding the horse backward. He has a real fall off the horse and gets dragged or forced run for a mile due to being tangled in the reins; shucking the reins, he goes back to the race car and recruits the driver to bring him up side by side to the train. (Distance is pretty relative in this part of the movie.) His effort to transfer from the car to the train is a real nail-biting couple of minutes, ending with an oncoming train blasting the abandoned car to smithereens as Banks swings aboard. He and Corbin then climb up to the top of the railcar; this allows the camera to be set up to show us beyond any doubts that the train is a real one and really running on a precipitous mountain route of immense frightfulness. We are genuinely shocked to our souls when Banks falls off the caboose and pitches down the steep mountain slope. In an extreme long shot, his dummy lands on the train's roof as the rails wind the caboose back under him, but that doesn't erase our amazement that Banks really did fall off. Harvey Parry was Banks's stunt double for some of the scenes on the train, but Banks made sure the camera was on his face when he fell off so we could see it actually was him.

Comment: This is sheer brilliance, no question about it. It is audacious, terrifying, exciting, scary, and convulse-on-the-floor funny all rolled up in one. Aside from Harold Lloyd's best movies and a few isolated exceptions such as Laurel and Hardy's *Liberty* and Buster Keaton's *Steamboat Bill, Jr.*, nothing can equal the spine-tingling thrill and laugh-out-loud hilarity of *Chasing Choo-Choos*. It is a timeless bit of cinematic perfection, already as hilarious 90 years after it was made, as it will be 190 years after it was made. I look forward to watching it again in the year 2117, when I will be a sprightly 162 years old, or approximately as old as Jack Duffy appeared in his films.

   Bonus: One of the earliest of the true child stars, Virginia Lee Corbin got her start in the movies at the age of six in 1916. She was one of the Fox Sunset Kiddies, a somewhat creepy series that cast little children in adult roles in classic tales such as *Aladdin and the Wonderful Lamp* (1917), *Jack and the Beanstalk* (1917), and *Treasure Island* (1918). She made about twenty-one of these kiddie films before taking a two-year break. At the age of, unbelievably, just fourteen, she made a comeback as one of the quintessential flappers of the silent screen. She kept up that jazz-baby persona for five years through such films as *Wine of Youth* (1924), *Bare Knees* (1928), *Jazz Land* (1928), and *Jazz Mamas* (1929); but at the same time, she was spreading her wings with more mature roles in features such as *The Cloud Rider* (1925), *Hands Up!* (1926), and *No Place to Go* (1927). A very beautiful blonde with a winning smile, Corbin sadly never had much of a chance at extending her career into the talkies. Marriages and children took up most of her time in the 1930s, and she died in 1942 of tuberculosis at only thirty-one years of age.

CHICAGO

(1928, De Mille Pictures/Pathé)

Director: Frank Urson (and Cecil B. De Mille)
Writers: Lenore Coffee, Maurine Watkins
Titles: John Krafft
Camera: Peverell Marley
Editor: Anne Bauchens
Cast: Phyllis Haver, Victor Varconi, Robert Edeson, Warner Richmond, Roy Barnes,
   Sidney D'Albrook, Eugene Pallette, May Robson, Viola Louie, Clarence Burton,
   Otto Lederer, Virginia Bradford, Julia Faye
Running Time (Length): 104 minutes (nine reels)
Availability: DVD (Flicker Alley)

Background: Leave it to the city of Chicago to make murder an icon of Jazz Age glamour; it was that city's practice run for making murder an icon of Prohibition Era glamour. Some real-life tawdry killings of their jilting sugar daddies by beautiful, brainless young tarts were conflated into the story of one fictional killer, "Roxie Hart," and how the media made her a star. The author of the resultant 1926 stage play, Maurine Watkins, was in truth precisely the reporter who was single-handedly responsible for doing so, consciously and deliberately using a mixture of lurid details and prickly wit to get the story on the front pages. Her play was a big hit, and within a matter of months it was adapted into a screenplay for the two-faced moralist Cecil B. De Mille. His fascination with sexual hypocrisy led him to become so titillated by the *Chicago* story that he took over direction of the movie from Frank Urson; then, being the virtuous fraud that he was, he kept his own name out of the credits except as producer. His behavior proved the whole point of *Chicago*.

Synopsis: Handsome young entrepreneur (he runs his own prosperous tobacco store) "Amos Hart" adores his bottle-blonde wife, "Roxie." She's an incorrigible flirt and a gold digger on the side. The side happens to be Eugene Pallette, before he got so obese as to have no sides. When Pallette, visiting "Roxie" while she's still in her negligee and wrapper, tells her he's decided to take his gold elsewhere and gives her a knockdown shove for emphasis, she grabs the conveniently loaded gun nearby and kills him. The reporters arrive at the same time as the police. A bit of cop trickery leads to dumb "Roxie" blurting out the truth. Sensing a career-making situation, the reporter brings up a photographer to put the beauty on the front page: she poses for his camera as "Remorse" with a gigantic grin on her face and the wrapper falling off her shoulders. In an instant, she's world famous as "The Jazz Slayer." Awaiting trial in the women's jail, she competes with other lady killers for sensational articles and photos. Exulting in the publicity, mistaking infamy for fame, she hardly cares that "Amos" can't afford the slick defense lawyer he's lined up. The only way he can get the money to pay "Lawyer Flynn" is by stealing it from "Lawyer Flynn" himself; though torn and miserable at the depths to which he's sunk, he'll still do anything for "Roxie."

Phyllis Haver pleads her innocence in *Chicago* (1928). *Courtesy of Derek Boothroyd*

"Flynn" prepares "Roxie" for the trial by putting her in a pink Bo Peep dress, all chiffon and bows, with a bridal bouquet to bring it to the peak of parody of virginal innocence. Of course, the all-male jury responds on cue, ugly old men preening at "Roxie's" entrance, their feet rising tumescently when she hikes her skirt up over her garters, and then drooping back down into their shoes when she covers her knees again. De Mille was nothing if not subtle, and he wasn't subtle.

"Roxie" may not know emotional expressionism or have any kind of a brain rattling around in her empty, vain head, but she instinctively knows how to play to the crowd, and does so in spades. One of her mental dullnesses is that she also doesn't know where to draw the line, so her courtroom portrayal of violated chastity goes way overboard, and everybody knows she's lying outrageously. They don't care, though: they eat it up, vindicate her with the verdict, and then instantly move on to the next female murderer. De Mille, still subtle as ever—which is to say *not*—illustrates her new situation with his usual heavy-handedness by having her front-page photo get washed down the gutter drain.

Comment: A winner in all of its film versions (and stage versions too, for that matter), *Chicago* is a foolproof property. No one has yet done a dead-serious, existentialist attempt at the story, probably, but even that version would be dynamite, and if they miscast it, it would be unintentional dynamite. You really can't go wrong with it.

The opening sequence, with Victor Varconi doing a terrible, awkward attempt to convey "Amos's" fawning worship of "Roxie," gets neatly (and deservedly) undercut by Phyllis Haver's sneaky glances at him puttering away in the kitchen, and from that moment on it's Haver's picture. She sets the tone for every scene. She decides the murder scene will be played melodramatically, and that's how it comes across. She decides the investigation will be played as farce, and that's how it goes. She decides to ramp up the satire in the rest of the scenes she appears in, and that turns a good comic property into a great comic property. She didn't have any say in how Varconi would play his tense scenes of thievery, so that's one of the main reasons why there's nothing amusing (or believable) about those particular scenes. Still, Haver's own performance is not spotless. Called upon to do more demanding acting for more minutes than she had ever done before, she's up for the challenge; there are just a few false notes, and they usually occur when she's *trying* to hit false notes and gives it just a little bit too much, notably in the pre-shooting confrontation with Eugene Pallette. The enthusiasm and authenticity with which she embraces the flapper aspects of "Roxie" are palpable, for Haver in real life was every inch the flapper; she knew intimately the ins and outs of living that role.

And what fun this film is! It's a romp of the sort Marilyn Monroe would make her own in the 1950s; you can very easily imagine Haver playing "Sugar" in *Some Like It Hot* (1959) and Monroe playing "Roxie" in *Chicago*. (Why didn't Monroe? She could certainly have handled the later musical version, too, if it had been made a half century or so earlier than 2002.)

The intertitles are full of snappy one-liners. When "Roxie" and "Two Gun Rosie" brawl in the prison, the matron chides them, "This is a decent jail—you can't act here the way you do at home!" Lawyer "Flynn's" price is too high for "Amos" to afford, so his wife begs the self-answering question, "Please, Mr. Flynn, shouldn't blondes be cheaper?" The reporter, asked if it's true "Roxie" will likely be found guilty and hanged for murder, snorts, "Hang a woman with a face like that? Say, justice ain't so blind!"

Bonus: Ginger Rogers was a highly unlikely choice to play the leading role in the first talkie version of the film, *Roxie Hart* (1942); this was part of her deliberate decision to leave behind her dance romances with Fred Astaire and prove her versatility in a wide variety of other roles. She's surprisingly convincing as twenty-three-year-old "Roxie" (Rogers was thirty-one at the time). A highlight is when she faints in the courtroom, then surreptitiously flips her hem above her knees for the benefit of the lecherous jurors while still pretending to be unconscious.

Acting even more against type in the 1942 version was Adolphe Menjou as the lawyer. Although he's right at home when the lawyer is being his smooth, dressy self outside the courtroom, he's a carefully disheveled mess inside the courtroom, and it's jolting to see him making sure his hair is hanging wildly in faked sweaty desperation. He's great, as usual, especially when delivering walls-come-tumbling-down orations during the trial.

Roxie Hart played the story for big, broad laughs from start to end. The modern musical version, *Chicago* (2002), which won the Academy Award for Best Picture, is a flashy, splashy epic with a bit of everything, though more a musical than a musical-comedy. Renée Zellweger plays "Roxie" less like a brainless sleaze and more as if the character were intuitively shrewd but psychologically disturbed. To that extent, it's a much more rounded character than either Haver or Rogers essayed, but that does tend to dampen the comedy quotient. This version of the film, being very closely based on Bob Fosse's stage revival, obviously echoes his earlier *Cabaret* (1972), and that's not necessarily a bad thing, although it does define it as overblown and historically imaginative. As mentioned, the property is fail-safe; all three film versions are extremely enjoyable.

CHICKEN FEATHERS

(1927, Christie)

Director: Walter Graham
Writer: Frank Conklin
Cast: Jack Duffy, Anne Cornwall, Billy Engle, William Irving, James Harrison
Running Time (Length): Two reels

Background: Jack Duffy is one of those supporting actors who pops up in everything—at least during the 1920s, his heyday—and whenever you spot him, you bounce a little in your seat in gleeful anticipation of big laughs to come. Losing all of his teeth at an early age, he decided to make the best of it by leaving out the dentures and makingup as an old goat, complete with an old goatee. He died at age fifty-seven, not having lived long enough to reach the age he looked onscreen.

Being young while portraying age allowed Duffy to provoke laughter as an improbably energetic and athletic octogenarian, but that wasn't all: he colored in

The off-screen Jack Duffy looks nothing like the white-haired, toothless, goa-teed, bespectacled old man he plays in *Chicken Feathers* (1927). *Author's collection*

a full characterization by also being an irrepressible skirt-chaser, an uncontrol-lable greedy-puss, an explosively tempered papa, a befuddled yet overly decisive judge, and an avaricious Scotsman. It was a great character, and Duffy made it an irresistible one.

Synopsis: Fleecing the Russians out of $5,000 in a deal, Duffy races to the bank to deposit his fortune before the bank closes for the day. Alas, he is about two seconds too late. Returning home, he decides the best place to hide the money temporarily is inside a throw pillow. Daughter Anne Cornwall, however, donates the pillow to a bazaar being run by her college chums. Not only are Duffy and Cornwall now in pursuit of the pillow, so are pint-sized crook Billy Engle and phony iceman William Irving. They all scramble around town chasing the pillow, eventually tracking it down inside a cleaning place. While Anne manages to find the money there, Duffy falls into a starch tub and then gets coated with the feath-ers flying around from broken-open pillows. With his goatee jutting straight out like a beak and his coattails jutting straight out behind (stiffened by the starch) and covered from head to toe in feathers, he really does resemble a giant chicken, and somehow ends up becoming the love object of a farmful of ostriches.

Comment: The pace of this film is terrific: Duffy really liked his movies to *move*, and move *fast*. (I'm not discounting the cranking speed.) Even when he affects to be slow moving, he's fast: he anticipates Tim Conway's old-man shuffle of about one inch forward at each step, but he does it quickly, as if he's in carpet slippers and deliberately working up to give someone a tremendous static-electricity shock.

Cornwall, Engle, and Irving are adequate, playing their roles broadly. Duffy, though, can't even enter a car without being a riot to watch: he pitches himself head first into the rumble seat of the boyfriend's car as it takes off, and it's killingly funny how he does it. After everybody else has jumped through the window of the cleaners, Duffy attempts to follow suit and flails about as the ledge meets his knees and the window pounds his back, and if that's a very old slapstick bit, he makes it completely new and gut-bustingly hilarious.

Other than a slightly nervous moment when one ostrich corners him—we know from Billy Ritchie's fate that an ostrich attack is no laughing matter—there is not a quiet moment in *Chicken Feathers*. It is an overlooked gem.

Bonus: Pretty much any Jack Duffy film from the 1920s is guaranteed to supply a fun time, especially if it's a short. His ability to amuse in features depends upon how much screen time he gets: very little time can be effective, albeit a bit of a waste of his talent, whereas a lot of time can bring out the sandpaper too much. He's fine in several Larry Semon films because Semon's ego wasn't going to let Duffy run away with the picture; he's a bit overbearing in *Madame Behave!* because he's given too much exposure. It's best to stick with his own starring two-reelers such as *Long Hose*, *Hot Scotch*, and *Loose Change* (all 1928), *Hoot Mon!* (1926), and *Hot Papa* (1927). In fact, any Duffy film whose title consists of two words is probably a safe bet.

THE CIRCUS

(1928, United Artists)

Director: Charles Chaplin
Writer: Charles Chaplin
Camera: Roland Totheroh
Editor: Charles Chaplin
Cast: Charlie Chaplin, Merna Kennedy, Henry Bergman, Allan Garcia, Harry Crocker, Tiny Sandford, John Rand, George Davis, Steve Murphy
Running Time (Length): 71 minutes (seven reels)
Availability: DVD (Warner Home Video)

Background: Long before 1928, Charlie Chaplin was fed up with short films. He had already proven, first with *The Kid* (1921) and then with *The Gold Rush* (1925), that he could make superior feature films. Between those two mileposts, he had whipped off three short films to terminate his First National contract, and had written and directed *A Woman of Paris* (1923) for Edna Purviance as his first contribution to the new United Artists company that he had formed with Doug Fairbanks, Mary Pickford, and D. W. Griffith. It was time to move on.

His critics and his fans alike were not entirely in synch with his artistic development; although they appreciated his growing deftness in mixing pathos with his comedy, they were disgruntled that he seemed increasingly to prefer wandering away from the laughs in pursuit of the tears. They wanted more of the old Chaplin, the one who fired off gags and funny business at a relentless pace and let the storytelling be damned.

So with *The Circus* he set out to, essentially, shut them up by giving them a barrage of pure comedy. By giving them what they wanted this time around, he could hopefully make the following film one that *he* wanted to make. It actually did work out that way for him, although it would take three years of tumultuous change in the entire industry before he could release *City Lights* in 1931, a silent feature film stubbornly made in the face of moviedom's total switchover to talkies.

Creating *The Circus* turned out to be three years of tumultuous agony in Chaplin's life, too, and not because of the impending doom of the silents. The tax man got after him and hauled him into court. It must be stressed that, contrary to the lies of the Chaplin haters, it was never an issue of Chaplin *evading* taxes, it was an issue of disputing *how much* tax he should be paying . . . and it was his "tax expert" brother, Sydney, who had not only miscalculated the amounts Charlie owed but had been accused of evading payment of *his own* (Sydney's) taxes.

Feeding into that legal frenzy was the disgusting, venal campaign of his second wife, Lita Grey (and her stage-managing, criminally gold-digging mother), to smear Chaplin's reputation in divorce court in hopes of landing the biggest alimony payout on record. Like the IRS, the Greys succeeded both in getting fistfuls of Chaplin's money and in destroying him personally and professionally in the eyes of too many gibbering cretins looking for excuses to hate him.

When Chaplin tried to escape these incredible stresses by burying himself in the work of making *The Circus*, he found the film gods were as merciless as the court judges and the court of public opinion. Bad weather destroyed some of the sets; the first few weeks of filmed scenes were entirely ruined by lab errors; fire destroyed the set a second time; and the uncut film had to be spirited away to a secret location to keep Grey's lawyers from seizing it.

Synopsis: The film opens with a brilliant extended gag sequence in which Charlie tries to escape from pursuers in and around a funhouse at a carnival. The inside has a mirror maze, and Chaplin the filmmaker does a brilliant job with the multiple exposures this setting naturally creates, long before Orson Welles ever attempted it. The outside of the funhouse has mechanical figures, and Chaplin again does a brilliant job of eliciting laughter when he is compelled to play one of the figures.

The movie then segues seamlessly into the circus that is the heart of the carnival. Charlie unwittingly gets involved in the clowns' routine and transforms it from a limp, wheezy bomb into a dynamite belly-buster. The conniving ringmaster hires him as a prop man so that Charlie can continue to enliven the clown act without realizing he is now the star clown. This turns around the fortunes of the circus, as why wouldn't it, with Charlie Chaplin as the lead comedian?

The ringmaster abuses his equestrienne stepdaughter, with whom Charlie has fallen in love and who in turn has fallen in love with the tightrope walker (played by Harry Crocker, Chaplin's offscreen collaborator and soon-to-be factotum). When the walker doesn't show up for a performance, Charlie decides to prove his love for the girl by taking his spot. This leads into one of the most killingly funny scenes in movie comedy history, as Charlie is beset by a barrel of monkeys on the high wire.

Once the real walker shows up and the girl swoons with relief and love, Charlie realizes he has no future with this particular circus. He does the Chaplin thing: sacrifices his heart so the girl he loves can have a presumably good future with a more suitable man, then kicks up his heels and waddles off alone into the sunrise of "another day."

Comments: The comic genius—and there is no hesitation in using that superlative—of Charles Chaplin is given perfect illustration in the set pieces with the clowns. Sure, sure, sure, he arranged these pieces to show himself off to best advantage, but listen to this: he picked timeless, *standard* pieces that had been integral parts of clown acts for literally centuries, going back to sixteenth-century commedia dell'arte, and he had the other clowns (led by the indefatigable Henry Bergman) play them exactly in that timeless manner.

The "barbershop piece" and the "William Tell piece" are first played out for our benefit the way they have always been played out (and were still to be played out, in the same fashion, by the Three Stooges and even by Harpo Marx in times to come après Chaplin). He didn't cheat by designing faux standard acts or by having standard acts played deliberately badly by the clowns. He used the real thing, played accurately. And then he followed these performances by playing them again with himself, putting his own spin on them.

The difference is like having an alien come down to Earth and participate in something he had never seen before. The two skits come alive. They become fresh, wild, impossible to predict, glittering with creativity and wit. Two skits that could barely raise one corner of the viewer's mouth in slightly derisive amusement suddenly put that same viewer spinning on the floor in convulsive laughter.

Bonus: Which is the best representative of a Charlie Chaplin feature comedy? Almost everyone picks *The Kid, The Gold Rush,* or *City Lights,* with a few giving the award to *Modern Times.* The lame dog in the list is *The Circus.* It never gets picked, for a number of good reasons—principal among them being the fact that Chaplin himself suppressed it for nearly forty years because it brought back too many traumatic memories for him.

I picked it because none of the other films are such pure comedy. Any viewer, even a rabid Chaplin fan, will sit through long stretches of the other films without cracking a smile because each of them has such extended stretches of serious drama or plot breaking up the comedy. *The Circus* does have its serious sections, but they are brief, and the ratio of serious-to-comedy is much lower in *The Circus* than in the other films. Simply put, it is the last wall-to-wall laff festival Chaplin ever made, and one of the best comedy films anyone has ever made.

Still recommended are all of the other silent feature films Chaplin made. Think of it: no one else ever made a set of just five films of which each one was very nearly perfect and of which at least one has appeared in nearly every "top 100" list of movies ever created, whatever the defining measure: top 100 comedies, top 100 films, top 100 silent films, top 100 family films, etc.

When he finally abandoned the silent film in 1940, Chaplin once again proved his unmatched genius—he really deserves that title—by making three talkie films that are among the most profoundly artistic, intellectually and politically ambitious, and simply fascinating movies in history. *The Great Dictator* (1940) matched *Shoulder*

Arms (1918) for dazzling audacity in finding comedy gold amid the grotesque idiocy of war *while a world war was actually raging*. *Monsieur Verdoux* (1947) was a postwar black comedy that raised pointed issues about mass murder; not entirely successful, it was still light-years beyond the reach (let alone the grasp) of all other filmmakers of the day in putting important human questions into amusing situations and seeking serious answers from the resulting Sennett-like anarchy that was both its fuel and its consequence. *Limelight* (1952) kept the comedy and the life-lessons philosophy (it contains more aphorisms and "wise sayings" than all the rest of Chaplin's oeuvre put together) but took them out of the context of warfare and into the context of human aging; again, not entirely successful, but again, far beyond anything being attempted by other filmmakers of the era.

All three films met with decidedly mixed reactions, or more accurately, with extreme reactions. For many, the older Chaplin remained the genius Chaplin; his fearlessness in exploring controversial topics and making them the objects of both laughter and philosophy confirmed him as one of the most supreme artists of the century, if not of all time. For the loud and ignorant and blinkered, the older Chaplin was a communist, an anti-American, an Antichrist, a priapic pervert, a pretentious pinko, a self-important bore, and a traitor to whatever class they thought he belonged to (or should belong to), whether it was upper or lower.

It would be counter to Chaplin's own intentions to tell viewers to put aside their political opinions and watch these three films with an open mind. They *are* deliberately political films, even *Limelight*. You *should* watch them from a political perspective. But try for the open mind, too; Chaplin has things to say that are worth listening to. He may be somewhat naïve and idealistic, but he is *thinking*, and the only respect he asks of you is the respect of listening and thinking as he goes along.

Chaplin's last two films, *A King in New York* (1957) and *A Countess from Hong Kong* (1967), are, however, nothing more than the films of an old man who had become cinematically senile. He tried to bring back some slapstick comedy with *King*, but he no longer had the physical dexterity or the directorial timing to make it work; it sank under the weight of gag situations that were nothing more than old-man-baffled-by-those-darn-kids-today conceits. *Countess* was putrid, a compendium of outdated routines played by totally unsuitable actors (Marlon Brando and Sophia Loren?!) being directed by an exasperated perfectionist who could not get them to do anything "right." If you must watch them, do not watch them as "Chaplin films."

A CLEVER DUMMY

(1917, Sennett)

Directors: Herman Raymaker, Ferris Hartman, Robert Kerr
Writer: Uncredited (supposedly Mack Sennett)
Camera: Elgin Lessley
Cast: Ben Turpin, James Donnelly, Claire Anderson, James DeLano, Juanita Hansen, Chester Conklin, Wallace Beery, Marvel Rea, Baldy Belmont, Eva Thatcher
Running Time (Length): Two reels
Availability: Alpha Home Entertainment

Background: Ben Turpin was a man of limited intelligence and equally limited education. It shows in both his career arc and his comedy. Wandering away from home and school at an early age, he spent some years going door to door begging handouts in Chicago. Wandering into live theatre, he found himself drafted into the title role of a farce about "Happy Hooligan," a cross-eyed goof. Wandering around the country playing this role for years, the formerly straight-eyed Turpin discovered his eyes had become permanently strabismic: he didn't have the common sense to limit his runs in this play to preserve his health. Wandering into the movies, he became the house comic at Essanay despite thoroughly pedestrian comedy skills; the only thing he had learned to do well so far was acrobatics and falls. After ten years in this position, Essanay reduced him to sidekick status; fortunately for Turpin, the lead comic to whom he was made sidekick was Charlie Chaplin, so you could say he wandered into an intern position under one of the two greatest comedians in history.

Wandering over to Sennett's studio, Turpin found himself once again being anointed the lead comedian on the lot, still despite his inability to think up anything funny to do when he didn't have a gag writer or a creative director around to instruct him. Wandering into the talkies, he kept his unforgettable image before the public in very minor roles off and on for about four years before finally packing it in for good (and promptly dying before learning how to enjoy his retirement).

How did a nonentity of such limited talent become—and remain—one of the most beloved, popular, and successful comedians in screen history? For one thing: by being one of the most *recognizable* comedians in screen history. One must never, ever underestimate the importance to audiences of being able to recognize performers; it's one reason why actors who are masters at changing their appearance from one film to another are rarely popular stars. (I give you a silent comedy example: Andy Clyde. "Who?" you ask. Right.) Turpin's physical appearance was unmatchably unique: crossed eyes, strings of fading hair, unexpectedly strong moustache, missing-in-action jawline, and like so many of the silent comedians he was a tiny fellow (only 120 pounds and 5'4", according to Brent Walker's authoritative *Mack Sennett's Fun Factory*, 2010). See him once and you forget him never.

A second reason for his success was his willingness, even eagerness, to make fun of himself. Or, no, we have to get more specific: he made fun of his own *appearance* onscreen, not of himself. Reading his press clippings, interviews, articles, etc., as gathered up by Steve Rydzewski in his biographical pastiche *For Art's Sake: The Biography and Filmography of Ben Turpin* (2013), one is struck by Turpin's offscreen personality as a bitter, sour, vengeful loner who took himself very seriously indeed, including being resentful of his physical appearance. Onscreen, it was a vastly different story: he made his indelible mark on comedy by choosing films that played up his goofy looks to the *n*th degree. It was sidesplittingly funny to see this amoebic schlub aping the suave ladykiller Rudolph Valentino or the intimidating, imperious war-hawk Erich von Stroheim. Turpin didn't have to do anything to get laughs except pose in Stroheim's uniform or in Valentino's patented seduction bend-over. He did it willingly in the movies, but it shriveled his soul in real life.

Synopsis: A Clever Dummy has a slightly complicated storyline, and you really need to watch it closely from start to finish. (I own a one-reel cutdown in addition to the full two-reel version; the cutdown is incomprehensible.) An inventor has built a wonderful full-scale dummy; his assistant, apparently the brains of the duo, had created the brains of the dummy, incarnated in the form of an electrical box with switches that programmed the dummy's movements (a wire from the box was plugged into the dummy's back). The janitor (Turpin) had modeled for the dummy, and therefore it is a dead ringer for him. Through a series of romantic complications—Turpin loves the inventor's daughter, who in turn loves the brainiac, whom the father hates—the janitor ends up substituting for the dummy during a stage demonstration.

Comment: The reason *A Clever Dummy* works so well is because it depends entirely upon Ben's one and only actual skill: the seemingly boneless flexibility of his body. He was considered the best man in Hollywood for falls because of that boneless quality. Here, he doesn't do any falling, but his physical dexterity and control is superb. As the dummy, he boxes, dances, slumps, contorts, all in all giving a most persuasive impression of a mechanical figure constructed out of rubber and foam.

Bonus: Originally filmed as a one-reeler called *The Automaton Figure* (according to Steve Rydzewski) or *The Automatic Figure* (according to Brent Walker), this film impressed Mack Sennett sufficiently for him to order a second reel. Thus there are two casts and two main locations in *A Clever Dummy*. The first reel takes place almost entirely in the inventor's room and features James Donnelly, Claire Anderson, and James DeLano supporting Turpin. The second reel takes place almost entirely in the theatre, and features Sennett stock players Chester Conklin, Wallace Beery, Marvel Rea, Juanita Hansen, Baldy Belmont, and Eva Thatcher.

One of the wittiest visual puns in the history of intertitles pops up in this film. Turpin writes a fake note to Anderson; when she discovers it, the intertitle identifies it as "The Forged Note," and accompanies these words with a line drawing of . . . a blacksmith hammering out a paper in his forge.

The most notorious visual, however, is Turpin's robot dance, which consists almost entirely of him repeatedly thrusting his middle fingers in every direction. It has to be seen to be believed.

CONDUCTOR 1492

(1924, Warner Bros.)

Directors: Frank Griffin, Charles Hines
Writer: Johnny Hines
Camera: Charles Gilson
Editor: Clarence Kolster
Cast: Johnny Hines, Doris May, Dan Mason, Fred Esmelton, Robert Cain, Michael Dark, Byron Sage, Dorothy Vernon, Ruth Renick, Billy Armstrong, Al Cooke
Running Time (Length): 75 minutes (six reels)
Availability: DVD (Alpha Video)

Background: Entering films in 1914, Johnny (sometimes "John") Hines mucked around until 1920 when he hit popularity as a recurring comic character called "Torchy." After two dozen of these shorts, Hines graduated to feature films,

Johnny Hines (*Conductor 1492*, 1924), publicity still. *Author's collection*

many of which he not only wrote but directed through the puppet of his brother Charles. Utilizing the formula of Harold Lloyd—he certainly wasn't alone in doing so, so that's not a criticism of him—Hines's features cast him as a relentlessly upbeat and infinitely competent go-getter whose financial and romantic success was precipitated by exciting chases and stunts. These went over big throughout the 1920s and they are still rousing crowd-pleasers every time they pop up in festivals of vintage cinema today.

Synopsis: "Terry" is about to leave Ireland for "Americky," but he's having a problem transporting his luggage via mule cart. His father, grandfather, and great-grandfather are called upon in turn to find a solution. It's "Terry" himself who finally has the necessary brainstorm: he'll use blarney instead of bricks when (not *if*) he gets into fights, so he can afford to remove about 25 bricks from his suitcase. Problem thus solved, the four generations head back into the house where a wake is being held to mourn his departure. The mourners brighten at the sound of a jug sloshing, and the party is on. "Terry's" dad gives him an Irish doll for luck, adding that there is something inside the doll that might be worth a shilling or two someday.

We next see "Terry" charming an Irish landlady into accepting him as a boarder . . . one of forty, in a house with two baths. The equally charming (in a different definition) Dick Sutherland is one of the forty battling for access to the baths. After some horseplay in disguise as a chair, "Terry" sneaks in and proceeds to lather himself thickly from head to toe, including the boxer shorts he is obviously wearing in the shower, using up a bar of Castile soap the size of a full rack of barbecue ribs; a nice tracking shot moves in on him as he starts to rinse it off.

He gets the same job his dad had held twenty years earlier—a period of time that makes us wonder how old "Terry" is supposed to be, since Hines is visibly nearly thirty years old—as "motorman," that is, a trolley driver in the town of "Lotedo," an anagram of "Toledo" as lame as his badge number, "1492," an anagram for the year the film was released. No matter. In this job, he makes a great pal of a little boy who likes to race the streetcar in his souped-up soap-box jalopy. All is well until the boy is T-boned by a truck, whose driver rolls off unconcerned even as the injured boy crawls out of the wreckage and staggers onto the trolley tracks. "Terry" manages to scoop the boy to safety as the latter's sister watches.

Sister, naturally, turns out to be the beautiful young daughter of "traction" (public transportation) magnate "Connelly," and "Terry" the heroic rescuer is immediately tagged as potential son-in-law material. "Connelly" is locked in a power struggle with his vice president, "Langford"; to settle it, he must find "Louis Rosenthal," who owns the deciding stocks in the company. Meanwhile, "Terry's" dad has come to visit him from Ireland and reveals himself to have adopted the name "Louis Rosenthal" during his own tenure in "Ameriky," and confesses to having stuffed the all-important stock certificates inside the Irish doll.

Despite a lengthy diversion in the story for a comic interlude involving a two-man camel disguise at a roller-skating party, "Terry" and his dad rescue the doll from a huge fire, "Terry" marries the gal, and they honeymoon back in Ireland to bring everything full circle.

Comment: Normally I dislike Johnny Hines. In *Conductor 1492*, however, he's not as smarmy and self-satisfied as he is in his other films. The result is unquestionably the best comedy he ever made, and one of the most enjoyable of 1924. It's episodic in structure, and while the episodes don't always hang together very well, they all hang separately quite successfully. The opening in Ireland is very good, playing on the stereotypes of dumb micks who spend all their time fighting and drinking, or vice versa. The second episode, set in the boardinghouse, also contains nothing groundbreaking or unique; it's just nicely done comedy, especially the extreme close-up of the immortal, lovely mug of Dick Sutherland and the zoom in on Hines's preposterously oversoaped body in the shower.

If the quick friendship between "Terry" and the "Connelly" family is developed too easily, it has the virtue of not being allowed to take up too much time. It also hosts an amusing variation of the switching-drinks routine, in this case "Terry" and "Langford" trying to stick one another with a bad cigar while snagging the good cigar for oneself.

Blatantly contrived, the camel skit is nevertheless very effective and very funny. Hines and Billy Armstrong (or maybe their doubles) revel in their skill in dancing the "camel walk" on roller skates while wearing the heavy camel disguise. One can't help comparing it to the two-man horse disguise in Syd Chaplin's *The Better 'Ole* two years later.

Dan Mason is fun as the father. Doris May is interestingly pretty as "Connelly's" daughter; one wishes for more close-ups of her intriguing face. Robert Cain as bad-guy "Langford" looks remarkably like Robert Duvall in the latter's moustache-and-slicked-back-hair days. Even Byron Sage as the little boy (who looks way too much like a little girl) is natural and pleasant, not at all obnoxious or "cute." There are no bad performances.

Bonus: None of the actors in this film had any kind of career in the talkies except for Dorothy Vernon, who made more than 100 appearances in sound films up to 1957. The rather sad track record for the other main performers:

Hines: Nine films in the 1930s, two of them shorts
May: no talkies
Dark: no talkies
Mason: died in 1929, so no talkies
Cain: One uncredited appearance, 1932
Renick: Nine movies in the 1930s, but only four credits
Esmelton: One uncredited appearance in 1931
Sage: Three talkies in the 1930s
Armstrong: Died in 1924, so no talkies
Cooke: Fewer than 20 talkies, all but one of them either shorts or uncredited
Sutherland: A half dozen talkies, all of them uncredited

THE COOK

(1918, Comique/Paramount)

Director: Roscoe Arbuckle
Writer: Roscoe Arbuckle
Camera: George Peters
Editor: Herbert Warren
Cast: Roscoe Arbuckle, Buster Keaton, Al St. John, Alice Lake, John Rand, Bobby Dunn
Running Time (Length): Two reels
Availability: DVD (Image Entertainment)

Background: Buster Keaton was seduced into the movies by Roscoe Arbuckle in 1917. Between that day and 1920 when they went their separate ways, the two men made fifteen films together in which they were a team in all but name. They were a team because they worked together in perfect harmony, perfect synchronicity, and perfect sharing of laughs. Offscreen, too, they were the best of friends; the only disagreement they had during this period, according to their own accounts, was over the intelligence of the average audience, with Arbuckle believing it to be very low and Keaton not.

The Cook was the twelfth of their fifteen collaborations, so by this time they were supremely attuned to one other onscreen and could pull off exquisitely timed interchanges without blinking or even looking at each other—a fact they didn't hesitate to demonstrate in this film. After it was completed, they had a one-year hiatus while Keaton went into the army (he didn't get into combat before the Armistice); when he returned, they proved with *Back Stage* (1919), *The Hayseed* (1919), and *The Garage* (1920) that not even time and war had been able to dislodge the perfect interlocking of their comic skills.

Synopsis: The Bull Pup Café is the hotspot for suave, sophisticated diners. Not quite as suave and sophisticated are the staff working there. Chief among them is the imperturbable cook, "Fatty," and the equally unflappable head waiter, "Buster." Utilizing full cups of coffee, bowls of soup, and humungous butcher blades, this blank-faced duo perform amazing juggling stunts with the indifferent aplomb of circus clowns who have been doing this stuff twice a day for twenty years. They even manage to incorporate not one but two Cleopatra dance parodies to perk up their act.

Al St. John, humbly identified in an intertitle as "The toughest guy in the world" and who clearly does not belong in this classy dining establishment, disrupts their day by forcing his attentions upon the beautiful cashier, "Alice." When "Buster" remonstrates with him, "Toughie" responds by using "Buster's" head to knock the top off a bottle of beer, chewing the bottle and spitting the shreds into "Buster's" face, and then smashing the rest of the bottle over his skull. Subtle he is not. Fortunately, Luke the dog latches onto "Toughie's" posterior and then chases him out the door.

An intertitle advises us: "The next day . . ." Lo and behold, Luke is still chasing "Toughie" all over town, up ladders and down, across rooftops and hilltops, all the way to Coney Island and out to sea, while "Buster," "Fatty," and "Alice" enjoy themselves fishing, romancing, and unintentionally swimming.

Comment: Arbuckle's Comique two-reelers are often two one-reel films tacked together with only the flimsiest of connections. And quite often, one of those reels is forgettable routine shtick while the other reel is superb horseplay.

The second reel of *The Cook* is noteworthy only for capturing some of the fun that was the Coney Island amusement park at its peak. Many other films of the era did the same thing, from Laurel and Hardy's *Their Purple Moment* (1928) to Harold Lloyd's *Why Pick on Me?* (1918) to Paul Fejos's melodrama *Lonesome* (1928), so *The Cook* isn't unique in that respect. The "Goatland" feature, which consisted of goats pulling couples in dogcarts, is bizarre and, in our modern view, appalling. I did find it interesting to watch Arbuckle place Luke on a post set in the water; Luke barks violently and gets very excited about a giant fish Arbuckle appears to capture, so much so that he (Luke) falls into the water; but that's hardly enough to make this reel a classic.

The first reel is something else, though. The interplay between Arbuckle and Keaton begins with Arbuckle bringing down the butcher's chopping knife with full force square on Keaton's neck as the latter sprawls across the cutting table. We had just seen "Fatty" use the same blade to hack off the bone end of a raw leg of lamb with a single swipe. Bringing it down on "Buster's" neck without any apparent fakery causes the viewer to audibly gasp and cover one's mouth in horror and shock. I do not know how they pulled this off without decapitating Keaton.

The scenes in the kitchen showcase Arbuckle's dexterity, as he flips knives and pancakes with tossed-off skill to rival W. C. Fields. More conventionally, he uses an industrial-size coffee dispenser to produce all of the liquids on the menu: juice, coffee, soup, gravy, milk, ice cream, and then reveals he uses the same pot as a safe dry place to store his hat and coat.

Keaton has kept busy in the dining room, taking orders and yelling their restaurantese translations to "Fatty" ("oinker slab," "cup of mud," "flip-flap a flap-flip," etc.) and dealing with peeved customers who attempt to send unsatisfactory dishes back to the kitchen. Keaton wheels in and out of the kitchen, smooth teamwork typified by "Fatty" throwing a full cup of coffee with saucer at "Buster" who not only catches it but flips it upsidedown and around without spilling a drop. "Fatty" throws a hot steak across the room and "Buster" does a behind-the-back catch with a plate; then they double it by flinging two pancakes that land in the separate dishes "Buster" is wielding as part of his Egyptian dance.

Al St. John, Arbuckle's real-life nephew, was a far more limited comedian than either Arbuckle or Keaton. What he did have, at this youthful stage of his life, was boundless energy and physical athleticism, which he and/or his uncle decided would be best channeled into extremely violent antics. He could "run funny" and leap like a basketball player while doing the splits, so that's basically what he did throughout the entire portion of his career in which he worked for Arbuckle. (In the talkie era, he was very popular as a hirsute comic sidekick in innumerable Westerns.) That, and smashing things over the heads of other people, running around with a dog at his heels (and often at a spot a lot closer and higher than his heels), and mugging furiously in outrage or gleeful villainy were pretty much his complete comic arsenal until he was old enough to grow a beard.

Bonus: The Cook was lost for 80 years until most of it was unearthed at the Norsk Filminstitutt in 1998 and further portions turned up at the Nederlands Filmmuseum in 2002. In 2003, the American film expert Dennis Doros of Milestone Film and Video produced a DVD of the combined elements that, at 22 minutes, constituted nearly the entire film. It was a remarkable and lovely example of international collaboration to recover, restore, and re-release a long-coveted "lost" film featuring major silent comedians. (In addition to Arbuckle, Keaton, and St. John, Alice Lake was a notable female comedian, especially at Sennett; John Rand was a longtime supporting performer in Charlie Chaplin's entourage; and Bobby Dunn was a very minor but prolific supporting comic who made his slight mark on history as the one-eyed runt of the Keystone Cops litter.)

COPS

(1922, Comique/First National)

Directors: Buster Keaton and Eddie Cline
Writers: Buster Keaton and Eddie Cline
Camera: Elgin Lessley
Cast: Buster Keaton, Joe Roberts, Virginia Fox, Eddie Cline
Running Time (Length): Two reels
Availability: DVD (Quality Information Publishers, Inc.)

Background: Like Charlie Chaplin and Stan Laurel, Buster Keaton was born into a theatrical family. Unlike Chaplin and Laurel, Keaton didn't waste any time going through babyhood, infanthood, and childhood before getting onstage—that was for saps! He crawled out there while only a few months old, and by age three he was a bearded trouper. Literally. His parents' act was a stereotypical Irish vaudeville turn, and father Joe put a red Celtic-style beard on the babe that matched the one Joe wore, just in case anybody had questions about the identity of Buster's progenitor. And then Joe flung the kid around and mopped the floor with him—again, literally. That's why tiny Buster was publicized as "the human mop."

Joe Keaton liked his drink, and eventually he liked it so much that his extremely violent onstage interplay with Buster became too dangerous. Mind you, it took 18 years for that point to be reached. Buster and his mother abandoned Joe, and Buster went to New York City looking for work in legitimate comedy revues. He found it, too, and immediately ditched it (before even opening day) for the world of film comedy at the behest of Roscoe Arbuckle, who was to become his lifelong mentor, best friend, and idol.

Buster was 21 years old and had never known anything but vaudeville, pickup baseball, and how to survive on the never-ending tour grind. The story goes that he spent one day in school and got kicked out on that one day for wisecracking. Unexpectedly, he turned out to have an ungodly bent for camera technology, or perhaps for technology in general, since his film gags turned out to be as intricately (yet instinctually) technologically constructed as a spider's web. To this day, it is probably safe to say, no one filmmaker has ever been his match for devising in-the-camera effects; given the reliance upon computer-generated imagery in 21st-century cinema, it is also probably safe to say no one filmmaker will ever match him in the future.

Keaton learned filmcraft as part of a team with Arbuckle, who was the most generous comedian in Hollywood and never failed to treat Keaton on- and off-screen as his equal and partner. Arbuckle's nephew, Al St. John, usually made it a three-man team. In barely three years, the apprenticeship was over and Keaton was launched as a solo comedian.

In 1920, he made both a feature film (*The Saphead*) and a short (*The High Sign*) before making *One Week*, but it was the latter short that was released first. It made him an instant sensation. A masterpiece, it displayed a total command of the grammar of filmmaking and matched this technical skill with otherworldly comedic talent and skill. He followed up with nine more shorts of similar quality that forced the universe to sit up and take notice of a genius. And then he made *Cops* and took his place alongside Chaplin in the two-person ultimate level of the pantheon of film comedy.

Synopsis: A preface sets the stage for two acts and a coda. In front of what appears to be a prison—but is actually the gates of a mansion—Buster is rejected by his snobby rich girlfriend for being a loser. As usual in his modus operandi, when Buster gets dumped by a girl for failing to make something of himself, he dutifully sets out to make something of himself.

Act One sees our cunning businessman get duped out of his money by a con artist who sells him furniture the con doesn't own. When Keaton loads the furniture onto a horse cart, its real owners show up and assume he is the mover, so they give him directions to their house. Keaton takes a turn up a main street and finds himself in the midst of a policemen's parade. He strikes a pose whose officious authority so impresses an anarchist that the latter tosses a lit bomb into the seat next to Keaton. After using its burning fuse to fire up his cigarette, Keaton does what anyone would do with a used disposable match: tosses it. Unfortunately for him, it lands in the midst of the parade and sends dozens of cops reeling and falling. Those who aren't hurt immediately set out to run Bomber Keaton down to earth.

Act Two consists of one of the loveliest comedy chases ever made. Keaton used literally hundreds of cops, or actors dressed as cops, to turn this into the all-time epic chase after one man. *Les Miserables* has nothing on this gendarmerie pursuit.

The ending winds back to the beginning. Having lured all of these flatfeet into their own station house and then locked the doors on them, Keaton presents himself as a success to his erstwhile girlfriend. She snubs him again, so he turns around and unlocks the prison doors and allows himself to be hoisted back behind bars, just as he was in the opening shot.

Comment: Jim Kline, author of *The Complete Films of Buster Keaton* (1993), wrote, "If the film weren't so breathtakingly hilarious, it would be the perfect subject for a psychological thriller or a tortured existential novel." He's on to something there. As soon as I read that sentence, the thought popped into my mind: "Kafka's *The Trial*." Like that great existentialist noir novel, that black comedy masterpiece of paranoia, *Cops* is about the inescapability of mass, monolithic (those cop uniforms) faceless authority. But only if you're an academic determined to parse the subconscious meaning of Great Art; for ordinary people, it's just a gigantic pile of laughs, one of the best of its kind (to paraphrase another great comic novel, Sterne's *Tristram Shandy*).

Bonus: For reasons of space, *Cops* is the only short Keaton film I have chosen for this book. (He gets three feature films to make up for it, as well as the Keaton–Arbuckle collaboration *The Cook* [1918].) I could have picked eight more: *One Week* (1920), *The Scarecrow* (1920), *Neighbors* (1920), *The Goat* (1921), *The Playhouse* (1921), *The Boat* (1921) (a real favorite of mine), *The Frozen North* (1922), and *The Balloonatic* (1923). He's not the only silent comedian whose two-reelers are so consistently outstanding; the Chaplin of the Mutual period, Charley Chase, and Laurel and Hardy all score equally well in that category. But while Chaplin, Chase, and Laurel and Hardy each turned out at least one stinker among the shorts made in their prime, not one of Keaton's solo shorts is less than very good. He made nine others in addition to the above; those lesser nine make for a wonderful three-or-so hours of comedy film binge-watching.

THE COWBOY SHEIK

(1924, Roach)

Director: Jay Howe
Writers: Will Rogers, Hal Roach
Titles: A. H. Giebler, Will Rogers
Camera: Robert Doran, Arthur Lloyd
Editor: T. J. Crizer
Cast: Will Rogers, Earl Mohan, Marie Mosquini, Billy Engle, Helen Gilmore, William Gillespie
Running Time (Length): 21 minutes (two reels)

Background: It's a challenge to describe Will Rogers's status in the eyes of Americans in the first 35 years of the 20th century. He was a bit like Jon Stewart during the latter's best years on TV's *The Daily Show*: the most insightful and the most listened-to political commentator, with his main stage being in New York City but his words being heard across the nation. Except that, unlike Stewart, his jokes were without malice or, indeed, any kind of emotion, let alone outrage.

Another major difference was that Rogers was a true cross-media sensation. In his day there was no television, let alone the Internet, but he was ubiquitous in all other media: live stage shows, circuses and rodeos, radio, newspapers, books, and movies. And he was wildly popular and beloved in all of them. That's right: beloved. People truly loved Will Rogers because he was just such a nice guy, never had a mean word for anyone, had an aw-shucks personality that was perfectly legitimate to his nature, and epitomized America's self-mythology of the cowboy hero of homespun wisdom and wit. His personal motto was "I never met a man I didn't like." You try disliking a man like that.

He delivered his off-the-cuff observations (he was "observing" long before Jerry Seinfeld was born) in an unbroken monologue, all the while performing eye-popping tricks with his ranch rope. This posed a bit of a problem when he started making silent movies, and all of his silents include long stretches of him yakking away unheard, with only a sentence or two being translated into intertitles. Most of the intertitles are really amusing; still, it's awfully hard not to feel you're getting less than half of his act. He fared better, obviously, when the talkies came along, but his silents are still quite good.

Picking just one Will Rogers silent comedy for this book was no less of a challenge than explaining him to generations born in another century. His best-known silent, at this point, is *Two Wagons, Both Covered* (1924), with *Big Moments from Little Pictures* (1924) and *Don't Park There* (1924) close behind; all are highly enjoyable. In his own day, his most highly regarded silents were a trio based on the character of "Congressman Doolittle": *Going to Congress*, *Our Congressman*, and *A Truthful Liar* (all 1924—that was certainly a good year for Rogers), but I found that trilogy the least representative of his work, except for an opening sequence in the first film, when he provides scripted answers to set-up questions from fellow cracker-barrel philosophers in a country general store.

The Cowboy Sheik may be typical only in portraying him as a shy cowboy, and its story is standard hokum, yet it is a funny film and it does give the viewer a good idea of his charm and attraction for the American public of the day.

Synopsis: Farmhands are competing for the right to ask the pretty teacher (Marie Mosquini) to the dance. Their macho means of competition: tiddlywinks. Not unexpectedly, "Slicky" the tough cowboy (dressed in black, naturally) rides up, kicks the wink out of the tiddlys, and informs the weaklings that he is the only one who will ask the teacher.

And that goes for you, too, "Two-Straw Bill" (Rogers), off there behind the barn practicing your dancin' skills with a large log that you have decked out prettily in an apron and bonnet. "Bill" is constantly making decisions by playing "short straw, long straw" against himself, and cheating himself when he doesn't like the way the game is going.

Charley Chase (left) and Will Rogers (right) in an off-screen comedy consultation (*The Cowboy Sheik*, 1924). *Author's collection*

The teacher evasively tells "Slicky" she'll be going to the dance with her folks, so at least all the farmhands know they still have a chance with her. "Bill" has his master plan in hand: he orders a fancy city-slicker three-piece suit from the Sears, Roebuck catalogue. All duded-up now, his efforts to get a dance with Mosquini are repeatedly interrupted either by his too-tight shoes or by "Slicky." When "Slicky" gets drunk enough to manhandle Mosquini, he and "Bill" lock into a very real-looking fight. It destroys the hard-earned suit but wins Mosquini's heart.

Comment: Earl Mohan had his own not-very-good series of short films as a not-very-good comic boxer; he sets out his credentials for that role in *The Cowboy Sheik*. His brawl with Rogers includes an apparently genuine mouth-bloodying exchange that leaves the latter looking shocked as the blood wells up over his lower lip like water over a dam.

The scene in which Rogers measures himself for the new suit elicits real guffaws and demonstrates the "extra" he could bring to a cliché. He crouches down to measure his inseam from the boot up, which eventually results in his being sent a pair of short pants. When he runs the tired old gag of unwittingly incorporating a post into his own waist measurement, he elevates it by expressing surprise at the result *and repeating the attempted measurement* (with the same result); the repetition provokes the laugh we were reluctant to give to the first effort.

Bonus: While the character he played in performances was an artifact of the past commenting on the follies of the present, Rogers himself was enthusiastic about the promise of the future. He saw aviation as a keystone to a greater civilization, and he both talked the talk and walked the walk (or flew the fly?). He proselytized tirelessly for air travel, including a military air force, and he flew every chance he got. A big selling point of aviation, he insisted, was its safety. You can guess how he was killed in 1935.

THE CRUISE OF THE JASPER B

(1926, De Mille Pictures)

Director: James Horne
Writers: Tay Garnett, Zelda Sears, and John Krafft
Camera: Lucien Andriot
Editor: Jack Dennis
Cast: Rod La Rocque, Mildred Harris, Jack Ackroyd, Snitz Edwards, James Mack, Billy Engle, Otto Lederer, Tiny Sandford, Fred Kelsey, Philip Sleeman
Running Time (Length): 62 minutes (approximately five reels)
Availability: DVD (Grapevine Video)

Background: The pirate film was, surprisingly, rather slow to become a popular genre in American cinema. There were a few things like *The Captain's Captain* in 1919 and the original filming of *The Sea Hawk* in 1924, and finally Douglas Fairbanks's *The Black Pirate* came out in 1926 (notice the gaps in time). Nonetheless, pirate films were grist for the mills of satire throughout the 1920s, especially in short comedies: Laurel, Chase, Turpin, Langdon, Keaton, and many other comedians all took their shots. Fairbanks's outstanding adventure seemed likely to inspire dozens of copycat features—his great films always did so—and the comedy veterans behind the scenes (Horne, Garnett, Krafft, De Mille) moved with alacrity to take the mickey out of the imitators before they could get under way.

Rod La Rocque was a marvelous choice to parody Fairbanks: he was almost as beautiful as Fairbanks, and almost as athletic too. And he had an even better sense of humor about himself than Fairbanks did. Having made his name (and it was a real one, not a Hollywood invention) in social comedies, he relished the opportunity to get practically naked in an out-and-out slapstick parody.

Synopsis: In 1725, a pirate named "Cleggett" takes over the good ship *Jasper B* (a name never explained) and weds the wench he saved aboard it. Eight generations and 200 years later, the last of the "Cleggett" men must follow the tradition set by the pirate ancestor of marrying on board the ship on his 25th birthday, lest he lose the family fortune. Alas, he has apparently already lost the fortune, for auctioneers and repo men seize everything in the house as he awakens on his birthday. Everything, that is, except the shortest towel-wrap in world history and the original pirate's outfit, which latter has somehow survived two centuries in perfect condition. These two outfits, along with extended bedroom and bathroom scenes, allow Rod La Rocque to spend literally the entire movie with his hairless chest on bold display; the fact that the pirate outfit includes very modern hemmed leather beach shorts leaves most of his legs bared, too. Despite the anomaly of biceps that look like they never lifted anything heavier than the razor Rod used to shave his pecs, he has quite the buff bod, and the Jolly Roger moustache goes well with the whole ladykiller pin-up physique.

Real-life Lolita, Mildred (Mrs. Charlie Chaplin) Harris, is the girl who improbably gets a contentious will imprinted on her bare back, which provokes the greedy pursuit of evil Snitz Edwards and necessitates the romantic protection of studly Rod. Fleeing to the scuttled remains of the *Jasper B* in order to be married by its befuddled captain, Rod and Mildred are attacked by the entire U.S. Army, Navy, and Air Force because they had commandeered a U.S. Post Office truck, which of course is a federal offense. Rod orders his hapless servant to "Answer them, Wiggins, shot for shot!" as he successfully marries Mildred and she inherits the fortune assigned to her in the real will.

Comment: This film has no pretensions to being anything but silly fun, and it succeeds in that ambition even though it slides downward from satire to cartoon at the end. It's Sennett slapstick, Sennett "farce comedy," broad and unapologetic humor. Sometimes it gets a little too self-congratulatory in its determination to have fun, as when an intertitle challenges the viewer: "What *else* do you suppose is happening?" Every comedy is entitled to its share of eye-rolling dud in-jokes.

Rod La Rocque obviously had a ball showing off his astounding chest and shoulders and sending up Fairbanks. Mildred Harris has little to do; she manages to inject a bit of twentieth-century naturalness into her naughty bits, which suggests a bit of sly typecasting. The rest of the characters are caricatures, with Jack Ackroyd being the most egregious offender as Rod's mugging butler.

The best running gag has gaggles of snooty, proper ladies at the auction ogling the more-than-half-naked La Rocque repeatedly and unabashedly. Ordered to turn their backs while he gets out of bed (he had forgotten to put on the bottom half of his pajamas before retiring for the night), they all whip out their compacts and pretend to powder their noses while angling the mirrors just right to see behind themselves.

But where's the "cruise" referred to in the title?

Bonus: There's a rather mild movement to rehabilitate the offscreen reputation of Mildred Harris, which for years had been damaged by Chaplin's bitter portrayal of her as a calculating gold digger who first cornered him into marriage by lying about pregnancy and then sought to ruin him in divorce by asserting she had been underage when he had allegedly seduced her; she scored a stinging financial hit in the courts, which only served to reinforce the gold-digger image. In addition, Chaplin made no bones about finding her incredibly boring, empty-headed, and uninteresting, to the extent that for weeks at a time he could not stand to interact with her. No doubt there is a bit of unfairness in his spiteful drawing; there is no doubt a lot of truth to it, too, since the false pregnancy, shot-gun wedding, complete incompatibility of minds, and wallet-bending divorce settlement are all indisputable facts. Harris presented her side of the marriage in an autobiography after many years had cooled memories; her helplessness to connect with Chaplin intellectually arouses sympathy in her account even as it confirms the shallowness of her mind.

She does not need to apologize, nor do her modern-day loyalists, for her work as an actress, however. She may have expected Chaplin to boost her career, but she was already a known quantity with a good resume to her credit. She was the child star in three movies made from L. Frank Baum's "Oz" series of books, and she had had a small part in D. W. Griffith's leviathan, *Intolerance* (1916), as well as the prestigious *The Warrens of Virginia* (1915) made by Cecil B. De Mille. After the divorce, she made more than thirty films but none of them were anything special, not even the titillatingly titled *Lingerie* (1928).

D

A DOG'S LIFE

(1918, First National)

Director: Charles Chaplin
Writer: Charles Chaplin
Camera: Roland Totheroh and Jack Wilson
Editor: Charles Chaplin
Cast: Charlie Chaplin, Edna Purviance, Albert Austin, Granville Redmond, Tom Wilson, Sydney Chaplin, Henry Bergman, Charles Riesner, Loyal Underwood, Minnie (Mrs. Sydney) Chaplin, Alf Reeves, Bob Wagner, James T. Kelly, Mut [*sic*] the dog
Running Time (Length): Three reels
Availability: DVD (Synergy Entertainment)

Background: A Dog's Life was the first film Charlie Chaplin made at the First National studio after leaving Mutual. The two-reelers he made at Mutual remain some of the greatest comedy ever put on film, a virtually unbroken string of absolutely top-drawer laughter. And having accomplished it, it was time for him to move on to new challenges. With *A Dog's Life*, he started boldly enough by stretching out to three reels and creating a real story structure to frame the comic set pieces, and by injecting pathos to an extent he had hesitated to attempt since *The Vagabond* (1916).

Synopsis: The Tramp has been sleeping on a vacant lot, just inside its fence. Awakened by the smell of food on the other side of the fence, he works quickly to sneak some of the food and then to evade the cop who spots him. After an interlude in an employment office, where he is always in the wrong lineup to get hired, he comes across a canine parallel: Scraps the dog has worked quickly to snatch some food and has then been pounced upon by police-minded enemy dogs. Made fast friends by their shared predicament, Charlie and Scraps proceed to fleece lunch-wagon chef Sydney Chaplin out of his sausages and cakes in a nice little family sleight-of-mouth scene.

The action shifts to the Green Lantern, which is not a superhero comic book but a sleazy dive run by Granville Redmond, an implacable and intimidatingly burly autocrat. He has an enthusiastic house band that is rendered, like his customers, sobbingly sentimental by the singing of an extremely nervous ingénue (Edna Purviance). The sobbing endures only until the last note of her song fades, then it's right back into the boisterous hot jazz and jive dancin' that rocks the place. Redmond, perhaps dissatisfied because the customers were crying into their beers instead of drinking them, orders Edna to flirt with them and coax them into buying replacement drinks, presumably watered down only by Redmond's taps and not by tears. When Edna proves as big a failure at allure as she was a success at tear-jerking, the merciless Redmond promptly fires her. For good measure, he also throws out Charlie, who had wandered into the pub and attempted to defend Miss Purviance.

Two of the other unrefined patrons of Redmond's establishment have removed a heavy wallet from an inebriated gentleman. For some reason not trusting their fellow lowlifes in the Green Lantern, they take their leave, hustle into the streets where the same cop (Tom Wilson) whom Charlie had evaded is still loitering, and wisely ditch the evidence by investing it in soil. It happens to be the same soil that serves as the Tramp's bed, to which he now returns. While he naps, Scraps does the doggy thing of digging up treasure and delivering it to his master.

Returning a wealthy man to the Green Lantern, Charlie vows to liberate Edna. As bad luck would have it, the thieves too have returned to the scene of the crime, which they promptly replicate with Charlie as the victim this time. They retire to celebrate with drinks in a private booth. Charlie occupies the adjoining booth (separated by a curtain), knocks out one of the thieves (Albert Austin), and reclaims the money, then proceeds to play the arms and hands of the comatose Austin in order to allay the second thief's suspicions until opportunity arises to conk him, too.

The film ends with a coda in which Charlie, Edna, and Scraps joyously cultivate an improbably huge farm purchased with the stolen money—one of the extremely few (try: "the only") silent comedies in which the Tramp ends up not only happily married but owner of a vast property.

Comments: Critics of Chaplin's longer films—in which I include the three-reelers—complain that they are merely set pieces or skits strung together on the flimsiest of narrative threads. It can't be denied that you could extract almost any episode from these films and present it as a stand-alone mini-film. To leave it at that, however, is to turn a blind eye to the care and artistry he brings to this style of filmmaking.

What Chaplin strives to accomplish is to have his set pieces reflect or parallel each other, or play upon the theme of the storyline. In *A Dog's Life*, the opening scene of the Tramp battling a hot dog vendor and a policeman to secure a bit of food is reflected in Scraps's battles with bigger dogs to hang on to the little bit of food he scrounges. The two of them are then brought together in the scene in which they both do battle with lunch-wagon magnate Sydney Chaplin to swipe a bit of food. Each of these scenes can stand alone; each of them parallels the others and the theme of survival against bigger adversaries (it should be remembered Syd Chaplin was considerably larger than his shrimpy half-brother). They are all neatly brought to fruition in the epilogue, in which the Tramp is planting his own food while Scraps has spawned and prospered on a healthy diet. It takes special skill to accomplish this method of deepening characters and reflecting parallels through a series of comedy skits that can each stand on their own two feet.

The lunch-wagon scene also presents the consistent element of deception in the pursuit of survival. The Tramp's pretense of innocence is a disguise for his theft of the food he needs to live; it parallels his pretense of being the hands of a comatose Albert Austin in the Tramp's pursuit of financial survival, i.e., the stealing back of the money he needs to live.

The Austin scene is hysterically funny. Chaplin's animation of the inanimate Austin is matchless pantomime, featuring boisterous hand rubbing, moustache smoothing, tie straightening, beer-glass clinking. . . . And Austin deserves special commendation for the perfect, immaculate canvas he provides for Chaplin's manipulation. Their chemistry is seamless in all of their many films together—they started out in the same Fred Karno troupe of comedians that brought them both (along with Stan Laurel) to America in 1913—and never more so than in this unforgettable scene.

Bonus: Granville Redmond has the juicy role of the tough bar owner, undoubtedly the second-best role he ever had in Hollywood. He was the preeminent deaf actor in the movies up until Oscar winner Marlee Matlin nearly seventy years later. This didn't amount to much, frankly; he was never more than a background actor except in this film and in Raymond Griffith's *You'd Be Surprised* (1926). The latter film, his best-ever role, gave him the second lead, as a non-deaf officer pretending to be a deaf butler, of all things. It also gave him the opportunity to use American Sign Language onscreen; he taught Griffith enough that the two of them engage in signed conversation throughout the movie, which I can confirm is authentic, if frequently difficult to decipher due to camera angles and a preponderance of fingerspelling over actual signs. Griffith also correctly signs "I'm deaf" in *White Tiger* (1923), and goes on to make a few other signs that, without Redmond's immediate guidance, fail to make sense or to look like actual signs.

Redmond was primarily a painter, and successful enough that he considered acting a very secondary career. Chaplin used him in at least six films between 1918 and 1931: *A Dog's Life, Sunnyside, The Kid, The Idle Class, A Woman of Paris,* and *City Lights*. Redmond said often that he was also in *A Day's Pleasure* and in Douglas Fairbanks's *The Three Musketeers*; although there is no reason to suspect him of inventing credits for himself, he isn't listed in the casts of those films and I am unable to spot him in them. His appearance in *City Lights*, after the talkies had already thrown deaf actors out of work, must have been bittersweet. Redmond was one of only four deaf actors known to have been active in silent Hollywood films, and he was by far the most notable.

Albert Ballin published a memoir/polemic called *The Deaf-Mute Howls* in 1930, only three years before he died at age 66. In it, he blames his deafness for his inability to crack the film industry but claims to have appeared in such prestigious productions as *The Man Who Laughs* (a very famous film widely available today on DVD and Blu-ray) and *The Woman Disputed* (by highly respected director Henry King and featuring huge stars Norma Talmadge and Gilbert Roland). He cannot be spotted in these films, but that does not mean he isn't in them, as he was never more than a space-filler in a crowd scene. His book includes photos and anecdotes that certify to his friendship with Laura La Plante, Neil Hamilton, Betty Compson, Thomas Ince, and Mary Pickford; he also knew Lon Chaney and painted a portrait of Tom Mix's daughter. Ballin did star in an all-deaf slapstick film called *His Busy Hour* (1926), a copy of which still survives in the Gallaudet University archives, but this film never received official studio release or sufficient financial backing.

Emerson Romero made a few short silent comedies under the *nom de rire* of "Tommy Albert." At least one of these films survives complete (*Great Guns*) and shows him playing a character who appears to be "normal" (i.e., not deaf) except for a fraction of a second when he involuntarily begins making the sign for "deaf." Romero apparently had a small role in a Harry Langdon film, *The Cat's Meow*, which is currently unavailable for viewing, and may have been an uncredited performer in at least one Bobby Vernon comedy. When the talkies came in and pushed him out of Hollywood, Romero invented one of the earliest forms of captioning by painstakingly creating his own captions and pasting them onto the frames of sound films, then staging public showings for the benefit of deaf communities. He also created and promoted deaf theatre troupes and participated in some all-deaf films. No wonder they adored him.

Louis Weinberg (stage name David Marvel) only technically qualifies as a deaf actor in the silent film era. Primarily a vaudeville dancer, he is part of a group of Indian princes in *The Woman God Forgot* (1917), a Cecil B. De Mille epic starring opera diva Geraldine Farrar that has been shown in silent film festivals as recently as 2011.

It is interesting that all four of these deaf silent-film-era actors remained in the arts all their lives: Redmond as a painter, Ballin as a painter and writer, Romero as an actor and writer, and Weinberg as a dancer. In contrast, when nondeaf actors of silent films left or were evicted from moviemaking, only a handful took to stomping the theatrical boards, less than a handful became painters, and only a fingerful made a new living as writers (and even then they achieved it mainly with the aid of ghostwriters or "as-told-to" memoirists); mostly they retired, got nonacting (and nonwriting) jobs around movies, got into politics, became small crafts-workers (interior decorators, jewelry designers, etc.), or simply subsisted on the compassion of fans and self-appointed "companions."

DON JUAN

(1926, Warner Bros.)

Director: Alan Crosland
Writer: Bess Meredyth, based on the poem by Lord Byron
Titles: Walther Anthony and Maude Fulton
Camera: Byron Haskins
Editor: Harold McCord
Cast: John Barrymore, Mary Astor, Warner Oland, Estelle Taylor, Montague Love, Myrna Loy, Philippe De Lacy, Yvonne Day, Joseph Swickard, John Roche, Jane Winton, John George, Lionel Braham, Phyllis Haver, Willard Lewis, June Marlowe, Nigel De Brulier, Hedda Hopper, Helene Costello
Running Time (Length): 113 minutes (10 reels)
Availability: DVD (Warner Bros.)

Background: We're approaching the talkies revolution when we arrive at *Don Juan*. There had been many, many experiments with sound on or with film over the preceding decades (yes, decades). *Don Juan* introduced the Vitaphone process of synchronizing recorded music and sound effects to the visual action. It is fortunate *Don Juan* proved to be a tremendous success with both critics and audiences; Warner Brothers attributed its popularity to the sound experiment and decided to build up the technology further in the following year with *The Jazz Singer*. The rest is history.

Synopsis: John Barrymore is introduced as "Don Jose," father of "Don Juan." "Don Jose" catches his beloved wife trysting with another man; in a slight over-reaction, he has the lover sealed up inside a brick wall and then trains his boy to distrust, seduce, ruin, and abandon women before they could betray him. Years on, the grown-up "Don Juan" (also played by Barrymore, although not exactly as a tribute to his own versatility) has become not only The Great Profile but also The Great Lover. He uses his servant and the multiple rooms of his castle-like mansion to service high-falutin' beauties on a schedule broken down into five-minute segments: apparently he is also The World's Fastest Lover, although this doesn't appear to discourage any of his seductees.

Unfortunately, he is living under the rule of the notoriously cruel and dissolute Borgias, and is targeted for the love/hate of "Lucrezia." If you thought it was dangerous to be loved by "Don Juan," you've never been loved by "Lucrezia Borgia"—she makes Glenn Close's character in *Fatal Attraction* (1987) look like Barbara Billingsley's "Mom" in TV's *Leave It to Beaver*.

Complicating the game is "Lucrezia's" pal "Count Donati," who decides he's going to prove his manhood by abducting and raping "Juan's" true love, "Adriane." The enactment of all these bipolar passions involves poisons, swordfights, horseback riding, swordfights while horseback riding, scuttling up and down towering house walls, breaking out of dungeons by way of flooding them from a river, and all sorts of such fitness routines.

Comment: A rousing, old-fashioned, comic-dramatic-romantic, pseudo-biographical, swashbuckling, epic spectacular as only Old Hollywood could make them. The last ten minutes are so full of absurd plot contrivances and superhuman heroics that they almost spoil the fun, but by that time we've been put in the mood to accept anything in the name of entertainment. The direction is pedestrian at best, especially in the action scenes (and why the fights were so obviously fast-forwarded is a matter Alan Crosland must have had to take up with God when he died). The acting is as full of ham as a piñata is full of candy; the exception, amazingly enough, is Barrymore, for this is the only film of his I've seen in which he doesn't overact outrageously. Not that he eschews grandstanding altogether; he just makes a rare effort to control it. He doesn't look drunk all the time, either, which is another novelty. Douglas Fairbanks might have made the acrobatics more believable, but he would have lacked the deep soul Barrymore puts into the role.

Bonus: This is a hell of a cast! Obviously John Barrymore is the legend; he hardly stands alone for distinction, though.

- Warner Oland sealed his own legend playing "Charlie Chan" in the 1930s.
- Nigel De Brulier played similar key historical roles in *The Three Musketeers* (both the 1921 and the 1935 versions), *The Hunchback of Notre Dame* (1923), *Ben-Hur* (1925), *The Iron Mask* (1929), and fictional roles in an enormous number of other major movies including *Intolerance* (1916), *The Four Horsemen of the Apocalypse*

(1921), *A Doll's House* (1922), *Salome* (1923), *Wild Oranges* (1924), *The Beloved Rogue* (1927), *Wings* (1927), *Noah's Ark* (1929), *Moby-Dick* (1930), and so on.

- Estelle Taylor developed from a vamp and decadent gold digger (*Blind Wives*, 1920) to a biblical saint (*The Ten Commandments*, 1923) to, well, whatever she was in the title role of *The Whip Woman* (1928).
- Bad guy Montague Love, typecast against his own surname, bedevilled heroes in films with titles like *Friday the 13th* (1916, not the modern horror franchise), *The Brand of Satan* (1917), *Rasputin: The Black Monk* (1916), *Vengeance* (1918), *The Grouch* (1918), *Three Green Eyes* (1919), *Rough Neck* (1919), *Shams of Society* (1921), *The Devil's Skipper* (1928), and hundreds more.
- June Marlowe split her silent-film years between supporting Rin Tin Tin and supporting fantastic comedians (Laurel and Hardy, Our Gang, Charley Chase, Harry Langdon).
- Phyllis Haver was a fantastic comedian in her own right; I ranked her the greatest female silent comedian except for Mabel Normand in my book *The 100 Greatest Silent Film Comedians*.
- Helene Costello had a strong career in the silents, although her films are now either unavailable or have aged quite badly; she's equally as well known (in her own era, at least) for being the sister of the more successful Dolores Costello and the daughter of the even more successful Maurice Costello, as well as the wife of the yet-more-successful Lowell Sherman.
- Hedda Hopper stepped away from being a truly bad actress to become the most powerful gossip columnist in movie history.
- Joseph Swickard started out with D. W. Griffith, moved on to Mack Sennett's studio where he supported Charlie Chaplin in five films (including the first feature-length comedy, *Tillie's Punctured Romance*, 1914) and supported Mabel Normand and Roscoe Arbuckle in several "Mabel and Fatty" comedies, then supported Larry Semon in *The Wizard of Oz* (1925) and *Stop, Look, and Listen* (1926), and still had time to appear in dramas like *The Four Horsemen of the Apocalypse* (1920).
- Philippe De Lacy, orphaned (and deprived of five siblings) by the Great War, was a child actor who appeared in *Peter Pan* (1924), *Beau Geste* (1926), *The Student Prince in Old Heidelberg* (1927), Greta Garbo's *Love* (1927), two of the most famous "lost" silent films, *4 Devils* (1928) and *The Way of All Flesh* (1927), and then as a grown-up he directed Buster Keaton in the latter's TV show in 1950.
- As for Mary Astor and Myrna Loy, their futures as extremely popular and deservedly respected lead actresses, immortal as "Brigid O'Shaughnessy" in *The Maltese Falcon* (1941) and as "Nora Charles" in the *Thin Man* movies, respectively, need no elaboration; suffice it to say that in *Don Juan* Astor is breathtakingly beautiful, and Loy proves that even as a 21-year-old she was one of the most subtle scene-stealers in silent history.
- And lost in the background of this dazzling cast were luminaries Gibson Gowland (curly-haired blond lead actor in the indomitably brilliant *Greed*, 1925), Dick Sutherland (legendary comic villain in dozens of slapstick two-reelers with Harold Lloyd, Lloyd Hamilton, Laurel and Hardy, etc.), and Gustav von Seyffertitz (another legendary villain who pops up in hundreds of films, both comic and serious).

E

EXPLOSION OF A MOTOR CAR

(1900, Hepworth Manufacturing Company)

Director: Cecil Hepworth
Producer: Cecil Hepworth
Running Time (Length): About 90 seconds

Background: Actual movies, as opposed to flip-card "motion photos" such as those pioneered by Eadweard Muybridge, more or less began in 1894, and immediately the comedy film became a staple genre even if it wasn't as prolific a genre as the actualities, or the porn (which didn't waste any time in becoming a prosperous subterranean genre). The first film ever to be registered with the Library of Congress was *Fred Ott's Sneeze*, a comedy masterpiece, at least of its kind—that is, 10-second sneeze movies. That was a comic documentary—well, it *was!*—so the next year (1895) Louis Lumière in France made the first fictional comedy, *L'Arroseur Arrose* (*The Sprinkler Sprinkled*), in which someone watering flowers with a hose gets suckered by a practical joker who squeezes the hose to stop the water, then releases it so the puzzled gardener gets a faceful of water. This gag went over so big, it was promptly ripped off all over the world (e.g., England's *The Biter Bit* [1900]), became a mainstay of silent slapstick, and was still being recycled 100 years later.

Because cast and crew were never listed in the earliest films, the credits are usually limited to *l'auteur*, and for once that term is accurate: it was usually the same person who came up with the idea for the film ("wrote the script" doesn't apply in this period), cranked the camera, directed the action, did the postproduction, and turned it over to a studio for marketing.

Here are some good examples of the earliest comedy films that are still readily accessible, thanks mainly to the preservation and restoration work of David Shepard of Film Preservation Associates:

- *Explosion of a Motor Car* (1900): Do you get the feeling "motor cars" were practically brand new in 1900 and that they generated tremendous excitement about their movie possibilities? If only the makers of these films could see the *Fast and Furious* franchise! This one is hilarious because the cop, with characteristic British phlegm, diligently writes out tickets for all the pieces of car, clothing, and human bodies that rain down on the street as a result of the titular explosion; he also dutifully organizes the various body parts into lots by gender.

- *Seminary Girls* (possibly filmed in 1895 but usually fixed as 1897): In a dorm room, some schoolgirls have a mild pillow fight that brings down the ire of the dorm mistress. One girl tries to crawl under a bed and gets dragged out. (Edison Manufacturing Company; 30 seconds)
- *Photograph* (1895): Not an actual photograph but rather the attempts of a photographer to take one of a man who is constitutionally incapable of following his orders to sit still. (Lumière Brothers; created by Louis Lumière; cast: Clement Maurice, Auguste Lumière; 35 seconds)
- *How It Feels to Be Run Over* (1900): Title tells the story of this creative little gem from England, which features one of the earliest usages of intertitles to deliver the punch line. (Hepworth Manufacturing Company; produced and directed by Cecil Hepworth; about 1 minute in length)
- *The Big Swallow* (1901): One way to stop the annoying paparazzi from bothering you is, apparently, to eat their camera, and the cameraman, too. Except in this case, the eater then steps back, munching on the machine and licking the figurative gravy off his lips . . . while the camera continues filming him from the outside. Someone, somewhere, is going to insist this is a continuity error. (Williamson's Kinematograph Company; produced and directed by James Williamson; about 1 minute in length)
- *A Chess Dispute* (1903): The power of suggestion through visual means—invented by the Russians/Soviets as the theory of montage, right? Watch this one, in which a chess game degenerates into a clothes-ripping, jumping and stomping, arm-windmilling, blood-letting brawl . . . below the frame, so we're being fooled. Creative and funny. (R. W. Paul; produced and directed by Robert W. Paul; about 70 seconds in length)
- *Airy Fairy Lillian Tries on Her New Corsets* (1905): The "airy fairy" part of the title has nothing to do with Lillian's proclivities; it is a gibe at her enormous obesity (clearly visible through her diaphanous petticoat when she stands sideways to the camera; this is early porn). Her husband tries to help her into her too-tight corset until he collapses from exhaustion. (American Mutoscope/Biograph Company; produced by Wallace McCutcheon and Frank Marion, directed/photographed by Fred Dobson; about 1 minute in length)
- *That Fatal Sneeze* (1905): A somewhat older man pranks his son or grandson with pepper, making him sneeze. (The relationship between the two is never made clear, and is further obscured by having the lad played by a young woman in drag; her true gender is given away by her thick hair, the feminine way she uses her arms, and her penchant for skipping along instead of running.) The lad gets revenge by saturating with pepper the old man's clothes, handkerchief, hairbrush, and everything else he can think of except, oddly enough, the two pairs of slippers that he stumbles over in the middle of the bedroom. What follows in the morning is a series of increasingly violent sneezes by which the old man comically destroys his room, houses,

and stores in the street, vehicles of all kinds, and so on until his final sneeze destroys himself. The destruction is terrifically well done technically and is consistently funny. Fred Ott must have been proud. (Hepworth Manufacturing Company; produced by Cecil Hepworth; directed by Lewis Fitzhamon; about 5:40)

- *The Policemen's Little Run* (1907): Clearly the inspiration for Mack Sennett's Keystone Cops, this little film consists entirely of two dozen policemen chasing a dog, and then being chased by the dog. The wall-to-wall chase, the pratfalls and unrestrained mugging of the cops, the sheer ineptitude of everything they do, the exaggeration and film tricks utilized (they climb up, and then fall down, the entire outside wall and rooftop of a building in pursuit of the dog), their heroic cowardice, and their sheer funniness is everything Sennett "borrowed" for his cops. And it's still laugh-out-loud funny today. (Pathé Frères; directed by Ferdinand Zecca; scenario by André Heuzé; about 5:40)

THE EXTRA GIRL

(1923, Keystone)

Director: F. Richard Jones
Writer: Mack Sennett
Titles: John Waldron
Camera: Homer Scott, Ernie Crockett
Editors: William Hornbeck, Ray Enright
Cast: Mabel Normand, Ralph Graves, George Nichols, Anna Hernandez, Vernon
   Dent, Ramsey Wallace, Charlotte Mineau, Louise Carver
Running Time (Length): Six reels

Background: At the turn of the decade, Mabel Normand's career and private life alike were in turmoil. She had finally given up on Mack Sennett as a lover and fiancé, and wanted to extend the split into their professional lives. Sennett, a mama's boy and most likely a closeted homosexual, was unhappy to lose his "beard"; more than that, though, he didn't want to lose his star comedienne. He tried to accommodate Normand's insistence on moving away from two-reelers and into feature films. Together they made *Mickey* in 1916, but for various reasons/excuses Sennett didn't get it into theaters until 1918. The delay led to Normand severing their professional relations.

However he may have misused and subverted her career even as he kept her up on the screen throughout the 1910s, Sennett had been good for Normand in their personal lives. He provided an anchor and fatherly guidance even if he didn't provide marriage. Adrift from him, she spiraled into chaos, becoming the prototype for the Hollywood party girl, using drugs, drinking heavily, and generally behaving irresponsibly. It turned out that her health was a lot more fragile than anyone had ever suspected; it could not stand up to this lifestyle. As if ill health weren't enough, scandal after scandal erupted to destroy her reputation and make her a shaky proposition at the box office. *The Extra Girl* was her last work of excellence.

Synopsis: Rural girl "Sue" (Normand) loves the boy she grew up with, "Dave" (Ralph Graves), but her parents intend to marry her off to a fat man with a good job (Vernon Dent). "Sue's" resistance to marriage is also driven by her movie-fan dream of winning a magazine beauty contest, the prize of which is a screen test in Hollywood. A predatory "merry widow" (Charlotte Mineau), who has plans to seduce "Dave," gets rid of her rival by ensuring she wins the contest. The news reaches "Sue" as she is desperately stalling on the wedding ceremony that will handcuff her to Dent forever; with "Dave's" help, a frenzied chase ensues in and around the house, and although their original scheme for escape is broken by discovery and pursuit, "Sue" still manages to get away and catch the train for Los Angeles.

Once there, the movie studio spokesman points out that she won the contest by fraud (thanks to the widow's machinations) and therefore they don't owe her the screen test. She'll get one eventually, though, and it will turn out to be an unintentional hoot; until then, she'll have to work as a lowly assistant in the costume department, where she is treated rather brutally by Louise Carver as the wardrobe mistress.

"Sue" also helps out with some of the animals, setting up the justly famous sequence in which Normand unwittingly leads a real lion through the studio. The lion breaks free and commences to chase her and other hapless film people in a genuinely terrifying scene. The creature repeatedly leaps through transoms (i.e., window frames set above doors; they were common in homes and business offices throughout the first half of the 20th century) in pursuit of Normand. At one point, she and two men take refuge in a cramped washroom; the lion smashes the bottom panel of the door and continually slashes its paw through the hole, quite visibly snagging Normand's leg at least twice. She was injured not only in these shots but in others as well. It must have been a traumatizing experience for her.

By the time of the lion's rampage, "Dave" has joined her in Hollywood, getting work as a stagehand; he, of course, is the one who saves her from the lion by turning a fire hose on it. Her parents also join her, "selling out" (their words) for a retirement they hope to fund by investing the proceeds of their "sale." The investor whom "Sue" helpfully chooses for them turns out to be a crook. "Dave" saves the day by beating up the crook, just as he had beaten up his romantic rival Vernon Dent back in the boonies, never mind the fact that Ralph Graves doesn't look like he could beat up Bambi in real life. The money is returned to the parents, "Dave" marries "Sue," and they all return to their contented home in the country.

Comment: The more I watch and rewatch this film, the more I believe it to be one of the two or three best films Mack Sennett ever supervised. And along with *Mickey* (1918), it's the best film Normand made in her lengthy career.

The main criticisms that have been leveled at *The Extra Girl* over the years are that the storyline is hackneyed and the "dramatic interludes," in Leonard Maltin's phrase, "don't really work" (*Leonard Maltin's Classic Movie Guide*, 3rd ed., 2015). I disagree. Sennett, who gets sole writing credit but almost certainly relied upon his entire stable of writers to help out, put every element of great storytelling into this movie, and then hired actors who could all put across exactly the effects he wanted in each scene.

There is comedy of every type in this film: verbal, situational, slapstick. There is pathos and melodrama. There is thrill comedy, scare comedy, excitement comedy. There is crime, dastardly doings, hissable villainy. There is heart-pounding tension and drama. There are dogs, lions, and babies, trains, buggies, and cars. There's social realism and exposure of intolerable working conditions for the lower classes. There is a behind-the-scenes documentary of the film industry and a behind-the-façade documentary of the rural oppression of women. There's love of all kinds, family love that can be both crushing and supportive, romantic love that refuses to concede to barriers. There's running away from home, and reconciliation, and perpetuation of home life with subsequent generations.

All of these different elements are handled with a skill that elevates the film above its clichés and predictability. George Nichols, who had already proven himself the perfect father for Normand in *Mickey*, is the glue whose nuanced performance holds the high standard for all the other actors to aim for. I don't think *The Extra Girl* would have been nearly as good with anyone else in his role; he is just plain wonderful, incredibly subtle, able to make his character believable in his veering back and forth from forcing Normand's wedding to Dent to supporting her elopement with Graves, from opposing her acting pretensions to supporting them, and so on. He is given an awful lot of pathos to handle, and he manages to win our sympathy with it instead of our cynical scoffing at it.

Normand may not have been in the best of health at this time, but she performs superbly. There isn't a minute that we don't feel intensely for her, feel intensely *with* her. We really feel sorry for her at having to marry Dent; we really cheer for her when she desperately scurries in and out and about the house in her broken plan to escape the wedding.

The coda, in which Normand tells hubby Graves that hearing their baby call her "mamma" means more to her than any Hollywood career, is an unfortunate but unavoidable concession to the social norms of the time. Knowing what the next few years holds for Mabel Normand offscreen, the viewer may feel this ending is in extremely bad taste. Onscreen and off, it bows to the moralistic Grundys that deplored the Hollywood lifestyle and product and demanded that society punish girls like Normand and "Sue" who had the temerity to want a life and career of their own. Don't let the finale spoil the pleasure and the fun of watching *The Extra Girl*.

Bonus: Mabel Normand was one of the faded stars whom Hal Roach signed up in the late 1920s, not just because they were now cheap talent but also because Roach hoped to help them revive their doomed careers. Normand was arguably the most pathetic of this lot; the viewer of her final films can't help cringing at her appalling physical appearance in *Raggedy Rose* (1926), *The Nickel-Hopper* (1926), and *Anything Once!* (1927), even though she is still intermittently capable of showing her great acting chops and comic timing in the first two of those films.

Contrary to myth, she did *not* die from drugs or other unnatural means. From adolescence she had lived with tuberculosis; by the time she was a prematurely old 35, it had progressed to the point where pneumonia easily carried her off.

F

THE FALL GUY

(1921, Vitagraph)

Director: Larry Semon
Writers: Larry Semon, Norman Taurog, and Edward Moriarty
Camera: Hans Koenekamp
Cast: Larry Semon, Norma Nichols, Oliver Hardy, Frank Alexander, Bill Hauber, Al
  Thompson
Running Time (Length): Two reels

Background: It's somewhat tempting to call Larry Semon the Miles Davis of silent comedy. Like Davis, Semon attracted and trained some of the best in the business. He was idolized by everybody else in the same business. He cut new trails and produced works of a greatness that was indisputable even when you didn't actually *like* it. While recognized as a genius in his art, he also sold a hell of a lot of tickets, at least for a time. And in the later part of his career, he was lambasted as a tyrant, an egotistical browbeater, a squandered talent, a brooding and angry loner. Davis, though, will never be forgotten, nor will his seminal place in the history of jazz music ever be dissipated by the mists of time. Semon, to the contrary, is forgotten, or if not forgotten, then disparaged and downgraded and made a minor figure even among silent comedy aficionados.

In his heyday—roughly between 1917 and 1925—Semon was one of the most popular silent comedians with the public, with the critics, and with his peers in the business. Budding and seasoned talents alike, such as Stan Laurel, Oliver Hardy, Frank Alexander, and others, clamored to play mere supporting roles in his films, learning from him how to put over the big gags and how to sell the comedy of confrontation. Bill Hauber, a dexterous and fearless if not particularly funny secondary player, left a solid career with Mack Sennett to become Semon's stunt double—and Hauber wasn't the only person to consider it a promotion.

Son of a theatrical family, Semon spent a few years as a cartoonist, and then spent the rest of his life living the cartoon. His films are like real-life trial runs for "Bugs Bunny" or "Tom and Jerry" 'toons: unbelievable scales of stunts and props and personal violence, from which all characters emerge with clothes tattered and faces blackened but no limbs damaged, let alone lost. Moreover, Semon made sure his films were cranked at a speed that paralleled the fast editing of Looney Tunes productions.

Semon took the thrill and spectacle aspects of Sennett's violent slapstick and made it the major part of his comedy. In this, he was roughly simultaneous with Harold Lloyd, who was developing his thrill comedy at Hal Roach's studio part and parcel with the development of his "glass character." Both Semon and the "glass" Lloyd proved immensely popular with the public and gave rise to the genre of thrill comedy or action comedy that combined the best features of cliff-hanger serials and mad slapstick.

Synopsis: Oliver Hardy is a two-faced guy (he needs two faces to cope with the bushels of hair allotted to his eyebrows and upper lip). He's the elegant, suave "Gentleman Joe" on the surface; not very far beneath, he's the dastardly "Black Bart," the terror of the Old West. He's plotting to steal something-or-other . . . maybe Norma Nichols's heart, maybe her jewels, maybe both. The only thing that stands in his way, apparently, is happy-go-lucky "Larry." Hardy does his best to eliminate this nuisance, forcing him to attempt suicide by blowing out his brains (he blows out the seat of Sheriff Frank Alexander's pants instead, which is a pretty fair metaphor for the original target) and removing a guardrail so "Larry" will fatally fall two stories to the floor of the local bar (he survives, somehow). Suffice it to say nothing works and "Larry" saves the day, the girl, and the jewels.

The Fall Guy (1921). Frank Alexander (white shirt) in center, Norma Nichols to his right, Larry Semon holding up the barn. *Courtesy of Claudia Sassen*

Comment: There are an awful lot of visual gags about cars in this film: cars with saddle extensions in back, cars possessed by the devil, cars pulled by mules, cars speeding around while housed inside garages, cars whose radiators shoot multiple fountains of fluid, cars stuck in muddy potholes, cars with mismatched wheels, and cars that won't start when "Larry" cranks 'em until he gets the bright idea of disguising himself so the car won't recognize him. These jokes are dominant in the first reel, and you can be forgiven for wondering when the film is going to get really hilarious, because the car gags don't always work.

Once the setting switches to the inside of a typical Old West bar, however, *The Fall Guy* becomes a riot. It mocks the conventions of the Western film with barbs so piercing only Keaton's *Go West* is in the same class. Keaton doesn't appear to have loved what he was chaffing—it is generally agreed his aim in making it was to ream out William S. Hart for Hart's sanctimonious denunciation of Roscoe Arbuckle—whereas Semon displays a knowledgeable affection for the genre's tropes and clichés. His comic take on those tropes is consistently inventive and truly hilarious; there are no misfires among his gags in this section. (*Caveat emptor*: make sure you are watching the print that includes *all* of the intertitles used in the bar setting. Some available prints cut out the two intertitles that provoke the biggest laughs of the entire film.)

Bonus: Like Raymond Griffith, Larry Semon had the ability and the willingness to work with talented and beautiful women comedians, which was not particularly common in the silent era. And like Charlie Chaplin, Semon had the questionable habit of making his female costars his offscreen lovers.

Around the time of *The Fall Guy*, Semon was living with Lucille Carlisle, and yet it happened to be one of the "off" moments in their on-and-off liaison. After her excellent work as Semon's leading lady in 1920's *The Grocery Clerk*, *The Fly Cop*, *The Stage Hand*, *Solid Concrete*, *The Suitor*, and *The Sportsman*, Lucille took off for New York partly to try her luck on the stage and partly to cool off Semon's marital intentions, which apparently she didn't share. The exact nature of their romantic entanglement is open for speculation, with at least one contemporary account blackening Carlisle's reputation by presenting her as a cold, methodical gold digger looking for a sugar daddy in NYC, and other accounts or hindsight analyses suggesting she had to escape Semon's autocratic control for a while.

In either case, Semon spent much of 1921 experimenting with other leading ladies, much as Miles Davis experimented with other saxophonists following John Coltrane's departure from his band. Unlike Coltrane, Carlisle returned to the fold in 1922, mainly because she failed to make her mark in other venues. Her eventual on- and offscreen romantic successor, the sublimely gorgeous Dorothy Dwan, loyally stuck it out with Semon on both sides of the projector until he became more or less incapacitated (health-wise and/or finance-wise).

The Fall Guy features Norma Nichols, one of the test replacements for Carlisle who managed to last more than one Semon film (she lasted four). She puts up a feisty performance, taking the physical abuse and dishing it out with all the spirit of someone who had already served a long and successful drill in Sennett comedies, "Ham and Bud" (Lloyd Hamilton and Bud Duncan) punchfests, and some early Charlie Chaplin shorts (*Dough and Dynamite, Gentlemen of Nerve* [both 1914]). Her sister married Hal Roach, who promptly gave Norma a job writing scenarios at his comedy factory as testimony to the respect the industry had for her comic chops. Given this impressive curriculum vitae, it is worth seeking out *The Fall Guy* just to appreciate the efficiency and skill of a less-heralded female slapstick artist.

FATTY AND MABEL ADRIFT

(1916, Keystone)

Director: Roscoe Arbuckle
Writer: Roscoe Arbuckle
Cast: Roscoe Arbuckle, Mabel Normand, Al St. John, Frank Hayes, May Wells, Wayland Trask, James Bryant, Joe Bordeaux, Glen Cavender
Running Time (Length): 30 minutes (three reels)

Background: There's no question Roscoe Arbuckle and Mabel Normand were the biggest stars in Mack Sennett's stable, from the moment they were teamed up in 1913 to the moment Arbuckle left in 1916. Each was immensely lovable, on- and offscreen, and both were embraced—separately and as a team—by viewers from the get-go. Each was a wonderful and even today an oft-underrated comedian of great skill and creativity. Equally important, if not more so, they had a rare genuine affection for one another that came across as possibly the best screen chemistry in the silent era (aside from Laurel and Hardy, who could scarcely be expected to romance one another in that era). The improvisatory nature of early comedy films enhanced this impression: because they were often making it up as the camera was cranked, their smiles and laughter and flirting were manifestly real, natural, spontaneous.

Sennett showed some appreciation for what they had meant to his studio and his box-office returns: he gave them the resources and the unusual three-reel length to make probably the best and most elaborate of their films together, *Fatty and Mabel Adrift*. They made at least two more films, but *Adrift* was effectively the finale to their exquisite teamwork.

Synopsis: Fittingly, since so many of their comedies had been set in rural locations, *Fatty and Mabel Adrift* finds them and their usual third-wheel Al St. John living on farms—Arbuckle and St. John both in their rather shopworn "feudin' hayseeds" roles, Mabel in her customary "pretty milkmaid/daughter" slot. After some routine rivalry-on-the-farm shtick, "Fatty" marries "Mabel," and they move into a little cottage on the seashore.

The scenes of their first day of married life in their own home are the apex of the romance and love between the two stars. Gentle humor enlightens some standard gags about "Mabel's" cooking and baking skills, they generously share the limelight and the jokes with Luke the dog, and then they spend their wedding night in separate beds, which is more a reflection of their endearing innocence than it is a bowing to the moral purists in the audience. An unexpectedly imaginative expression of both the love and the innocence is the filming of the shadow of Arbuckle kissing Normand goodnight.

In the morning, they find a fair bit of damp in the house. In fact, it's out in the middle of the lake and sinking, thanks to jealous St. John who had enlisted some cronies to cast it adrift in the night. Luke the dog foreshadows Lassie by desperately swimming, running, jumping, and running some more to fetch help that saves "Fatty" and "Mabel" from a watery demise.

Comment: The pervading feeling within this film is one of sweetness and charm. The humor—and there is quite a bit of good comedy—mostly underpins the sunny bliss of the first days of married life, even as the newlyweds thrash about in neck-deep water, which is probably not how they envisioned their initial morning-after as husband and wife. Both Arbuckle and Normand are effortlessly engaging. The wedding seems to have graduated them from yokel sensibilities, too, as they quickly drop the rural mannerisms once they are ensconced in their house. In contrast, St. John never grows up; he's got manure on his shoes and in his soul, as if he never wants to follow his costars out of hick slapstick and into social comedy. And with a few exceptions, he never did.

Bonus: Arbuckle seldom reprised the yokel character after he left Sennett. He didn't really get much more sophisticated in his subsequent series for Comique Films with Buster Keaton and St. John, but at least he was now playing urban types. After three years (1917–1919), the trio split up, and Arbuckle began testing the waters of light comedy features, completing his evolution from slapstick stubble-jumper to suave social comedian. And then, of course, came the disaster of scurrilous accusations and court trials that ruined his career and his life, despite his being totally exonerated of the charges.

FIREMAN, SAVE MY GAL!

(1919, Gayety/Christie/Mutual)

Director: Craig Hutchinson
Cast: George Ovey, Lillian Biron, Al Haynes, Harry Rattenberry
Running Time (Length): 12 minutes (one reel)

Background: In any era, in any business, there is the realm of the great, the realm of the good, the realm of the bad, and the realm of the unremarkable in any way. Comedy of the silent era was no different. You had Keaton at the top, Ton of Fun as the good, Billy West as the bad, and hundreds of unremembered toilers off to the side. George Ovey was one of the unremembered.

After a lifetime of bare subsistence in most of the lower kinds of live entertainment such as vaudeville and minstrel shows, a chance acquaintance with David Horsley got Ovey into the movies in 1915, a very visible 45 years old. Horsley was a seat-of-the-pants producer whose various studios never spluttered along for more than a few years, but he took Ovey with him in the lifeboat every time another of his ships went down in the briny deep. Ovey wasn't talented enough to be in demand elsewhere, so he gratefully accepted the boss's charity, until about 1920; thereafter, he scrounged hundreds of supporting roles in both comedies and dramas, his fifteen minutes of fame long since gone but his vigorous swimming keeping his head above water.

Synopsis: George Ovey and Al Haynes are rivals for the hand of the underwhelming "beauty," Lillian Biron. While she leisurely bathes, visibly naked (at least from the armpits up), the rivals engage in competitive byplay that at one point sees Ovey hike his chair right into Biron's bathroom by mistake. Haynes, an intimidating though not large type, is easily winning the competition until Ovey falls through a trapdoor into a convenient basement liquor stash. Emboldened by a swift swig or two, he gets back up to the main floor and challenges Haynes to various forms of violence, all of them stylized and harmless, including a swordfight during which they politely trade weapons.

Al loses by driving his sword into the well-upholstered buttocks of Biron's father, who happens to be the fire chief, and who promptly fires Haynes out of his house in favor of Ovey as his prospective son-in-law. Haynes vows revenge: he recruits some disreputable fellows to burn down the father's house. Being extremely bright boys, the arsonists light a small fire under the icebox in the kitchen. The fire melts the ice, which drips straight onto the fire and puts it out. The brave fire chief arrives just in time to stamp out the dead embers and present himself as the exhausted hero of the hour.

Comment: The fact that Ovey is not a noteworthy comedian, that the Gayety Comedies produced by Al Christie for Mutual distribution are an unsubstantial lot, and that the meager resources available to these filmmakers meant they had to use an ordinary house for a setting, doesn't mean *Fireman, Save My Gal!* is a weak film. To the contrary, it's an excellent example of the skill and charm and easy amusement that can be found in many a film whose only ambition was to fill the bottom of a movie-house bill.

Ovey and Haynes have fine teamwork, coordinating their movements perfectly. The swordfight earns chuckles, even if it isn't very imaginative. There are some weird gags involving a large hole in the wall between the bathroom and the sitting room, but the fire scenes are very funny.

Ovey is another small guy—it sometimes seems three of every four silent comedians was less than 5′6″ tall—and a string bean to boot. He's a self-confident shrimp but not an arrogant one, and not one who fights above his weight. You can see why he never really made it, although he did have a modest following outside the big cities and the more sophisticated theater circuits. This is a nice film that probably shows him at his best and is worth seeking out to get a measure of how enjoyable even an average silent comedy film can be.

Bonus: Most of Ovey's films are gone, lost, unavailable, or squirreled away somewhere. They just weren't good enough or unusual enough for care to be taken for their preservation. Darren Nemeth and Ben Model got together to recover most of *Fireman, Save My Gal!* and put it up on YouTube, and for that we owe them warm thanks. A second film on YouTube, *Holding His Own* (1917), isn't nearly as good, unfortunately.

FLAMING FATHERS

(1927, Roach)

Directors: Leo McCarey and Stan Laurel
Writer: Uncredited (probably Laurel)
Titles: H. M. Walker
Editor: Uncredited, probably Richard Currier
Cast: Max Davidson, Martha Sleeper, Edward Clayton, Tiny Sandford, Lillian Leighton, Charles King
Running Time (Length): Two reels

Background: Remember Mack Sennett's "formula" for making comedies back in the 1912–1915 era? Take a (male) comedian, a cute girl, a policeman, and a villain to the park, and just crank the camera as they make it up on the spot, right? Stan Laurel was such a protean talent that this still sounded like an easy, quickly made barrel of fun to him in 1926—no comic possibility, however shopworn, could faze him—and Leo McCarey was nothing if not an amiably willing master of comedy direction. So they loaded up Max Davidson, Martha Sleeper, Tiny Sandford, and Edward Clayton in a jalopy—filming the mechanical mayhem that befell Davidson as they went along, naturally—and wheeled out to the nearby beach. Nothing could be more normal than to invite all the kids to be in the movie (free of charge, saving the studio a bundle) and to film Davidson amusing them with his funny faces. And use the crowds already present: just have them race over to where Davidson is going through his antics and surround him when told.

Synopsis: Daughter Martha Sleeper is suspected of planning to elope with boyfriend Edward Clayton under the ruse of spending a day at the beach. So "Papa" Max Davidson invites himself to chaperone them. Payback starts with the drive to the beach, which apparently takes the same grooved road Harry Langdon's friends took him along in *Saturday Afternoon* the year before (1926); the results are the same, too, as Davidson and Langdon both slipped down in the rumble seat and found themselves rattling around in various interesting locations inside the auto's mechanisms.

When they arrive at the shore, everybody rents bathing suits, a Twenties commonplace that has today's viewers cringing in hygienic hysteria. Everyone makes fun of Davidson's oversized suit, which looks as though it was on hold for Roscoe Arbuckle. You know a dog is going to yank it off him, and you know Davidson will spend the rest of the movie in makeshift outfits such as a Tarzan seaweed suit and an extra-long policeman's coat. Weaving in and out of those two themes are a multitude of amusing storylines: a running battle with a beach bully, which attracts crowds of bathers and keeps interrupting a cop's luncheon; Davidson's attempts to catch Sleeper and Clayton hand in hand, or bum in lap; a couple's futile attempts to enjoy a picnic; a pile of kids racing around having a grand time chasing Davidson and laughing at the faces he makes; the timid arrival of "Mama," whose timidity morphs into outrage the instant she lays eyes on "Papa"; and finally his arrest and escape from the Black Maria police wagon.

Comment: Flaming Fathers is a trifle that delights. The gags are classic Stan Laurel gags, or at least they would *become* classic Stan Laurel gags when he reused many of them in future Laurel and Hardy films. And it's a joy to watch Leo McCarey stitch all the various storylines together so that they flow smoothly into and out of one another. This is a beautifully constructed comedy, displaying all the aplomb with which McCarey would create his great talkie features such as the Marx Brothers' all-time classic *Duck Soup* (1933), W. C. Fields's *Six of a Kind* (1934), Mae West's *Belle of the Nineties* (1934), and *The Awful Truth* (1937).

Bonus: Mack Sennett had Mabel Normand. He also had the stupendously talented and infinitely gutsy Phyllis Haver, gorgeous Marie Prevost, and criminally underrated Minta Durfee. But Sennett was an old-school guy who didn't believe women could be funny, so he routinely underused all of these skilled comedians. Hal Roach was probably about as sexist as all the other men of his generation, but he did believe in using accomplished women as foils in his films, strong ladies who were rarely wilting wallflowers. His four best were the riveting Anita Garvin, the melting Jobyna Ralston, spirited Bebe Daniels, and sweet Martha Sleeper.

Of the four Roach beauties, Sleeper was the one who got the Minta Durfee end of the stick—that is, she never seemed to catch the wave that carried all the others to feature films and fan reverence. Certainly she had a track record that would leave any silent comedy fan writhing in envy: she was leading lady to Charley Chase, Harold Lloyd, Max Davidson, Stan Laurel, James Finlayson, Glenn Tryon, Oliver Hardy, and others. She was lovely, she was natural and unaffected, she had excellent timing, and she was immensely likable. Her career didn't disappear when the talkies came along—she averaged more than three films per year between 1930 and 1936—but her roles were small, sometimes uncredited, and quite disillusioning.

Aside from a small role in *The Bells of St. Mary's* (1945), which a retired Sleeper essayed as a favor to director McCarey, she devoted herself more and more to creating one-of-a-kind jewelry. These items became quite sought after and she evidently made a good sideline out of them: they still sell for rather high prices on eBay today.

FOX-TROT FINESSE

(1915, Vitagraph)

Director: Sidney Drew
Writer: Maurice Morris
Cast: Mr. and Mrs. Sidney Drew, Ethel Lee
Running Time (Length): 16 minutes (surviving print)

Background: Sennett's Keystone Studio had Roscoe Arbuckle and Mabel Normand as its top comedy couple; Vitagraph had Mr. and Mrs. Sidney Drew. The difference, obviously, was that the Drews were an actual married couple offscreen as well as onscreen. This state of affairs had a real influence on their films. The

Arbuckle–Normand movies are all about wooing and flirting and breaking up and reconciling, innocent kids playing at love. The Drew movies show the couple as already veteran (middle-aged, in Sid's case) marrieds, no innocence left, no breakups or reconciliations or flirting (except, for Sid, with *other* women), just a comfortable life together, knowing each other's little quirks and accepting them.

The Drew films, consequently, are rarely about romancing. Instead, they deal with situations that arise between long-marrieds, or between them and external forces. They are mature comedies, even when Sid is indulging in a little bit of immature behavior.

Synopsis: The opening scenes are a reworking of *Jerry's Mother-in-Law* (1913): the Drews' house is darkened by the presence of a pterodactyl mother-in-law who rules the breakfast table and everything else in the lives of a cowed Sidney and a seemingly indulgent Lucille. Ethel Lee plays the mother-in-law as a woman so frosty she wouldn't melt in a *ménage à trois* with Warren Beatty and Jack Nicholson. When she finally departs and demands that Sid "Kiss . . . me . . . goodbye!" he instantly breaks into a despairing sweat, tremblingly gathers up his courage, dusts off her fossilized lips with his hanky, and can just barely muster a nanosecond-long peck before nearly collapsing. It's still hilarious: exaggerated as it is, it never *feels* exaggerated to the viewer, and that makes it all the funnier.

Now that they're alone together, Sid and Lucille can get back to doing what she loves best: fox-trot dancing. They're old marrieds, not young marrieds, after all. Sid, though, being twice Lucille's age, has done enough dancing in his lifetime; he'd rather just sit at home reading magazines and smoking. He connives to get

Mr. and Mrs. Sidney Drew, *Fox-Trot Finesse* (1915). *Author's collection*

out of the nightly pirouetting by faking an ankle injury; the ruse lasts only a short while before Lucille catches on. She writes a letter asking her mother to return to them to help Sid manage with his lame foot, lets him read it, and it proves to be the magic cure for his injury.

Comment: Like all of the Drews' films, this one succeeds entirely on the delightful personality of Sidney Drew and his tremendously witty pantomime. He never overplays even when he's mugging it up; he's playing it straight even when he's laughing to himself; and above all, he's totally natural even when he's performing. He has the little touches of a genius comedian: watch him gleefully kiss the mother-in-law's luggage goodbye as it is trundled out of the house, such a joyful contrast to the suicidal kiss he was forced to give the mother-in-law herself. Chaplin might have done the same, but Chaplin would have done it as a comedian pulling a gag for the benefit of an audience; Drew does it as an old uncle pulling it spontaneously for only himself secretly, with no awareness of an audience watching.

Bonus: The fox-trot, of course, was a dance craze popularized by Vernon and Irene Castle in 1914, recent enough that this movie was a timely response to it and an accurate reflection of its incredible popularity across America: the average married couple really did attend house parties among their friends where everybody did nothing but dance the fox-trot.

Throughout the 20th century, it was spelled as both "fox-trot" and "fox trot." In the 21st century, for some reason, it is now being spelled "foxtrot." I have not seen the original title-card for the film—all the various copies I have seen have used replacement cards made in the last quarter of the 20th century—so I am unsure of the punctuation Vitagraph adopted in 1915. I have chosen to use the hyphenated version herein.

G

THE GENERAL

(1927, Buster Keaton Productions/United Artists)

Directors: Buster Keaton and Clyde Bruckman
Writers: Clyde Bruckman, Al Boasberg, and Charles Smith
Camera: Dev Jennings and Bert Haines
Editors: J. Sherman Kell, Buster Keaton, and Harry Barnes
Cast: Buster Keaton, Marion Mack, Frederick Vroom, Glen Cavender, Joe Keaton,
   Mike Donlin, Jim Farley, Charles Smith, Frank Hagney, Edward Hearn, Frank
   Barnes, Tom Nawn, Ray Thomas, Bud Fine, Red Rial, Red Thompson, Jimmy
   Bryant, Ray Hanford, Charles Philips, Al Hanson, Tom Moran, Ross McCutcheon,
   Anthony Harvey
Running Time (Length): Eight reels
Availability: DVD (Alpha Video)

Background: Ever since the Civil War, a story has floated around the United States about a soldier who stole an entire locomotive from under the enemy's nose. Clyde Bruckman, one of the most crucial behind-the-scenes players in silent film history, found a print version of the tale, showed it to Buster Keaton, and the two of them speculated how it could be best brought to the screen. It was simply an interesting possibility until Keaton thought of flipping the real story around: the North heisted the train, but what if the South had heisted it back?

Imbued with legends of the Confederate army being filled with true gentlemen, noble exemplars of chivalry and graciousness, bravery and high principles—legends that were still virtually unquestioned 60 years after the war, even in the Northern states—Keaton reasoned that no one could help sympathizing with a Confederate man, at least if he were a harmless engineer rather than a soldier. This shaped the lead role to fit him: the apparent loser who was repeatedly rejected by the army (more sympathy for him from the audience) but who overcomes incredible odds to achieve something that his superiors couldn't have done. Even if the Confederate army was the bad guys' army, the audience would root for Keaton's character to succeed.

Once he had worked out that twist on the premise, Keaton became consumed with the enterprise. No expense was too great, no amount of extras or props was too many, and no amount of care or time was excessive in making this a perfect film.

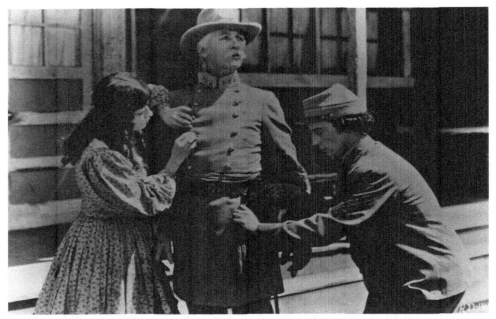

Marion Mack and Buster Keaton make sure Frederick Vroom's uniform is immaculate in *The General* (1926). *Courtesy of Bruce Calvert*

Synopsis: It's war! The Civil War, at that, and we unexpectedly find Buster Keaton as Confederate loyalist "Johnny Grey" (what, would "Johnny Reb" have been too obvious?). As a railroad engineer in charge of the good locomotive "The General," "Johnny" is deemed too valuable to be wasted as cannon fodder. Unfortunately, the recruiting officer doesn't explain this thinking to "Johnny," so he is helpless to refute charges of cowardice from his girlfriend "Annabelle" and her war-going father and brother.

He gets his chance to be a hero when the Union army steals "The General" and plans to take it north while destroying Southern lines as it goes. Actually, "Johnny" doesn't see this as a chance to be a hero; all he knows is that his personal locomotive has been swiped and he is going to get it back if it kills him. He doesn't know that his second and lesser love, "Annabelle," is a hostage aboard the train.

"Annabelle" and the Southern cause become "Johnny's" greater motivation only when he holes up in a house that happens to be the Union headquarters and he (1) discovers "Annabelle's" plight, and (2) overhears Union plans. It's only after these new motivations introduce themselves to him that he finds "The General" in a Union-held station. Now he can combine all three of his inspirations: rescue "Annabelle" and "The General" together and bring them back home along with the Union army plans, delivering all three to the Confederate army.

The military planning in this film is so diligent, it took me a couple of viewings to appreciate it; the first few times, it just kind of flowed over my attention as being intricate and unnecessary to one's enjoyment of the movie. When I watched it again with conscious alertness to the army maneuvers, I realized it was the key to ensuring the massive climax could happen: if "Johnny" hadn't recovered "The General" when he did and managed to bring it to the crossing bridge just ahead of the convergence of two parts of the Union army, he would not have reached Confederate lines in time to warn them so they could ambush the enemy troops that survived the tremendous collapse of the burning bridge under the weight of the pursuing train.

Such attention to detail is totally characteristic of this marvelous film. Its planning is outstanding; its performances are note perfect; its technical aspects are beyond ideal; its story is believable; and its comedy is sublime.

Comment: Universally regarded as one of the greatest films of all time, let alone as one of the greatest comedies, *The General* actually flopped with critics and crowds alike on its initial release. We can understand its financial failure: the cost of just one of its scenes, the train falling through the burning bridge, was about half the cost of an entire average film of the day. It didn't take "Hollywood accounting practices" to run up a deficit, it just took a great artist's complete indifference to budgets in his pursuit of great comedy. But how could it have failed in the opinions of critics and moviegoers?

Keaton onscreen was still Keaton onscreen, but the storyline that supported his gags was something completely different for him: an actual historical event that he treated with great respect and veracity rather than as a template for satire and exaggeration. This approach required discipline and all the elements of modern screen storytelling, as opposed to extemporization from a napkin-jotted "situation." There is always an underlying seriousness to the action and to the plot developments. Even when "Johnny" gets his foot caught and inadvertently lifts the connecting rod between the locomotive and the cannon car, the slapstick aspect is cut by dramatic tension in a way it never was in any other train-centered silent comedy. This kind of parallel drama and comedy was something the audience and the reviewers, apparently, were not yet ready to take on its own terms; thus, they complained the film was "not very funny."

The comedy is, in fact, a steady pulse throughout the film; see, for example, the scene in which "Johnny" and "Annabelle" are trying to sneak away from the Union army–occupied house in pitch darkness and "Annabelle" gets her foot caught in a trap. "Johnny" gets the trap off her foot by getting *both* of his hands caught in it. One hand would have been standard comedy; *both* hands elevates it into a priceless laugh.

American film, in particular among national cinemas, has always conflated the "motion" of the term "motion picture" with "violence." You would think a film about the most violent conflict to ever occur on American soil would revel in this opportunity, and it's true there is quite a lot of violence in it, what with cannons pitching bombs, railroad destruction of all kinds, ignorant armies clashing by night (and day), etc. Yet the "motion" in *The General* is actual *motion*, not mere violence. The camera is constantly traveling, and when it isn't physically rolling along the line, it is panning, scanning, sweeping.

Which brings me to exclaim: "What incredible camera direction!" It's not just the motion of the camera, it's also the placement of the camera. Every single shot in this film is perfectly placed. Every camera setup is brilliantly chosen. Every visual composition is absolutely exquisite.

Bonus: Keaton's legacy has been dogged by accusations that he treated his actresses poorly, at least onscreen. All of these accusations seem to be rooted in a single film: *The General*. He's got to have a love interest, so he's got to have a girl in every film, but his comedy post-Arbuckle was always a solo act. This means the girl is necessarily only a motivating force for his character. With few exceptions—the father in *Steamboat Bill, Jr.* comes immediately to mind—the male performers in his films fare little better than the female performers; they just get a rougher treatment because he doesn't have to marry them in the end, and because in the first half of the 20th century the villain in any mass entertainment story was always a male.

Marion Mack suffers a lot of indignities in *The General*, such as being stepped on while hiding in a sack. That's a gag, not an anti-woman act of cruelty; I can think of a dozen silent comedies in which men are stuffed into sacks and subjected to far more vicious treatment, versus this one single instance of a woman being sacked and slagged. If "Johnny" had been trying to sneak a male Confederate soldier out of a Union campsite by putting him in a sack, Keaton wouldn't have changed a thing about this skit; he would still have flung the sack into the railcar and later stomped on him in attempting to find him.

"Annabelle" is a dumb person. As a pampered and pillar-topping beauty of the old Southern aristocracy, she was raised to be useless and brainless, to lack all common sense, to be shielded utterly from the tiniest responsibility for herself, and therefore to be completely incapable of fending for herself in the real world without dozens of slaves and noble Southern gentlemen to do everything for her. Plop her into a real-life threatening situation, and the very practical-minded "Johnny" (he's an engineer, after all, the most practical-minded men on Earth) will certainly be exasperated by her idiocy because it gets the way of their survival against all odds. "Johnny" may love her but he knows firsthand that in this situation she can't be anything but a nuisance and a hindrance.

Marion Mack fills this brainless persona extraordinarily well. I don't know if she really was this stupid or if she was simply playing the role with exceptional naturalness: she betrays absolutely no actressy affectations or stretching for effect in *The General*, and that's what makes it hard to figure out how much of the airheadedness of "Annabelle" was really Marion Mack and how much of it was a very skillful actress playing a part. Mack made only a few films, most of them almost anonymously (under her real name, Marion McCreery) for Keystone, but she later wrote a few films and went into real estate, so she must have had something going for her. On the other hand, everything she did in the films other than *The General* was so totally unremarkable that no one remembers her for anything else.

If she were a brighter girl offscreen than on, it would have made no difference to Keaton: every thing and every person was fodder for his comic brain, whether brilliant or moronic.

THE GREAT K&A TRAIN ROBBERY

(1926, Fox)

Director: Lewis Seiler
Writers: Paul L. Ford, John Stone
Titles: Malcolm Stuart

Camera: Dan Clark
Cast: Tom Mix, Dorothy Dwan, William Walling, Harry Grippe, Carl Miller, Edward
  Peil, Curtis McHenry, Tony the Wonder Horse
Running Time (Length): 63 minutes (five reels)
Availability: DVD (Grapevine Video)

Background: The (supposedly) first real American film ever made was a Western, *The Great Train Robbery*, in 1903. It wasn't actually the first anything, but its *popularity* created the myth that it was the first everything. What it undeniably *did* do was to launch the Western as a staple genre of the American movie industry, a status it held for 90 years.

Broncho Billy Anderson, who had played several roles in *The Great Train Robbery*, parlayed the experience into an output of more than 400 one-reel films that made him the first great Western star, or cowboy star. As his career peaked, around 1910–1912, rivals began surging forward to usurp his crown; the most important and most successful of these was Tom Mix. William S. Hart came along a bit later, in 1914, to elevate the Western into something complex and sophisticated enough for an adult audience.

What Tom Mix had that Anderson didn't was showmanship. He displayed this talent early by inventing a personal history of aristocratic lineage (*and* "primitive" Native American heritage) and extensive military success: he claimed to have fought in the Spanish-American War, the Philippine War, the Boxer Rebellion, *and* the Boer War . . . with time left over to serve with distinction as a Texas Ranger and who knows what else. The truth was that he had been born dirt-poor to a couple of nobodies, had dropped out of school in the fourth or fifth grade, and was officially an army deserter who had never served on any battlefield. His showmanship developed further as a fancy rider and rodeo star in Wild West shows, where he learned how to work a crowd and how to dominate an act and make sure he was the center of attention.

All of these traits he brought to the still very young film industry. Dismissing the plodding, stagey "action" of the movies made by the overweight and over-aged (and therefore underathletic) Anderson, Mix went full out for flamboyance and excitement, flash and stunts, fancy roping and fancy riding and fancier clothing. He targeted his films at little boys, the most appreciative and noisiest audience, and knew exactly what they needed to set them off like strings of firecrackers popping with deafening delight: action, thrills, action, stunts, action, comedy, action, showing off, action, violence, and action.

There is never a dull minute in a Tom Mix film; hell, there is never a dull *half* minute in a Tom Mix film. He would dismiss today's *Fast and Furious* films as too slow, too talky, too tame, and too mushy-romantic. And besides, the *Fast and Furious* guys didn't ride horses.

Mix was not a quick learner. From 1910 to 1916, he poured out more than 100 one- and two-reel films whose entire plot would consist of one dim practical joke perpetrated by him and some fellow cowboys. Their production values were execrable. Only starting in late 1916 or early 1917, when he moved from the Selig studios to Fox, did his movies start to have something resembling a storyline that didn't revolve around one drawn-out gag (although they were still classified as "action comedies"). Even then, it wasn't until 1921 that he wised up enough to buy an actual story written by an actual writer of Western fiction, Max Brand, so that his films would take narrative shape. The production values were still negligible; but the next year, with *Sky High* (1922), he at last got direction, photography, and editing of a standard to match the improvements to the writing.

By 1925, he had finally arrived at the point where he could take a story by the superb Western novelist Zane Grey and make a great movie out of it: *Riders of the Purple Sage*. Ironically, the material and the cast and crew were all so far beyond Mix's own limited acting range that he is the only one who doesn't fit into his own film. It took yet another couple of years before he was able to achieve an acting performance commensurate with his material and crew.

When the talkies came in, he rode off to the circus for three years before coming back to make a last handful of films and some radio shows. By that time, John Wayne was ready to take over the serious saddle, while Ken Maynard and Gene Autry moseyed the unserious saddle over into "singing cowboy" territory.

Synopsis: A bunch of the boys were making a fine living by robbing the K&A trains every week, and beleaguered railroad president "Eugene Cullen" is made even grumpier by the failure of his specially hired "detective" (Mix) to show up

Lobby card for *The Great K&A Train Robbery* (1926), starring Tom Mix. *Courtesy of Derek Boothroyd*

for the job of stopping the bandits single-handedly. The "detective" (he's more a cowboy-mercenary than a private investigator) is actually on the job already, convincingly enough that "Cullen" mistakes him for the bandit responsible for the holdups. This is a double problem, because "Cullen's" daughter has naturally fallen for the mysterious stranger, and because "Cullen's" male secretary is secretly the leader of the bandits.

Through a variety of exciting chases and ambushes and plottings, spiced with humor from Mix's typical Western comic sidekick and "Cullen's" black butler, and highlighted by Mix's spectacularly nonsensical leap on horseback from a second-story balcony into a swimming pool, the bandits manage to make off with a strongbox of gold bonds. Mix trails them to their hideout, a cave reached by swimming under a reef; he does this underwater torpedo act with his enormous hat and flapping chaps staying intact on his body. Moving from the improbable to the preposterous, he rounds up all 25 or so members of the gang, apparently by surrounding them like Chaplin did with the trench full of German soldiers in *Shoulder Arms* (1917), and makes them all swim back to the train where the posse is waiting to arrest them.

Comment: It's pretty much the tour de force it's reputed to be: nonstop action, great stunts, fantastic photography, constant excitement, and genuine humor, the latter thankfully being well above the yokel slapstick of Mix's earliest films. In that respect, it shares a certain similarity with William S. Hart's *Tumbleweeds* (1925): a pull-out-all-the-stops, give-him-a-decent-budget-for-once epic that could stand as either man's career capper, and certainly the most amusing films either of them made. Whereas Hart very visibly kept his distance from the abysmal idiot-level humor that was forced upon him (he left it to Lucien Littlefield, who is unendurable), Mix readily partakes of the slightly more urbane wit in his film, comfortable no doubt thanks to his beginnings as a slapstick cowboy.

The Great K&A Train Robbery is also notable for the generous footage given over to "Snowball"—why did so many silent filmmakers think "Snowball" a hilarious name for a black man?—who, name and spoonful of caricature aside, is a genuinely funny thread of comic relief.

The opening scenes are fantastic. The first shot is a breathtaking overhead—far, far, *far* overhead—vista of a mountain gorge, with a tiny train winding its way on a narrow track hugging the foaming waters. The second shot is taken by a camera mounted on top of the same train, treating us to a mesmerizing first-person view of that same winding track beside the rapids. The sequence wraps up with the camera shooting up from a hole in the ground between the tracks, the train bearing down upon us until it runs right over us. It's a bravura performance by the photographer, Dan Clark. Clark keeps it up, too: the entire film is filled with wonderful camera work outside, inside, and all around the train.

Bonus: Mix's early shorts play like 19th-century nickelodeon flip-cards in their crudity; it's incredible that something like *Local Color* (1916) and *An Angelic Attitude* (1916) were being made *after* D. W. Griffith's *The Birth of a Nation* (1915) and John Bunny's well-constructed short comedy *Hearts and Diamonds* (1914). In 1914's *In the Days of the Thundering Herds*, Mix had still not given us even one close-up shot; if you go through his available films chronologically, in 1916 you will still not know what he looks like, other than that he has a phenomenal honker under his cowlick of black hair and that he wears way too much lipstick. (Note: I am using Robert Birchard's chronology from his 1993 book, *King Cowboy: Tom Mix and the Movies*. Other sources have given differing dates for the release of the Mix films mentioned in this paragraph; Birchard seems to me the most trustworthy source.)

We finally get the close-up in *The Heart of Texas Ryan*, made in 1917 (according to Birchard). Jumping ahead four years, in 1921's *Trailin'* Mix has gotten a Max Brand story that has the effect of really lifting the quality of his output henceforth. The script is full of holes, mind you, but the plot progressions are solid and our interest is sustained. Everything comes together in 1922's *Sky High*, a technically accomplished film in which Mix even shows how hip he is by blending autos and planes into a conventional Western giddyup with impressive naturalness, bordering on nonchalance: no apologies to the horses-and-guns fans, no contrived conflict between the old Western ways and the new encroaching urbanization, no big deal made over the casting of his character as a border guard instead of as a "true" cowboy.

I mentioned above that Mix's best (but not his most amusing) film, the Zane Grey epic *Riders of the Purple Sage* (1925), is better than he is. Let me explain. Grey likes to shade his plots with moral ambiguity, which is a quality Mix has never come even moderately close to attempting. As a result, Mix the man seems out of place even though his character is drawn as an integral element of the whole film. His complete lack of anything less than total self-confident "goodness" is at odds with the ambivalence of the story and of the other characters. When he closes the film by telling the little girl that someday the grand canyons that are their death-trap will bloom with flowers, it has no poignancy because Mix delivers it like just another self-assured declaration of his supreme abilities to do everything perfectly. It's a problem because Grey's story is very strong, but its strength is built upon the theme of ambivalence and the contrast between perception and reality, the very qualities Mix lacks. John Wayne in *The Searchers* (1956), an obviously similar film, would color the statement into a show of bravado that he doesn't really feel; and William S. Hart might turn it into a quiet celebration of spiritual resignation. Tom Mix was definitely a much lesser actor than either of those stars, which is a paradox for a man so completely an actor's creation himself.

H

HAPPINESS

(1934, Moskino Kombinat)

Director: Alexander Medvedkin
Writer: Alexander Medvedkin
Camera: Gleb Troiansky
Cast: Peter Zinoviev, Elena Egorova
Running Time: 65 minutes
Availability: VHS (Kino Video)

Background: Russians—what a bunch of crazy madcaps! Well, they did always have some fun people around, such as Gogol and the early Bulgakov and Arkady Boitler. Even before the communist revolution, however, the Western image of Russians was one of gloomy, vodka-guzzling, philosophically agonizing drama queens, typified by the writhing losers of Dostoevsky and the doom-laden pomposities of Tolstoy.

And then came the Commies, and the Bolsheviks and Mensheviks and other -sheviks. The stuttering beginnings of a Russian cinema were forcibly detoured into the service of propaganda of a technologically impoverished and dramatically lethal sort. Lenin, a psychologically insightful man whatever one may think of his politics, knew the value of film and wasted no time in setting up a department to control and develop it, under the direction of no less an authority than his own wife.

He pretty well had to take this step, because almost the entire existing Russian movie industry either had fled the country or were openly defying nationalization (even before nationalization of the industry had begun). In other words, Russian cinema was almost completely wiped out one way or the other and had to be replaced with pliable newcomers.

Contrary to what one might expect, the new people had tremendous talent, and they blossomed in the hothouse atmosphere of revolutionary upheaval. It took time, in part because of a near-total lack of film stock and technology, but by the early to middle 1920s Russian movies were back in force. In the middle to late 1920s, shortly after Lenin's death, the industry enjoyed a phenomenal burst of creativity and outright cinematic genius. Lev Kuleshov, Vsevolod Pudovkin, Alexander Dovzhenko, Dziga Vertov, Leonid Trauberg, Abram Room, Esther

75

Shub, Boris Barnet, Fedor Ozep, and most famously Sergei Eisenstein all took the Soviet cinema and put it right up there among the most interesting and innovative on earth.

Alexander Medvedkin was very much a minor among these titans, yet he managed to produce one of the most outrageous, rambunctious, impertinent, surrealistic, daring, and amusing films of the period. Moreover, he did it in 1934, after Stalin had begun crushing the spirit and insouciance out of all the other filmmakers.

Synopsis: What is happiness? Not a magazine title, unlike *Life* and *Time* and *Mad*. The movie called *Happiness* combines life and time and madness into one hour of the kind of crazy slapstick you never could have believed the Soviet Union of the Stalinist era was capable of producing. Stalin couldn't believe it either, which is why it was banned for forty years from being shown in his evil empire.

We're introduced to "The Loser" and his wife, "Anna Loser," peasants in czarist Russia. They are ground down under all the machines of the czar, especially by a devil-man of a landlord named "Foka" who is so demonically exalted that food flies into his mouth untouched by human hand, and also especially by frenziedly genuflecting religious leaders and other purveyors of flagrantly hypocritical piety. After "The Loser's" father is killed by "Foka" for trying to steal a dumpling, "Anna" casts him out of their pitiful sharecrop with the command, "Go find good luck, and don't come back empty-handed."

Amazingly, he carries out this order to the letter, sneaking off with a drunken merchant's dropped purse while pious ascetics fight each other over it. He buys a polka-dot horse with the money; alas, it is more mule than horse—that is, stubbornly uncooperative. He's forced to put his wife in the traces and together they attempt to plow an impossibly steep, rocky, and barren hilltop. With the assistance of trick photography and camera angles, it's such exhausting work that "Anna" collapses. "The Loser" responds in a lovely scene of pathos without sentimentality (are you paying attention, Mr. Chaplin?); he casts flowers around "Anna's" sleeping body, covers her in a bearskin, and sings a dream song of prosperity while playing an accordion.

They end up with a great harvest, only to have it all taken away by taxmen, "Foka" the landlord, church humbugs, and a couple of—incredibly enough—nuns wearing sheer black see-through habits that do nothing to cover their bare breasts. To add insult to injury, during the night thieves break into the couple's locked chest to steal . . . nothing, because there is nothing stored within the chest that had been protected by locks, sheds, and dogs.

Fed up, "The Loser" resolves to die and builds himself a coffin. This brings in "Foka," the police, the religious leaders, the court representatives of the czar, and the army, all upbraiding him for having the temerity to end his life without their permission. As punishment, they beat him half-dead, send him to the war front where he is killed seven times, and chain him up for 33 years.

During those 33 years, the revolution takes place, and "The Loser" returns to the lowliest position in the farm collective of which "Anna" is the star laborer. "Anna," we are told, is enjoying "the happiest life imaginable"; apparently, the most romantic dream of Soviet women was to drive a monstrous thresher. Being a Soviet agricultural collective, they quite naturally have a harvest so enormous, it causes the food storage buildings to literally burst apart.

The religious renegades, now outcasts thanks to the rational eradication of the church, steal an entire storeroom of food, but are routed by "Anna" and her incredibly old father. "Foka" takes revenge by attempting to burn down the entire barn, orchard, and fields, but "The Loser" manages to overpower him at the risk of his own life. "The Loser" is rewarded, in a peculiar coda, by the present of a three-piece suit picked up at a department store. He throws his old rags to the religious outcasts and has a good laugh as they fight over the shreds. It is not clear how he will continue farming in nothing but a three-piece business suit; maybe that's a story for another film.

Comment: One reason I love silent comedy, more than even silent drama, is that it is truly eternal. The stories, characters, plot twists, even the dialogue of the silent dramas have become so shopworn and historically distanced from us that even when we know we're watching a "first" (say, the realistic gangster groundbreaker, *Regeneration* [1915]), it's nearly impossible to fully appreciate them. But no matter how many times a Laurel and Hardy routine has been copied over the decades—and no matter how many times we've watched the originals over and over again—the original is still fresh and hilarious every time we reel it off.

Which is a roundabout way of saying that while silent Russian dramas can be unwatchable because time has made their self-admiring tricks so annoying, it is still easy to truly enjoy their comedies. *Happiness* is inventive, quirky, and laugh-out-loud funny. Although it has immense debts to American slapstick and French surrealism, it benefits from a true inherent idiosyncrasy due to its very Russian/Soviet mind-set. It's impossible to imagine any American comedian making it—not even Mel Brooks, or Albert Brooks either.

Bonus: A much more widely praised Soviet comedy is Lev Kuleshov's *The Extraordinary Adventures of Mr. West in the Land of the Bolsheviks* (1924). It is a pretty good film, too. However, I find too many of Eisenstein's mannerisms in it. More to the point, it is much too obviously a Russian filmmaker's idea of a Russian comedy as made by Harold Lloyd. Apparently Kuleshov wasn't aware that Lloyd had already made his Russian comedy, *A Sammy in Siberia* (1919), which is also funnier than *The Extraordinary Adventures of Mr. West.*

HEARTS AND DIAMONDS

(1914, Vitagraph)

Director: George Baker
Writer: Eugene Mullin
Cast: John Bunny, Flora Finch, Ethel Corcoran, Ethel Lloyd, William Shea, Charles Eldridge, Arthur Cozine, Kalman Matis, Lenny Smith
Running Time (Length): 23 minutes (two reels); some restored versions run 30-plus minutes due to inappropriate film speed

---

Background: Who was the first superstar of American comedy movies? Well, you could make a case for the improbable Mary Pickford or Mack Sennett in their pre-1912 Biograph Studio days, or the somewhat more probable Augustus Carney who began his film career in 1909. But Pickford was an actress, not a comedian, and Sennett was never a superstar on the screen. Carney's reputation was made as "Alkali Ike," a character created in 1911, not 1909. Mabel Normand was a genuine comedian and got started in 1910, but she didn't become a superstar until Sennett made her one at Keystone in 1912. Likewise Fred Mace. And although Ben Turpin starred at Essanay beginning in 1907, he was a dud and demoted to supporting comic until transitioning to Sennett in 1917.

It is widely agreed that John Bunny was the first. In 1910, he made the momentous decision to abandon a quarter-century's worth of stage fame that had made him a well-paid performer and to pour all his energy into a new career as the first dedicated screen comedian. A man of unbridled egotism, he wanted something that greater stage actors like Edmund Keane never had: immortality of actual performance. That's what the movies promised. That's what Bunny thought he had secured. The Immortals had the last laugh, though: almost all of the hundreds of films Bunny made are gone now. His immortality rests on a threadbare handful of surviving reels, and when I say "handful," I'm thinking of Three-Finger Brown's pitching hand.

Synopsis: Bunny is so disappointed by the wussies whom his two daughters have chosen—disappointed? Hell, he's outraged to the extent of bodily flinging them out the door!—that he decides to show the girls how it's done. Presenting himself as a teenaged stud of fifty years' standing and no family baggage to speak of, he pursues the purse of a wealthy widow. (An inserted newspaper article calls her the "daughter" of a wealthy man, but the intertitles all refer to her as his "widow.") Finding out that she is cracker-jacks for "base ball," as it was then spelled, Bunny doesn't let his gigantic gut and old age get in the way of faking-up his own ball team to impress her.

His opponent, professional ace pitcher "Matty Christheson" (i.e., Christ-the-Son), promises to throw the game, not just the ball. This is a nice dig at real-life pitching idol and ostentatiously moralistic super-Christian Christy Mathewson of the New York Giants. Even if you're going to make fun of pious, clean-living Mathewson, though, you have to wrap up your story fully in accord with the revered ballplayer's values: Bunny ends up blessing his daughters' romances and hanging up his own cleats to lead a sober, chaste, wise-old-man's sedate life in pursuit of goodness rather than gelt.

Comment: Though not very funny today, this is by far the best of the extant "Bunnyfinches," as their fans called the films that paired grossly obese John Bunny with bag'o'bones Flora Finch. Finch, who makes "Olive Oyl" look like Jayne Mansfield, has little to do here, which gives viewers some relief from the formula that dogged most of their films together: hubby Bunny does something that gets him into trouble with wifey Finch until he good-naturedly agrees she was right and he was wrong, and the universe is set right on its axis again.

This time, Bunny is an aggressive money-grubber, satyr *manque*, grossly abusive paterfamilias, and fake but hustling athlete. He completely dominates, throwing himself (sometimes literally) into every shot. When he overpowers a demented ballplayer who breaks into Finch's house, you honestly fear you're about to see the man's heart burst from the strain. As it was, he made only three more films before exhaustion led him to take a break—by going out on the road with a vaudeville tour! As everyone must have warned him at the time, that was a suicidal thing to do, and he dropped dead from Bright's disease right after cutting the tour short in 1915.

Bonus: For the longest time, the only John Bunny film that seemed to be readily available for public viewing was *A Cure for Pokeritis* (1912). Because it appeared to be the entire surviving legacy of an indisputably pivotal figure in motion pictures, viewers and historians felt obligated to exalt it as a great comedy; Robert Klepper, always a source of gobsmacking opinions, called it "a truly hilarious comedy classic" in his book *Silent Films 1877–1996* (1999).

The truth is that *A Cure for Pokeritis* is a singularly lame "light comedy" that became instantly a quaint artifact of a bygone era. Its story of a wife inveigling her cousin to fake a raid on a poker game in order to "cure" her husband of his passion for cards was obsolete and silly long before 1912. Sure, it's nice to see Bunny and Finch in a genuinely historic piece of nitrate (now, of course, a genuinely historic piece of digitalization), but the movie is unfunny and labored. It's even low in unintentional laughs, the only one being the startling physical resemblance of the cousin to Oscar Wilde: when a fluttery, fey Wilde leads the moralistic pseudo-cops in a raid on the depravity of men who are having fun together, it's not easy to stifle an ironic giggle or two.

HEARTS AND FLOWERS

(1919, Sennett)

Director: Eddie Cline
Camera: Fred Jackman and Perry Evans
Cast: Ford Sterling, Louise Fazenda, Phyllis Haver, Heinie Conklin, Jack Ackroyd, Billy Armstrong, Harriet Hammond, Eva Thatcher, Edgar Kennedy, Kalla Pasha, Bert Roach, Baldy Belmont, Pat Kelly, Grover Ligon
Running Time (Length): Two reels
Availability: DVD (Classic Video Streams: *The Producers: Rare Films of Mack Sennett,* vol. 2)

Background: One of the original Sennett stars, Ford Sterling achieved tremendous popularity in 1912–1914 as "Chief Teheezel," leader of the Keystone Cops, and as a generic "Dutch" villain so comically evil that he could—and did—steal candy from babies. With his rimless glasses and paintbrush goatee, he had an instantly memorable appearance; he rendered his image indelible in audience minds by playing everything with the greatest possible exaggeration for comic effect. No one has ever been quite so deliberately cheesy in his performance, so over-the-top that the viewer couldn't help falling on the floor in convulsive laughter—which, of course, was exactly what Sterling wanted.

He got so beloved in this persona, he decided he deserved his own imprint, so he left Sennett to make "Sterling Comedies" for Universal in 1914. This didn't work out, either behind the screen or at the box office; he grudgingly returned to Sennett in 1915 and put in another two-year stint before escaping again, this time to Fox. Once again, that arrangement lasted only one year before Sterling crawled back on his knees to Sennett for a third go-round. Times had changed, though, and "Teheezel" was an outdated characterization. He might have misjudged the audience's willingness to follow him out of Sennett's orbit, but Sterling didn't misjudge the audience's own movement out of the Sennett orbit by the end of the Great War: he tossed the old makeup and the old routines, and played different kinds of new characters with different looks (usually an ordinary moustache and no glasses, wearing ordinary clothes that actually fit him). He also lowered the exaggeration level of his acting, but he was born and trained to play to the last row of cavernous vaudeville houses and mammoth circus rings, so even in his more sophisticated impersonations he still performed broadly enough to ensure he dominated the screen. *Hearts and Flowers* comes from the middle of his final period with Sennett, and as such is an excellent example of the transition slapstick was going through, discarding the wild abandon of earlier Keystone films and moving toward the less grotesque and less anarchic comedy of the Twenties.

Synopsis: Penniless and homely flower-girl Louise Fazenda is hopelessly in love with flamboyant nightclub conductor Ford Sterling. During one evening performance, Sterling makes eyes with society hottie Phyllis Haver. Both Fazenda and

Gorgeous Phyllis Haver proved her immense comic talents in *Hearts and Flowers* (1919). *Author's collection*

Haver already have boyfriends; both are ready to overthrow the hapless wimps in a flash if Sterling favors them with a wink. Faced with a choice of willing femmes, Sterling quite naturally chooses the hottie over the nottie . . . until he gets punk'd with a fake note stating that the nottie is heiress to millions. Fazenda, unexpectedly swept off her feet, calls in her mama and three hulking brothers to witness her instant wedding to Sterling and maybe to make sure the groom-to-be doesn't weasel out of it. He does, though—this is Ford Sterling, after all, a dyed-in-the-wool villain with firm if shallow values that prize sex over anything but money. Fazenda's jilted boyfriend wins the competition, not just by default of Sterling's absconding but also by somehow finding the gumption to lay out the brothers.

Comment: Hearts and Flowers turned out to be a showcase for nearly everyone who has a key role. Nominal star Fazenda gets a lot of screen time and does what she can to deserve it, whipping herself through comic dance steps and pratfalls and yokel-romantic moués. She's competing with one of cinema's most flagrant scene-stealers in Sterling; he's hilarious as the amoral cad who can't resist either Fazenda's supposed wealth or Haver's indisputable sex appeal, until the first proves mythical and the second vanishes into a transvestite turn.

Haver is a revelation: not only is she a two-timing sexpot every bit as amoral as Sterling, she's also an impressively convincing male impersonator, even dancing like a man and giving Fazenda not one but two big, long, juicy kisses. There seems to be no rational for the transvestite act; it just gives Haver a glorious opportunity to showcase her talents, and boy! does she ever make the most of it.

Bonus: For no discernible reason other than Sennett's standard modus operandi, there is an episode at the beach to indulge in a lengthy ogling of the Sennett Bathing Beauties. It goes without saying that their beachwear, the raciest in America in 1919, will leave today's audience laughing uncontrollably: baggy one-piece suits with knickers and skirts, knee socks, and shoes. They play some variation of sand football with a beach ball, the camera leering in at gang tackles, trying to find some wriggling in the behinds that are encased in at least two layers of heavy wool. It is totally gratuitous, of course, and Sterling and Fazenda as onlookers run out of reactions to fake; Haver, ready as ever to do anything and everything as the go-to girl, boisterously leads the players with her kicking, throwing, catching, running, and tackling, a gal who never hesitates to jump into the thick of the action.

HIS PICTURE IN THE PAPERS

(1916, Fine Arts)

Director: John Emerson
Writers: Anita Loos, John Emerson
Camera: George Hill
Cast: Douglas Fairbanks, Loretta Blake, Charles Butler, Homer Hunt, Clarence Handyside, Renee Boucicault, Jean Temple
Running Time (Length): 62 minutes (five reels)
Availability: DVD (Alpha Video)

Background: Douglas Fairbanks is so indelibly etched in cultural memory as the hero of wonderful, extravagant adventure features, it often amazes people to learn that this larger-than-life stardom was actually the third stage of his career. He first made his mark, as so many silent comedy stars did, in live theater. Imagine how his overwhelming personality must have come across to audiences in that medium! No wonder the Fine Arts movie studio courted him assiduously for the movies: he exploded live stages like nitroglycerin in a wooden box, whereas films provided him with a boundless environment ideally suited to his boundless energy. His first film, *The Lamb*, was a smash, and he was off and running. *His Picture in the Papers* was only his third film, but it demonstrated he was already the complete master of his new realm. The second stage of his audience-delighting career had launched.

Synopsis: Somebody other than Heinz has made a fortune out of manufacturing gag-inducing synthetic foods—namely, "Proteus Prindle," a mighty handle for a fat old man famous for "27 Varieties" of nauseating semi-edibles such as "pre-digested prunes," "puffed peanuts," and "perforated peas." This ostensibly vegetarian smorgasbord has fattened not only "Prindle" but also his two hefty adult daughters; his only son, "Peter," is suspiciously svelte and muscular, which we soon learn is due to his regular secret scarfing of tombstone-sized steaks, foot-high steins of beer, and copious amounts of martinis.

A fellow secret carnivore is "Christine Cadwalader," daughter of the railroad magnate who is the loudest devotee of "Prindle's" product. "Peter's" less than wild enthusiasm for his job of shilling Dad's products leads to both fathers not only forbidding his marriage to "Christine" but ordering him to get out there and make a man of himself before they'll even consider changing their minds as to his uselessness.

"Pete" has already shown the audience he's more than capable of coming up with inventive ways of bettering himself. This is a guy, after all, who gets his body moving in the mornings by doing a standing jump over his bed, pumping weights, and twirling Indian clubs, then arriving at work "punctually late" and pouring himself a martini from hidden ingredients, then washing his glass in a small basin he surreptitiously built into a desk drawer.

Faced with the paternal ultimatum, it's off to the races for "Pete." He buys a lemon of a car, deliberately smashes it over a cliff, pretends it's a drunken crash, distributes his elegantly posed photo to reporters, and then is vexed when their articles mention his name but do not publish his photo—it's the *photo* he needs to get into print.

After a wild locomotive adventure that somehow includes snipping the beard off a goat (and Fairbanks really does wrestle the goat to the ground), he arrives at a boxing match, takes on the champion and whips him, poses for photos for the newspapers, then is frustrated again: police raid the illegal fight and smash all the cameras.

A drunken spree ends up with "Pete" being put aboard a ship bound for Vera Cruz. Through the haze of a hangover he realizes the error and jumps ship, swimming *sidestroke* all the way back to Atlantic City. Gosh, do you think anybody might be able to do that in real life? Never mind, this isn't real life, this is Doug Fairbanks's life. He not only makes it back to shore, he still has enough energy and presence of mind to beat up two cops and make sure the local reporter gets his picture in the papers. Unfortunately, they refuse to name him, to spare his family the disgrace of his conduct. Curses, foiled again!

Eventually, "Pete" ends up vanquishing a gang of seven or eight toughs. How tough? Erich von Stroheim plays one of the *lesser* members of the gang, that's how tough. "Pete" single-handedly saves an entire train from being derailed. "Christine" and her wealthy dad just happen to be on board, and everybody is sufficiently impressed to allow the wedding of "Christine" and "Pete" to go ahead. After all, he finally managed to get his picture in the papers.

Comment: One of the movies marking Fairbanks's transition from short films to feature films, *His Picture in the Papers* clocks in at a slightly clumsy one-hour length: too short to allow for a fully developed "A" picture, too long to make it a snappy hustle. Good thing it's funny at any length.

Fairbanks never stops racing: even when he's buttering up "Christine" and priming her for a kiss, he's in a rush. He keeps the moving picture moving; anytime there's a chance for exposition that might slow it down, such as his joining "Christine" in a nonvegetarian restaurant, Fairbanks simply cuts the scene and moves on to something else. Move, move, move!

His Picture in the Papers might be seen as an anti-vegetarian tract. Making all the "Prindle" devotees corpulent, except for weedy "Melville" who doesn't long survive being "Christine's" fiancé, is Fairbanks's way of lambasting the movement as "unhealthy." (What did they know about nutrition in the Twenties? Answer: Not much.) It was his belief that a hearty variety of foods was essential to a strong constitution, and vegetarianism didn't provide that hearty variety. None of the veggie addicts in this film could have jumped over their beds, let alone run through Grand Central Station not once, not twice, not thrice, but four times in the space of a few minutes. And that's not even to consider them getting into the boxing ring with a champion.

The first half of the film is rather traditional; its humor rests on joke intertitles and on prop gags such as the martini glass washer. The second half is much more in the spirit of soon-to-be-classic Fairbanks and therefore is a lot more obvious in its ability to entertain us and keep us giggling.

Bonus: Loretta Blake, who plays "Christine," was an obscure and thoroughly undistinguished actress whose career, entirely in the silents, lasted only six years and eighteen films. (The majority of them are shorts; *His Picture in the Papers* is one of only seven longer than two reels.) Although a competent enough performer, she did not photograph particularly well and was too ordinary looking to stand out. Fairbanks, ever sensitive about appearing much more youthful than his years, did not like the fact that she looked mature onscreen: he wanted love interests whose age was more in tune with the boyishness of his personality than with the maturity of his own age. He never again used a leading lady who didn't look as youthful as he felt.

HONEYMOONIACS

(1929, Educational/Jack White Productions)

Director: Stephen Roberts
Camera: John Shepek
Cast: Monty Collins, Betty Boyd, Harold Goodwin, Maxine Jennings
Running Time (Length): About 16 minutes (two reels) survive in home video releases
(all of which seem to have been copied from the same source print)

Background: The last year of the silents in America was 1929, give or take a few anomalies such as Chaplin's two 1930s silent features and the "goat gland" movies that were released in both sound and silent versions in 1929 and 1930 (and a few in 1931). Mary Pickford famously said that it would have made more sense for movies to have progressed from talkies to silents, rather than the reverse. She wasn't talking about the technological developments involved in the evolution; she was talking about the skill level of the creative crew and cast. It's easy to explain a storyline in dialogue (or monologue, for that matter); what's difficult, and requires a lot of skill and experience, is to explain it *without* dialogue, even without sound effects other than mood music from an organist.

Substantiating her suggestion is the quality of films being produced in these last few years of the silents, specifically 1927–1929. Among the most brilliant productions of these years one finds the original *Beau Geste*, the second (and by far the best) *Ben-Hur*, seminal films including *Berlin: Symphony of a Great City* and *The Cat and the Canary*, Beatrice Lillie's only silent film *Exit Smiling*, Keaton's all-time classic *The General*, Clara Bow's immortal *It*, Harold Lloyd's great *The Kid Brother*, Cecil B. De Mille's *The King of Kings*, a bunch of Greta Garbo star-making vehicles, astounding German films such as *The Loves of Jeanne Ney* and *Metropolis*, Pickford's own crowning achievement *My Best Girl*, France's breathtaking epic *Napoleon*, the Soviet Union's pivotal *October*, the first Academy Award winners *7th Heaven* and *Sunrise* (the latter often cited as the greatest silent film ever made and the apotheosis of the silents), a delightful version of *The Student Prince in Old Heidelberg*, a whole bunch of significant Lon Chaney films, and the epic *Wings* . . . and that's just in *one* year, 1927!

"Mere slapstick" also reached its apogee in this brief period. (Anybody who has ever essayed it has discovered there is no "mere" about slapstick.) It's the time in which Laurel and Hardy were finally *really* teamed up, when Buster Keaton was producing his last great movies, when Chaplin created *The Circus*, when Harold Lloyd and Harry Langdon and Charley Chase were all waving their last goodbyes to genius comedy. And by this point, even a fourth-rank comedian like Monty Collins was so accomplished in silent slapstick that he could toss off, almost as an afterthought, a cripplingly funny comedy like *Honeymooniacs*.

Synopsis: There could scarcely be anything more romantic in the 1920s than to honeymoon in Niagara Falls, notwithstanding Oscar Wilde's lethal gibe that the Falls must be the second greatest disappointment of the new bride. Newlyweds Monty Collins and Betty Boyd are so dewy-eyed with anticipation on the train to Buffalo, they need to open the window to clear the mist from their glims. The window has other ideas. Collins fights with it, and when he finally pries it open, fights with his fellow passengers who are inundated by soot, water, and sundry atmospheric entities.

A whole series of gag situations follow and are carefully milked to just within an inch of their laughter limits. These include such hoary old situations, given delicious new life by Collins, as the passenger whose hat is repeatedly crushed by him, the jealous couple whose wife repeatedly finds Collins ensconcing himself in her lap, the taffy that encases Collins's hands and anything with which he comes into contact, and the reliable old sleeper berth jokes that were still being recycled by no less a perfect comedy than *Some Like It Hot* thirty years later.

Monty Collins, his hair slicked back instead of combed forward in his on-screen "dumbbell" bangs, writes the motto of all comedians to a fan. *Author's collection*

Comment: No one could blame you for expecting a tired compendium of fourth-rate repetitions of worn-out old gags from Monty Collins (ranked an unprepossessing #69 in my *100 Greatest Silent Film Comedians*), especially from a Jack White Production; the White Brothers were to comedy what the Smith Brothers were to coughs: pills that subdued the most energetic of practitioners.

How astonishing, then, to discover *Honeymooniacs* is a great overlooked laugh machine! Truly the acme of Collins's career, it shows him as someone who, at least this once, was able to pull together everything he knew about comedy in his lifetime (he had been in entertainment since the age of ten), and to toss it out there for the audience with an offhandedness that adds to its unexpected charm.

Collins, as already noted, milks each gag exactly to its furthest extent. His accidental crushing of a train passenger's hat is done four times, and those four times are a perfect construction: the original crushing, a repeat crushing to set up a pattern for our expectations, a surprise alteration that uproariously gets the same results, and finally a payoff version. This is the kind of competence in structure that we never saw in movies before Charley Chase started making "pattern" stories work within his urban settings.

In my previous book, mentioned above, I singled out the gag in the train washroom with a hand towel as one of the best-ever elaborate visual gags in all of silent comedy. I repeat that assertion—it is such a perfectly executed throwaway!—and I add that it is, in fact, typical of this extremely funny movie.

Bonus: Betty Boyd didn't have much of a career. She was certainly attractive, and as indubitably sexy as hell in the sleeping-car scenes in *Honeymooniacs*; it was not, alas, an unusual kind of prettiness in Hollywood, then or now. The character she played in *Honeymooniacs* probably didn't help her career, either; she's quite the termagant in it, after softening us up with a demure false front in the first few minutes. When she starts egging on Collins to do physical violence to an unruly fellow passenger, she loses a lot of our sympathy, and probably got herself typecast as an unpleasant sort of girl. That was no help in an industry that was in high anxiety about alienating its patrons by either adding or not adding soundtracks to the dying silent format; they wanted complacent beauties whose demure subservience would soothe the disgruntled, show-me audience expecting to hear the movie talk to them.

I

THE IMMIGRANT

(1917, Mutual)

Director: Charles Chaplin
Writer: Charles Chaplin
Camera: Roland Totheroh and W. C. Foster
Editor: Charles Chaplin
Cast: Charlie Chaplin, Edna Purviance, Eric Campbell, Albert Austin, Henry Bergman, John Rand, Janet Miller Sully, James T. Kelly, Frank J. Coleman, Loyal Underwood
Running Time (Length): Two reels
Availability: DVD (AFA Entertainment, LLC)

Background: After breaking into films with Mack Sennett's Keystone Studios and rising to stardom, Charlie Chaplin went for the money: he signed with Essanay in 1915. The fourteen or fifteen films he made there (a few others were crapped together by Essanay after he left, as they tried to squeeze every penny out of his discards) were occasionally awkward comedies; they reeked of anxiety as Chaplin dealt with a lack of confidence in the onscreen character he was still developing, and with the pressure he felt to justify his salary. After three years in movies, he still believed it could all end tomorrow when audiences grew tired of his antics or when he ran out of ideas. The flop sweat can be smelled through the first nine Essanay films. Only with *The Tramp* and *The Bank* did he seem to gain control and assurance over his conceptions.

Leaving Essanay after just one year, Chaplin again went for the money and signed with Mutual. This time, he also gained total control over the filmmaking by setting up his own production company; he had artistic autonomy while sticking Mutual with the business responsibilities.

The result was one of the greatest strings of unfettered comedy brilliance ever created: an even dozen films in less than a year and a half, with ten of them deserving of five stars in a four-star rating system, and the other two worthy of three and a half stars each. When people talk about Chaplin being funny, these are the films they have in mind even if they can't remember the titles: *The Floorwalker, The Vagabond, One A.M., The Pawn Shop, Behind the Screen, The Rink, Easy Street, The Cure, The Immigrant, The Adventurer,* and the two slightly lesser efforts, *The Fireman* and *The Count.*

Chaplin recalled the Mutual years as the happiest time of his career, and it shows on the screen.

Synopsis: On the deck of an immigrant ship, Charlie fleeces menacing but gullible "friends" out of their money at dice and cards. He gives the money to a girl and her mother who have been robbed. Landing penniless in America, Charlie finds a coin that—those were the days—is sufficient to pay for a restaurant meal. Meeting with the same girl, whose mother has since died, Charlie treats her to a meal and then discovers he has lost the coin. The subsequent interplay with terrifying waiter Eric Campbell is one of the best and most sympathetic scenes Chaplin ever devised; it must truly have been the revelation that told him sympathy and comedy could work together to create brilliant comedy while putting the audience solidly on the side of his character.

Henry Bergman, playing a dedicated "society artist" who wants to paint the girl (Edna Purviance), unwittingly saves the day by producing a coin that Chaplin manages to double-clutch into paying his own bill. Chaplin and Edna, with a little coaxing, then find shelter at a justice of the peace office, where they are presumably married.

Comments: This is one of the truly great, fully realized comedy stories of the two-reel slapstick era. Each sequence is perfect in itself and in developing both character and plot, while being filled with exquisite gags and "bits of business." From the first meeting of Edna and Charlie on board the immigrant ship, to their climactic dodging into the marriage-license office out of a teeming rainstorm, everything unfolds logically and credibly.

Charlie's handling of cards in the gambling sequences—they're not "card tricks"—is a panic, as is his handling of the dice. The inadvertently shared soup scene on board the rolling ship delightfully illustrates his sharing nature, even when he doesn't really want to share: it foreshadows his reluctant sharing of his coin and meal in the restaurant, confirming for us that he really does have a generous and empathetic nature and will do the right thing even when his conscious ego would rather not.

J. Edgar Hoover, chief hoodlum of the Federal Bureau of Investigation, set off the unending streams of hatred that a crazed portion of the American public has subsequently poured upon Chaplin, all because of a brief scene in which Chaplin kicks the behind of an immigration officer who had bullied the ship's travelers upon their arrival in America. Never mind that the officer eminently deserved the kick for his brutal handling of the immigrants. Never mind that the officer had treated them like animals instead of like the builders of a greater nation that they would prove to be. Never mind that *the officer gets his own revenge by kicking Chaplin later in the same scene.* Never mind that Chaplin's kick is but one split second out of a film that confirms America as the shining dream of millions who had lived in poverty and oppression in other lands. No, in the minds of these perverse "patriots," Chaplin had forever identified himself as the Antichrist by taking a quick poke at American "authority" when the latter happened to step over the line of human dignity, equality, and freedom—you know, all those things we revere as uniquely American virtues.

Bonus: Eric Campbell was one of the all-time great heavies of film comedy. Another of the many Fred Karno veterans who gravitated into silent comedy films, he worked exclusively with Chaplin, performing in about a dozen of their films in just two years (1916 and 1917). Their physical contrast—Chaplin was extremely slim and short, Campbell was extremely corpulent and tall—was fairly standard: see, for example, the early Oliver Hardy with Billy Ruge in a series of cheap chaos called "Plump and Runt," or the many early efforts both human and cartoon to bring *Mutt and Jeff* to the screen, or the unofficial teaming of Harry Langdon and Vernon Dent or Marvin Loback and Snub Pollard, and that's not even to mention Laurel and Hardy. Campbell's florid and evilly curving moustaches even contrasted with Chaplin's neatly cropped little toothbrush, notwithstanding that the latter was soon to become a symbol of ultimate evil thanks to Adolf Hitler.

Like Dent and Hardy, Campbell brought something extra to the teamwork: he was a masterful comedian who sacrificed ego to forge a true team. He never tried to run away with a film or to upstage the partner whose name was first in the cast list; instead, he did everything he could to bolster that partner, feeding the latter's brilliant comedy even as he earned deserved laughs for his own supportive actions. And unlike Dent and Hardy, Campbell always played the antagonist, the villain, the opposite to the lead comedian's good guy: he willingly played up the sympathetic nature of the hero by being the irredeemably horrible, nasty, awful—but funny—bad guy.

Campbell's death by car crash in 1917 deprived us of a performer who might have gone on to a lengthy career as a second banana, a professional villain, a cartoonish hoodlum, and a social hypocrite but also a misunderstood gentle monster in the vein of *The Hunchback of Notre Dame* or even *Frankenstein*. It is noteworthy that Chaplin never attempted to replace him; in future films, he used a variety of nondescript actors in the villainous roles, and none was ever presented as being as knee-shakingly frightening as Campbell.

INNOCENT HUSBANDS

(1925, Roach)

Director: Leo McCarey
Writer: Charley Chase (uncredited)
Titles: H. M. Walker
Camera: Len Powers
Editor: Richard Currier
Cast: Charley Chase, Katherine Grant, Martha Sleeper, Lucien Littlefield, James Finlayson, William Gillespie, Kay de Lys, Jane Sherman, Jack Gavin
Running Time (Length): Two reels
Availability: DVD (Kino Lorber Films: *The Charley Chase Collection*, vol. 2)

Background: Next to Buster Keaton and Charlie Chaplin, Charley Chase was arguably the greatest single comedy force in silent films, and one of the greatest in the entire history of the motion picture. I say this because he wasn't just an onscreen comedian. He was a comedy writer, director, leading actor, supporting actor, gagman, prop man, producer, re-writer/script doctor, comic dancer, comic singer, factotum, mentor and teacher, consultant and advisor. He was among the top three in every one of those roles. He, more than anyone, designed and implemented the

Roach Studio comedy machine whose influence still has an impact on every comic movie and TV series today, 100 years later.

What makes him even more of a true rival to Keaton and Chaplin is that he did it all for dozens of other comedians, not just for himself (unlike Keaton and especially Chaplin). He made Lloyd Hamilton and Snub Pollard and Max Davidson look like brilliant comedians. He elevated Billy West from totally unendurable to barely tolerable. He made even the Three Stooges funny. He contributed some of the best stuff done by Laurel and Hardy and Our Gang. In his earliest days, although not yet in a position of authority, he brought shape and subtlety to the Mack Sennett "farce comedies" that influenced the likes of Chaplin, Roscoe Arbuckle, and Mabel Normand. He helped create Harold Lloyd. He taught Leo McCarey everything McCarey knew about comedy, according to McCarey himself. Who else did Keaton and Chaplin ever mentor into effective comedians? Elsie Ames and Marlon Brando?

Synopsis: Husband "Melvin" has had enough of wife "Mame's" jealousy; he's going to shoot himself in the privacy of his bedroom, where he can fire his pistol into the floor and then flop down beside it uninterruptedly . . . repeating as necessary, which turns out to be repeatedly necessary. Giving up, he resolves on a quiet night at home for himself while "Mame" goes off with her girlfriend. Proving herself susceptible to every kind of groundless fantasizing, the wife and her pal attend a "spiritualistic meeting" in which the mystic declares "Melvin" is flirting with a slender sylph even as they speak.

Katherine Grant's leg-show shocks William Gillespie (in bed) and Charley Chase (under bed) in *Innocent Husbands* (1925). *Courtesy of Derek Boothroyd*

The slender sylph in question is actually a chubby party girl whom "Melvin" has been forced to squire to his neighbor's jazz party; "Melvin" thought he was joining the neighbor (William Gillespie) for a demure game of checkers in their dressing gowns. The suspicious desk clerk (James Finlayson, whose lack of a moustache here makes him look like a fish) and the even more suspicious hotel dick (Lucien Littlefield, an actor so hammy he smokes himself) try to catch him two-timing his wife. They don't succeed, but now "Mame" orders her entire spiritualist troupe to decamp to their home so *she* can catch him in the act before a disapproving audience of confirmed, er, skeptics.

With the neighbor, the party girl, and another party guest (Martha Sleeper) all trapped with "Melvin" in his bedroom, he takes advantage of the phony mystic's conjurings to sweep each person in turn out of the apartment in the guise of materializations of "Mame's" ancestors. Everything ends well, with the innocence of all husbands confirmed beyond dispute for all time, or at least until the next Charley Chase film.

Comment: Chase's facial reactions to Kay de Lys (the party girl) are priceless, if a tiny bit cruel. In fact, with the exception of the final sequence with the spiritual materializations, the entire film depends upon Chase's incomparable expressions and body control to "put over" the gags. His plaintive, frustrated, had-enough-of-it discouragement in the face of wife Katherine Grant's unreasonable suspicions strike any married person as honest and accurate and, consequently, funny. His reaction to the storm of keys landing around him on the sidewalk after whistling three times as a signal to de Lys conveys all the disgust and hopelessness anyone would feel in the situation. His panic when his wife comes up to the apartment while de Lys is sprawled unconscious within it is not the least exaggerated, which again makes it honest and true and therefore hilarious.

The manifestations are ingeniously done, and Chase smartly embellishes their potential as comic props by adding broad interplays in the hallway with the house dick. All in all, the film is very skillfully stitched together with comic needles.

Bonus: Viewers who enjoy lip-reading obscenities in silent films are advised to watch the scene of Chase with de Lys in a taxi. Chase chalks the message "DON'T SLOW UP" on the sole of his shoe and shows it to the cabbie. Unluckily for him, the standard taxi rules posted on the screen between them obscures the first word. When Chase realizes the cabbie is doing the exact opposite of what he instructed him to do, he explodes a clearly readable F-bomb.

IRENE

(1926, First National)

Director: Alfred E. Green
Writers: June Mathis, Rex Taylor, and Mervyn LeRoy
Titles: George Marion
Editor: Edwin Robbins
Cast: Colleen Moore, Lloyd Hughes, Kate Price, Charlie Murray, George K. Arthur, Betty Francisco, Edward Earle, Lawrence Wheat, Eva Novak, Bess Flowers, Ida Darling, Maryon Aye, Lydia Yeamans Titus, Cora Macey
Running Time (Length): 94 minutes (eight reels)

Background: Clara Bow was the quintessential 1920s flapper as the good bad girl, the don't-care flirt who cares, the reckless hedonist who sees the error of her ways; her movies reassured an extremely nervous parental generation that their wild, overexuberant, scofflaw youngsters would eventually settle down into sedate, demure, pious conformity. Colleen Moore was the quintessential 1920s flapper as the good girl, the sweet and innocent virgin, the practical optimist; her movies reassured vastly relieved grandparents that their grandkids were exactly the happy, prudish, harmlessly adventurous do-gooders the old folks devoutly prayed they were.

Irene was churned out more or less at Moore's peak, depending on how you view the trajectory of her career—by quality or by length. She started early, in the late 1910s, and was playing lead roles by 1918. She didn't come up with her perennial character and iconic haircut in full until the early 1920s, particularly with the big hit *Flaming Youth* in 1923. Her best years, both at the box office and in terms of film quality, were undoubtedly 1926 and 1927, a period in which she made seven very good films (although *Lilac Time* was not actually released until 1928). Yet she was basically out of the business by the end of 1929, and not entirely because of the switchover to talkies or her marriage issues; although she appeared in four films in the middle 1930s, her time was well past, she didn't need the money, and she had other offscreen interests (principally her dollhouses, which became world famous and are now in museums).

Kate Price, Charlie Murray, and Colleen Moore (left to right) are pop-eyed about *Irene* (1926). *Courtesy of Bruce Calvert*

Irene is quintessential Colleen Moore, and about as good as her films get. *Flaming Youth, Orchids and Ermine, Twinkletoes, Lilac Time,* and even *Ella Cinders* could just as easily be celebrated as representative Moore films; I have chosen *Irene* because I think it has more amusing moments and overall tone than the other films.

Synopsis: When young Irene gets kicked out of the house by her irate mother, there's nothing an idealistic girl can do but—of course!—head straight for New York City and a supposed life of glamour. After the requisite hand-to-mouth struggle, her luck changes through the usual movie ruse of mistaken identity: wealthy bachelor Lloyd Hughes falls for her and persuades his partner in a dress shop to feature her in the fashion show that will make everybody's future happy and secure.

Comment: It is completely fair to say all of Moore's films follow the same blueprint, even those that might seem superficially different, such as *Little Orphant* [*sic*] *Annie* (1919), which in any case somewhat preceded her ascent to full-fledged stardom. All of her films use the same simple story of a nice, enthusiastic "girl" (she was in her middle and late twenties when she made the best of them; by the standards of that era, she was actually an old maid) whose positive spirit and impregnable virtue triumph over penury and dissolute temptation to land her the rich man of her dreams. There are never any real complications or strong subplots, never any real threats to the happy denouements. And you never believe for one second that Moore's naïve character could really survive in New York, let alone live out her one fantasy of marrying happily and wealthily. And did I mention that she always ends up wealthy?

So why is she considered a major star of the silent era? Because she's adorable. Yes, even F. Scott Fitzgerald called her the perfect flapper and the epitome of the era, but the plain truth is that she's adorable, and it has nothing to do with flapperdom. She's Shirley Temple as a happy "teenager." The resemblance in Moore's and Temple's acting styles, tricks, and mannerisms is striking: they smile the same, they do the "dreamy look" the same, they roll their eyes the same, they dimple-up the same, they do their three close-up expressions ("oh!" and "ooooh!" and "ohhhhh!") the same, they even move their heads and bodies the same. It's not exactly creepy—they're both too genuinely endearing to be annoying—but Temple's performances retroactively impart an infantilism to Moore's performances. It doesn't make them any the less winning, though.

Bonus: The majority of comedy in this film comes from three veteran slapstick artists. Kate Price and Charlie Murray play Colleen's parents as Irish stereotypes, roles these two old-timers had been playing in films since starting out in 1912 or thereabouts, Murray at Biograph with D. W. Griffith, Price at Vitagraph with John Bunny. Both appeared, not exclusively, in Mack Sennett productions for a dozen years along with doing guest spots in several other studios. These two knew their stuff and never phoned-in a performance, even for those films in which they weren't given a lot of time or space to let it rip.

The third veteran comedian is George K. Arthur, for whom *Irene* was a bit of a turning point. Although he had been involved with Joseph von Sternberg's *The Salvation Hunters* the year before (1925) and had scored a five-year contract in 1923, in 1926 he was only starting to get noticed. He teamed with Karl Dane in a popular series of comedy shorts, nearly all of which are unavailable today.

Unfortunately, that turned into a bit of an "all his eggs in one basket" situation: the talkies arrived only a year later, and Dane's accent dashed the basket to the asphalt, putting both of them out of film work basically forever. Arthur survived the 1950s and 1960s packaging TV shows.

Arthur is truly wonderful as the gay couturier, Madame Lucy. He manages to be "light in the loafers" rather than effeminate. No shrieking, mincing, fainting, hankie-waving hysteric, he's simply one of those fastidiously dressed males of impeccable taste in design, able to build a woman's wardrobe thoughtfully and objectively because he has no interest in her as a sexual partner: she's simply, as a beautiful visual metaphor illustrates, a stick upon which he exercises his artistry.

Interestingly, when Arthur does do an overtly gay gesture or expression, it is the women who giggle derisively; the men seem more accepting and unquestioning. And it's not because they're too dull-witted to realize what he is; they certainly recognize his orientation.

IT

(1927, Paramount)

Directors: Clarence Badger and Josef Von Sternberg
Writers: Elinor Glyn, Hope Loring, Louis Lighton
Titles: George Marion
Camera: Kinley Martin
Editor: F. Lloyd Sheldon
Cast: Clara Bow, Antonio Moreno, Priscilla Bonner, William Austin, Jacqueline
   Gadsdon, Julia Swayne Gordon, Gary Cooper, Eleanor Lawson, Rose Tapley,
   Lloyd Corrigan, Elinor Glyn
Running Time (Length): 69 minutes (seven reels)
Availability: DVD (Image Entertainment)

Background: Clara Bow lived the twentieth-century American girl's dream: she was plucked from the most grinding poverty and family dysfunction by winning a fan magazine beauty contest whose prize was an expenses-paid relocation from Brooklyn to Hollywood and a screen test, and the screen test led directly into worldwide adulation as the most popular (and most lusted after) movie star on the planet.

It is not really true that she struggled in bit parts for a long time before hitting it big. She played in about 15 films before she could be said to be a star, which sounds like a lot, but those 15 films were all made within a period of only one and a half years (1922–1924). She had become a popular lead by the middle of 1924, still only 18 years old (she turned 19 in August).

In 1925, ambitious and heartless producer Budd Schulberg at Paramount made the fateful decision to turn Bow into the biggest star in movies. His method of doing so was to drive her into exhaustion and mental breakdown through overwork. She never got a bit of relief: he pushed her through film after film after film with no break. Worse, each film was either the same or lousier than the one before. She made 15 films in 1925 alone—the same number she had made over 1922–1924, but in those earlier films she wasn't responsible for carrying the whole picture, whereas in 1925 she was the star in everything, on the screen almost all the time in every movie, and that does make an enormous difference in the physical, mental, and emotional strain put upon an actor.

Clara had such a powerful joy in life, such a thrilling exultation in youth and its limitless horizons, that she was able to live through this professional abuse to reach her apex in 1927 with *It*, as well as the superb *Wings* the same year. After that, though, the pace of Schulberg's inhumane exploitation swiftly took its toll. Bow's health and career suffered just as the talkies revolutionized the industry. Contrary to myth, she performed very well and very winningly in the sound films she made; like her contemporary Mabel Normand, sadly, it was her health and the years of abuse (human and recreational abuse) as well as the call of marriage that dictated her time was up.

Synopsis: The son has stepped into his father's shoes as the head of "Waltham's" department store, and he's a dapper dreamboat who definitely has "it" in quantities to cause his own salesgirls to cluster in sighing, staring infatuation. Not least

This unusual pose doesn't show off Clara Bow at her best, which is why it is rarely seen (*It*, 1927). *Author's collection*

among them is Clara Bow, who has enough "it" of her own to infatuate William Austin, playing "Waltham's" idle-rich pal, "Monty."

Romantic at heart though she is, Bow's "Betty Lou" character is a thoroughly practical gold digger too. She plays "Monty" for all the free shopping she can get out of him, not to mention dinner at the spiffy Ritz so she can send the first dart of love into the heart of fellow diner "Waltham." Pretty soon, "Waltham" is off to Coney Island with her for the time of his life, notwithstanding that his suit and tie never get loosened, not even when Bow's skirt is blown sky-high and her rolled stockings are put on public display three or four times.

"Betty" shares a walk-up apartment with a friend and former co-worker, helping care for the latter's baby during the woman's illness. Fortuitously on the spot when responsible social workers attempt to remove the child to "the Home," "Betty" fends them off by declaring she is the mother of the fatherless infant. Even in the New York City of 1927, this is front-page scandal, thanks to reporter Gary Cooper in a very brief early career appearance. The expected misunderstandings ensue, which "Betty" resolves by inviting herself via "Monty" to join "Waltham's" yachting party for the purpose of creating romantic mayhem. All's well that ends up in the water, with "Waltham" and "Betty" pledging their drenched troth while "Monty" and his pal's discarded ex-fiancée face the fact that they themselves are "itless its."

Comment: Elinor Glyn's success in the Twenties as not just a popular writer but a public quote-machine is not really inexplicable: the lack of any real talent other than for promoting oneself and being carefully risqué is an enduring American type that has actually become a mass phenomenon in the 21st century thanks to YouTube, Twitter, and other social media. Glyn is woefully homely, stout, middle-aged, and self-important, all qualities that could easily be overlooked if only she were a decent writer. As pompous and wordily inarticulate in person as she is on the printed page, she has presented us with a trite and formulaic story, cardboard characters, the shopgirl's fantasy of romance with a prince (of industry, this being business-worshipping America rather than royalty-besotted Europe), and melodramatic material that by 1927 was already the most overworked set of clichés in feature movies.

And here's where the actors prove their worth: Clara Bow, Antonio Moreno, William Austin, and Jacqueline Gadsdon all give such fine and feisty performances as to turn this silly and predictable stuff into a very fun romp.

Bow's eyes have never been more beautiful, huge, and impossible to resist. This is almost unanimously considered her best film, in the sense of it being the film that most successfully gives her a stage upon which to show us everything she can do. Bow bounces with energy and joie de vivre; she even bounces when she's standing still, she's so effervescent. Or, as Moreno's would-be fiancée stiffly observes, Bow is "rather lacking in reserve." Hopping around and tossing her gorgeous curls and flapping her giant eyelashes as she does, she even forces the camera to behave in a lively fashion just to keep up with her. In the era of the stationary camera, *It* is full of tracking shots, tilting shots, *moving* shots; when it pauses to fix on her incredibly expressive face, it almost feels like the cameraman is trying to catch his breath.

Austin does go overboard in his silly-ass British-twit caricature, and it seems out of place in a film where Bow, Moreno, and Gadsdon (not to mention the overwrought and underused Priscilla Bonner) are working hard to keep their own characters credible and human; we don't need comic relief in a comedy, at least not in a comedy that is succeeding in being funny without him. But he does put in such an effort that we have to acknowledge he adds considerably to the pleasure of the film. And he does get some good lines, such as this one: "They've been friends for years. Some day they'll marry and end it all."

And you've got to love the ending that has Clara swimming fast enough and far enough (in a sidestroke, yet) to win an Olympic gold medal . . . without losing her high-heeled shoes in the water.

Bonus: Probably the single most amusing thing about Elinor Glyn's real-life idiotic, preening persona and vastly overblown contemporary reputation as a writer is her three—count 'em, three—attempts in this film (in person and in her quoted publications) to define "it." She grasps that "it" has something to do with "magnetic sex appeal" and irresistibility to the opposite sex, but she conflates it with "charisma," a concept she has even less sureness of understanding. All of her definitions wind down to a somewhat desperate insistence that a lack of self-consciousness is (practically the only) requisite for "itness." She doesn't mean "self-consciousness" in the sense of painful shyness; she means it in the sense of "self-awareness." If one thinks of charismatic epitomes—Presidents John Kennedy, Ronald Reagan, and Bill Clinton come to mind—and of sex-appeal catnips like Marilyn Monroe or George Clooney, it should be obvious that no one with "it" could possibly be lacking in self-awareness. (I chose post-Glyn examples, but I could as easily have mentioned Rudolph Valentino, Wallace Reid, Theda Bara, Houdini, Liszt, Oscar Wilde . . .) Every person who has "it" knows it, can't help but be made aware of it through the adulation or adoration of others, and consciously wields "it" all the time he or she is in company or on display. Rock stars know they are rock stars.

THE ITALIAN STRAW HAT

(1927, Albatros [France])

Director: René Clair
Writer: René Clair, based on the play by Eugène Labiche and Marc Michel
Camera: Maurice Desfassiaux and Nicolas Roudakoff
Editor: Henri Dobb
Cast: Albert Préjean, Marise Maia, Vital Geymond, Olga Tschekowa, Yvonneck, Jim Gèrald, Alex Allin, Paul Ollivier, Louis Pré fils, Alexis Bondireff, Alice Tissot, Andre Volbert, Mlle. Chouqette, Valentine Tessier
Running Time: 105 minutes
Availability: DVD (Flicker Alley)

Background: The silent film in France underwent some interesting metamorphoses. Contrary to American self-mythology, of course, it was France that essentially invented the motion picture and originated the concept of the documentary (in the form of *actualités*), the science fiction film, the trick/magic film, and even the slapstick comedy film. This history indicates the inventiveness that kept the French cinema churning in new and different directions continuously from the middle 1890s until the middle 1920s, which is almost the entire lifespan of the silent era.

Then something happened in the middle 1920s. Russia had always extravagantly admired the language and culture of France, and when the Revolution overturned the old czarist order, those who had the means to flee made a beeline for Paris after 1919. This included hundreds of artistic leaders, who in the next half dozen years proceeded to overthrow the old order in French culture with their own revolution. Dance, music, art, theatre, and film all suddenly experienced an earthquake that both undermined and invigorated French culture.

The received wisdom is that French movies had grown sclerotic and uninventive, bogged down in adaptations of preexisting books and plays instead of continuing to build on the innovations of Méliès, Linder, Gance, and others. Considering that Gance, for one, didn't even hit his stride until the early to middle 1920s, and that *Cyrano de Bergerac* had presented astoundingly creative use of color and spectacle in 1925 (albeit *Cyrano* itself was, indeed, a theatrical warhorse), this seems a peculiar perspective. But then, France was traditionally as fascinated by Russian culture as Russia was by French culture, so any inflated rationale justified their embrace of the Russian film colony. Alas, this proved fatal to French cinema, which became undistinguished with a few exceptions until the New Wave shook it awake in the 1960s.

Alexander Kamenka, the émigré who ran Albatros Studios, had made it a headquarters for Russian filmmakers and performers; in 1924 those capricious talents, led by Ivan Mosjoukine, pulled yet another revolution and emigrated to their own new studio. To keep his business afloat, Kamenka recruited French talent and put them to work with his remaining Russians.

Thus we get René Clair, no longer quite the struggling neophyte filmmaker but still not yet making his mark as a premier talent, reviving and updating a chestnut play from 1851 with a cast of mixed Russian, French, and Swiss performers and a similarly mixed Russian and French production crew. *The Italian Straw Hat* is about as pretty and as witty as the Russified French cinema could achieve in the later 1920s; although it is indeed pretty and witty and frequently inspired, it also carries with it a sheen of international diplomacy, and no one ever called diplomacy a cutting-edge discipline.

Synopsis: It's the wedding day of "Fadinard" (sometimes referred to as Ferdinand by translators) and "Hélène" in the happy year of 1895. While the bride and her family struggle with tight shoes, missing gloves, and pins falling down inside the back of gowns, "Fadinard" is leisurely making his way into the city driving a horse and cart. He encounters a lady's discarded hat, which his horse partially eats while "Fadinard" seeks out the errant woman. She proves to be a dazzling brunette rolling in the bushes with a hot-tempered military officer. Because she is a married woman (not to the military officer) and this is 1895 rather than 1995, her reputation will be ruined by the telltale clue of the half-eaten hat; it is "a rare Italian straw hat" given to her by her husband, so if she does not return home with a perfectly intact topper he will know what cuckoldry she has been playing on him.

The lady and her lover take up residence in "Fadinard's" house and threaten to destroy everything in it if he does not find a replacement hat immediately. "Fadinard" must juggle his desperate search for the hat with the progress of his own wedding. The latter event features the kind of supporting characters invariably described as "colorful" because each is given a single trait or situation that makes them easily and immediately identifiable: a missing glove, supposedly "hilarious" deafness, pince-nez that keep falling off the nose, a tie that keeps falling out of the collar, and so on. The wedding itself is quite odd looking: a civil ceremony in which the members of the wedding party sit in five leather easy chairs while the mayor lectures them at great length with great dullness. There is also a lively and entertaining post-wedding dance that evolves first into a mass invasion of the wrong house, then into a street chase, then into an attempted mass invasion of the right house, and finally into a mass ushering into a police station, before everyone gets shooed back into their own homes so the bride and groom may finally enjoy a happy ending.

Comment: I have no hesitation in including *The Italian Straw Hat* as one of the 100 essential silent film comedies; however, I caution the reader not to expect gut-busting, bawdy belly laughs in the manner of a Feydeau bedroom farce. This film is *belle époque* social satire draped over the framework of a sex romp, which means there is no sex and no romping; instead, we get elegant and discreet fun poked at the moral strictures that govern the expected/approved behavior of the social class. We are entertained in a civilized manner; we do not guffaw. Sometimes, especially in the early going when "Fadinard" and the soldier quarrel repetitively and overlengthily, the movie verges on dullness; it is only after "Fadinard" flees his own home that the film starts to awaken.

The set design, by Lazare Meerson, is quite beautiful. "Fadinard's" home is replete with bright, complicated bric-a-brac, while the other settings are simple but well rendered. Although occasionally indulging in artsy-fartsy overhead shots, for the most part Clair keeps to classical camera framing, letting the physical activity of the performers push the visual compositions into liveliness (which is another reason why the early repetitious, stationary arguments between "Fadinard" and the soldier slow things down and make us aware of a certain lethargy).

The two young female leads are fascinating in their appearance. Neither is anything more than mildly attractive, but their hairstyles—one brunette, the other blonde—create an illusion of great beauty in both. Professional movie hairstylists of today would be well advised to pay attention and learn something from the past.

Be sure to watch the full 105-minute version and not the 84-minute American cut that was the only available version from 1931 until 2010. The shortened version is akin to cutting the string that holds together a stuffed tenderloin before it is put in the oven: bits and pieces and shreds fall out and leave behind a loose collection of chunks that do not cohere into a tasty whole.

Bonus: Although I had no hesitation in including *The Italian Straw Hat* as a great silent comedy, I had considerable hesitation about including *Lady Windermere's Fan* (1925), and ultimately decided against it. Why the *Hat* but not the *Fan*? It is deserving of a brief explanation.

Both films are based on classic comedies of the 19th-century stage, plays that have endured in theaters around the world for more than a century and continue to be revived to popular acclaim in the 21st century. Their popularity is attributable to a verbal wit that has proven virtually timeless. Both have been turned into glossy silent features by European film geniuses, in *Fan*'s case the much-adored Ernst Lubitsch. Both are, really, very good films.

René Clair kept the essence of the stage *Hat* and transformed the spoken wit into vigorous physical comedy informed by the slapstick that was the uniquely successful blossom of silent comedy. Lubitsch, on the other hand, threw out everything Oscar Wilde had put into the stage *Fan*. He literally did not use a single word from Wilde's play, not even "and" or "the" (to paraphrase Mary McCarthy's evisceration of Lillian Hellman's writing). Instead of replacing it with physical comedy, he chose to create a melodrama of social tension.

Lubitsch's sets are splendid, so enormous and spacious that everyone appears to be living in Versailles; the sets are busy being symbols of the emptiness of social conventions, a role that renders them intrusive, whereas Clair's sets are fully integrated into *Hat*'s storyline and are used cleverly as props supporting the action.

"Lady Windermere's" brush with social convention is made into a reinforcement of oppressive social mores, completely contrary to Wilde's intention of deriding them. Wilde's characters go on living the conventions, knowing full well how ridiculous they are, because that is the institution with which they remain comfortable and contented even within their cynicism. In Lubitsch's version, they are neither aware of the absurdity of the conventions and the institution nor are they cynical about it; instead, they are dedicated to shoring up its pillars.

In the end, Lubitsch's *Fan* is impressive and a good film that has nothing to do with Oscar Wilde and has very little humor in it. The sole scene that even mildly amuses is a collage of binocular-wielding toffs observing the sexily disreputable woman sitting in ostracism at the racetrack. Clair's *Hat*, in contrast, is impressive and a good film that adheres to the delightful play and is consistently amusing, even if there are few out-loud laughs in it.

IT'S A GIFT

(1923, Roach)

Director: Hugh Fay
Titles: H. M. Walker
Editor: Uncredited, probably T. J. Crizer
Cast: Snub Pollard, Marie Mosquini, Wallace Howe, William Gillespie, Mark Jones
Running Time (Length): One reel
Availability: DVD (Classic Video Streams: *Anthology Series: Forgotten Comics*, vol. 4)

Background: The year 1923 was the last year in which Snub Pollard sustained a volume of product that averaged at least one film per month. Beginning the next year, his production was reduced quite a bit. The success of both the Our Gang series and the development of Charley Chase's self-starring comedies of embarrassment in 1924 reduced the need for Pollard's films to fill holes in Hal Roach's distribution contract; it also drastically reduced the amount of attention Chase could devote to Snub, and the drop-off in quality was definitely noticed. *It's a Gift* was the last really good film Pollard made, and one of the very few that turned out well without Chase's help.

Synopsis: As we all know so well, billionaire oil tycoons deserve to make themselves into *trillionaire* oil tycoons. They fret over how this worthy goal might be achieved in 1923, a year when that mere ballplayer Babe Ruth was being overpaid a scandalous $80,000, and the president of the United States was making even less than the Babe. The selfless tycoons decide to consult a mysterious man known to the world only as "Inventor Pollard," whom rumor whispers has invented a liquid that turns car engines into rocket engines with a single drop.

It's morning in the Pollard home. Snub is awakened by an automated foot-tickler. Sitting up in bed, he proceeds to make breakfast by manipulating a formidable set of pulleys dangling from the ceiling. Then another bunch of pulleys dresses him, makes the bed, and pulls it up to reveal a roaring fireplace where the box spring would normally be found; he must have had a warm bed in any kind of weather.

Outside the house, his garbage can serves as the garage for his vehicle of choice: a torpedo in size and shape and also in its lack of an engine of its own; instead, Pollard uses a giant magnet to coast in the slipstreams of other vehicles. (In those days, cars were made of metal, not plastic—hence their vulnerability to magnets!)

When he arrives at the meeting with the underpaid oil bosses, no one thinks to ask him why he drives a vehicle without an engine if he has invented a serum that transforms engines into warp-speed rockets. He proceeds to prove the potency of his invention by dripping it into the gas tanks of about a dozen cars, which instantly careen out of control at the highest speeds that can be achieved by undercranking a camera. Aghast at the realization that this could mean the end of the oil industry instead of its complete takeover of world power, the tycoons (or at least their public flunkey, the cop) give chase to Pollard. He dives into his torpedo and it fires off into the air as if it had become a real rocket . . . despite that lack of an engine!

Comment: It's a Gift is possibly the most popular and most highly regarded film Pollard ever made. That doesn't mean it was his best, but it ranks up there with *Sold at Auction* and *On Location.* For many people, it was the one Pollard silent film they might have stumbled across from the 1960s through the 1990s because it was readily available in fan circles and was excerpted in Robert Youngson's compilation *When Comedy Was King* (1960).

It's an uneven film. The opening scenes of "Inventor Pollard" using Rube Goldberg gizmos to awaken, cook his breakfast, get him dressed, and put away his Murphy bed are extremely well done and entertaining, notwithstanding their rip-off of Buster Keaton. The second section, in which he buzzes around town in his bullet car, starts with cleverness and then becomes repetitive. The final section, the demonstration of his gasoline substitute, is kind of desperate, a flaying-about of cars in search of Keystone-style laughs. And the very last scene is just an awful ending by any standard.

Well worth viewing for its lively wit and for the insouciant elaboration of the Keaton material, *It's a Gift* is an especially good diversion for people who have never seen a silent comedy before.

Bonus: Pollard's long run of good luck at the Roach studio hit a brick wall called "Laurel and Hardy" around 1927. Snub had survived far longer than his minuscule talents deserved because Charley Chase made him a pet project, his films broke even while filling huge portions of Roach's production schedule requirements, and he did what he was asked to do with nary a demurral. Once "The Boys" took off, however, Pollard was pushed to the sidelines where he belonged. Disgruntled, he betook himself to the Weiss Brothers at Educational Pictures; there, to everyone's horror, he was handcuffed to the execrable Marvin Loback in the world's most revolting copycat version of Laurel and Hardy. This broke Pollard's inflated reputation, and he spent the talkie era sneaking up on the audience in cameos (often uncredited) in Three Stooges films, Westerns, and TV shows right up until his death in 1962.

IT'S THE OLD ARMY GAME

(1926, Paramount/Famous Players)

Director: Edward Sutherland
Writers: W. C. Fields, Joseph McEvoy, Tom Geraghty, and J. Clarkson Miller
Titles: Ralph Spence and W. C. Fields
Camera: Alvin Wychoff
Editor: Tom Geraghty
Cast: W. C. Fields, Louise Brooks, William Gaxton, Mary Foy, Mickey Bennett, Elise Cavanna, Eugene Pallette, Blanche Ring, Josephine Dunn, Jack Luden, George Currie, John Merton
Running Time (Length): 72 minutes (seven reels)
Availability: DVD (CD Baby)

Background: The luminous Louise Brooks, owner of the most distinctive female haircut of the Roaring Twenties as well as the most perfect and beautiful back (not backside) in American film history, was on the cusp of graduating from teendom when she made this motion picture, which was just her third significant appearance on nitrate if one excludes the tiny bit part with which she had made her debut in *The Street of Forgotten Men* (1925). One can forgive her, therefore, the limitations of her performance. As with all actresses in Fields's films, she is given nothing to work with. Fields divided the main female roles in his scripts into two unidimensional types: the intolerant, intolerable termagant and the adoring, forgiving ingénue. Cast in the latter, Brooks spends the entire film laughing in a loving way at Fields's antics, and amateurishly playing coy with would-be lover William Gaxton, who has plenty of desperate energy yet still is no match for a girl who in real life is all too clearly out of his league.

Brooks and Fields had already worked together on stage in the Ziegfeld Follies. Born rebels, they had become fast friends and lasting ones; she wrote a fine tribute to him in her excellent book of film essays/reminiscences, *Lulu in Hollywood* (1982). In *It's the Old Army Game*, it is clear she is genuinely tickled by Fields's comedy even though she had seen it all countless times before; in turn, he obviously enjoys her laughter, quite sincerely pleased to have amused someone he likes very much indeed.

Both performers, though no longer novices to film, were still at the early stage where their producers were trying to build them up to stardom. Both wobbled quite a bit in silent-era Hollywood. Brooks bookended *Army Game* with winners in *The American Venus* (1925), *The Show-Off*, and *Love 'em and Leave 'em* (both 1926), but at the same time she was also in clunkers like *A Social Celebrity* (1925), *Just Another Blonde* (1926), and *Evening Clothes* (1927). After the superb *Beggars of Life* (1928), she temporarily gave up on American cinema and went to Germany to make the greatest and most influential films of her career: *Pandora's Box* (1929), *Diary of a Lost Girl* (1929), and *Prix de Beauté* (1930). Filled now with a self-confidence and an artistic contempt that never left her, she returned to Hollywood to find herself virtually ostracized, forced to accept menial roles in crapulent movies until she retired and spent the rest of her life as a semi-recluse, a lowly sales clerk, a writer, and a celebrated cult figure.

Fields's twelve silent films (seven of which survive) were by and large failures, despite the fact that D. W. Griffith was in charge of two of them—or maybe because of Griffith, since he was notorious not only for having no sense of humor himself but for being incapable of having fun onscreen. *It's the Old Army Game* was actually designed to be the relaunching of Fields as a star film comedian, Griffith's *Sally of the Sawdust* (1925) having landed with the thud of a dud. As someone whose personality simply did not permit him to accede to the orders of others, Fields ignored direction and continued, throughout the silent era, to perform as though on the stage. For that matter, he also continued to perform his stage *acts*. Any Fields fan, and any Fields hater, can check off the man's short list of skits: the golf skit, the pool-table skit, the blind-man-in-a-pharmacy skit, the picnicking-on-a-private-estate skit, and so on. From the start of his film career, critics complained that he was recycling his stage repertoire; far from letting this criticism upset him, Fields perversely provoked it further by recycling his recyclings. *It's the Old Army Game* recycled bits from *Sally of the Sawdust* and was in turn remade in part as both *The Pharmacist* (1933) and *It's a Gift* (1934), while one of its key lines (already recycled within twenty minutes of itself in *Army Game*) gave the title to *Never Give a Sucker an Even Break* (1941).

Synopsis: W. C. Fields is "Elmer Prettywillie," a brilliant sobriquet that no one seems to have realized is Fields's tribute to his own aesthetically pleasing male organ. (You can be quite sure Louise Brooks got the joke.) Befitting the man with such a manly name, he is a druggist, which in those days and in small-town America made his store the epicenter of the community. When he is not selling cough drops, malteds, telegrams, illicit gin (it was the Prohibition era) or postage stamps—for the drugstores of that era were also luncheonettes, telegraph/telephone offices, bootleggers, and post offices—he is dealing with unreasonable customers, freeloading volunteer firemen, freeloading checker players, freeloading friends, demanding female relatives and their budding psychopathic offspring, and one beautiful and mutually affectionate young girl who needs his kindly guidance in finding a husband.

Into his store bursts one such candidate, a hustler with an intriguingly counterintuitive scheme. Hucksters are flooding New York City to sell Florida lots to suckers; why not reverse the flow by flooding Florida with hucksters selling New York City lots to suckers? Suckers being suckers wherever they are found,

Norman Z. McLeod (left) and W. C. Fields (right) argue over Carmen the dog in this candid publicity shot that has nothing to do with *It's the Old Army Game* (1926). *Author's collection*

"Elmer" is the first to buy into it, to the extent that his store is turned into a bucket-shop churning Brooklyn deeds into cash faster than even the prestidigitous Fields can pocket.

Idly wealthy now, "Elmer" takes a break to introduce filmgoers to another of Fields's longer and more elaborate repertoire pieces. He had earlier subjected us to the silent version of the "Carl LaFong" skit in which he is constantly disturbed when trying to sleep on the back porch of the three-story house in which he lives; it actually works well without the incessant repetitions of the "LaFong" dialogue. Now, he piles his noxious family into his jaunty jalopy and drives onto a ritzy private lawn for a quiet, genteel family picnic. This bucolic outing features more blowing trash than a city dump in a hurricane, as many smashed statues as ancient Rome, and the wholesale destruction of everything the pestiferous nephew can pilfer from the mansion. Fields is unfortunately equally obnoxious in this version of the skit, guffawing at the destruction, chortling and giggling at the criminal (literally) vandalizing by the boy; the viewer does not sympathize, no matter how antisocial or anticapitalist he or she may be.

Back at the drugstore, the air has abruptly departed the tires of the land scam as the police move in, and "Prettywillie" faces the not-so-pretty specter of bankruptcy as he resolves to go to NYC to get the straight story. After some desultory turns and turnabouts, the Manhattan deeds turn out to be worth the full value of the paper they are written on, Louise unpersuasively surrenders to the marital tweets of twitty William Gaxton, and everybody is made wealthy and happy.

Comments: In the 1930s and early 1940s, W. C. Fields immortalized himself as one of the truly great, truly original, and truly unique film comedians in a frequently broken string of classics such as *The Bank Dick, Tillie and Gus, Never Give a Sucker an Even Break, You Can't Cheat an Honest Man, You're Telling Me!, It's a Gift, The Man on the Flying Trapeze,* and *My Little Chickadee;* the breaks in this string usually involved mediocre programmers in which he perked up the dullness as the comic relief in supporting roles (*Big Broadcast of 1938, International House, Six of a Kind*) and even undertook a fairly straight character role as Mr. Micawber in *David Copperfield* (1935).

One of the many assets that made his character so distinctive was his voice: an odd hybrid of hurriedness and drawl, a volubly articulate mumble, a monotone that cut and drew blood, inaudible yet overheard, and inevitably detoured from the mouth whose corners curled like a villain's mustachio to instead emerge honking through the chrysanthemum nose (how could it have come from anywhere else?).

The voice and the proboscis-based mutter are such integral parts of the Fields persona that to have cast him in silent films strikes one as little short of perverse. Yet Fields made an even dozen silent films in which his voice is never heard. The fact that sound recording had not yet become an element whose absence from a movie is unthinkable did not give Fields pause in the making of these early films. He trusted—because he participated in writing them—the ability of intertitles to convey his witticisms; and as a many-decades star of stage and vaudeville, beginning with a mute juggling act and visual tricks that relied upon physical action to distract live audiences, he had justifiable confidence in his visual comedy.

Bonus: In all of his silent films, Fields adopted cinema's most deliberately fake moustache prior to Groucho Marx's painted Fuller brush. Usually it appears to be a set of cultivated nose hairs, being set right at the wide-open doors of his nostrils and far from the expected nesting place just above his mouth. In *It's the Old Army Game,* he loses all interest in pretending the moustache has any relation at all with reality. Most scenes show he has applied a bare smudge of glue to only one side of his upper lip, leaving the other half of the moustache unattached to any part of his face. Why bother?

Why indeed? In subsequent films, especially *Running Wild* (1927), he didn't even trouble himself to paste it on straight. It wasn't until *Million Dollar Legs* (1932), one of the stupidest and most hilarious screwball comedies ever made, that Fields threw away the silly bit of horsehair and allowed his massive nose to flourish in all its undiluted, attention-grabbing nakedness.

I WAS BORN, BUT . . .

(1932, Shochiku [Japan])

Director: Yasujiro Ozu
Writers: James Maki (i.e., Yasujiro Ozu), Akira Fushimi, Geibei Ibushiya
Camera: Hideo Mohara
Editor: Hideo Mohara
Cast: Tatsuo Saito, Mitsuko Yoshikawa, Hideo Sugawara, Tokkan Kozo, Takeshi
   Sakamoto, Teruyo Hayami, Seiichi Kato, Shoichi Kofujita
Running Time: 90 minutes
Availability: DVD (Criterion Collection: *Silent Ozu: Three Family Comedies*)

Background: As a child and teenager, Yasujiro Ozu was a pretty spectacular failure.
Exiled from Tokyo by his father, who sold poop for a living (I'm not making this
up!), Ozu was spoiled by his mother. He wasn't much of a student and failed all
attempts to get into postsecondary institutions. Despite that, he got hired as an
assistant teacher, proving the axiom that those who can't do, teach. He did a bit
better in his various army stints, which stretched off and on from the 1920s to the
end of World War II, after which he was interned as a POW for half a year. More
importantly, however, he had fallen in love with silent movies at an early age and
got into the creative side of the industry when he was barely 20 years old.

To take a brief diversion here: the year Ozu entered the film industry was the
same year a massive earthquake hit Tokyo and Yokohama particularly hard. It
put the domestic film industry in suspension for a long time—we're talking years
here—and when it came back, the influence of overseas films that had filled the
gap in movie theatres was palpable. Japanese cinema abruptly grew up or reinvented itself. The only carryover from the pre-earthquake era, more or less, was
the role of live narrators called *benshi*; their occasionally violent activism on behalf
of their jobs caused lengthy delays in Japan's transition to talkies, and that is why
we find Ozu still making silent films deep into the 1930s.

In 1927 he had made his first film and very quickly became an assembly-line
director and scriptwriter, pouring out as many as seven films per year, in all kinds
of genres and styles. It wasn't until 1931 that he could get off that intensive apprenticeship treadmill and start making the films that would lead him to become
one of the greatest and most respected directors in the world, even if he never
really had any successes in the Western markets.

Synopsis: A father has moved his family to the suburbs (which in this case looks
like a dismal, abandoned landscape of trails worn through grass) in order to be
closer to his employer, to whom he assiduously grovels with an eye to future
promotion. The move has put his two young sons squarely in the sights of bullies.
The bullying reaches the point where the brothers prefer to skip school altogether
and fake positive reports from their teachers to fool their parents.

The parents, little suspecting what is going on, praise the boys and daily en-
courage them to work hard and make something of themselves. Watching their
father be the lickspittle of his boss (whose son is one of their tormentors), the boys

realize *he* hasn't made anything of himself despite working hard, getting a good education, and sucking up to his betters. This revelation, one that kids every-where discover eventually, saturates the boys with a contempt that makes them bold enough to strike back at, first, their neighborhood bullies, and second, their father himself. When forceful discipline makes them only more bitterly stubborn, the father realizes he must find other ways to conciliate and build bridges to them if the family is to remain whole.

Comment: Japanese comedy, not including their poker-faced monster movies and what used to be derisively referred to as chop-socky martial arts films, is quite different from the comedy of any other country, especially the loud, obvi-ous, slapstick comedy of Hollywood. For some Western viewers, indeed, it is hard to recognize as comedy: it seems rather to be glum drama in which the actors incongruously grin and laugh politely and bow incessantly. It's comedy in the same way the medieval morality plays of Europe were comedy. You don't laugh much at it unless you're immersed in the culture and the times, just as you won't laugh much today while watching a medieval morality play that slayed audiences in 16th-century Europe.

In 2008, the good people at the Criterion Collection issued *I Was Born, But . . .* along with *Tokyo Chorus* (1931) and *Passing Fancy* (1933) in a DVD set called *Silent Ozu: Three Family Comedies*. The set is not exactly Image Entertainment's *The Slap-stick Encyclopedia*. I was hard pressed to decide whether to include it in this book or not. The first two films do have fleeting instances of amusement, and they do absorb the attention fully. *Passing Fancy* has its merits but is definitely a downer, with hardly a moment's smile in it.

The comedy in *I Was Born, But . . .* (a title never explained) lies mainly in the two boys' unsmiling and careful negotiations with life in new surroundings, and the lessons learned through hard experience. The desolate surroundings—was there ever a bleaker undeveloped suburb in America?—emphasize the working-class realities of their existence. This isn't Hollywood's idea of poverty; this is the real thing, as lived every day on the other side of the world.

There are no jokes, few humorous intertitles and incidents, nothing that will elicit a burst of laughter from the viewer. Yet the film works: you do smile gently as it patiently unscrolls its subtle wit and family truths.

Bonus: I like *Tokyo Chorus* rather more than *I Was Born, But. . . .* Both films are wonderful at balancing the realities of a hardscrabble working life with under-stated comic bumps, most particularly as both impact on a conventional family life. *Tokyo Chorus*'s comic bits are more overt: the universal slapstick of army recruits (or school cadet corps) trying to master the most basic of military skills such as showing up on time and standing in a straight line, and the farce of male employees going to the washroom in turn to fake urination just for the chance to review their paycheck in privacy.

The added despair of *Tokyo Chorus* is ultimately why I decided to follow conven-tional opinion and pick *I Was Born, But . . .* instead. The father in the former movie provokes his own firing and is unable to find new work. That's when you realize this film was made in 1931, when the world was plunging into the most terrible years of the Great Depression. If you have any historical sense, you cannot help feeling a real anxiety about the plight into which the father's impetuous ethical stand has plunged the entire family. You know he's not going to get a good job again for years, the very years in which his young son and daughter will be growing up into teenagers and will most acutely experience the agonizing adolescent embarrassment of being very poor. His wife already shows alienation: she is devastated to the depths of her soul by the sight of her husband trudging the streets wearing a signboard advertising a cheap restaurant, and although she eventually overcomes this marital "betrayal" and pledges to support her husband, you just know the rupture is there and will not be wished away. The film is emotionally depressing, and you don't watch comedies to be depressed.

J

Background: The wonderful social comedy skills of Sidney Drew were built equally on stage experience and genetic heritage: he was part of both the Drew and the Barrymore clans of legendary actors, today combined into actress Drew Barrymore. Sidney's unpretentious personality delivered his impressive talents at the humble level of genial-old-uncle lovableness; he was so *genuine*.

We remember him mostly as half of "Mr. and Mrs. Sidney Drew." The other half was his second wife, Lucille McVey, whom he married in 1914, about a year after joining Vitagraph. McVey shared in the act's name and she almost always made onscreen appearances in supporting or "wife" roles (I'm hard-pressed to remember any time she appears onscreen *without* Sidney in the same frame); however, this self-effacement belied the fact that she was the brains of the pair, the one who wrote almost all of their Vitagraph scenarios.

The Drews were unquestionably the monarchs of short social comedies from 1913 to 1919. It was a position they earned on merit: every film was creative and imaginative, every film had at least a few hearty laughs in it and several were endlessly side-splitting, every film demonstrated intelligence even when it was going through a dopey scene, and almost every film featured the Drews as a truly next-door couple with whom you could entirely identify. Moreover, they weren't afraid to experiment with black humor, adventurous storylines, serious themes, and the kind of backyard home movies look that silently revealed the lack of resources put into their films—possibly because they were making so many of them, more than thirty per year, that they couldn't afford either the money or the time to build fancy sets or to rent expensive studio space.

Synopsis: Horrors! Sid's mother-in-law is coming to stay with them! Not only is she a domineering bully who demands to be the center of attention, she's also a moral crusader. Sid has been invited to a costume ball, which Mom disapproves of on principle. Wife Clara Kimball Young—Lucille McVey wasn't Mrs. Drew yet, so Young was recruited as the leading lady for this film and a couple of others—soothingly talks Mom into granting permission. The cost to Sid: he must give Mom a kiss. Again: horrors!

Once he's free to go, Sid promptly substantiates all of Mom's condemnations of parties as the conduit to depravity: he smokes, he flirts, he gets so drunk he falls down the steps outside his house and sleeps there. In a borrowing from Max Linder, Drew is wearing a knight's armor as his party costume, and the coincidental theft of the local museum's prize display of a knight's armor causes him to be mistaken for the stolen outfit. Drew gets stripped by the museum's security people. Missing footage would bridge the gap between the stripping of Drew and the "next" scene in which he's taking a bath and Mom walks in on him. She reacts to his nakedness as if acid has just been thrown into her eyes. (Imagine Sid's reaction if their positions had been reversed. Horrors!)

Next, Drew gets inspiration from a hypnotist: maybe he can learn how to mesmerize Mom and program her to never darken his door again! When that attempt fails, he coaxes two friends to dress up as cops and then pretend to get hypnotized by Drew in Mom's presence. Their antics are terrifying enough to finally evict Mom from the house, and Sidney and Clara are once again free to be together.

Comment: The storyline, even with the crib from Linder, was not quite entirely shopworn in 1913. And thanks to Sidney Drew's ineffable natural talent, it seems fresh and newish more than a hundred years later. Sometimes the touches of timelessness are subtle: the Drews' maid may be black, but she openly laughs at them, and Sid's reactions to her mockery when she catches husband and wife kissing are those of a schoolkid whose enemy and equal has caught him in an act that will harm his status in the neighborhood pecking order—not the reaction of a racial superior.

On other occasions, the timelessness is in the gags and in Sid's (it's hard to keep referring to your very own Uncle Sid by his surname) mugging. The best example of the latter is his attempt to deliver the kiss demanded by Mom. After wiping his lips with a handkerchief, steadying his buckling knees, moaning for mercy from God, and trying to find the least repulsive spot on her head for the smooch, Sid barely pecks her on the forehead, and immediately recoils violently in falling-down-dead horror at the touch. He's an absolute scream.

For the timelessness of the gags, a brilliant one that is almost impossible to catch until the second or third viewing takes place when Sid pays his friend (or "friend") the rental fee for borrowing the latter's knight armor costume. Sid peels off five bills from a roll of money and hands them to the "friend," leaving himself with only one bill that he shoves into his pocket. The first time you watch it, you won't notice the friend lifting the solitary remaining dollar out of Sid's pocket.

Less sly, but no less funny, is when Sid has donned the armor and insists on having a burning cigarette put in his mouth before he lowers the visor of the helmet. You expect, from seeing this gag done in other films (Chaplin and Keaton both come to mind), that he will asphyxiate and gasp for the visor to be opened, but that's not what Drew does: he puts the viewer rolling helplessly on the floor in hilarity by continuing to smoke like a chimney, the exhaust pouring out from the grills of the helmet.

Bonus: "Jerry" was an amazingly popular name for slapstick characters in the very early silent comedies. George Ovey was only one among many who adopted it; I mention him in particular because he usually put the name into the title of his films, and he made more than 100 shorts in which his character was named "Jerry." Sidney Drew used the onscreen name "Jerry" a couple of times, but when Lucille McVey took over the offscreen leadership of the team, she changed it to "Henry" in an attempt to set Drew apart from Ovey and his ilk. It was a wise decision, like separating the cream from the cow pee.

K

KID BOOTS

(1926, Paramount)

Director: Frank Tuttle
Writers: Luther Reed and Tom Gibson
Titles: George Marion
Camera: Victor Milner
Editor: F. Lloyd Sheldon
Cast: Eddie Cantor, Clara Bow, Malcolm Waite, Lawrence Gray, Natalie Kingston, Billie Dove, William Worthington, Harry von Meter, Fred Esmelton
Running Time (Length): 59 minutes (nine reels)
Availability: DVD (Original Cast Record)

Background: It can be difficult for today's audiences to comprehend the importance and influence of live New York City theater on the entertainment industry of the United States in the first quarter of the twentieth century. It wasn't just that there was no Internet back then, there was no television either, and radio was just starting to spread at the end of the 1920s. Entertainment that covered distances meant one thing only: vaudeville. Oh, sure, there were things like chautauqua and traveling theatrical troupes, but those were just smaller, less prosperous, more "educational" streams of vaudeville.

The movies followed in the footsteps of vaudeville and quickly surpassed it in reach and impact. As the motion picture industry grew, so did its need for popular personalities and experienced talents. Those personalities and talents, as proven successes, were to be found on Broadway. And so were the vehicles that propelled them to the top and that were ready-made sources for new film scripts.

Eddie Cantor, in common with a lot of the Broadway stars, may have been a big splash in the big pond of New York City, but that didn't mean he was known anywhere outside of the NYC–Boston–Philadelphia–Chicago city limits. But he was wildly popular where he was known, and he had a terrific theater contrivance to showcase his shtick, a comedy called *Kid Boots*. He had been building his resume to that point for about ten years and felt he had nothing more to prove on the stage. It was time to find new fields, or rather new media, for him to conquer.

Eddie Cantor had his greatest impact onstage using the now-disreputable gimmick of blackface (*Kid Boots*, 1926). *Author's collection*

It was time to spread his fame across the rest of America. It was time to invade the movies.

Synopsis: "Tom" (Lawrence Gray) was finagled into what he calls "a frame-up marriage" by "Carmen" (Natalie Kingston); they are in the final stages of divorce when he just so happens to inherit millions and she discovers she loves him as a rich man. Through plot convolutions that take some twenty minutes of screen time to arrange, "Kid Boots" (Cantor) is whisked off by "Tom" to a resort in order to preserve his mortality as "Tom's" unimpeachable witness in divorce court. "Carmen" follows with her retinue of lawyers, still seeking to entrap "Tom" in such a way as to nullify the divorce and gain painless wifely access to his millions.

So does "Big Boyle" (get it? get it?), a burly bully whom "Kid" had had the misfortune to antagonize by flirting with his delectable girlfriend "Clara" (the ever-vivacious Clara Bow). While "Kid" and "Clara" resume their amours and "Carmen" endeavors to compromise both "Kid" and "Tom," "Tom" has fallen in love with "Eleanor" (Billie Dove), which turns out to be the only dull romance in the film, alas.

Somehow this mélange of couples propels "Kid" and "Clara" into a frantic sprint to the courthouse via car, airplane (nope, almost, but it won't be ready to fly for another hour, so they resort to other means), horseback, swinging rope, and finally parachute. Still not exhausted after this chase—heck, they haven't even broken a sweat, dirtied their clothes, or dislodged a hair—the two athletes wrap things up with a marathon run while the judge marries them from a moving car.

Comment: What a female cast: Clara Bow, Natalie Kingston, and Billie Dove! None of them are really given a whole lot to do, especially not Dove, but they're all at the peak of their beauty and sexiness, so they all seem to be doing very, very well by any male viewer.

Over the course of her career, Bow ended up with the darnedest homely men: Donald Keith (in at least four films), Edward Everett Horton, Ernest Torrence, and now Eddie Cantor, who looked like a lemur. Unlike Keith, Cantor is amusing; unlike Horton, he's clearly heterosexual; unlike Torrence's character in *Mantrap* (1926), he's every inch a born-and-bred city dweller (just like Clara). Nonetheless, he's no more convincing than they are as a credible aspirant to Bow's love.

Cantor took too much of the masseuse scene from Chaplin's *The Cure* (1917); however, he makes up for it by taking the whole thing to another realm with some real yoga contortions for which he did not use a double. His physical comic dexterity also gets a vigorous workout with a scene in which he uses his own left arm to fake a two-person love-making gag, and it's worthy of Chaplin. Cantor could really use his body.

Some of the gags in this film are spotted a mile in the distance. The climactic scene of Bow and Cantor parachuting into the courthouse is taking our indulgent suspension of disbelief way too far. And the closing scene of Bow and Cantor running the distance of a mile or two behind a car as they go through the wedding ceremony is beyond silly. Yet this is undeniably a very enjoyable film.

Bonus: Cantor's career in silent films lasted only one more outing: *Special Delivery* (1927). Despite its being directed by Roscoe Arbuckle under a pseudonym and costarring Jobyna Ralston and William Powell (and the ubiquitous, unappealing Donald Keith), it was a bomb. In true Broadway star fashion, Cantor blamed its failure on everyone but himself. He scurried back to New York, had a couple more stage successes to reassure himself, and returned to the movies three years later, when the talkies had arrived to give him a fair platform to let his patter-and-song style of comedy flourish. Although not all his talkies were great pictures, he managed to achieve satisfying results with the likes of *Whoopee!* (1930), *The Kid from Spain* (1932), *Roman Scandals* (1933), and *Kid Millions* (1934).

Cantor was fond of relating a story about how Clara Bow helped him bridge the distance from his frantic stage style to a more subdued style that better fitted the movies. Apparently she told him, "What rehearsals are to the stage, spontaneity is to the screen." This seems to have made perfect sense to Cantor, but I'm still puzzling out how you can rehearse spontaneity.

THE KID BROTHER

(1927, Paramount)

Directors: Lewis Milestone, J. A. Howe, Lex Neal, and Ted Wilde
Writers: John Grey, T. J. Crizer, Ted Wilde, Lex Neal, and Howard Green
Camera: Walter Lundin and Henry Kohler
Editor: Allen McNeil
Cast: Harold Lloyd, Jobyna Ralston, Constantine Romanoff, Walter James, Leo
   Willis, Olin Francis, Frank Lanning, Ralph Yearsley, Eddie Boland, Gus Leonard
Running Time (Length): 72 minutes (eight reels)
Availability: DVD (New Line Home Video: *The Harold Lloyd Comedy Collection*, vol. 2)

Background: By the time he made *The Kid Brother*, Harold Lloyd was the number
one comedian at the box office. His "glass character" shorts and semi-features
had boosted him to the forefront of silent comedy; his full-length feature debut,
Grandma's Boy (1922), was hailed as a cinematic breakthrough; subsequent films,
including *Safety Last!* (1923), *Girl Shy* (1924), and *The Freshman* (1925), were indisputably works of comic genius as well as being top-grossing products, well
ahead (in receipts) of anything Keaton was putting out, and going toe to toe with
Chaplin's decreasing outputs. With the steady, steeply rising growth in quality
and appeal of his work over the past few years, it makes perfect sense that *The Kid
Brother* would be the most nearly perfect film Lloyd would ever make.

Synopsis: A male version of the Cinderella story, *The Kid Brother* casts Lloyd as
the slavey bullied by two brothers and a widowed father. The latter is sheriff of
the rural district, and he appears to be a Jim Thompson kind of sheriff, so stiff-
necked and controlling that he won't even issue a permit to a traveling medicine
show anchored by the glowing Jobyna Ralston. Ralston is, of course, Lloyd's
female counterpart, which is to say she's the sweet, innocent slavey to a couple
of sharpers who are out to fleece the hicks. While "Sheriff Jim" and his two bully-
boys are busy at a town meeting taking protective custody of monies raised to
build a dam, "Harold" dresses up in an extra tin star and gets accosted by the
medicine show sharpers, who realize and exploit his awkward playacting to extract the necessary permit from him.

When his father finds out "Harold" has flouted the rules, he sends the boy to
the medicine troupe's performance to rescind the permit. Naturally "Harold" is
rebuffed and humiliated, which firmly puts the audience in his pocket; naturally,
too, this scene serves to bring him and Ralston together in a romantic pairing.
Their bond is displayed in a striking scene: as Ralston parts from him and walks
away, "Harold" repeatedly climbs higher up a tree and calls out questions that
she pauses to answer; the camera climbs with "Harold" as he ascends, a directorial touch that greatly impacted audiences and fellow filmmakers of the day, and
which is still both effective and affective today.

Through various contrivances, Lloyd and Ralston end up in her makeshift
"bedroom" (quite chastely, of course) when the brothers come a-courtin' the purty
gal. "Harold" pretends to be her, and for once manages to make fools of his bul-

Harold Lloyd and Jobyna Ralston in *The Kid Brother* (1927). *Courtesy of Derek Boothroyd*

lies. It's one of his most endearing scenes and serves to foreshadow "Harold's" turning the tables on all the other bullies in his life.

The money for the dam has been stolen by Ralston's crooked keepers, one of whom kills the other as they hide out in a half-sunken old ship. The movie climaxes with an astoundingly vicious and lengthy brawl between the surviving scoundrel and "Harold"; Lloyd must have been striving to outdo the brutality of the climactic fight in Buster Keaton's *Battling Butler*, released the year before. That's not all: he then adds an almost equally ferocious attack on the town bully to wrap things up.

Comment: One of the factors that makes *The Kid Brother* a truly great film by any measure is the intricacy of its structure. There are about five or six different story threads in it—one can understand why it took five writers (six including Lloyd, who almost never gave himself a writing credit)—and these threads all fit together so seamlessly, the end result feels like a single straight plotline.

Thread "A" is "Harold's" wish to change his Cinderella status among his family. It leads directly to Thread "B" (the town bully who articulates the same Cinderella status "Harold" has among those outside his family), Thread "C" (the threat against the father as an accused thief to be lynched), and Thread "D" (the medicine showmen's exploitation of "Harold's" desire for authority). Thread "D" goes straight to Thread "E," the romance with Ralston. Then Threads "A," "C," and "D" wrap themselves up into Thread "F," "Harold's" destruction of the thief and restoration of the money, which in turn leads to the resolution of Thread "B" and the culmination of Thread "E."

Bonus: More than any other silent comedian, Harold Lloyd benefits from an audience. For argument's sake, let's consider the other top comedians. Keaton, Chaplin, and Langdon are the kinds of comedians a viewer either finds killingly funny or else watches in slightly bored silence; the dichotomy is so decisive that the reactions of fellow viewers can rarely influence whether one enjoys it or not. Charley Chase and Laurel and Hardy are just flat-out uproarious to nearly everyone, regardless of whether or not fellow viewers are laughing, too; they can be extravagantly enjoyed in complete viewer isolation. Raymond Griffith, Max Linder, Lupino Lane, Sidney Drew, and Douglas Fairbanks all compel admiration: laughter is optional, and may be expressed a little more freely (or not, as the case may be) by an audience's reaction, but won't be determined by it.

Lloyd is funny when watched without companions. Watched with other people, however, the laughter builds along with the excitement he provokes with his speed, action, daring, and thrills. It picks up volume and intensity, just as a terrific hockey game with nonstop end-to-end rushes and booming shots and spectacular goals or saves stimulates a crescendo of roars of excitement from the viewers.

Watching Lloyd movies alone is wonderful; watching them in a crowd is extraordinary.

L

LIBERTY

(1929, Roach)

Director: Leo McCarey
Writer: Leo McCarey
Camera: George Stevens
Titles: H. M. Walker
Editors: Richard Currier and William Terhune
Cast: Stan Laurel, Oliver Hardy, Jack Hill, Harry Bernard, Sam Lufkin, James
   Finlayson, Tom Kennedy, Ed Brandenberg, Jack Raymond, Jean Harlow
Running Time (Length): Two reels
Availability: DVD (Image Entertainment: *The Lost Films of Laurel & Hardy: The
   Complete Collection,* vol. 3)

Background: Although they were reaching new peaks of incredible popularity, Laurel and Hardy had followed up *Two Tars* (1928) with a pair of weaker efforts, *Habeas Corpus* (1928) and *We Faw Down* (1928). Talking films were at last starting to climb up to dominance in the industry, and if The Boys were going to make the transition to sound within the first six months of 1929, they needed to solidify their grip on the world's funny bone with an outgoing string of top-notch silents. They responded with a half-dozen superb efforts, four of which rank among their best ever. The first of these was *Liberty.*

Synopsis: Dangerous criminal masterminds—or, more likely, petty vagrants—Laurel and Hardy have somehow conspired to escape from prison. They switch into civvies in the getaway car driven by two henchmen before hopping out on to a street and instantly pretending to be auto enthusiasts casually examining a parked car. So far so good, except they have inadvertently donned each other's pants. Given the disparity of their sizes, this is a major nuisance. They seek privacy in which to drop and swap their trousers; this privacy, regrettably, is repeatedly interrupted by individuals who, even more regrettably, make ill-informed assumptions as to why two grown men might be dropping their pants in furtive locations.

At last they find an open-ended box wherein they can exchange the bottom half of their suits, albeit with an annoyed crab hiding in one pair. Emerging in relief from the box, they discover to their horror that it was an elevator that has now deposited

119

"What does it *look* like we're doing?!" Laurel and Hardy caught in an easily misunderstood situation in *Liberty* (1929). *Courtesy of Bruce Calvert*

them near the top of a skyscraper, as yet unfinished beyond the skeleton of girders. Bedeviled by red-hot rivets, loose beams, vanishing ladders, ill-timed elevators, plunging sandbags, and other inconveniences as well as the pincer-exercising crab, The Boys scramble desperately around the unreliable bones of the building until finally managing to crawl into the elevator and back down to safe ground.

Comment: Despite its being quite obviously inspired by Harold Lloyd's *Never Weaken* (1921), *Liberty* is brilliantly tapered to the Laurel and Hardy gestalt. Lloyd's self-absorbed persona doesn't have any real reason to end up teetering on an unfinished building; it takes a thoroughly unrealistic contrivance to get him into that spot, and once there, he has little to play against other than a hot rivet, a crane-borne girder, and his own fear. Laurel and Hardy's prison escape and the necessity of donning civilian clothes in the cramped confines of a car are brilliant comic motivations; from thence, moreover, they are constantly in conflict with other people as well as with the building materials, even as they play off each other's distinctive personalities.

Lloyd himself, his supporters, and his detractors alike have made it accepted opinion that he was a comic actor rather than a comedian. Comparing him with Stan Laurel when they are placed in the same set of circumstances resoundingly supports this claim. Laurel's reactions to his predicament, especially his incredibly funny terror, are those of a born comedian, and he is never more than a couple of seconds away from yet another shriekingly hilarious physical incident. Lloyd's reactions are those of a desperate young man trying to think his way out of an unthinkable dilemma; since Laurel is incapable of thinking, this automatically makes Laurel funnier in the situation.

Hardy is no less proficient in ad-libbing uproarious bits. They range from simple physical acts, such as his reaching behind his back to try to hoist his huge bottom up on a beam, to H. M. Walker–assisted verbal gems such as the outraged reproach to Laurel, "What did you do *that* for?!" Lloyd has no one to whom he can issue similar bon mots.

In praising to the skies the sequence set in the incomplete skyscraper, one must not neglect the cleverness and wittiness of what went before (and what led directly to The Boys going aloft): their earnest attempts to swap trousers. This is deliciously risqué material, one of the very few times Laurel and Hardy permitted others to suspect their onscreen relationship was something more than platonic. Especially delightful is their shamefaced, little-boys-caught-in-the-act, trouser-buttoning exit from a vehicle into which luscious Jean Harlow is being helped by her gentleman friend—and her subsequent cautious peering into the cab to make sure there are no other odd fellows inside before she enters it again.

Bonus: Laurel and Hardy went out of the silent era with a bang, or even six bangs. Perhaps only Buster Keaton finished his silents career with a comparable string of rib-ticklers, and Keaton was making only features by that time.

All made in 1929, *Liberty* was followed by the underrated *Wrong Again* in which The Boys confuse a horse named "Blue Boy" for a famous painting of the same name, leading them to endeavor to place the horse atop a piano in a rich man's home; *That's My Wife*, arguably the funniest of all the films (sound as well as silent) that were built around the necessity of Laurel donning his dame persona; *Big Business*, cited by most aficionados as their best-ever silent short; *Unaccustomed as We Are*, produced in both silent and sound versions (they were the same film; the soundtrack was removed and intertitles were inserted for the silent version); and finally *Double Whoopee*, in which a blisteringly hot 17-year-old Jean Harlow served notice of her future as the movies' first indisputable sex bomb.

That's not all, though. *Bacon Grabbers* and *Angora Love*, both also made and released in 1929, were silents held back until after a few sound films had tested the talkie waters for Stan and Ollie and confirmed those waters were warm and pleasant. Both are excellent comedies, ranking with the other silents made in the same year. The sound films—*Berth Marks*, *Men O' War*, and *A Perfect Day*, again all made in 1929 (what a year that was!)—were released as talkies but were also made available with intertitles in pseudo-silent versions. Possibly because of this intentional hybrid approach, they are a bit less successful than the pure silent movies.

LIZZIES OF THE FIELD

(1924, Sennett)

Director: Del Lord
Writer: Mack Sennett
Titles: John Waldron
Camera: George Spear and Bob Ladd
Editor: William Hornbeck.
Cast: Billy Bevan, Andy Clyde, Sid Smith, Spencer Bell, Tiny Ward, Barbara Pierce, Jack Lloyd, Jack Richardson, Barney Hellum
Running Time (Length): 14 minutes (two reels) are available
Availability: DVD (Alpha Video: *Mack Sennett Sensations*)

Background: By 1924, Sennett was slipping behind Roach as the premier short-comedy producer. There were a lot of reasons for this state of affairs, some of them having to do with booking and distribution shenanigans, others having to do with Sennett's perpetual search for funds, and still others having to do with the public's increasing sophistication and urbanization, which had frankly outgrown the Sennett lowbrow formula. But another reason was that Sennett had run out of really good comedians.

He used to say with some bitterness that the mantra of comedians was "Start with Sennett, get rich elsewhere." It wasn't always money that drove them away, although that was usually a factor because Sennett couldn't or wouldn't pay competitive salaries; it was also a case of the comedians, like the audience, outgrowing the Sennett formula. Plus, if you ever look at the filmographies of the comedians of the silent era, you are struck by the peripatetic nature of their careers. Almost every one of them, including Chaplin and Keaton, hopped from studio to studio. It was the nature of filmmaking, then and now; only the three fleeting decades during which "the studio system" chained actors to seven-year contracts (roughly, the 1930s, '40s, and '50s) nailed them to the same studio for long periods of time, and even then, they could be loaned out to other studios.

When all the good ones had gone away, Sennett was left with Billy Bevan, Andy Clyde, and Ben Turpin as his star comics, with even lesser talents like Sid Smith, Jack Cooper, and Johnny Burke to come. There was an air of desperation to his product throughout this decade. It presented a good opportunity for an innovative, kinetic young director named Del Lord.

Synopsis: Rival garages compete for customers with dirty tricks such as throwing boat anchors at passing cars and reeling them in. There's a pretty girl and $25,000 at stake in a road race, enough for the winning garage to stay afloat and for its owner to get married. Whatever. It's just an excuse to move quickly to ten minutes of road racing, some of it exciting, some of it appallingly destructive, and some of it very funny indeed. The film ends with a very good dialogue card.

Comment: The pre-race stuff, like the pre-race stuff in the real world of car racing, is perfunctory and quite dull. Fortunately, in this movie (unlike in the real world), it is also brief. There are somewhere between six and eight cars in the race at any one time, and their speed is well presented. There's a bit too much spinning-around-kicking-up-dust; that, however, was the actual nature of car racing in those days, with bald tires trying to find a grip in parched dirt roadbeds. Some of the antics are, shall we say, traditional—a wayward vehicle blasts through a barn, a "detour" sign is reversed, etc. We can forgive these old warhorses because the filming itself is so exciting.

What's really jaw-dropping is a climactic scene in which car after car roars along a ski jump and smashes down in a splintered heap. Each subsequent car *lands directly on the ones before it,* and there are real live drivers still sitting inside every open-top car, getting crushed as the next vehicle lands like a gigantic hammer on them. One of the last cars, upon landing on two others, plows ahead a bit on momentum and blasts into one of the drivers who had gotten out of his own broken car, visibly firing the poor man ahead for at least twenty feet. There is no fakery or camera trick, let alone computer-generated imagery: these are real crashes pulverizing real drivers. Director Del Lord, who specialized in these predecessors of the *Fast and Furious* franchise while at Sennett, applied what he had learned to Three Stooges movies later in his career. After the experience of the drivers in *Lizzies of the Field*, he must have secretly considered the Stooges a trio of wimps for pulling their punches and not *really* killing one another.

Bonus: In 1913, Sennett made a huge splash with *Barney Oldfield's Race for a Life*, an extremely exciting comedy that featured the day's most famous professional race-car driver, Barney Oldfield. Being a big fan of the sport himself, Sennett pondered how to convey the speed and thrills of a race despite the stodgy, bulky nature of the camera. He concluded that the only two ways to do it were to squeeze a camera into the car itself, and to jam another camera into a car that could speed fast enough to keep parallel to the racers. He put his technical crew to work at the challenge. The result led directly to the in-the-car cameras that are still being used today to give audiences a driver's-eye viewpoint.

LONG HOSE

(1928, Christie)

Director: William Watson
Writer: Sig Herzig
Titles: Al Martin
Camera: Jack Bremer, Edgar Lyons
Cast: Jack Duffy, Gale Henry, Gail Lloyd, Jimmy Harrison, Eddie Baker
Running Time (Length): One reel

Background: From 1921 to the end of the silents in 1929, Jack Duffy made more films almost every year than he had the year before. It was a nice testament to his growth in popularity and the high demand for him as a supporting actor. He always worked best as part of an ensemble; one of his key strengths as a comedian was the ability to play off other comedians rather than carry a film on his own. What makes this particularly admirable is that Duffy had such a powerful screen presence; like Ford Sterling, he effortlessly dominated the frame with his crackling personality, and unlike the tall and well-built Sterling, he had only a small, short body, so it was his kinetic energy that grabbed attention: he physically imposed himself on the viewer even as he worked in smooth tandem with his colleagues.

Synopsis: Widower Duffy is the fire chief in a town so small it has only one fire hall, so it can only handle one fire at a time (as the intertitles tell us). His daughter is being wooed by the son of the widow who runs the grocery store (Gale Henry), and Duffy is determined to put a stop to it. That's what dads do in silent comedy films. Henry's rival sets her store on fire, and Duffy must rescue the widow. The end result, of course, is a double romance: daughter and son, widower and widow.

Comment: Even the plot's perfunctoriness is perfunctory: it's just an excuse to get Duffy booming away in fire-chief mode. He does the role proud. I love the way he can dive comically into narrow entrances: in *Chicken Feathers* he dove into the rumble seat of a car, in *Long Hose* he dives down the pole in the firehouse, and in both cases he makes it look like an unplanned fall that turns him completely

Compare Jack Duffy in costume here with the photo of him out of costume (*Long Hose*, 1928). *Author's collection*

upside down. He drives the fire truck as if *it* were on fire. He bowls people over, literally, from his sheer speed and aggressiveness. He's an absolute scream.

When he pulls Gale Henry out of a second-story window while standing at the top of a none-too-secure extended ladder, there's the quickest of cuts to replace them both with dummies—so quick, you don't have time to register it before the two of them horrifyingly pitch head over heels *twice* down the ladder; you really gasp with shock at what looks like a terrible unplanned tumble.

That quick switch plays upon your expectations, which have been deliberately built up by the film's unvarying use of *real* props-of-disaster. The fire that engulfs the store is a *real* fire, no question about it, and at one point a flaming beam falls within inches of Duffy, who didn't know it was coming *quite* that tightly in on him. When he takes a swig of water and discovers it's gasoline, that's *real* gasoline in his mouth, because he promptly spits it out and it sets off a fresh burst of fire. A trail of trickled gas on the ground is traced back by the fire to the garage where the gas was stored: the garage *really* blows up. Thus indoctrinated, you "know" the dummies who fall down the ladder are "really" Duffy and Henry in the flesh. It's a masterful job of manipulation by the filmmakers.

Bonus: One of the funniest running gags in the picture is the town's traffic cop. In the middle of the intersection—apparently the little place's only intersection, so small is the population—he has set up a beach lounger and a sun shade, so he can direct traffic at leisure.

In my previous book, *The 100 Greatest Silent Film Comedians*, I had a brain cramp and credited Louise Fazenda as the actress playing the widow. It is Gale Henry who plays the role.

LOVE, SPEED AND THRILLS

(1915, Keystone)

Director: Walter Wright
Cast: Mack Swain, Chester Conklin, Minta Durfee, Josef Swickard, Edwin Frazee, Billy Gilbert, Grover Ligon
Running Time (Length): One reel
Availability: DVD (Quality Information Publishers, Inc.)

Background: Mack Swain and Chester Conklin were the bromance version of Mabel Normand and Roscoe Arbuckle, which is to say Mack Sennett put them together in an early film and immediately recognized their onscreen chemistry (not to mention their physical contrast), so he wasted no time in creating an ongoing series of quick, short comedies in which they meet up in a variety of situations that had nothing to do with plot and everything to do with set-ups in which the two veteran comics could play off against one another.

Swain is the prototype of the physically enormous but psychologically timorous, adorable teddy-bear comedian. He differs from, say, John Goodman or John Candy in that he palpably has no street smarts (which is not the same thing as having no brains), nor does he swagger with Oliver Hardy's self-deluding confidence. He's easily flustered; he's needy and insecure; he has a pretty good grasp of the chaos going on around him but can't think fast enough to cope with it. This, at any rate, is the "Ambrose" character he created under Sennett's guidance in 1914. Occasionally, "Ambrose" can be successful (he's even a bank president—and cuckolding Conklin, to boot—in *The Home Breakers* [1915]); in those cases, however, his veneer of assurance and achievement is easily smashed and the character flounders desperately in multiple attempts to restore his perceived status. Although the "Ambrose" series of films ended more or less in 1917, Swain struggled to break free of its typecasting until Charlie Chaplin rescued him with key roles in some of the latter's greatest films, particularly *The Gold Rush* (1925). Chaplin, a friend from those earliest Sennett days, knew Swain was capable of great versatility in both comedy and drama; his adroit use of the big fellow helped to extend Swain's career into the talkies and almost to his death in 1935.

Where Swain was skilled and capable of great nuance, Conklin was pretty much one-dimensional (despite his second series of comedy shorts as an ordinary bumbler named "Droppington") until, ironically, he lost his starring status in the late 1920s and found a new niche as a comically skeptical supporting player. As with Swain, this artistic rebirth kept him working almost to his death, which in

Conklin's case was in 1970 (his last film credit was in 1965). Conklin's exaggerated villain character in Sennett shorts was called "Walrus" in tribute to his extravagant moustache; he kept the fake soup-strainer in virtually all of his subsequent films, for it was an instantly recognizable trademark and his ticket to continual work.

There was an obvious Mutt-and-Jeff quality to the pairing of the huge Swain and the short, slightly built Conklin; aside from that, what gave their pairing its chemistry was whatever emotional response Swain threw up against Conklin's aggressive chicanery. In *Love, Speed and Thrills*, he shows both sides of "Ambrose." He's the jittery jelly-man henpecked by wife Minta Durfee, but when she gets abducted by the irredeemable "Walrus" he is fearless and resourceful in his energetic attempts to rescue her. In the first case, "Walrus" can taunt him and attempt to cuckold him; in the second case, "Walrus" has to flee him in terror and desperation. Conklin, being a comedian of lesser subtlety, doesn't much vary in character or in approach between the two sets of circumstances; Swain, on the other hand, paints his character in full dimension. Both comics are pretty funny, so psychological depth doesn't necessarily equate to additional laughs. It does equate to cheers of hilarious sympathy, though, and that's what you want with your comic hero, not with your comic villain.

Synopsis: "Ambrose," mighty man of the pioneer wilderness and incidentally sheriff of a town as yet too small (and too cheap) to be made visible on the movie screen, floridly departs his house to massacre innocent animals so wife Minta can serve him a dinner sufficiently copious to satiate the hunger pangs of his massive, manly physique. Villain-by-rote "Walrus," lurking in those same woods for reasons unexplained but clearly nefarious, gets brained by a heavy branch blasted off a tree by "Ambrose" in a futile attempt to slaughter a cat. Displaying exceptional compassion, and possibly concern about word of his hunting non-prowess spreading around town, "Ambrose" slings the KO'd "Walrus" over his shoulder and brings him home for repairs and the bribe of nourishing food. This does not sit well with Minta, who tears strips off "Ambrose" until the latter flees their cabin for peace.

"Walrus," who was never quite as comatose as he had led the sheriff to believe, seizes the opportunity to attempt dastardly deeds upon Minta's chaste lips. "Ambrose" bursts through the door in the best D. W. Griffith style to save the reputation of his wife. Alas, "Walrus" manages to escape with Minta in his clutches. There follows the standard Sennett chase sequence, utilizing horses, motorcycles, tirelessly running Keystone Cops (it really is hilarious to see cops sprinting at top speed for miles because the police department apparently has only one car in its fleet), collapsing bridgeworks, rope rescues, and more cats running wild and upending the mighty "Ambrose."

Comment: The Mack Sennett films of this period (which roughly parallels the duration of the Great War, 1914–1918) are pretty much interchangeable. The plots, written on the back of a cigarette package, can be summarized thusly: "Boy gets girl, boy loses girl, cut to the chase." At both Biograph and Keystone Studios, Sennett insisted that the title card must identify each film as a "FARCE COMEDY." The redundancy of the description serves a purpose, albeit one Sennett may not have been deep enough to articulate: it is a license for absurdity and exaggeration and fancy, a cavalier treatment of logic and credibility, all in the pursuit of laughter. Like Bugs Bunny and Road Runner cartoons, everybody gets killed and nobody ever dies, even after spectacular death spirals and self-stranglings (see Ford Sterling in *Barney Oldfield's Race for a Life*, *Dirty Work in a Laundry/A Desperate Scoundrel*, and, well, practically all other Ford Sterling films made for Keystone).

Love, Speed and Thrills was selected for inclusion in this book because it features the standard Sennett chases, offers a sample of the immensely popular "Ambrose and Walrus" series, and almost incidentally showcases Minta Durfee's under-rated comic skills. It has energy and action and laughs to spare.

Bonus: Minta Durfee has historically been hard-done-by. A successful musical-comedy stage performer before she was even 20 years old, she married Roscoe Arbuckle when he was still a nondescript stock player; he may have weighed 2.25 times more than she was, but she was 2.25 times more successful than him at that point. Five years later, she joined him at Keystone and was installed as one of the many extremely talented women whom Mack Sennett couldn't bear to feature as star comics; instead, they all had to subsume their gifts in thankless supporting roles as shrewish wives or helpless girlfriends to the primary male comedians. Naturally, that meant she never realized her potential as a screen actress, whereas Arbuckle's career took off for the stratosphere until scandal blew it to smithereens.

In the first half of *Love, Speed and Thrills*, Durfee makes the most of her atypi-cal amount of screen time. She shows just how effective a supporting player can be when given the opportunity to work up a scene in collaboration with a lead comic, instead of merely providing a foil against which the latter may shine. The best example of this occurs when Swain brings home the semi-stunned Conklin and tries to ease him into a chair. While she distracts us by yapping incessantly at the hangdog Swain for constantly dragging home mooching bums like Conklin, Durfee whips out a chair upon which the apparently expiring con man might collapse. Just as quickly, though, her ongoing tirade against Swain causes Durfee to almost unconsciously fling the chair aside so that she can get further into her husband's face. Conklin, of course, plonks down hard on the floor instead of softly into the expected chair. Durfee doesn't even notice him, she's so busy giv-ing Swain several pieces of her mind. It's a beautiful, perfectly executed bit of slapstick at its purest.

M

MADAME BEHAVE!

(1925, Christie)

Director: Scott Sidney
Writers: Jean Arlette and F. McGrew Willis
Camera: Gus Peterson and Alex Phillips
Cast: Julian Eltinge, Ann Pennington, Jack Duffy, Lionel Belmore, Tom Wilson, Stanhope Wheatcroft, David James, Evelyne Francisco, Tiny Sandford
Running Time (Length): Existing print runs 54 minutes (six reels)
Availability: DVD (The Film Detective)

Background: "Dame" disguise was one of the oldest devices in live theatre, going back at least to the beginnings of traveling troupes in medieval times, if not all the way to Greek and Roman plays. Logically enough, it was also one of the oldest devices in silent movies. Most silent comedians came out of vaudeville, music hall, and traveling troupes, where doing a drag act was simply another gag in their bag of laughs. There was nothing, it must be repeated, *nothing* titillating about it; putting on a dress was no different or kinkier than putting on a soldier's uniform, a judge's robes, or a chef's hat and apron in the pursuit of laughter. It was a *prop.*

Stan Laurel became noted for the frequency and adeptness of his dame disguises. It sometimes seems the only male screen performer who used a skirt more than Stan was Julian Eltinge (born William Dalton), and then only because female impersonation was Eltinge's whole act. He began it at age ten and basically never stopped until the moralists forced him out of business in the Dirty Thirties. That was quite ironic, because Eltinge was exceedingly scrupulous never to be overtly gay, camp, effeminate, or deviant in his performances. He played either a woman from the get-go who only later revealed himself to be a man (in the manner of Julie Andrews in *Victor/Victoria* [1982]), or made it very clear he was a straight man who was temporarily forced by circumstances to masquerade as a woman.

Madame Behave! is apparently the only extant silent film he made; ten others are lost, but at least one of the two publicity films he made exists (*How Molly Made Good,* an elaborate promotional film for the 1915 Broadway season, in which he plays himself). He was sensationally popular in live theatre, one of the biggest and

Julian Eltinge, both photos (*Madame Behave!*, 1925). *Author's collection*

best-paid stars, so much so that he had the then-rare honor of having a theatre named after him. This film is, essentially, all we have left of an actor who played a quietly effective role in bending the genders in the early years of the cinema.

Synopsis: As in most bedroom farces (although bedrooms rarely figure in the action), the plot of *Madame Behave!* is comically overcomplicated. Eltinge and his (presumably platonic) roommate, David James, are getting kicked out of their apartment by crusty old landlord Jack Duffy. To add insult to injury, Duffy is suing James's uncle for a car accident witnessed by a woman who has disappeared. The quarrel between the two old coots devolves into a competition to find the woman and marry her for the purpose of winning the court case—she can't testify against the uncle if he marries her, but she can be forced to testify against him if the landlord marries her.

Meanwhile, Eltinge uses the rent money in pursuit of an engagement ring in order to gain the advantage in his competition (with the impossibly named Stanhope Wheatcroft) for the hand of Ann Pennington. David James has a girlfriend in there somewhere, too. The two romantic (or practical) pursuits collide when Eltinge gets into drag, is assumed to be the missing female witness, and gets her/himself engaged to both elderly men.

Comment: When these kinds of dizzy romantic comedies click, they are loads of fun. The fact that Eltinge was a professional female impersonator and not just a comedian doing a dame turn gives *Madame Behave!* a bit of elegance and sophistication that raises it out of the ordinary.

Stanhope Wheatcroft's character has a name every bit as improbable as his real one: "Percy Fairweather." You can easily guess what kind of character would bear that sissy name: a British twit, who at one point is derided with the insinuating term of "cake eater." Jack Duffy abuses the free rein he is given to enact his feisty-old-hellraiser persona; he's not so much an old goat as he is an old guy hopped up on goat glands. The highly attractive Ann Pennington, otherwise given very little to do, puts her Charleston dancing skills on display, albeit far too briefly.

Tom Wilson plays a valet who, for some reason, wears an unbuttoned barber's jacket. Wilson was one of the many supporting comics from the silent era who posted an incredibly durable career: 50 years in films, and nearly 300 productions. In the days of the silents he carved a niche as a white actor specializing in what might best be described as off-brown characters: he didn't black up, but he did brown up, using such a soft color that he barely even looked tanned. The inter-titles for his dialogue were custom written for the blackest of black characters, or rather, caricatures. The result is not only uncomfortably racist but also puzzling, at least if you're not aware of Wilson's specialty; it makes no sense that this huge white man is allegedly talking with the worst sort of Uncle Tom accent: "De only way out am in Mrs. Stimson's clothes," "A skirt in de house is better dan two pants in de hoose-gow," and so on. To top it off, Wilson does an extended shuffle dance in de wuss cullu'd folks' stylin'.

Other than Wilson's misguided "black-speak," and also other than the forced humor of the insulting names Duffy and Belmore inflict upon each other (always with initial capitalization, for some reason) such as "you Rusty Rhino!," the in-tertitles are really funny and clever. A quarrelling couple was "married by the Secretary of War," and the jealous husband introduces his wife to a playboy friend with the instructions "Meet the wife—but not too often."

Eltinge in drag opens the door for the title writer to get off the expected double entendres. A deeply amorous Belmore sweet-talks him/her: "I can see you're not a bit like other women." Eltinge responds to a marital proposal with "When I marry, I must wear the pants"—slightly obvious but nonetheless irresistibly giggly.

For those looking for such things, the in-drag Eltinge and the unsuspecting Pennington get off a really eye-popping hot pseudo-lesbian kissing scene. For those just looking for good laughs, Duffy has a splendid throwaway sequence in which he tries to take a taxi ride.

Bonus: Reviews of Eltinge's act sometimes criticized (or complimented?) him for "not really *impersonating* a woman." The sense was that he played his dames as a guy wearing a dress, not as a guy attempting to *be* a convincing woman. He sure as hell wasn't setting the mold for Michel Serrault's performance in *La Cage aux Folles* (1978). I don't see the merit in this criticism. He doesn't stuff his bra, but even without man-boobs (he doesn't have them, either), he's less flat-chested than his female costars; let's not forget the 1920s were the era when fashionable young women actually *wanted* to look completely undeveloped in the bust. And in *Madame Behave!* he has a sequence in which he prances very girlishly while leading Duffy and Belmore on a lovers' chase. He plays exaggeratedly coy, repeatedly, during an extended set in which he and Wilson are trying to fool a nosy cop in their apartment. If he's too husky to flutter and simper, he can still be flirtatious in a definitely female manner.

One can only extrapolate from the little known of his private life, but it does seem almost certain that Eltinge was gay. At the least, beginning with his pre-cocious prepuberty debut as a dame, he was surely a real-life transvestite. The viewer cannot help comparing him in male attire to him in female attire while watching *Madame Behave!* and concluding that he seems more comfortable in the latter costume than in the former. As a man, he is puffy-faced, displays the discretion and politesse of a very reserved homosexual of the era, and wears the uniform of a dapper-but-not-attention-drawing upper-class "confirmed bachelor" of the 1920s: straw boater with custom-tailored, double-breasted blue blazer, white duck pants, and white shoes. It is a deliberately assembled look, a sharp contrast to the casual, subdued dark suits thrown on indifferently by all of the "real" men who never need to think about their own masculinity and how to project it. When he puts on a dress, wig, and lipstick, the puffy face becomes a woman's soft, round cheeks, and the clothes look like what would be worn by a slightly matronly lady whose gender has never been in question. If this is not the real Julian Eltinge, then it is all the more reason to watch this film and admire one of the best female impersonators of all time.

THE MAD WHIRL

(1925, Universal)

Director: William Seiter
Writers: Richard Washburn Child, Fanny Hatton, Frederic Hatton, Edward T. Lowe,
    and Lewis Milestone
Titles: Harvey Thew
Camera: Merritt Gerstad
Editor: Thomas Pratt
Cast: May McAvoy, Jack Mulhall, Myrtle Stedman, Barbara Bedford, Alec Francis,
    Ward Crane, George Fawcett, Marie Astaire
Running Time (Length): 65 minutes (seven reels)
Availability: DVD (Alpha Video)

Background: It has become the accepted wisdom that the twentieth century saw the invention of Youth, particularly Rebellious Youth. As a cultural phenomenon, Rebellious Youth couldn't have existed until the development of mass media. As a social phenomenon, they couldn't have existed until the development of mass production and modern technology, because prior to that time, young people were too busy working to earn a living for themselves and their parents, siblings, and grandparents. They didn't have spare time to fool around, nor did they have the means to fool around with; you can't really go street cruisin' with a horse and cart.

Idle hours, growing prosperity, extended schooling, and the convergence of large groups of peers into the target-rich urban environment fostered youth culture. And no sooner were Billy and Susie roaring around to speakeasies in their Model T's than the elders were up in arms about "those darn kids," preachers were preaching against the sinfulness of the young people, police were grimly proclaiming that those punks were out of control, parents were wailing that they didn't know what to do about their "children," and . . . Hollywood jumped upon the gold mine.

The Jazz Era was the first to mythologize/demonize Rebellious Youth in America as a group (there had always been *a* lone rebellious youth in books and plays, of course, but never the entire generation), and that meant Hollywood spent the 1920s firing out movie after movie about them. *The Flapper* (1920), *Flaming Youth* (1923), *Jazz Mad* (1928), *Jazz Land* (1928), of course *The Great Gatsby* (1926), *Our Dancing Daughters* (1928), *Our Modern Maidens* (1929), *Dancing Mothers* (1926), *Fascinating Youth* (1926), *The Perfect Flapper* (1924), . . . and *The Mad Whirl* (1925).

Many of these films were as totally clueless as the TV shows of the 1960s that thought they were doing a great job of accurately portraying the Rebellious Youth of *that* era by tearing off the head of a mop and plopping it on the head of a thirty-year-old male and having him exclaim, "That's groovy, man!" Virtually all of them, needless to say, showed that the wild ways of youth were empty, unsatisfying, and destructive, but that all Rebellious Youth would quickly realize it was much better to give up that life and settle down to suburban banality. *The Mad Whirl*, let us say, did not buck that trend.

Synopsis: "Jazz . . . a new form of measles . . . !" screams the opening intertitle, implying we are in need of inoculation before watching any further. So break out the, er, ginger ale. That's right: ginger ale. And apparently they don't mean it as a euphemism for, you know, . . . *ale* ale. We never see anyone actually drinking the stuff, or anything else but coffee. We see empty bottles and glasses, mind you, but never anyone drinking. As for food, they gorge on sandwiches, and slices of roast beef, and banana splits (which they hate; too sinful, apparently). The scenes of horrifying mass dissipation and orgy consist of youngish people lying around sleeping, fully clothed, their arms wrapped around piano legs and vases and bearskins but never around each other. Sex is indicated by couples sedately sitting in porch swings . . . just *sitting there*. Even the decadent beach party consists of girls in Victorian beach attire and boys in two-piece gym suits, playing ring-around-the-rosie. I kid you not!

Blame the parents for this disgraceful conduct. Yep, it's young Jack Mulhall's 60-year-old father and 40-year-old mother who are out there partying with their son and his dissolute, ne'er-do-well gang until all hours of the night, encouraging the fun because "parents must be *companions* to their children," else just think how wild things might get if the old folks weren't there to "exercise restraint." What kind of restraint, you ask? Dad gives Jack a pile of money and orders him to go out and have a good time . . . at *eleven o'clock in the morning*.

But Jack meets May, an old school friend, and instantly knows she is the one for him, despite her ultra-square ways. Just to make sure we get the equation clearly, Jack is out there sinfully breaking his promise not to drink anymore while May is in church with a heavenly light streaming in on her. (Again, I tell you, I'm not kidding!)

May whips Jack across the face, he finds God in this biblical scourging, and they promptly elope, leaving it to her dad to tell off Jack's parents for their misguided assumption that they should behave as flaming youth's "Friends for excitement—cards—jazz"—wait a minute: *cards?!*

Comment: Every list of best or essential comedy films should include at least one film that was never intended to be funny but ended up being so absurd that it provokes a laugh every minute. *The Mad Whirl* is mine. This film works as serious hilariousness by presenting everything in extremes. The kids don't just party, they do nothing *but* party, 24 hours a day, 7 days a week—they're apparently done with school, and the only reference to work is as a big joke. The heroine isn't just an old-fashioned virgin, she still drives a horse and cart and slaps any man who makes a pass at her. The rakish son doesn't just give up partying and settle down to trite domestication with the heroine, he runs off with her to that epitome of bourgeois respectability and romantic stodginess, Niagara Falls. His parents don't just immediately stop partying all the time with the kids as the result of getting a good talking-to about acting their age, they instantly transform themselves into 80-year-old, stoop-shouldered, tired frumps unable to get out of their easy chairs unaided. The girl's father doesn't just try to protect her from the decadent rich, he brings down biblical curses on their heads. All of this extremist nonsense makes the picture entertaining as hell, and it explains why five writers got credits: no one person could possibly dream up all of this craziness. Well, maybe Tod Browning.

Bonus: Not one of the actors in this film is known to any but the most rabid devotees of old movies these days. In the silent era, though, the entire cast formed an impressive gathering of names: second- or third-tier performers, yes, but they were by no means negligible players. They were respected and moderately popular minor stars, established or developing supporting players, and sturdy backgrounders who toiled for decades before and to come.

May McAvoy, a quite pretty and very petite brunette, is almost completely unremembered today other than as Al Jolson's gal in *The Jazz Singer* (1927), the film that launched the talkies. That's like being remembered as the girl partnering John Travolta in *Saturday Night Fever* (1977)—quick, what's her name? McAvoy was, in fact, a low-riding genuine star with impressive acting skills; she's very good in the lead of *Lady Windermere's Fan* (1925) and as "Esther" in *Ben-Hur* (1926). Mostly, though, she carried forgettable and forgotten product like *Mrs. Wiggs of the Cabbage Patch* (1919), *The Truth about Husbands* (1920), *A Homespun Vamp* (1922), *The Enchanted Cottage* (1924), and films whose titles mutely testify to her prudery both onscreen and off, such as *Morals* (1921), *Her Reputation* (1923), *Tarnish* (1924), *Slightly Used* (1927), and *A Reno Divorce* (1927).

Jack Mulhall had an incredibly prolific career: nearly 450 films over nearly 50 years, from the silents of 1910 to the TV shows of 1959, and he had the lead in many films of the '20s. Barbara Bedford played key roles in a lot of glossy "women's pictures" of the era, balancing them unconventionally with a lot of Westerns, including William Hart's outstanding *Tumbleweeds* (1925). Alec Frances supported John Barrymore in *Beau Brummel* (1924), Sydney Chaplin in *Charley's Aunt* (1925), and Harry Langdon in *Tramp Tramp Tramp* (1926). Myrtle Stedman was another who supported William Hart (*The Whistle*, 1921) and made a lot of Westerns, women's pictures, and jazz babies warnings.

One of the really humungous stage attractions for many years, George Fawcett got into films as a favorite of D. W. Griffith and also appeared in *Manslaughter* (1922), *Java Head* (1923), *Tess of the d'Urbervilles* (1924), *The Sporting Venus* (1925), *The Merry Widow* (1925), Valentino's *Son of the Sheik* (1926), Garbo's *Flesh and the Devil* (1927) and *Love* (1927), *Captain Salvation* (1927), and Erich von Stroheim's *The Wedding March* (1928)—a very impressive resume.

THE MARK OF ZORRO

(1920, United Artists/Douglas Fairbanks Pictures Corp)

Director: Fred Niblo
Writers: Eugene Mullin, Douglas Fairbanks (as Elton Thomas), Johnston McCulley
Camera: William McGann, Harris Thorpe
Cast: Douglas Fairbanks, Marguerite de la Motte, Robert McKim, Noah Beery, Charles Hill Mailes, Claire McDowell, Sydney de Grey, George Periolat, Walt Whitman, Snitz Edwards, Tote Du Crow, Noah Beery Jr., Albert MacQuarrie, Charles Stevens, John Winn, Charles Belcher, Gilbert Clayton, and allegedly Milton Berle
Running Time (Length): Seven reels (There are at least three different versions available, each with a different running time; AFI catalogue says eight reels.)
Availability: DVD (Cobra Entertainment, LLC)

Background: "*The Mark of Zorro* is a landmark, not only in the career of Douglas Fairbanks, but also in the development of the action adventure film," writes Jeffrey Vance in his impressive and beautifully produced book, *Douglas Fairbanks* (2008). As he goes on to explain, Fairbanks had made 29 films in just five years, nearly all of them successful with critics and crowds alike, and he was slipping into the complacency that traps performers into the same routine for decades. *The Mark of Zorro* was far from being his first full-length feature, and wasn't even his first historical feature; it was, however, markedly different in casting him as a larger-than-life semi-mythic hero in a historical costume adventure liberally spiced with comedy. It was this film that convinced him his future lay in the past, and lay in playing it up big, big, BIG! DOUG-SIZE BIG!

Vance's second point is that *The Mark of Zorro* also gave a shot in the arm to the costume picture in general. The genre had quickly and easily become bogged down into a boring procession of sumptuous outfits, formula stories, ho-hum romances, and overall lassitude. Fairbanks effectively reinvented it, infusing it with energy, wit, speed, and athleticism. He reinvented it by inventing the swashbuckler picture.

Synopsis: Surely everyone is already familiar with the Zorro story, not least from the 1940 remake with Tyrone Power and the 1998 reboot (*The Mask of Zorro*) with Antonio Banderas. As great as both of those two later films are, the original still outshines them because no one has ever matched Douglas Fairbanks for the sheer joy he imparts to the role and to the audience. No one has ever had as much fun in the movies.

In old California, the Spanish controllers tyrannize and terrorize the Mexicans and natives and plunder the wealthy caballeros at their pleasure. Only one man seems able to do battle with the overseers: a mysterious masked and caped swordsman named "Zorro." But who is "Zorro"? No one seems to know, and no one seems to care less than the depleted dumbbell "Don Diego Vega," aristocratic wimp corrupted into flaccidity and cluelessness by a sojourn to dissolute Spain: he's Eurotrash before there was Eurotrash.

Of course, this enervated, torpid wuss is none other than "Zorro" in disguise, or rather, vice versa. As "Zorro," he sweeps the moderately lovely "Lolita" (Marguerite de la Motte) off her feet with his dash, his élan, his bravery, his macho manliness. As "Don Diego," also a would-be suitor, he sloshes around doing handkerchief tricks, always preceded by the rhetorical question, "Have you seen this one?" No wonder she snarls to her parents, "He isn't a man, he's a fish!" Indeed, he moves as slowly and with as little expenditure of muscle power as a snoozing bottom-feeder.

Slimy "Captain Ramon" wants "Lolita" far more aggressively than "Don Diego" does, and he takes action to compromise her to try to force her into accepting his suit. He's got the blustering "Governor" alongside him in support, and a host of caballeros with nothing better to do than fight on his behalf, at least until "Zorro" shames them into readily switching loyalties. Once "Zorro" does that, and marks "Captain Ramon" with his signature "Z" scar on the forehead as well as the neck, "Ramon" and the "Governor" accept with alacrity the command to clear out of California, which will then be pure and innocent forever after.

Comment: It's impossible to say anything bad about *The Mark of Zorro*, and impossible to do anything but praise Fairbanks for the brilliance of invention and production he brought to this glorious film. He's a riot as "Don Diego," and an irresistible rascal as "Zorro." All of the performers do well, with Noah Beery (Sr.) giving one of the greatest deliberately bad shows in film history: Beery stomps around with legs wide apart as if he's wearing iron underpants, he's terrific at kicking the bar stools out from under people's bums, he clears tables of food and drinks and candlesticks with a single sweep of his sword, he's a perfect bullshitter of a manly man. Marguerite de la Motte certainly doesn't top Linda Darnell or Catherine Zeta-Jones for gorgeousness or hot Latina sex appeal, but she's got their feistiness and stubbornness, a feminist rebel ahead of her time. Charles Mailes ("Don Pulido"), Sydney de Grey ("Don Alejandro"), and Claire McDowell ("Doña Catalina") are superb as the three parents; they are veteran actors who have long since learned exactly how to walk the fine line between expressiveness and restraint that is required for effective acting in silent films.

A lot was written at the time about the sensational chase of "Zorro" through the village by the soldiers and "Captain Ramon." In the past few decades, American cinema seems to have turned into one endless chase scene, and whether it's car chases or superhero chases, it's always about 90 percent dependent on CGI and special effects, and 10 percent dependent on professional stunt performers. In *The Mark of Zorro*, it's just plain human beings running after other human beings: visibly out-of-shape soldiers falling into pigpens that Douglas Fairbanks himself visibly cleared with a single leap. When he climbs walls, he's not doing it with the aid of CGI-synthesized "spider webbing," he's climbing them literally by himself with the aid only of a few strategically placed handholds and footholds. He pitches himself through a window more in the manner of Tarzan than Batman. There's enough *esprit* for him to pause long enough to gulp down a quick breakfast and offer the landlady the sage advice that "nothing should be done on an empty stomach—but eat!" He's making more hairbreadth escapes from danger than "Jason Bourne," but unlike "Bourne" he's doing it on his own without any computerized effects, super-technology gimmicks, or obviously impossible indestructibility. The chase scene is human, hilarious, exciting, and so, so easy to cheer.

Bonus: It is not generally known that Fairbanks was the one who invented the eponymous "mark of Zorro," namely, the letter "Z" carved into the flesh of the enemies of the people. This was typical of the ingenuity of silent moviemaking: find a way to visually convey information to the audience, to visually play on their expectations and emotions, to visually provoke tension or laughter or surprise or recognition or any combination. The mark of Zorro does not appear in the stories upon which the film was based until *after* the film was released, whereupon it was incorporated as a recurring motif.

THE MARRIAGE CIRCLE

(1924, Warner Bros.)

Director: Ernst Lubitsch
Writers: Paul Bern, Lothar Schmidt
Camera: Charles van Enger
Cast: Marie Prevost, Adolphe Menjou, Florence Vidor, Monte Blue, Creighton Hale, Harry Myers, Esther Ralston, Dale Fuller
Running Time (Length): 85 minutes
Availability: DVD (Image Entertainment)

Background: Ernst Lubitsch made his name in Europe with two kinds of movies: frenetic farce comedies that seemed more like a condescending parody of American slapstick than a real attempt to emulate it; and lavish, often melodramatic costume spectaculars in keeping with the European love of opulence, decadence, and ennui. Both kinds of films were so well made that it was inevitable he would be lured to Hollywood.

Mary Pickford, knowing nothing of the director's working style, chose him to direct her in *Dorothy Vernon of Haddon Hall* (1924) but, in a foreshadowing of the clash of egos to come, Lubitsch imperiously dismissed the script out of hand. They agreed instead to make *Rosita* (1923). Although it turned out a critical and box-office success, both Pickford and Lubitsch regretted the collaboration: the self-regard of each, and their need for absolute control, made it impossible for them to cooperate.

With this obligatory debut out of the way, Lubitsch was free and sufficiently established to command full autonomy from Warner Brothers to make *The Marriage Circle*. It is the film most often cited as planting the style and craft that became identified as "the Lubitsch touch."

Synopsis: Ever suave, ever dapper Adolphe Menjou needs an excuse to divorce his self-absorbed and trashy wife, Marie Prevost. Conveniently, she is summoned to her old friend Florence Vidor, who has just discovered that Prevost moved to Vienna recently, the same city where Vidor already lives in contrasting marital bliss with Monte Blue. Once Prevost gets a whiff of Vidor's happiness, the bile of jealousy rises in her gorge and she makes an enormous play for Blue.

Florence Vidor and Monte Blue toast their perfect marriage . . . while it lasts. *The Marriage Circle* (1924). *Courtesy of Derek Boothroyd*

All too suddenly, Vidor is converted from totally trusting, devoted wife into suspicious virago, except her suspicions settle on the wrong "other woman," and she sends Prevost into action to divert Blue, which of course is exactly what Prevost has already been doing. Vidor's perplexing mistrust leads Blue into asking his colleague Creighton Hale, with his perpetual smarmy grin, to "console" Vidor while Blue focuses on rejecting (or not) Prevost's attentions.

This being a Hollywood movie, Prevost as the trashy woman must be the only one punished, while Menjou gets his wish for freedom and the Vidor–Blue marriage is made stronger through adversity. This being a Lubitsch movie, Prevost bounces back by picking up Hale in the street and driving off into the mists with him as her latest conquest-to-be.

Comment: There is an inviolable rule that any sizable list of great comedy movies must include at least one Lubitsch film. If the list is just one of "great films" or "enjoyable films" or "arty films," I have no trouble including his *Passion* (1919) and *The Student Prince in Old Heidelberg* (1927). When it's a list of comedy films, however, I feel at a loss.

Lubitsch's films are never about jokes, gags, antics, or even situations. They hardly even qualify as "comedies of manners," the default term used to excuse the unfunniness of the trivial pursuits of the idle rich. They are the kind of films whose admirers insist on describing them as "witty" rather than "funny." In other words, there are no actual *laughs* in them.

What you will get from the likes of *The Marriage Circle* are smiles and a few chuckles. An essential element of the Lubitsch "touch" is that the chuckles almost always come from the facial reactions of the actors, which Lubitsch invariably films head-on in extended, motionless takes. For this approach to succeed, obviously, he needs supple and skilled actors. He certainly has those in spades for *The Marriage Circle*.

They are led by the irreproachable Adolphe Menjou, a favorite actor of mine and of practically everyone else who enjoys classic movies. He is one of the very best practitioners of the art of "acting with the eyes" (and in the case of *The Marriage Circle*, acting with the mouth; Menjou never used his adaptable smile quite as delightfully as he does here). Marie Prevost, playing the bad wife, has a challenge for someone who came up through the ranks of Mack Sennett's Bathing Beauties; she does a credible job of conveying her character's narcissism and what we would nowadays call her "gossip girl" combination of jealousy, vengeance, pettiness, and cattiness. Monte Blue is probably the weakest cast member, even if one overlooks his awful makeup (especially those femininely contoured plucked eyebrows); his face is overexpressive, and its features seem incapable of lining up attractively regardless of the emotion or thought he is trying to arrange them to display. Florence Vidor and Creighton Hale are valiant performers who are called upon to wrench themselves too abruptly and too unbelievably from their default emotions—joy and contentment, for both of them—into the opposites, dismay and unhappiness; their reactions are forced and artificial because their situations are forced and artificial.

This is one of the major criticisms I have for Lubitsch's films. In real life, no one acts the way he has them act in his films. An extremely adoring wife like Vidor is not going to react as her character does when she sees her beloved husband has accidentally lost the flowers she gave him. She instantly flies into a conviction of betrayal and infidelity; yet her love has already been demonstrated to have been so strong that such a tiny thing couldn't possibly overthrow it. She finds a pair of ladies' gloves on his office desk, and takes it as proof he is having an affair, a completely irrational response in view of the fact that she knows perfectly well he is a doctor with a large practice in treating hysterical women. Blue's character bursts into hilarious laughter at his wife's dream that his best friend is kissing her, and then again kills himself laughing when both the wife and the friend affirm that it happened in real life; no, this is not how real people react. And no one, male or female, sends their "best friend" (of the "wrong" gender) to "console" their spouse in privacy. All of the jealousy and mistrust that drives this film is simply false to the viewer.

Bonus: My preference among Lubitsch's films is for the ones he made in Germany, particularly those with the supple, beautiful Pola Negri. Each of those films has its weaknesses—including, sometimes, Negri's own performance—but they are lively, energetic, creative movies that entertain briskly. I would include the Hollywood-made *Student Prince in Old Heidelberg* among this group, because it recaptures the energy and joyousness of the German films (probably because it was set in that country). *Student Prince*, though, is saddled with the regrettable Norma Shearer and her immensely irritating "aren't I adorable?" performance. (No, you are *not*, Norma.) Grit your teeth and tolerate her, because *Student Prince* is definitely worth it.

MAX GETS STUCK UP

and other Max Linder Films
(Pathé Frères)

Director: Max Linder
Writer: Max Linder
Camera: Uncredited, possibly Lucien Nonguet
Cast: Max Linder, others usually unidentified
Running Times (Length): 6–8 minutes for one-reel films, 20+ minutes for two-reel films

---

Background: Let's have no quibbling about it: Max Linder was the first international movie comedy superstar. I have chosen those words carefully: challenge them at your peril.

André Deed and René Gréhan may have preceded Linder as comedy stars at Pathé; they were *stars*, not superstars, as is easily proven by the fact that their characters were passed on to Linder in much the same way each character in Our Gang/Little Rascals was passed on with a different name to succeeding performers. In contrast, Linder made the "Max" character his own and it could not be passed on to any following performer.

The likes of Arkady Boitler, Onésime, Little Moritz, and Fred "Pimple" Evans all came after Linder: they weren't the first of anything. All had limited international success. They were big in their own countries, and maybe in one or two other Old World nations, but that was the extent of their stardom. Again, they weren't international superstars.

Other predecessors or contemporaries weren't movie stars. Little Tich, for example, made only four very short films over a 10-year period; they were barely a footnote in his 50-year career on the stage, and were never the reason why English, French, and American theatregoers idolized him.

True superstars inspire others, including imitators. Chaplin inspired legions of imitators from the moment he trimmed his onscreen moustache into a toothbrush and pulled on Roscoe Arbuckle's oversized trousers. But who inspired Chaplin? According to himself: Max Linder.

Who imitated Linder? Raymond Griffith, for one, lifted himself out of obscurity by adopting Linder's groomed little moustache, tuxedo-and-top-hat outfit, constantly smiling self-assurance, noblesse oblige flirting, unflappable demeanor, and sophisticated comedy. Nobody was inspired by or imitated Boitler, Evans, or even Deed.

After a mediocre start in live theatre, Linder joined the movies in 1905. It took him a couple of years—and Gréhan's departure from Pathé—to find his feet; once he did so, he churned out hundreds of very short, one-joke comedies that were immensely popular all over the Western world. He took an enforced break due to illness in 1910 and then returned with a vengeance, still mostly limiting himself to one reel or less in length, but building full-bodied stories and routines and sketches into that fantastically constricted time frame.

As a true superstar, he anticipated the publicity machines of modern-day superstars by doing tours all over the Continent, and by making sure his jaw-dropping salary demands received more press than all the crowned heads of Europe could command on a given day.

No empty vessel, Linder had the talent, the magnetic personality, and the comic genius to produce films that thoroughly justified all the publicity, acclaim, and fame (and money). To give a fair sampling of his work, and because all of these pre–World War I films were so short, a selection of his most entertaining pre-American films is given below.

Max Gets Stuck Up (1906): Smooth bodily maneuvering gets Max stuck to flypaper in three different ways in a store. He joins his lady friend and her parents in a home dinner with one of the flypapers still stuck to him. This is the son of, and the father to, approximately 15 billion movie renditions of "the flypaper gag," and it remains the best one you'll ever see. That may not be saying much, but do watch it, and spare yourself from having to watch the other 15-billion-minus-one renditions by other comedians.

Max Takes a Bath (1906), directed by Lucien Nonguet. Just six minutes long, but beautifully laid out in four acts. Act One: Max buys a claw-foot bathtub and then struggles to get it home from the store. Act Two: There's only a single water tap for the entire floor of his apartment building, so Max has to place his tub underneath it in the hallway in order to fill it for his bath, which of course makes it impossible to move the tub back into the privacy of his apartment . . . so he proceeds to bathe right there in the hallway. Act Three: Outraged tenants and the landlord call the police; collectively, they drag the tub with Max in it through the streets to the hoosegow. Act Four: Now Max is the outraged party, defiantly splashing the policemen as they try to pull him from the tub. He makes his escape, using the

The debonair Max Linder. *Author's collection*

emptied tub to hide his (presumed) nakedness as he scurries along the sidewalk, a nosy dog eagerly trying to join him under his mobile shelter.

Max's Hat (1908): An excellent example of Linder's ability to take one simple gag—his hat keeps getting demolished—and build upon it within the alarming limits of just six minutes or so. The climactic variation has to be among the first dog-pee jokes in movie history.

Max and the Quinquina (1911): One of his best-known shorts, this is a small triumph of a comic drunk act. Drunk acts were as common as hayseed acts in this decade and are not nearly as amusing to a modern politically correct audience; where Linder steps above his contemporaries is in making his intoxication not the result of willful boozing but of medical prescription, so it's less reprehensible to our sensitivities and we can relax and laugh without self-reproach. Be patient through the first several minutes, just past the point when he finishes drinking the quinquina and gets jolly, because the fun starts when he goes out on the town, and it doesn't stop until the final scene, in which the gendarmes converge to enjoy themselves by inflicting a jolly bit of police brutality on him. (Two reels, about 18 minutes)

Max and the Statue (1912): Max is excited about going to a masquerade party until the costumes store tells him the only available outfit is a knight's armor. To console himself, Max wastes little time in finding a party girl and sharing too much champagne with her. Since his armor left no place for him to carry his wallet, he gets thrown out into the street for nonpayment of his bill, and he lapses into a drunken sleep in the gutter. Meanwhile, an art gallery is burglarized of its prize display . . . a knight's armor. You can guess the next step, but you can't guess the final joke of this enjoyable short.

Max and the Lady Doctor (1909) is another of his amusing one-reelers; it loses its point, though, to a modern young audience, because it is based on both an outdated sexual modesty and an outdated sexist attitude. You need to know history to appreciate it on its own terms. *Max Plays at Drama* (1913) is also quite funny and is noteworthy as possibly the germ of the idea for *The Three Must-Get-Theres* (1922). On the other hand, *Max and His Mother-in-Law* (1912) starts off with some great laughs about his new mother-in-law interfering with Max's attempts to launch his wedding night; it then descends into a rather shocking display of elder abuse, with a really angry Max physically and verbally battering the old lady; worse, this is one of Linder's rare early two-reelers, so the abuse continues for a very uncomfortable 20+ minutes.

THE MERMAID

and other Georges Méliès films
(Star)

Director: Georges Méliès
Writer: Georges Méliès
Editor: Georges Méliès
Cast: Unidentified, usually includes Georges Méliès himself.
Running Times (Length): Various running time
Availability: DVDs (Flicker Alley)

Background: If Thomas Edison, the Lumière brothers, and several other claimants hadn't already invented the motion picture, it would hardly have been an exaggeration to proclaim Georges Méliès the inventor. Certainly, once the mechanisms had been created, he was one of the first persons in the world to seize and exploit the possibilities of the medium.

Starting out with the standard actualities—using a camera he designed and built himself—Méliès quickly graduated to magic and trick films, and why shouldn't he have? He was a longtime magician and illusionist who owned the theatre of the great Robert-Houdin. He whacked out 78 of these very short cinematic gems in little more than half a year (1896). He built the first film studio in Europe; with that resource, he was able to stretch his productions to include a broad variety of material, such as movie versions of great plays and novels. In 1902, he brought these different elements together into *A Trip to the Moon*. This was the *Birth of a Nation* of its era, the one film so stunningly innovative, so lengthy, so carefully developed in its narrative structure and drive, so monumental in scope and ambition, so technically advanced, that no one who saw it could help but feel a seismic shift in the progress of world culture and art.

By the time he was pushed out of the industry through bankruptcy and an inability to change in tune with the public, Méliès had pumped out more than 500 films in just 17 years. A lot of this output is superfluous: rip-offs of Lumière and Edison films, actualites that may have wowed 'em in 1897 but hold little interest today even as living records of the era, remakes of his own films, etc. A lot of it is no longer available to the general public, although the Internet is putting more and more of it online, usually without restoration. Fewer than half of his films have been recovered, restored, and assembled on commercial discs.

Synopses: The following is only a representative sample from the most-easily accessed films, chosen mainly for their comic elements. All are very brief films, seldom more than a couple of minutes, except where noted otherwise.

The Mermaid (1904): Méliès moves rapidly through a preliminary little skit in which he scoops water from an aquarium, dumps it into his hat, then scoops fish out his hat and dumps them back into the aquarium (where, curiously, they all immediately head for the bottom of the tank and stay there, although their tails move to let us know they aren't dead or fake). One of the fish enlarges as a mermaid, and then Méliès does various magic rituals concerning her as a woman and as a mermaid. The big laugh in this film is unintentional: one large fish, being a born ham and camera hog despite its piscine nature, plants itself right in front of the mermaid's head and refuses to move. Méliès has to do a quick edit to make the mermaid's lovely face visible again.

The Living Playing Cards (1905): Yes, it's a bunch of card tricks, but no, not the kind you can do in the comfort of your own home. Méliès has a jolly time enlarging the playing cards and turning them into real queens and kings. The punchline comes at the end with the king, and it's tremendous fun. Stick with this one even if you hate card tricks.

The Cook in Trouble (1904): The head chef of a large kitchen drives off a beggar who, unknown to the chef, is a disguised wizard. The wizard puts the whammy on the kitchen, and what follows is a fast-paced routine of imps running and tumbling, the chef and his assistants chasing and being chased, boxes changing sizes and contents in an instant, and at last the ultimate revenge of anyone who has ever eaten a bad restaurant meal and wished to give the chef a taste of his own medicine.

The Scheming Gamblers' Paradise (1905): Another speedy film with a good punchline at the end, this one eschews camera trickery, instead putting the trickery into the setting itself, which is that of an illicit gambling den. Watch this and you'll know where George Roy Hill and David S. Ward got the idea for *The Sting* (1973).

The Eclipse: The Courtship of the Sun and the Moon (1907): One of his longer efforts (five to seven minutes), this is a multipart movie, really three or four films cobbled together. Essentially about goofy scientists getting overexcited as they use their huge new telescopes to watch a solar eclipse, it is padded with a section showing the sun and the moon (both with superimposed human faces on them) in action, and a section on people/gods/other celestial beings riding shooting stars and planets in amorous pursuit of one another, etc. Some of it is amusing; the main reason for including it in this book is because it is probably the first gay comedy ever made. The raffish-faced sun moves behind the boyish-faced moon and the latter sighs, squeals, bites his lip, rolls his eyes ecstatically, and then pouts when the sun drifts away and doesn't even bother phoning him the next morning.

Comment: The films in which Méliès works more or less alone are usually better than those in which he has a large cast to work with. The reason is simple: all of the acting is visual bellowing, but with too many people being overactive across the entire width of the screen, you have difficulty figuring out where you should be looking. The cast is even waving and lurching frenetically and doing distracting physical business when they are all lined up seriously injured in hospital beds (*An Impossible Voyage*, 1904)!

Bonus: Inevitably, it will be asked why I have not included *A Trip to the Moon* (1902). After all, not only is it perhaps the earliest great feature film ever made, it is also a satire of Jules Verne's fantasies, and satire is comedy. My reason will probably not convince anybody but myself: I find it "comic" only in the Shakespearean sense, which is to say it is merely comedic in its structure. In plain English, it doesn't deliver any laughs. Some of the tantrums of the scientists will raise a smile, the idea that the moon is inhabited by a bunch of hunched-over tumblers wearing devil's horns will provoke a condescending guffaw, and you will snort at the idea that the moment the scientists arrive on the moon, they will get out their blankets and go to sleep out in the open, rather than excitedly explore the place. But you won't be laughing sympathetically at any point in the film.

Besides, Méliès provided a written narrative that must be read out loud as the film unwinds, and this is a book about *silent* comedies.

MIGHTY LIKE A MOOSE

(1926, Roach)

Director: Leo McCarey
Writer: Charley Chase
Titles: H. M. Walker
Camera: Len Powers

Editor: Richard Currier
Cast: Charley Chase, Vivien Oakland, Gale Henry, Charles Clary, Charlie Hall, Anne
   Howe, Malcolm Denny, Rolfe Sedan, Harry Bowen
Running Time (Length): Two reels
Availability: DVD (Kino Lorber Films)

Background: By 1926, Charley Chase was the most popular comedian in short films—Chaplin, Keaton, Langdon, and Lloyd had all abandoned the two-reeler format—but that status would end within a year and a half, as Laurel and Hardy overtook him. It must have been bittersweet for Chase, as he had relentlessly championed Hardy for many years and had become best friends with Laurel, whose temperament was very similar to Chase's. Nonetheless, the period of 1925–1927 was the peak of Chase's comedy output, and the very best of the best was *Mighty Like a Moose.*

Synopsis: How happy can a happy marriage be when the husband has horizontal front teeth and the wife has a honker proportionally bigger than that of a puffin? We're about to find out when "Mr. Moose" secretly gets his chompers fixed at the same time "Mrs. Moose" is secretly getting her schnozz planed. Their surgeons' offices are conveniently on the same floor of the medical building, so they get to "meet cute" at the elevator—not recognizing one another with their new visages—and end up arranging to meet later to attend a party together.

Entering their house from different directions, each discovers the other's presence without the other's knowledge. Since they're both getting dressed to cheat on each other, a grand ballet of near misses and split-second avoidances takes place, and they escape in separate taxis.

At the party, "Mr. Moose" is stuck partnering the 1888 polka steps of Gale Henry at her bony homeliest. When he finally does manage to sit down with his new flirt, "Mrs. Moose," the party is raided and their compromising photo is instantly splashed across the front page of the local newspaper, in one of those miraculously speedy journalistic productions that only ever existed in the movies. "Mr. Moose," now wise to the true identity of the lady thanks to that newspaper, plugs in the set of false buck teeth his dentist had thoughtfully provided for him, confronts his wife with the telltale newspaper, and stages a terrifying one-man (literally) fight to the death with her new lover . . . until she turns the tables on him.

Comment: The very idea that this deeply affectionate couple would be totally helpless to recognize each other after fairly minor cosmetic surgery (and instant healing) is preposterous, and Chase knows it: he satirizes it by having even the family dog fail to recognize "Mr. Moose" until the latter slips the set of fake buckaroos into his mouth, as if dogs don't recognize their masters by scent. With that in-joke, you're sucked into the premise and are rendered helpless to do anything but laugh almost without cease throughout the entire film.

The choreography of near misses in the dressing scene is brilliant. Just when you think one more of them will be one too many, Chase throws in a comic wrench by barging in through a door only to screech (silently) to a halt inches from bumping into Oakland who has her back turned to him: you can't help bursting into fresh laughter, the whole silly situation reinvigorated on the spot.

Chase's monumental brawl with himself is by far the best anyone has ever attempted. His mugging, his endlessly imaginative violence, the tireless racing back and forth and around and around and all the time switching clothes on the run, is just superlative and excruciatingly funny. There may have been editing involved, but there was certainly no CGI, masking, or special effects of any kind: it is pure Chase and pure hilarity.

Finally, one must mention the truly funny intertitles supplied by the ever-reliable H. M. "Beanie" Walker. When "Mr. Moose" is verbally invited to the party, he declines at first with the very reasonable explanation, "I've stopped having a good time—I'm married." And when the flirting couple escapes from the raid and finds about thirty taxis waiting in the street outside, taxis that the cops apparently plan to use to transport all the partygoers to jail, Chase instantly scatters all of them by warning, "The police are looking for a bootlegger!"

Bonus: Hollywood has always been the locale with perhaps the highest per capita rate of cosmetic surgery in the world. *Mighty Like a Moose* was not the first film built around it, and not even the first film to satirize it. That it could, in fact, make an entire comedy about it in 1926 and expect the rest of the world to appreciate the joke shows just how common it had already gotten by that time.

THE MISHAPS OF MUSTY SUFFER

(1915–1917, George Kleine Studio and Essanay)

Director: Louis Myll
Writers: Unidentified, but presumed to be mostly Louis Myll
Cast: Harry Watson Jr., Dan Crimmins, H. H. McCollum, Della Connor, Maxfield Moree, Rosa Gore, George Bickel, Cissie Fitzgerald
Running Time (Length): Originally five reels; released as three series of one-reel shorts
Availability: DVDs (Undercrank Productions: *The Mishaps of Musty Suffer*, vols. 1 and 2)

Background: George Kleine hired the circus, vaudeville, and stage revue (Ziegfeld's Follies) comedy team of Bickel and Watson to film, first, two five-reelers (*The Fixer* and *The Politician*, both 1915), and then the introduction of the "Musty Suffer" character in the five-reel *Keep Moving* (also 1915). Instead of releasing *Keep Moving* whole, however, he decided to chop it up, add new and previously edited footage, and launch it as a series of one-reel "whirls" in 1916. The success of this first set of ten "whirls" prompted a second set in 1917, which more or less exhausted the store of available material. A third set, also in 1917, was made with mostly fresh material and released rather negligently through Kleine's new partners at Essanay. Like most sequels to sequels, the third set drained the audience of interest, even though some of the surviving episodes are among the best of the "Mustys."

Despite the considerable popularity of the first two series, the films disappeared with time. Watson wandered back into live theatre before wandering right out of show business and ending up in—of all places—the little fishing town of Pene-tanguishene in northern Ontario, Canada. The character of "Musty Suffer" evaporated from the records and from the memories of silent film comedy.

In 2014, just in time for the centenary, silent film musician and preservationist Ben Model resurrected eight and a half (only six minutes of *Hold Fast* survives) of the one-reelers, glisteningly cleaned and repaired by the Library of Congress, and with the help of online donors, released them under the collective title of *The Mishaps of Musty Suffer*. This set proved such a hit that Model was able to follow up with a second volume in 2015, consisting of four more "whirls" and the earlier Bickel and Watson showcase film, *The Fixer* (1915). Each set included one newsreel in which Bickel and Watson made appearances in public events. In addition, researcher and fellow enthusiast Steve Massa assembled a booklet that fit nicely into the DVD case of either volume; most of the information in the paragraphs you are now reading is taken from Massa's diligent work.

Synopsis: Massa and Model fondly describe the series as "cartoony and surreal . . . an American descendant of the zany and anarchic early European comedies of Pathé and Gaumont." Harry Watson's lead character (George Bickel has significant roles in only four of the "whirls") is given the nom de guerre "Musty Suffer" for good reason: he's obliged to suffer exaggerated violence that, unlike the hyped-up brutality of Lloyd Hamilton's and Bud Duncan's

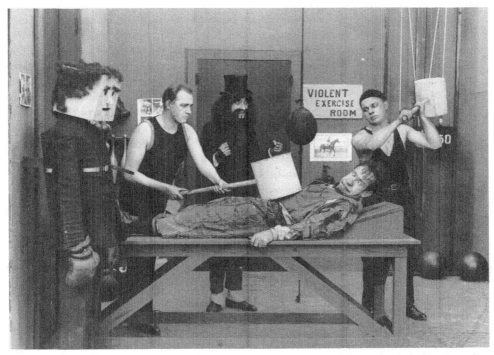

Harry Watson Jr. illustrates why his character is called "Musty Suffer" in the "whirl" released as *Cruel and Unusual* (1916). How can you not love the box-headed boxer on the left? *Courtesy of the Library of Congress / Undercrank Productions*

"Ham and Bud" films, is almost magical in its off-the-wall creativity. It infuses reality with the elasticity of a Bugs Bunny cartoon, not just the violence.

In a (probably unintentional) nose-thumbing at Charlie Chaplin's tramp character, Watson wears a hobo outfit so shredded, it seems to have been assembled from confetti streamers fished out of gutter water. He's blessed with a clown's face similar to that of the Sennett Studio's Frank Hayes or, later, Joe E. Brown of *Some Like It Hot* fame: eyes closer to their respective ears than to each other, leaving plenty of room in the middle for a nose bigger than the average lightbulb and a mouth whose corners are racing the eyes to be first to touch his earlobes. As hapless as he looks, "Musty Suffer" is a resilient little guy who can be provoked into feisty counterattacks, although his more frequent reactions to his sufferings are, first, endurance, and second, escape.

"Musty's" secret is that he has a fairy godfather, or more accurately, a fairy tramp: a tutu-waisted hobo with the power to make "Musty's" somewhat low-caste wishes come true. Such modest wishes include bathing in beer, chopping off the arm of a would-be food thief, wearing the fancy uniform of a ticket-taker or a cabbie, and getting a "soft job" as the guinea pig in experiments by crazed medical men.

The latter wish, alas, always turns out to be more of a nightmare than a dream. The wildest of the crazed doctors was showcased in the very last film, *Musty's Vacation* (1917), wherein he subjected "Musty" to revolving-door plastic surgery that Joan Rivers could only envy: a hammerhead shark nose job, the elongation of his forehead to a height several inches beyond the ability of his scalp to keep pace, feet stretched to water-ski length, and then each change instantly undone when either the surgeon or the patient expresses dissatisfaction with the results.

Close behind this plastic surgeon in the realm of medical malpractice was the dentist in *Local Showers* (1916), who was aided by a contraption that seized "Musty" by the feet, turned him upside down and shook all the money out of his pockets, propelled him into a chair, applied anesthetic by mallet, pulled his aching tooth, soaked him from head to toe to awaken him, and then turned him on a spit over a fire to dry, until "Musty" escaped by being shot through the inside of a chimney with the assistance of a high-pressure fire hose.

Not enough Suffer-ing? Well, in other "whirls," "Musty" is projected headfirst through a brick wall (*Showing Some Speed*, 1916), made the target in a shooting gallery (*Out of Order*, 1916), discomfited by having a car parked on his chest (*Blow Your Horn*, 1916), relieved of an unwanted beard by getting it soaked in gasoline and then blown off in a fiery explosion (*Keep Moving*, 1916), and force-fed a dinner by having a chicken injected into his stomach and peas shotgunned into same—no need for that sissified chewing-swallowing-digesting system everybody else uses (*Active Service*, 1916).

In short: anarchic, surreal, imaginative, unconventional, exhilarating, very funny, and definitely a unique brand of slapstick comedy.

Comments: Although the films work well as one-reel "whirls," they should really all be considered (and watched as) episodes in a single feature film, as George Kleine first conceived them. Treating them as 30 stand-alone films instead would leave me hard-pressed to limit myself to recommending fewer than three of them—they're that good, and that oddball.

Kleine's budget limitations necessitated the use of a lot of available lighting and settings. Where sets were artificially constructed, they were narrow and tight, requiring close camera work to keep within the boundaries. In *Out of Order*, "Musty" is a movie-house jack-of-all-trades; one of his weapons against sneaks and unruly patrons is an escalator that can run in both directions. Compare this very compact escalator against the full-scale double escalator Chaplin uses in *The Floorwalker*, or the staircase that can be flattened into a ramp in comedies by Bobby Vernon, Harold Lloyd, Buster Keaton, and others; the latter all get more laughs and more play out of theirs, but the size forces the camera to be set up far back enough to encompass the entire scene, creating a bit of distance between the performers and the audience. The necessary closeness of the camera in the "Musty Suffer" films, in contrast, keeps the audience directly invested in the manipulations of the stairs, allows a vivid exposure of Harry Watson's mugging, and sets a warmer tone to such scenes. They aren't better or funnier scenes than Chaplin's or Vernon's, but they are more intimate and immediate.

Among this jumble of fascinating creativity and cartoonery, a truly awe-inspiring supporting character upstages "Musty" throughout *Strictly Private* (1916). This is a two-man horse. Rather than have one man play the entire back end of the horse while the other man plays the entire front end, both men play only the horse's legs from underneath a one-piece hard-molded horse's torso-with-head. At first the viewer wonders why they came up with this peculiar variation of the standard stage horse. The answer is that it gives wonderful flexibility (counterintuitively, given the inflexibility of the shell) and even a bizarre believability to the phony animal . . . even, or especially, when it makes like a fireman and uses a rope pulley to swing itself up and down a hole between the first and second floors of a barn. The leg-men never break the perfect synchronicity of their steps and dances and pirouettes, except once for a fraction of a second when one of them slips while trying to gain traction to pull a very heavy hackney carriage. And they play a lovely role in one of the climactic gags: when they are too tired to continue pulling "Musty's" vehicle, he lights a fire between their legs, they jump and move forward just far enough to put the fire under the carriage and set the latter alight, and "Musty" unhurriedly proceeds to unspool a full-length fire hose from under the seat and pours water back inside the burning coach.

Bonus: In addition to Bickel and Watson, the "Musty Suffer" series features a second popular vaudeville team: Crimmons and Gore, a husband and wife who numbered the original stage version of *The Wizard of Oz* among their theatrical accomplishments.

Supporting actor Maxfield Moree contributes (among many characters, including the fairy tramp) a background persona whose physical contortions seem to set him up as the model for any number of swaybacked animated figures, including the various ducks (Donald, Daffy, Howard, etc.). Dressed in an excruciatingly tight white suit, he stuffed more padding into his seat than the average sofa and proceeded to maintain an S-curve posture that stuck out his posterior even further. As silly (and uncomfortable) as this stance looks, it fits right in with the overall cartoon design of the series.

MISS BLUEBEARD

(1925, Paramount)

Director: Frank Tuttle
Writers: Townshend Martin and Avery Hopwood
Camera: J. Roy Hunt
Cast: Bebe Daniels, Robert Frazer, Raymond Griffith, Kenneth MacKenna, Martha
Madison, Diana Kane, Lawrence D'Orsay, Florence Billings, Ivan Simpson
Running Time (Length): 62 minutes (seven reels)
Availability: DVD (Grapevine Video)

Background: Among the most prodigious careers of the generation of performers
who came of age during the first half of the 20th century was that of Bebe Daniels.
Like Buster Keaton and Stan Laurel, she had the good fortune (for a performer,
at least) to have been born into a traveling theatrical family, so the first lesson life
ever taught her was to be entertaining or else be murdered by audience silence in
some two-bit, 25-seat "opera hall" in rural Kansas or backwoods North Dakota.
After a half-dozen years playing leads in circuits, she swept into the movies and
immediately played everything from Westerns to cliffhangers to slapstick. She
hadn't even reached double digits in age yet!

By the time she was 14—for her generation, that was barely the start of physical
puberty—she was playing the grown-up girlfriend of Harold Lloyd in dozens of
his "Lonesome Luke" and early "glass character" films. At 19, she was the brazen predator losing a hellacious physical fight with Gloria Swanson (the biggest
female star of the movies) under the direction of Cecil B. De Mille (the biggest
director in the movies) in *Why Change Your Wife?* (1920) (see review in this book).

Unlike Keaton and Laurel, Daniels played all sides of the actorly spectrum: she
was as adept at serious, dramatic, melodramatic, and tragedy roles as she was
at slapstick, farce, screwball, and social comedy. It all made her not only one of
the most respected and admired actresses but also one of the most popular and
praised throughout the entire silent film era.

When the silents were done, she proved she could talk and sing onscreen. In the
mid-1930s, she and husband Ben Lyon were performing in Britain when World War
II started. Grateful for the success Britain had given them on stage and radio, they
elected to stay and uplift the bombarded Britons with their entertainment throughout the duration of the war; Britain repaid them by making them the biggest radio
stars of the era, right through the 1950s with only a brief interruption in the immediate postwar late 1940s when they spent a few years back in the United States.

In her versatility, her popularity, her ability to turn her real marriage into a
long-running sitcom, and her sheer professional longevity, Bebe Daniels was Lucille Ball before Lucille Ball.

Synopsis: It's so wearisome being a massive success in the Paris theatre. Somehow the English songwriter "Larry" and the French stage star "Colette" have
never met each other despite their parallel Parisian hits. Both become so *de trop*
with the adulation that plagues their comfortable lives that they decide to escape

Bebe Daniels and Robert Frazer in Miss Bluebeard (1925). *Courtesy of Bruce Calvert*

to England, "Larry" to go home and "Colette" to visit an English girlfriend she hasn't seen in years. In one of those just-plain-stupid-and-unbelievable decisions that motivate far too many movies, "Larry" decides to let his best friend, lady-killer "Bob," assume his identity. These three characters mix it up on the train so that the real "Larry" meets and falls for "Colette" but she farcically gets married to "Bob," thinking him "Larry." As if that isn't confusing enough, "Bob" is engaged to "Gloria," who happens to be the old school friend "Colette" is going to visit.

Almost the entire remainder of the film takes place in "Larry's" sumptuous apartment and in "Gloria's" parents' house. The two men juggle their aliases and their girlfriends/fiancées, as well as "Larry's" other miscellaneous girlfriends and sugar mamas. The juggling is aided and abetted by "Bertie," the sleepyhead hanger-on of "Larry," and to a much lesser extent by "Larry's" scandalized and uncomprehending butler, "Bounds." Eventually, the various liaisons get sorted out and "Colette" ends up with the right "Larry" for her husband.

Comment: So-called bedroom farces like *Miss Bluebeard* all seem to be the same film, so what matters in these cases are the strengths of the performers, the funniness of the one-liners, and the briskness of the direction. The plots (and the subplots, too) are simply variations on the same theme and can be dismissed from consideration.

On the plus side, *Miss Bluebeard* is piloted by two superb silent comedians: Bebe Daniels and Raymond Griffith. On the negative side, the navigators are two nondescript spear-carriers: Robert Frazer and Kenneth MacKenna. All four are competent; the navigators have energy and enthusiasm if they lack power and presence, while Griffith does well in a thoroughly undemanding role, and Daniels is strong enough that even her French can be lip-read as having a credible accent.

Florence Billings is given very narrow opportunities as "Larry's" sugar mama, "Eva," and is so good that we know the couple's entire relationship without anyone even hinting at it; her middle-aged yearning for young love as an escape from a tired old marriage is conveyed with beautiful subtlety. Subtlety is a difficult delivery to achieve in a broad farce.

The intertitles provide mild chuckles and smiles rather than belly laughs, but at least they don't detract from the good-naturedness of the film. And the direction keeps things moving, although the intercutting during the transition from France to England is a bit of a forced fit. Most of the staginess of the theatrical original is nicely disguised by utilizing the various separate rooms of "Larry's" apartment as separate sets, so that entire scenes can be played out in the main room, the two bedrooms, or the outside hallway, avoiding confinement to one large set.

Bonus: As has been pointed out in thousands of dissertations, lectures, books, and documentaries, the American film industry from its earliest days and right on into the 21st century has been obsessed with putting women "in their place" and with dictating that "place" to be firmly within a marital context. Even today, when the marital context can easily be that of a lesbian liaison, the American film will frame the sympathetic and therefore "correct" woman of the pair to be the submissive, vulnerable, feminine, "traditional" one. Hollywood, it seems, has never grown out of its past as the fantasy projections of stodgy but ruthless old white men from Old World backgrounds suffused with medieval orthodox religious beliefs about the place and value of the female sex.

Silent feature films with women stars—Bebe Daniels, the Talmadge sisters, the Gish sisters, Gloria Swanson, Colleen Moore, Clara Bow, the films in which Mary Pickford played females old enough to get married—all of them had but a single focus: to make a marriage, or if marriage was a preexisting condition, to repair or replace that marriage. Any other plot thread was nothing more than a means to that end. In *Miss Bluebeard*, for example, Daniels's career as a successful stage performer is established at the start, and then she promptly abandons it in order to get married and subsequently to get her inadvertently confused marital status straightened out. Little else is said about her work, and certainly nothing is said about her resuming her career once she has gotten married to the right guy. We're left to assume she will give up that French nonsense and retire to being a good little housewife for her big strong successful working husband.

Male characters in silent films of course also had to be married off in the final scenes; after all, marriage as defined by the Hollywood producers of the era required a husband as well as a wife. But whereas actress-led movies focused solely on the goal of marriage with any other plot considerations being secondary, actor-led movies focused on the exciting plotline and treated marriage/romance as the nuisance subplot whose climax (marriage) was desultorily jerry-built onto the very last scene of the film.

Were there exceptions? Of course, and they provide an interesting comparison. Bebe Daniels starred in *Feel My Pulse* in 1928; it was a virtual remake, with gender reversal and a politically corrected plot, of Harold Lloyd's *Why Worry?* (1923). Daniels and Lloyd both played extremely wealthy, self-obsessed, socially clueless, lifelong hypochondriacs who are cured of their illusions and their naiveté by experiencing a situation of extreme violence and danger, to which they respond with a most unlikely display of physical bravado, energy, and mental agility. In Lloyd's case, the event is a (presumably) South American revolution. Daniels genteelly avoided that implicit racism and U.S. superiority by replacing the foreign revolution with a good old all-American bootlegging shoot-out; she actually gets more bullets flying around her "isolated" sanatorium than Lloyd did with competing armies in an entire country.

Lloyd's character is accompanied by a gorgeous nurse, the drop-dead beautiful Jobyna Ralston, who (of course) secretly loves Lloyd; it is his efforts to rescue her and then protect her that fuel many of Lloyd's gags and gunfights. In *Feel My Pulse*, the drop-dead handsome Richard Arlen secretly loves Daniels; it is his efforts to rescue her and then protect her that fuel many of Daniels's gags and gunfights. (A beautifully hairy, unkempt, slightly potbellied William Powell plays the bad guy who lusts after Daniels, while a beautifully hairy, unkempt, not-at-all potbellied James Mason—not the later British actor of the same name—plays the bad guy who lusts after Ralston.)

In the final scene of both films, the hypochondriac throws away all the pills and salves and protective pampering that have been used to cultivate utter passivity, vows to live an exciting life henceforth, and—apparently in fulfilment of this vow—promptly announces marriage plans with the no-longer-secret admirer. In Lloyd's case, you actually feel trepidation for the future of his wife-to-be: any man so capable of resorting to impetuous violence as Lloyd is not a man who is going to be easy for her to live with. In Daniels's case, you feel it is less of a mismatch—Daniels has proven the alacrity with which she can resort to out-of-control violence, too, which means Arlen isn't going to be able to abuse her without a fight; what's going to be problematic for this couple in the future is that she is a rich aristocrat while he is a scrabbling, low-class reporter. So in both cases, the coming marriage is rife with a power imbalance, Lloyd–Ralston's marriage being an imbalance of *physical* power and Daniels–Arlen's marriage being an imbalance of *social* power. Daniels is being subversive of the accepted system; Lloyd is doing his hyperkinetic damnedest to reinforce that old-fashioned system.

THE MONKEY STORY

(1924, Roach)

Director: Len Powers
Camera: Burt Currigan
Cast: Our Gang, Robert McGowan, the Dippy Doo-Dads
Running Time (Length): One reel

Background: Hal Roach organized his comedy production into generic categories. He had a "kid" series (Our Gang), a "dumbbell" series (Snub Pollard), a "young urban man" series (Charley Chase), a "two-men" series (Laurel and Hardy), and made attempts at a "two-women" series (Anita Garvin and Marion Byron, others). Late in the 1920s, he had a series that could be very unkindly labeled the "old washed-up star" series (Mabel Normand, Theda Bara, Pola Negri, etc.).

One often-overlooked series was the "animal" series, led by "Rex the Wonder Horse." Of these animal efforts, one of the oddest was the Dippy Doo-Dads, a collection of little capuchin monkeys. These animals—some of them cute, some of them not; their fangs tended to make them a little scary in close-ups—were put through the paces of typical human movie scripts. The comedy, apparently, was intended to be found in the sight of monkeys pretending to be people—that and the intertitles, which spouted gag lines and quaint grammar (in a few occasions, regrettably, with African American "accents").

Synopsis: Our Gang members are being transported to the site of their next film. For some reason, they are driven in a car, while the Our Gang adult mastermind, Robert McGowan, arrives via train. Noticing the kids' fascination with a little monkey, McGowan sits them down to listen to him tell "the monkey story." The rest of this movie is the film of that story.

In the grand tradition of so many silent dramas, the son of farmers leaves his folks to move to the big city. After wandering the streets in hick awe, he realizes he is hungry and broke, always a dire combination of affairs. Being upright

Two of the Dippy Doo-Dads, circa 1924. *Courtesy of Steve Massa*

and honest, even if his farmwork had also proven him lazy and a goof-off, he applies for a job as a messenger "boy" in a bank, where the other staff members are all monkeys except for the gigantic security dog. He's immediately given the task of carrying a sack of money across town. A masked robber-monkey sticks him up and makes his getaway in a fast car. The farm-monkey chases after him by various transportation means, finally going up in an airplane and dropping a bomb or a rock (it's not clear which, in existing prints) that destroys the car.

Having recovered the money and proven himself, the farm-monkey marries the boss's daughter. She gets roaring drunk at the wedding reception and hangs upside down from the chandelier, displaying her underclothes to a shocked and titillated audience of guests of various species. (The rabbit looks particularly interested in what lies beneath the skirts.) A year later, notwithstanding that unpromising start to their marriage, the bride is in labor—a surprising little scene at a time when the movies couldn't even show a married couple sharing a bed, and one I would like to have heard McGowan narrate to his audience of six-year-olds—and eventually a baby monkey joins the family.

Comment: This is not "animal cruelty." If you want to fulminate about "animal cruelty," go watch one of the earlier Dippy Doo-Dads movies, *The Watchdog* (1922), in which the *monkey* is the one actor brutalizing other monkeys, a dog, goats, ducks, a mule, and a cat. (The cat also beats up the dog.) *The Monkey Story*, like the majority of Dippy Doo-Dads movies, merely puts the animals through human stories and actions. The sets are miniaturized to fit them, as are the props such as the airplane and the cars. The monkeys look comfortable in front of the camera.

The charm of the film, like that of the series as a whole, rests upon the cuteness of monkeys doing human things. The best and funniest example is the farm boy's reaction to the sight of pastries in a shop window: he licks his chops, slurps drool, rolls his eyes in a spot-on slapstick pantomime of food lust, and for good measure he pulls out the pockets of his pants (with a little aid from offscreen handlers) to show he hasn't the money to buy even a cupcake.

The monkey-wife almost comes from a different movie. Her drunk scene is a hoot, especially the reactions of the male lookers-on, who peek between the fingers covering their faces in fake consternation at the display of intimate finery. The scene where she is about to go into labor is also intensely fascinating and nicely detailed.

The Monkey Story is not a barrel of laughs, but it's a very interesting and absorbing experiment in comedy.

Bonus: Most available copies of Dippy Doo-Dads films are in poor condition, and there seems to be little heart in our politically correct times to restore them for public consumption. *Be Honest!* (1923) is mildly amusing, but the only accessible copy is difficult to watch; the tones have faded so that the print is alternately too murky and too light, and a lot of frames are missing. *The Watchdog*, as noted above, is full of animal-on-animal cruelty and is not fun, other than the closing (or near-closing) scene in which the monkey has finished eating a huge sack of peanuts and staggers around in slow motion with a (fake-) distended belly.

The most accessible Dippy Doo-Dads film is *North of 50–50*, a very well-done simian version of the old story of a bad guy in a Canadian gold rush town whose North-West Mounted Police pursuer is the boyfriend of the villain's sister. Although beautifully realized, the only laughs are in the intertitles (uncredited, but bearing the wit of "Beanie" Walker, Roach's go-to titles writer). Finding the villain's horse abandoned during the chase, Mountie "Dan" confidently deduces, "He won't go far on foot—it's too much like work." The villain, "Pete," begs his sister "Marie" to hide him from "Dan" in her house; after mulling over the possibilities, she gets the bright idea: "The attic! He'll never think to look there, he's only a policeman."

And in a delightfully sly jab at Prohibition, Walker's final intertitle has "Dan" tell "Marie" in a tender embrace, "Drink caused it all—we'll go to the States where there's a law against liquor."

MOVE ALONG

(1926, Educational)

Director: Norman Taurog
Writer: Norman Taurog
Camera: Len Smith
Cast: Lloyd Hamilton, Helen Foster, Glen Cavender, Jack Lloyd, Otto Fries, Anita Garvin
Running Time (Length): 22 minutes (two reels)

Background: For three years (1914–1917), Lloyd Hamilton wore a fake moustache the size of a submarine sandwich (with wilted lettuce drooping from both ends) and kicked around the near-dwarf Bud Duncan in a couple of hundred one-reel comedies as the team of "Ham and Bud." These films are unwatchable today; in their heyday, they were among the biggest box-office successes. It's unfathomable, like Adam Sandler's popularity 85 years later.

Freed of Duncan and the Kalem Company studio, not to mention the moustache, Hamilton switched to Educational Pictures and built a new onscreen character for himself. This turned out to be an intriguing process. Hamilton was a big man physically, not unlike Edgar Kennedy in height and beef (both were husky, not fat); he stood out because of it, and didn't need the getup of a grotesque in order to draw the viewer's eye. He adopted a po'boy cap, also known in the United States as a newsboy cap, which distinguished him from the boater, bowler, and porkpie hats all the other comedians sported. But most of all, he invented a poofter's sashay that no other male performer would even satirize, let alone steal, in terror of being labeled a homosexual.

One of the many troubles that beset Hamilton throughout his solo career was a chronic indecision as to which direction he should take this character. He continued to cherish the cartoon violence of his "Ham and Bud" days and made films like *Somebody's Fault* (1927), which were two reels of Wile E. Coyote blow-ups.

Right next to it, he made *Papa's Boy* (also known as *Who's Kidding Who?*, 1927), in which he took the "sissy" character to its limits by making him into a vastly overgrown "mama's little boy" complete with short pants and nerd eyeglasses. And somewhere in between these two extremes, he presented his po'boy persona in much more naturalistic surroundings and situations.

It should have been obvious that the last approach was the only viable way forward for him. The man-boy-sissy of *Papa's Boy* was an incredibly limited option for someone who was already 40 years old. Physical breakdowns—he broke a leg at least three times, according to some sources—and advancing age ruled out the "Ham and Bud" mayhem option. Yet because he couldn't make up his mind, he never pursued the development of the po'boy character beyond the props of the cap and the swish. The best he ever got out of it was *Move Along*, a film that hints at far more potential than he ever managed to deliver.

Synopsis: The plot of *Move Along* follows the simplicity of most great silent comedy shorts: it's essentially a two-scene set, with some small interstitial threads binding them, that allows the lead comedian maximum flexibility to show us what he can do.

In this case, Hamilton is out of work and out of money; he joins a lineup at the employment office where twenty jobs are guaranteed, and he's number twenty among the hopefuls. A pretty girl comes up and is despondent to find herself number twenty-one. Hamilton, not out of gender chivalry but out of respect for someone even more desperate than himself, gives up his spot and his chance at a job.

The second sequence finds him amid his belongings in the street, where the landlady has tossed them for nonpayment of rent. The earth apparently gets knocked off its axis, for the weather suddenly changes into a monsoon, and just as suddenly becomes a snowstorm of an intensity rarely experienced south of the North Pole. Hamilton fashions a snowhouse on the spot and is joined by the girl who had jumped the queue at the employment office, to whom Hamilton offers deliberately Chaplinesque hospitality.

The interstitial material mostly consists of Hamilton looking for a place to rest, always being pounced upon by a cop who orders him to "move on." The film may be titled *Move Along*, but that's never what the cop says in the intertitles.

Comment: A beautiful and well-constructed film, *Move Along* is widely recognized as one of the greats of the silent comedy era. This is despite the fact that there aren't really that many outright laughs in it. The interstitial material is where almost all of the laughs are to be found, not in the two set pieces.

The snowhouse sequence, in particular, seems to come out of nowhere, out of some other film, and out of some other comedian. Hamilton plays it very well, without mugging or other typical slapstick physical maneuvers. He's at home with this style of domestic comedy even though he's never done anything else quite like it before and even though it is clearly not the kind of comedy we associate with Lloyd Hamilton. It seems scripted, perhaps a bit too much so; and, as mentioned, it is self-consciously Chaplinesque, especially when Hamilton eats a frozen flower (*The Gold Rush* with its boot-eating dinner had come out the year before).

The snowhouse scene is the one scene people associate with Lloyd Hamilton today. It is, in a real sense, his only legacy. And it probably says a lot about his failure to fulfill his potential that he is remembered for the one time he stepped out of his multiple-personality morass and imitated a comedian who knew exactly who his own onscreen character was.

Bonus: A Lloyd Hamilton film that came very close to being included in this book was *Moonshine* (1921). Its opening section is absolute comedy brilliance: a backcountry war between hillbilly moonshiners and Prohibition-enforcing authorities, filmed in the manner of a baseball game with guns instead of balls and bats. As with so many other short silent gems of slapstick, it was designed by Charley Chase, who did everything, including playing at least three roles; since Hamilton's character is only being delivered by stork (literally) during the battle, Chase is even the star and lead comedian of this sequence.

Once the full-grown Hamilton is introduced, however, Chase retires into directing (he does show up later as yet another Prohibition agent among the undiscouraged enforcers of the law, but it is more or less a cameo), and *Moonshine* instantly falls off the cliff into a routine set of gags about hillbillies outwitting the authorities—well done, as anything by Chase must be, but ordinary.

A MOVIE STAR

(1916, Sennett)

Director: Fred Fishback
Cast: Mack Swain, Harry McCoy, Polly Moran, Frank Hayes, Julia Faye, May Emory, Nick Cogley, Phyllis Allen, Joey Jacobs, Louella Maxam, May Wells, Ray Grey, Grover Ligon
Running Time (Length): Two reels
Availability: VHS (Kino Video: *Slapstick Encyclopedia*, vol. 2)

Background: The movies have always been self-reflective, self-aware, quite willing to ally the audience with them in making fun of themselves; in 1901, *The Big Swallow* took just 60 seconds to portray a "star" fake-complaining about the paparazzi even as he moves closer within their camera range and eventually eats the camera in a none-too-subtle metaphor for a movie star's insatiable hunger for attention. Mack Sennett had already done a few farces of this sort by 1916, such as Chaplin's *A Film Johnnie* (1913). He was also fond of recording the absurd behaviors of movie audiences, including his own in *Mabel's Dramatic Career* (1913). With *A Movie Star*, he hit the jackpot, doing a film-within-a-film, showing it in a lively theatre, and having the "star" present in the audience to lead the cheers for himself. The result was one of the best and funniest films ever to deal with these subjects.

Synopsis: At 6'2" and 250 pounds in an era where men averaged 5'8" and 140 pounds, mighty Mack Swain is no shrinking violet. He likes to pretend he is, though . . . *after* making sure people notice him and recognize him as the famous movie star, "Handsome Jack." Where better to bask—with becoming false modesty—in the consequent adulation than in a theatre that, oh, what a coincidence!, just happens to be screening his latest epic, *Big-Hearted Jack*. The audience is large and appreciative, at least for the most part, and the largest and most appreciative is "Jack" himself: first to applaud, first to bow humbly at the applause, first to reinvigorate the applause as it threatens to die out, and last to sit down when it is exhausted.

The ladies in the audience deeply appreciate "Jack's" handsomeness and big-heartedness; the gentlemen somewhat less so. In fact, one Shakespearean-favoring male viewer jeers his onscreen work as "hammy," as if his offscreen personality were anything else. The film-within-a-film, *Big-Hearted Jack*, provides ample evidence for all of these descriptors, being a deliberately cornball Western featuring our hero as a paragon of virtue and chivalry, not to mention handsomeness and big-heartedness. He's also extremely brave and a fearsome fighter, traits the real "Jack" demonstrates in negative terms when his wife shows up at the theatre and wades into him with fists flying.

Comment: The interplay between Swain and the theatre audience is Sennett teamwork at its best and funniest. It is unfair to pick out any supporting player for special mention because they all work together so fluidly, but it's impossible to avoid singling out Polly Moran as an uninhibited and unapologetic fan sitting right behind Swain: mere portions of her physique are visible behind the giant, yet she is so skillful in pantomime than she delivers a complete and nuanced performance that leaves us prostrate with laughter—especially the dirty, flirty wink she slips Swain when we least expect it.

Harry McCoy has the supporting role of his life as the theatre's musician and sound effects man. A veteran in slapstick movies since 1912, McCoy had descended from co-headliner status with Max Asher, through supporting actor with almost every great silent comedian other than Charlie Chaplin and Charley Chase, and eventually he shifted into offscreen work, mostly for Sennett, although he did work briefly for many other companies. *A Movie Star* is his showcase almost as much as it is Swain's, even though he gets maybe 15 percent as much screen time: the energy, inventiveness, and sheer hilariousness he unleashes from his sounding board is without parallel.

As for Swain himself, he just lives his two-faced role to the fullest and most side-splitting extent possible. Always a huggable, bashful, and well-rounded (in both senses) teddy bear, he is irresistible as the insecure egotist. You know he must have been channeling dozens of his contemporaries for this role, if not peering into the future to set the typecast for the likes of Judy Garland; yet "Handsome Jack" also comes across as an unabashedly original characterization, a persona beautifully realized from imagination by a very clever comedian.

Bonus: Harry McCoy's character is hardly even an exaggeration of the antics some real-life musical accompanists routinely unspooled. We have in our cultural history the image of lavish orchestras in tailcoats settled in the pit before enormous screens, ready to pour out oceans of refined classical music to bolster silent dramas; that applied only to select theatres in the biggest cities. Most theatres actually had but a single musician, or perhaps a small group of between three and ten players. Rural theatres and small-town venues usually had just a pianist. Somewhere in scale between the lone pianist and the symphony orchestra was the organist. Though only one person, he (it was a rare female who could handle the physical demands of a Mighty Wurlitzer organ) played not only a multiple-keyboard organ but also entire panels full of sound-effect pulleys and buttons and props: he was indeed a one-man soundtrack for the entire theatre bill. The energy and verve Mc-Coy flaunts in *A Movie Star* is as much an admiring tribute to these lone stalwarts as it is uproarious.

MUM'S THE WORD

(1926, Roach)

Director: Leo McCarey
Writer: Charley Chase (uncredited)
Titles: H. M. Walker
Camera: Floyd Jackman
Editor: Richard Currier
Cast: Charley Chase, Martha Sleeper, Anders Randolph, Virginia Pearson
Running Time (Length): Two reels
Availability: DVD (Kino Lorber Films: *The Charley Chase Collection*, vol. 1)

Background: Charley Chase made nearly 50 films in the three-year period of 1925–1927, a prodigious output of excellence. It explains why all three of his films recommended in this book were made within less than a year (August 1925 to July 1926).

In 1925, he made 18 films of which seven are one-reelers, so this works out to about fourteen and a half two-reelers. Two are lost and one exists only partially, so let's say there are twelve available. Of those twelve, ten are delightful.

In 1926, he made twelve films, not including cameos in two others. Again, ten are killers.

In 1927, he made fifteen films, not including a cameo in an Our Gang short, but including his brief appearances in *Call of the Cuckoo*. The survival rate is a bit chancier here: two are lost, three exist only partially, so let's say only ten remain. Unfortunately, of those ten, just seven are readily available. But of those seven, five will have you rolling on the floor.

In summary, if you have a chance to watch *anything* Charley Chase created in 1925, 1926, or 1927, be sure to do so. And watch it while lying on the floor, so you have less distance to fall when laughter incapacitates you.

Synopsis: What a joy it is to watch Chase take the dopiest of plots and transform it into a perfectly logical storyline of sheer insanity! His middle-aged mother has remarried; nervous that the existence of a son well into his twenties (to be generous: Chase was 33 at the time of filming) will instantly age her into unacceptable decrepitude in the eyes of her new hubbie, she conceives the ingenious solution of passing off Charley as . . . hubbie's new valet. Disregarding the Freudian complexes that seem the inevitable result, Charley reluctantly agrees, hoping to ingratiate himself with a stepdad whom he quickly recognizes to be a cantankerous and domineering bully. The bully has his tender side, though: he's spotted embracing the comely housemaid with whom Charley has hit it off. All is innocent, however, as it turns out Martha is to Daddy what Charley is to Mommy, although we're left wondering how Charley will be to Martha the same way Daddy is to Mommy, since they are now stepsiblings.

Comment: The plot, as noted, is conventionally nonsensical and has been recycled from numerous movies both comic and (melo-)dramatic. Therefore, what matters is the individual permutations Chase puts it through, and what original gags he implements to make it stand out from its peers. More than up to the challenge, he turns it into a virtuoso farce, as reasonable on the surface as it is ridiculous under the surface, as uproariously serious as it is seriously uproarious. Nobody in the small cast lets on that what is happening is anything but ordinary and commonsensical, which of course feeds the utter absurdity of their actions and reactions.

One simple example will suffice. Charley is charged with polishing Dad's shoes. Distractions prevent him from completing the task before Dad, a man of no patience, confronts him and demands the instant production of his shining footwear. Well, there is only one possible pair of gleaming men's shoes in this entire house (since Dad has hitherto been the only male in it): the ones on Charley's own feet. With hardly a second's hesitation, Charley does the perfectly sensible thing and passes his boaters to Dad. And then he and Martha have to spend the best part of a reel trying to get Charley's shoes off Dad's feet and to put Dad's shoes on in their place . . . without Dad ever suspecting a thing. The strategies they employ in this pursuit are Einsteinian in their cleverness and creativity; at the same time they are unquestionably, certifiably harebrained; the combination of opposites is irresistibly funny.

Bonus: Chase stored a lot of his artifacts, mementos, film products, and peripherals, perhaps even some notes for a memoir, to such a prodigious level that he acquired a railway boxcar in which to keep it all. After his death in 1940, no one could find the boxcar. For all we know, it may still be out there somewhere, more than 75 years later, a lost treasure trove from one of the greatest and most talented people in the history of comedy.

MY BEST GIRL

(1927, United Artists)

Director: Sam Taylor
Writers: Allen McNeil, Tim Whelan, Hope Loring (Kathleen Norris)
Camera: Charles (Chuck) Rosher, David Kesson
Cast: Mary Pickford, Charles (Buddy) Rogers, Lucien Littlefield, Sunshine Hart, Hobart Bosworth, Evelyn Hall, Mack Swain, Carmelita Geraghty, Avonne Taylor, John Junior, Frank Finch Smiles, William Courtright, Harry Walker, Sidney Bracey
Running Time (Length): 78 minutes (some versions run 88 minutes; eight reels)
Availability: DVD (Image Entertainment)

Background: The story of Mary Pickford is so well known, it became somewhat the template for romantic dreams of would-be movie stars the world over. Born in Toronto into a family whose precarious financial situation became desperate when her young father passed away, Mary's natural talent was recognized by her mother, who promptly became the template for the pushy, ambitious stage mother living through her daughter's success. Along with much-less-attractive, much-less-talented sister Lottie and born-rascal brother Jack, the family moved to New York so Mary could flourish in the theatre. Eventually she condescended to enter films by joining D. W. Griffith's Biograph Studio; her beauty and lively character proved so luminous on the screen (she was not a light-up-the-room personality in private life) that she quickly became the biggest star in the business, and arguably the very first bona fide superstar of the movies, known far and wide as "America's Sweetheart."

History even now insists on pushing an image of Pickford as the perennial "little girl with the curls," playing archaic pantaletted-and-ringletted children when she was in her thirties. While she did play a lot of young girls, that wasn't all she played, and she didn't play them all as innocent angels. Few films about childhood are as terrifying and as poignant as *Sparrows* (1926); few double-role films were as brilliantly performed as by Mary in *Stella Maris* (1918); and in *Little Lord Fauntleroy* (1921) she upped the ante on double roles by playing a boy and the boy's mother! She made war films, she made immigrant films, she made films about people in appalling poverty, she made ethnic films, she made hillbilly films, she made Shakespeare films. She did everything, not just "Our Little Mary" films.

Being the family breadwinner since age five could have been crushing. For Pickford, it meant learning early how to do business and business deals, and how to grow a spine and reinforce it with steel. She treated business the way a Mafiosi did: mercilessly, coldly, uncompromisingly, and with an inflexible rule that she must extract huge money out of every contract even if that involved draining the last drop of blood out of the other party.

My Best Girl was her farewell to silent films—*The Taming of the Shrew* (1929) was made as both a silent and a talkie but the former was barely released, and both totally bombed—and it very definitely presents her as an adult woman in adult relationships. (This is one of the reasons why I have chosen it; I do not wish to play into the assumption that she only did child roles.) The public seemed uninterested, not because she had emphatically abandoned her child persona, but because they had swept away almost all silent movie stars as so many blacksmiths in the era of the automobile: those silent performers were from another medium, not just another era, and the new medium of talkie movies blew in a whole new generation of exciting young actors.

After four talkies, Pickford retired, and over the remaining 45 years of her life sank slowly into the twilight, looked after by her third husband and costar of *My Best Girl*, Buddy Rogers.

Synopsis: Even in the silent era, the plot of *My Best Girl* was overused to the point of being banal: rich man's son works in his father's business under a false name as training for the day when he will take over the business, he falls in love with a poor working girl on staff, his parents either disown the son or try to buy off the girl, and all ends happily. Unfortunately, *My Best Girl* doesn't put any fresh spins on this tired storyline. What elevates it and makes it worth watching once or twice is the cast and, to a lesser extent, the technical direction: there are a lot of very interesting camera setups, intriguing set designs, and robust lighting schemes.

Soon-to-be real-life couple Charles "Buddy" Rogers and Mary Pickford exchange a spark of love in *My Best Girl* (1927). *Courtesy of Bruce Calvert*

Comment: Nobody could handle cuteness scenes like Mary Pickford. In her hands they might still retain their implausibility and their silliness, but they never become icky. I'm thinking in particular of the scene in which Buddy Rogers persuades her to dine at the family mansion and they pretend to be his parents. This scene teeters on the edge, too calculated at tugging our heartstrings, yet imbuing their antics with just barely enough sincerity, reluctance, and wariness to be successful.

This film is a little uneven, probably because it was trying to do too much; there's even some Keystone slapstick at the very end, in their mad dash to reach the boat. And it's somewhat startling to see that Mary Pickford—still married to macho swordsman Doug Fairbanks at the time—apparently never learned how to kiss, at least not onscreen: she kisses Rogers by pressing her closed lips to a corner of his mouth, never puckering or making any other kind of motion with her lips.

As far as shop-girl romances go, Colleen Moore, who was certainly not lower class in real life, looks rather more believable as a lower-class girl. Mary may have been lower class in real life, but she doesn't *look* like something born into a slum; when she plays a slum girl like "Unity" in *Stella Maris*, she has to transform herself into an unrecognizable ragamuffin. Pickford, however, blows Moore out of the water as far as *acting* like a lower-class girl is concerned.

The closest Pickford comes to losing the audience is the semi-hysterical fit she throws near the end. She obviously wanted to pull out all the stops and prove she was a great actress, which she was (she had already proven it with *Stella Maris*), and the scene is very effective and moving, but it just goes on too long and becomes all-too-obviously a star turn.

Sunshine Hart and Lucien Littlefield, both longtime and long-in-the-tooth slapstick comedians with Mack Sennett and other studios, play Mary's parents for laughs, and earn those laughs with vigor. Less impressive is an overacting and unappealing "sexy" Carmelita Geraghty as the wild younger daughter whose involvement with an entirely inappropriate John Junior (as a greasy con man) leads the family to a night court presided over by a very serious, very professional, clean-shaven Mack Swain.

Hobart Bosworth, who could be either the world's biggest scenery-chewer or its most subtle underplayer as the whim seized him, surprises with his restrained performance here, though he still seems to think a variety of exaggerated smiles passes for great acting. Buddy Rogers starts out very uncomfortably, overplaying everything and acting with his great teeth, but he gradually settles down and becomes an effective performer. His somewhat gay aura meshes nicely with Pickford's distinctively female brand of toughness, and you can see why he (if not she) made it work the same way offscreen.

Bonus: A superstar as crucial as Pickford to the development of the movies and of the cult of stardom should probably have more than just one film in a list of 100 great comedies. Yet I found it unexpectedly challenging to identify *any* Pickford film that could reasonably qualify as a true comedy. Most of her films, even the earliest Biograph shorts, fall into the categories of sentimental romances, straight dramas, melodramas, and dramas with intervals of comedy. So right there, we have a problem finding a film that is *mostly* comic. You have to go back to her Biograph days to dig up *Wilful Peggy* (1910), in which Mary clearly has a lot of fun playing the title character, and it's fun to watch her, and the story is ridiculous enough that you look around for the young Mack Sennett and, yup, you find him in it; it's an enjoyable fast romp, but hardly typical of what we think of as a Mary Pickford film.

So *My Best Girl*, not strictly speaking a true comedy, is virtually by default the movie I have chosen as a representative vehicle for Mary Pickford.

THE MYSTERY OF THE LEAPING FISH

(1916, Triangle Films)

Director: John Emerson
Writer: Tod Browning
Titles: Anita Loos
Camera: John Leezer and Karl Brown
Cast: Douglas Fairbanks, Bessie Love, Alma Rubens, A. D. Sears, Tom Wilson, Charles Stevens, George Hall, Joe Murphy
Running Time (Length): Two reels

Background: In 1916 the drug scene in the United States was very different from what it would be in the 1920s, let alone 2016. Cocaine was not exactly illegal: it was a "controlled substance." Heroin was not illegal under any definition until 1924. Cannabis and marijuana were controlled haphazardly until the mid-1930s.

Drug-related deaths in the fledgling film industry were few and far between, and had no impact until matinee idol Wallace Reid died from withdrawal reactions in 1923. His widow, Dorothy Davenport, produced a couple of anti-drug films in his memory; this helped push legislators into enacting several drug control and drug prohibition laws, and both politicians and the medical establishment began to take addiction seriously, trying to curtail it by banning the substances that provoked it. The Volstead Act, which introduced the prohibition of liquor, was not a part of this campaign; it was enacted in 1919.

Still, that's three years *after* Douglas Fairbanks went totally against his offscreen beliefs and made *The Mystery of the Leaping Fish*, a film that celebrated extreme drug addiction as a hilarious gag and not incidentally was a rip at William Gillette's filming the same year of his lifelong role on the stage as Sherlock Holmes, he of the "seven percent solution," that is, cocaine.

That Fairbanks took on this film at all is quite a conundrum. Offscreen, he was famously a teetotaler who eschewed all artificial stimulants, legal or illegal, in favor of the most robust possible lifestyle of physical fitness and athletics. It is much more in keeping with his personal beliefs and character that, almost as soon as *The Mystery of the Leaping Fish* was finished, he disavowed it.

Many commentators have noted the irony that Alma Rubens plays a small role in this movie. She became, after Wallace Reid, the most famous victim of drug addiction in the silent era (although she actually died in 1931, long after the talkies had taken over). After making four films with Fairbanks early in his career, she, like Reid, veered into addiction to harder drugs after receiving some treatment with morphine. The last ten years of her life were years of addiction and failed treatment; although her death was officially due to complications from pneumonia, it seems likely that that illness would not have carried her off had her system not been ravished by the addictions.

Synopsis: He's the world greatest "scientific detective," whatever that is, and his suitably Sherlockian name is Coke Ennyday. Sounds real. He lives in one room behind multiple locked doors, and no wonder, with all those drugs he's got in there with him. He keeps his heroin close to his vest; in fact, his vest is composed of a line of about a dozen loaded hypodermics, which he pops into his hand veins every few seconds. In the intervals, he takes a giant powder puff, loads it up with cocaine from a cake-sized cookie tin, and powders his entire face with it, just to ensure he gets enough. And when he gets tired of that, there's a lobotomized-looking butler to mix him drinks entirely composed of poisons. What an old sobersides!

Duty calls the great "scientific detective" to the beach, where in short order he discovers a gang of cutthroats is smuggling opium from offshore boats into a Chinese laundry via "leaping fish," which turn out to be nothing more than inflatable mattresses for water fun. To make sure the opie is the real thing, "Ennyday" immediately consumes an entire tin of the stuff, with the punny result that he spends the rest of the picture "hopping" nonstop.

He's generous with the dope, too. When his own "leaping fish" isn't moving swiftly enough in the water, he kindly injects it with heroin, which sends it roaring off at motorboat speed. He overpowers the gang of smugglers by injecting them or by blowing an entire canister of cocaine into their faces, as well as beating up one and having girlfriend Bessie Love beat up another. Bessie finds this endearing enough to let her genuine giggles show, and you just know theirs is a match made in heaven.

Comment: Anybody who thinks "old black-and-white silent movies" are the ultimate in uncool, unhip entertainment needs to see *The Mystery of the Leaping Fish*. Nothing could be more eye-popping than those opening scenes of Fairbanks snorting cocaine by the faceful, pumping heroin into his veins every ten seconds, knocking back poison cocktails, and having a whale of a time doing it. Those checkered clothes are probably a bit too dressy for today's hipsters, but coordinating them with a checkered car is totally redeeming.

Even with official maniac Tod Browning writing the scenario, the film couldn't possibly maintain its opening level of insanity. It sure tries, though. This is druggie slapstick of a kind we've gotten used to, post–baby boomer, first with "Cheech and Chong" (Cheech Marin and Tommy Chong), later with "Harold and Kumar" (Kal Penn and John Cho); but *Leaping Fish* was the first and by far the funniest, even if you're watching it while not stoned. Plus, Fairbanks is doing everything solo that the later comedians needed a duo to attempt, and they still came up way, way, way short of Fairbanks's mark.

Bonus: As Fairbanks anticipated the druggie comics of two and three generations later, so Tod Browning anticipated the later weirdo writer-directors such as David Lynch. Browning got his start in films with, inappropriately enough, the stiff and straightlaced D. W. Griffith, not only as an actor but also as an assistant director. He didn't really let his freak flag fly until teaming up with fellow strange-guy Lon Chaney in several of the latter's last movies, beginning in 1925. He certainly hit his peak of idiosyncrasy with *Freaks* in 1932, a film that took horror into realms that would remain mostly untouched (other than by the sanitized grade-B monster movies of the 1950s) until the television series *American Horror Story: Freak Show* in 2014–2015. Obviously, the burst of insanity he unleashed in 1916 with the script of *Mystery of the Leaping Fish* turned out to be an isolated and anachronistic harbinger of bizarrities to come.

N

THE NAVIGATOR

(1924, Buster Keaton Productions/Metro Pictures)

Directors: Buster Keaton and Donald Crisp
Writers: Clyde Bruckman, Joseph Mitchell, and Jean Havez
Camera: Elgin Lessley and Byron Houck
Cast: Buster Keaton, Kathryn McGuire, Frederick Vroom, Noble Johnson, Clarence Burton, H. M. Clugston
Running Time (Length): Six reels
Availability: DVD (Kino Video)

Background: What would you do if you had $25,000 to squander and you were told it was enough to buy a steamship that would otherwise be scrapped? If you were a lifetime professional comedian like Buster Keaton, you wouldn't hesitate to plunk down that $25,000 on the spot because you would know a steamship could be comic gold. It's only later that you would gather your comedy brain trust and sit down with them to think up a movie to write around the boat.

Synopsis: A couple of unnamed countries are at war. One of them discovers the other has bought a steamship, the *Navigator,* and—since they are apparently all old men and have no one fit to lead a Doug Fairbanks–style takeover of the ship—they decide the only way to sabotage it is to set it adrift and hope it wanders out of reach.

Back in another unnamed country that looks a lot like the ritzier neighborhoods of the United States, Buster in his favorite rich-idiot role wakes up and decides to marry the rich-idiot girl across the street. Although he goes ahead and books the honeymoon voyage, his would-be bride demurs. He won't let that ruin his plans. He rips up her ticket and takes his own to the pier for a very early pre-boarding. Kathryn, seeking her abducted father—and that's the last we ever see of *him,* apparently a collateral victim of war—ends up on board the same ship at night. It is cast adrift by the dastardly fiends; they have successfully sabotaged it by leaving it to the care of Buster and Kathryn, which is almost as good as leaving it with two giant bombs, fuses a-burning.

They aren't really stupid; they simply have never had to do anything for themselves. This does not faze them. With the complete confidence of wealthy socialites who know their own value—because it's published right there in the Blue Book of bluebloods—they prepare breakfast in the galley that was designed to feed hundreds. Six raw beans in a pail of salt water ought to produce a lovely coffee, and the bacon looks so debonair after Kathryn ties each slice into a bow before burning it.

There follows a series of skits at night in which they are frightened by "natural" phenomena. These are basely contrived clichés of the old-haunted-house type: one banging door nudges a record player into singing the ominous song "Asleep in the Deep," a series of cabin doors swing open and slam shut in eerie syncopation, a portrait of a menacing old gob is mistaken for an evil spy, there just happens to be a warehouse-sized cache of fireworks (stored *in the boiler room*, for pete's sake!), and so on. They are all well done, but the material before and after them is so superior and so original that you can't help feeling rather disappointed about these silly old put-ons.

Things perk up again when the ship runs aground in the shallows in front of an island of cannibals. Kathryn helps Buster into a deep-sea-diver suit; being a good Second Amendment American, he sticks a handgun inside his weight belt. He goes below to perpetrate a terrifically funny underwater scene, one of the highlights of which is his conscientious washing of his hands in a scooped-up pail of water, "drying" them with his handkerchief, and pitching the dirty water into the, er, water. Meanwhile, above surface, the cannibals have taken Kathryn home to dinner—to *be* the dinner. Buster's rescue of her is another wonderfully entertaining sequence (nobody ever got so many laughs out of a deep-sea-diver suit). They do battle with the cannibals aboard the *Navigator*, escape from it into the limitless sea, and then are saved by a *deus ex machina* courtesy of the navy.

Comment: There are so many delightful belly laughs in this film that some fans consider it, pound for pound, the funniest that Keaton ever made—not the greatest, the funniest. Its weaknesses of construction make it look somewhat slapdash overall, but each set piece is beautifully constructed within itself. The early scenes of Keaton in his house with his butler are ingenious; the proof is that every element of these scenes has been stolen over and over again by other comedy films, particularly social comedies. The dancelike coordination of their search efforts when they each wake up on the *Navigator* and sense they are not alone—which has also been stolen countless times by other films—reminds one of the meticulous music boxes of the 18th century, in which figurines on three levels rotate elegantly in and out of a shelter in time to a waltz. And, as noted above, Keaton in his sea-diver's outfit is one of the greatest and most original extended gag sequences you'll ever see.

Bonus: As I have argued elsewhere, Keaton's characters (in the silent films, not his talkie films) are never dumbbells; they are merely inexperienced. His first experience with anything is uproarious because of his misguided confidence in his own ability to be the instant master of the unknown. The disastrous first results perplex him almost not at all; he quickly invents his own way of "correctly" getting the job done, which it does, only not in the way all the rest of us "masters" are accustomed to doing it. It's a series of disconnects from our expectations: you cannot anticipate a Keaton solution. You can only burst out in the laughter of someone caught off-guard by a hilarious joke on yourself.

THE NERVOUS WRECK

(1926, Christie)

Director: Scott Sidney
Writer: F. McGrew Willis
Titles: Walter Graham
Camera: Alex Phillips and Fred Jacquemin
Cast: Harrison Ford, Phyllis Haver, Hobart Bosworth, Mack Swain, Chester Conklin, Vera Steadman, Paul Nicholson, Charles Gerard, Clarence Burton
Running Time (Length): 73 minutes (seven reels)
Availability: DVD (Grapevine Video)

Background: Toughening-up wussy namby-pambys is one of the most enduring plots of American movies. It's peculiarly American because of the national myths: this rough'n'tumble country, the country of he-men, the heroic giants who conquered the West and then won every war ever fought (especially the wars that the United States didn't even participate in!), the land of football players and heavyweight boxing champions, the bullies of business . . . No other country's people were ever so fixated on proving their manliness, even when they're women.

By this ethos, anyone on American soil who is a wimp without the excuse of being a "foreigner" or a cowardly villain must need a kick in the pants to eject his *cojones* from their hiding place deep inside his pelvic cavity and get them down into his manly scrotum where they belong. In our own era, this is why American films are full of comic-book superheroes who are bespectacled pushovers in their "secret identities"; quaking-stomached spacemen who must undergo alien adversity to become fearless conquerors of the universe; and even benign, inanimate toy cars that get transform(er)ed into behemoth killing machines. In the silent era, this was the basis for dozens of films about young men who believe themselves to be at death's door but find themselves drawn (by love) into a maelstrom of action and violence that proves they were just deluding themselves when they thought they were ill little pussies. They're actually accomplished brawlers and therefore deserving of the beautiful girl who had been hanging around them unnoticed and unappreciated. Hurray for America!

Synopsis: He's gonna *die!* So delicate, pill-popping, hypochondriac "Henry" (Harrison Ford), one finger on his pulse and a thermometer in his mouth, comes to Arizona to die in the wide open West. The ranch he picks for his final days is owned by Hobart Bosworth, whose daughter "Sally" (Phyllis Haver) takes one look at the city wimp and decides she's going to marry him instead of the overweight sheriff to whom her daddy has betrothed her. "Henry," in turn, takes one forkful of her cooking and decides he might have found something to live for after all.

This doesn't sit well with the trigger-happy sheriff, especially when "Sally" impetuously leaves a note that she and "Henry" have eloped. Sheriff and daddy set out, separately but simultaneously, to head off the impertinent couple at a ranch "in another part of Arizona" (as the intertitles tell us). The reason the couple haven't gotten past this second ranch is because they've been shanghaied to cook and wait upon "the Governor" and his entourage, who happen to be the same carful of self-important snobs whom "Henry" had heisted for gas along the road.

Much noisy (but silent!) chaos ensues as people insult one another, fire off their guns, throw food, and generally do all those strenuous exercises necessary to release "Henry" from the lethal spell of his own hypochondria and to convince Bosworth that the wimp is worthy of his daughter's hand.

Comment: There are some weaknesses in this Wild West twist on the same story that had been used so often in other feature films. Even in a farce, there is no way "Henry" and "Sally" could have survived their car's plunge down a steep, long, rocky mountainside: it's not similar to the Keystone trope of having a car plunge down a short grassy *hillside*. The sheriff's fear of thunder and lightning is the worst sort of *deus ex machina* dredged up to give the scriptwriters a cop-out from the sheriff's otherwise-inescapable final confrontation with "Henry": he's got "Henry" not only with a tight noose around his neck but with a sharpshooter's gun point-blanking at his heart, but the sheriff is run off by a little rain. Sure. And the intertitles strain too hard for humor, missing by wide margins, as when "Sally" complains her life is so boring that she's half-willing to bite a rattlesnake for the excitement.

The cast gives this film an extra bit of cachet, as it usually does with this story-line. (It's a bit like seeing completely different but interesting casts tackle *Twelfth Night* each year at the Stratford Shakespeare Festival—not that this material is on the same level as Shakespeare.) Harrison Ford is Harrison Ford; it's nice to see him being feisty when he isn't being his usual clueless dork. Hobart Bosworth is not the guy you expect to find in a Western setting, but he's on his best be-havior here, other than laughing uproariously a bit too often. Mack Swain, *sans* moustache, and Chester Conklin, *avec* moustache, don't have scenes together; nonetheless, their mutual presence arouses smiles at the memories of "Ambrose" and "Walrus"; Swain gets ample opportunity to blow everyone else off the screen with his flamboyance and size, while Conklin gets some fun spots in the kitchen scenes. Vera Steadman appears to be contemptuous of the whole thing and is a bit of a drag, while Paul Nicholson as the sheriff is a doughy, overaged, numbingly uninteresting fiancé, a complete mismatch for "Sally," and you don't get the sense this character is much of a stretch for the real Nicholson.

Which brings us to Phyllis Haver. Her gorgeous, luminescent blonde beauty (even her skin looks glowingly peroxided) practically washes out the screen, it's so bright and light. She has a dynamite smile to go with it. As an actress and comedian, she handles everything she's given with professional aplomb and spirit, even when that involves sucking on a siphon hose to draw gas out of Swain's car . . . and then gag-ging on it, spitting it out, letting it dribble out of her mouth in genuine revulsion, and all this done in extreme close-up, as if director Scott Sidney wanted to deface her beauty in full view of the audience. She reacts to the disgusting mouthful of fluid with complete naturalness—it's not an act when she does everything possible to get the taste out of her mouth—and she's still professional enough to avoid smearing her makeup, even the heavy lipstick. Haver is *always* worth watching!

Bonus: Much is made of the license number on "Henry's" car, as it is the clue that Swain's entourage uses to identify the refugee at the ranch. What the film-makers could never have anticipated was the future significance of the second set of numbers on the plate: 007.

A NIGHT IN THE SHOW

(1915, Essanay)

Director: Charles Chaplin
Writer: Charles Chaplin
Camera: Harry Ensign
Editor: Charles Chaplin
Cast: Charlie Chaplin, Edna Purviance, John Rand, James T. Kelly, Fred Goodwin, Dee Lampton, Paddy McGuire, Bud Jamison, Carrie Clarke Ward, Leo White, May White
Running Time (Length): Two reels
Availability: DVD (Image Entertainment: *Chaplin's Essanay Comedies*, vol. 3)

Background: Although he had been noticed with praise in several theatrical endeavors both before and during his association with the Fred Karno Pantomime Company in England, as a very young man Charlie Chaplin really made his mark—his first mark—on the history of comedy in a skit called, originally, *Mumming Birds*. This was the same skit that had already proven the launching pad for wildly admired comedians of the British stage, notably Billy Reeves and Billy Ritchie, both of whom subsequently squandered the rest of their lives mewling about Chaplin having stolen their act. Stan Laurel also made his mark in this sketch, understudying Chaplin and then succeeding him in the main role; Laurel did not spend the rest of his life sniping at Chaplin but rather went out of his way to insist "Chaplin was the greatest" and a great friend too. Chaplin disproved his friendliness by eliminating all mention of Laurel from his autobiography; he never could bring himself to praise those whom he viewed as his true peers and rivals.

When the Karno troupe toured America, the show Karno himself had designed for overseas consumption (*The Wow-wows*) proved a dismal bomb. In desperation, *Mumming Birds* was retitled *A Night in an English Music Hall* and Chaplin's presence in a dual role ("Mr. Pest" and "Mr. Rowdy") guaranteed it would be recognized as an ingenious comedy. Mack Sennett saw this American stage version and made an offer to hire Chaplin for his Keystone Studio, which arguably turned out to be the one single act that created the motion picture as the cultural and entertainment colossus as we know it.

Synopsis: The English music hall of the late 19th century and early 20th century was virtually the same thing as the American vaudeville: that is, a troupe of diverse acts plied their talents in the lead-up to a long sketch or playlet (which could be comedy or melodrama) and traveled the country with the show, playing ten or so times every week to a live audience.

Prior to signing with Sennett, Chaplin had played these circuits literally all his life: his birth father and his mother were both music hall performers, and his elder brother, Sydney Chaplin (a comedian in his own right; see *The Better 'Ole*), created a third set of footsteps for Charlie to follow into the world of clown-white greasepaint.

As its title makes obvious, *A Night in* (or *at*; the latter rolls more naturally off the tongue but is incorrect) *the Show* presents a full bill of typical music hall performers, all of them inept and untalented: the phony strongman, the mismatched duet singers, the snake charmer, the fire-eater. Since these are verbal acts—all are seen talking or singing, without intertitles to tell us *what* they are saying or singing—the comedy is provided mostly offstage: Chaplin as the extremely drunk aristocrat "Mr. Pest" in the expensive seats and eventually in a box seat, and as the equally drunk and equally obnoxious "Mr. Rowdy" in the cheap balcony seats. Despite the huge cast of spectators and the many stage acts, it's a one-man, two-character show. And he is a riot in both roles.

Comments: One potential drawback to enjoying this blast from a very distant past is the amount of laughing the onscreen audience does. If you're one of those viewers who detests such scenes, be warned there are a lot of them, with a lot of people in each one. It isn't exactly Red Skelton, since Chaplin never laughs at his own antics in either of the roles he plays, and the audience really does appear to be laughing spontaneously rather than on cue; this should make it tolerable to all but the most irritable viewer.

This is also a quite violent film, although not in the sense that anyone gets hurt in anything other than his or her feelings. A great many things get thrown, including the powerful stream of water from a fire hose. Mr. Pest gets into several fights and near fights, and Mr. Rowdy gets into one. Musical instruments are abused and misused. Drunkenness, as was the norm for the era, is treated as a hoot-and-a-half in itself. But then, if you dislike comic violence, you probably shouldn't be watching a silent comedy, even if it does star Charlie Chaplin.

Bonus: We are truly blessed that Chaplin had the brainstorm of filming this phenomenally influential skit, for it preserved forever the British music hall bill at its Victorian–Edwardian peak, as well as preserving the best thing the legendary Karno ever created; it goes a long way toward explaining the astounding popularity, influence, and power Karno held in the British imagination for a generation. The man developed almost as many of history's greatest comedians as Sennett did, and his dominance in British humor was such that the British Empire's troops marched into World War I singing the satiric ditty, "We Are Fred Karno's Army," which includes the lines "Fred Karno is our Captain / Charlie Chaplin our O.C."

THE NOISE OF BOMBS

(1914, Sennett)

Director: Uncredited, possibly Mack Sennett
Cast: Charlie Murray, Edgar Kennedy, Lucille Ward, Dixie Chene, Josef Swickard, Harry McCoy, Eddie Cline, Charles Parrott (Charley Chase)
Running Time (Length): One reel

Background: The Keystone Cops were assembled incrementally over the earliest days of the Keystone Studio, which is to say 1912–1914. Brent Walker, the ultimate authority on all things Sennett and author of *Mack Sennett's Fun Factory* (2010), identifies *The Man Next Door* (1913) as the first "Keystone Cops" film. Although they didn't appear in as many films as people assume, the Cops became the indelible icon of Keystone films, then and now. Most of the best-known Keystone male comedians of the 1910s put in an appearance as a Cop at some point, including even Charlie Chaplin.

A single performer was forever pegged as the spirit of the Cops: Ford Sterling. As the incompetent, duplicitous, corrupt, mewling, groveling, hypocritical "Chief Teheezel," Sterling put his goateed and bespectacled face on movie history forever. It was a face contorted into wildly exaggerated emotions and loudly mouthed plot narration for the benefit of his devoted immigrant audience (who pretty much learned everything they knew about English from lip-reading him); he was famous for nattering on ceaselessly while acting for the unhearing camera because that was how he made himself comfortable while performing.

Without deliberate irony, I have chosen a Cops film that does not feature Sterling. In 1914 he was off on an ego trip, quitting Sennett with delusions of becoming a superstar under the totally inept guidance of Henry "Pathé" Lehrman. In true "Teheezel" fashion, he cringed his apologetic and humiliated way back into Keystone the next year, his reputation forever blotted. During his absence from the force, no real attempt was made to replace him; various veterans were wheeled in to fill the role of "chief" for one or two films, and the role itself was downplayed. That's why, in *The Noise of Bombs*, the focus is on a regular cop (Charlie Murray) with the chief (Edgar Kennedy) being still a key role but not the center of the gags as it was with Sterling.

Synopsis: Sergeant Charlie Murray isn't a bad cop; he's just a sleepy one. That's why he was resting his eyes on a park bench when he was disturbed by Chief Edgar Kennedy bum-rushing a quartet of toughs out of the bushes and pell-mell over Murray's bench. Despite this less-than-valorous example of his work ethic, Murray is entrusted with the chief's baby son by its nurse while she traipses off in search of a treat. The toughs, seeking revenge, force both Murray and the baby to vanish from the park and transport them to the gang's hangout, which proves to be a shack conveniently loaded to the rafters with clearly marked crates of dynamite and bombs. Perhaps they timeshared it with Larry Semon.

While furiously smoking away in the presence of all this combustible weaponry, the gang comes up with a great idea: they'll send Murray off to the chief's house with a time-fuse bomb, to be planted therein along with a note warning the chief that the bomb will go off in ten minutes and, by the way, his baby is in their adoring safekeeping.

Murray manages to get into the chief's house and leave the note, but before he can find a good hiding place for the bomb, the chief and his wife arrive home and find the note. Being a good cop, Chief Kennedy naturally panics and . . . calls the Cops, forgetting just how inept his underlings are. At the station, they are leisurely dusting, cleaning, swatting flies, nothing to do, no crimes to bust, so they leap into action at the phoned-in behest of their boss.

Meanwhile, Murray, being a Keystone Cop himself, has the brainwave (a flat-line in the case of every Cop) of hiding himself with the bomb in a large chest.

The time fuse on the bomb has the temerity to ignite at this point, but it's okay, because it's going to prove itself the slowest-burning fuse in history.

Somehow, eventually, Murray manages to flee the chief's house with bomb in hand (fuse still burning), chased by the Cops and the thieves in separate bunches, and ends up back in the shack. Trading the bomb for the baby, he climbs out on the rooftop and insanely gets away by hauling himself hand over hand on the electric wires, the baby dangling by its wrapper held in Murray's teeth. The thieves break back into the shack; now that Murray and baby are both safely away, the Cops settle back to watch the bomb finally explode and take everything in the shack with it, including (implicitly) the thieves.

Comment: It's the little jokes that make this a great Keystone Cops film. Without Sterling around to entertain us (and eat up the minutes) with his extravagant hamming, there is finally space for these little gags, and they are delicious. The Cops cleaning the station with the delicacy of refined maids earns a huge guffaw. The desperadoes all smoking up a storm in a dynamite shack elicits a steady stream of anticipatory giggles. Murray has a wonderful throwaway when the gang hands him the bomb: he accidentally pokes the end of the long fuse into his own eye, and as if that isn't funny enough, in a reactive fit of pique he almost flings the bomb down at his own feet, barely stopping himself in time to remember that doing so would blow himself up. While he's hiding in the chest, he briefly sticks his head out of one end in order to catch a breath, and Kennedy's wife unwittingly sits down on the chest; Murray's neck is visibly crushed, and you half expect his head to become detached and roll off the set.

Although the Cops don't really race around in their jalopy and this film is not representative of their antics on that score, *The Noise of Bombs* is still a terrific representative of the one-reel paeans to their madcap zaniness.

Bonus: One of the greatest, if not *the* greatest second-banana comedians in movie history, Edgar Kennedy is very much the second banana to Charlie Murray in this film, even though Kennedy is playing the chief. He is, however, unrecognizable in it. For one thing, he sports the usual Sennett horsetail across his upper lip. For another, he still has hair on the top of his head. Once he started losing his hair, Kennedy went completely bald on top very quickly; it's hard to tell from film and photographs, particularly because he used toupees to varying extents, but it seems he became a chrome-dome in the space of about one year, 1918–1919.

The Noise of Bombs doesn't offer him any opportunities to launch the "slow burn" reaction that became his stock in trade. Truth to tell, it doesn't give him any opportunity to stand out at all: he races around at a speed the mature Kennedy would find breathtaking, he gets angry at Murray instead of exasperated, and his frustration is not drawn out for comic effect but rather is the normal frustration of an efficient man at the bungling of an inefficient co-worker.

Kennedy freelanced a lot throughout the 1920s, building up his reputation as a supporting comic and a director. It wasn't until he joined Roach at the tail end of the silent era, 1928, that he finally hit the high points of his long, long career. *The Noise of Bombs* offers us a nice chance to see him before the glory crowned that shiny pate.

NOW YOU TELL ONE

(1926, Bowers Comedy Corporation)

Creator: Charley Bowers
Cast: Charley Bowers, all others unidentified
Running Time (Length): 22 minutes (two reels)
Availability: DVD (Image Entertainment: *Charley Bowers: The Rediscovery of an American Comic Genius*)

Background: One of the strangest, most accomplished, and mysterious creators in the silent era was a little man named Charley Bowers, who bore a distinct physical resemblance to the young (dark-haired) Charlie Chaplin crossed with Buster Keaton. Much like Larry Semon and Harry Langdon (among others), his youth and—some say—even his childhood found him immersed in the circus, live theatre, cartooning, and early film animation. Restless by his mid-thirties, he practically invented a form he called "the Bowers process" that combined all of his work genres into one outlet: live-action film integrated with stop-motion mechanical animation and puppet-animation methods that presented life as an engineer's stage fantasy.

He made about two dozen of these peculiar movies, if you include a couple he created in the talkie era as commercial promotions. Then they, and he, more or less disappeared. The discovery of a few of his films in French archives in the 1960s and 1970s did little to propagate his achievement. It took another 30 years for resurrection to take place: Image Entertainment and Lobster Films restored most of his available work and released them on DVD in 2003. This served to win him, at last, recognition as a true eccentric genius of the 1920s. If he was not a great comedian, he was most certainly a great filmmaker of a totally unique comic achievement.

Synopsis: The Liars Club has had a very disappointing meeting. Liar #1 told of 47 elephants marching into the Capitol building in Washington, D.C., to fete him and Mussolini (we are shown the elephants, but not the dictator). Liar #2 claimed to have swum the English Channel on the back of a cyclist, swathed in pepper body grease to make the sharks sneeze. Liar #3 found the lost chord, beating the Moody Blues rock band by 42 years. Liar #4 complains these lies all have too much truth in them, and he walks out in disgust. Spotting Charley Bowers trying to blow his own head off with a cannon, he brings Bowers into the Liars Club to tell his story.

Bowers explains he invented a process to graft anything. Grafting eggplant produces a gourd containing an egg and a salt shaker; a drop of his liquid on a straw causes it to grow into a straw hat right on his head; shoelaces grow from a planter and lace themselves into his boots. He goes outside to demonstrate his invention to farmers. The first farmer has an entire tree grow through his clothes. The second has a decorated miniature Christmas tree grow on the handle of his plow.

Entering the house of an attractive girl, Bowers finds it full of mice—gun-toting mice. He grows dozens of cats out of a pussy-willow graft to eat all the mice.

Thinking this has earned him the right to the girl's hand—this is a two-reel slap-stick comedy, after all—Bowers asks the elderly farmer for his approval. He can't give it, because the girl is not his daughter, she's his wife!

Comment: The liars' competition is a very good framing device for the tall tales Bowers tells, and he brings the film to a close with a fine return to the competition. It was not common for Bowers to take this much care to develop a storyline, which elevates *Now You Tell One* above most of his available output (about half of his films are still missing). Aside from that, of course, the amazing effects are the principal attraction of this extraordinary comedy.

What is really staggering is his skill in showing things grow while a nearby living prop creates the illusion of complete fluidity. While the straw is weaving itself into a hat on his own head, Bowers himself continues working and moving with complete naturalness and no time disruptions. Even more impressive is the scene of cats growing tail-first out of the pussy-willow plant; the third cat grows directly onto a shelf less than a couple of inches from the tree, from which it watches the subsequent cats grow and run off, *with its tail twitching and waving through it all in unbroken movement.*

As everyone who enthuses about Bowers's work keeps exclaiming, he did all of this without the help of CGI or even traditional animated drawings. "The Bowers process" proves to be every bit as incredible as his character's "process of grafting."

Bonus: Every film Bowers made in 1926–1928 is worth watching. But they should be watched at a rate of no more than one per day or per session. Watching even two of them back-to-back is a bit of an enervating experience. This is due in part to their mechanical nature. They are rather lacking in the human touch; you admire them immensely, you could spend a lot of time analyzing how they were made, you marvel at their seamlessness . . . but you never really feel affectionate about them.

OH! DOCTOR!

(1925, Universal)

Director: Harry Pollard
Writer: Harvey Thew
Camera: Gilbert Warrenton
Cast: Reginald Denny, Mary Astor, Otis Harlan, William B. Mong, Tom Ricketts, Lucille Ward, Mike Donlin, Clarence Geldart, Blanche Payson, George Kuwa, Martha Mattox, Helen Lynch
Running Time (Length): 63 minutes in surviving print (original length was approximately seven reels)
Availability: DVD (Grapevine Video)

Background: Another actor with an incredibly long career in the movies (47 years), Reginald Denny in the 1920s made a good living in light comedy features that often recycled warhorse storylines in bright new ways. The hypochondriac transformed by love into an adventurer whose recklessness would make Doug Fairbanks tremble was a plot already rendered hackneyed by Fairbanks himself, Harold Lloyd, Buster Keaton, Harrison Ford, even Roscoe Arbuckle. Denny and ace comedy director Harry Pollard (not the same person as silent comedian Harry "Snub" Pollard) even used the same situations as others, yet they created a sheen of freshness that enlivened the material. Denny was no slapstick comedian but a genuine comic actor with real chops.

Synopsis: Having been born prematurely, "Rufus" (Denny) is seen as a lifelong cash cow by a collection of un-Hippocratic medicos and insurance scammers, who together raise him as the hypochondriac to end all hypochondriacs. Notwithstanding their strict regimen of no excitement, no exercise, and pretty well no food, "Rufus" grows up to be a handsome fellow with a noticeably firm body, which they present to him as a weak, sickly near corpse. Word gets out that the father of "Rufus" has left him a fortune that, however, he cannot touch for three years. The Three Stooges of insurance—"Clinch," "McIntosh," and "Peck" (played by Harlan, Mong, and Ricketts, respectively)—have him sign over the fortune in exchange for a $100,000 advance to be used to hire a nurse to usher the premature baby to a premature death. The goal, of course, is to convince "Rufus" he is dying

177

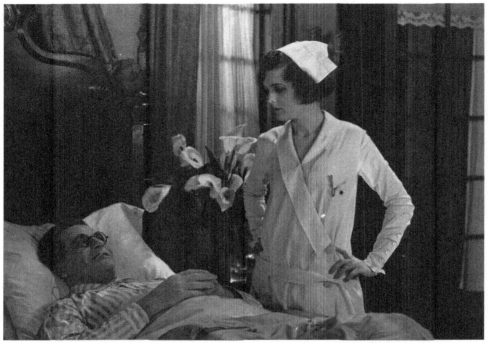

The indescribably gorgeous Mary Astor is not fooled by Reginald Denny's hypochondria in *Oh! Doctor!* (1924). *Courtesy of Derek Boothroyd*

well within the three-year marination period, and squeezing his last breaths just past the date when the money is his, whereupon it immediately becomes theirs.

The nurse they hire proves too right for the job: the splendidly nicknamed "Death Watch Mary" (Mattox) has no patience for the three-year timeline, preferring faster action. The triad of greed replace her with "Dolores Hicks" (Astor), whose beauty alone will certainly be medicine enough to keep any young man feeling coltish for three years, if not a lifetime. And the lifetime, of course, is precisely what entails, because "Rufus's" love of "Dolores" gets him out of his invalid's bed and living life to the fullest, up to and including climbing the flagpole at the top of a skyscraper.

Comment: This storyline, as noted above, was shopworn long before 1925, whereas Denny's 1926 version of the theatrical chestnut *Skinner's Dress Suit* was one of the freshest and most forward-looking productions of the era. Nonetheless, *Oh! Doctor!* is the equal of the later film in simple, easygoing funniness.

Denny's "type" was common in the Twenties: William Haines, Glenn Tryon, Charles Ray, Wallace Reid, Ralph Graves, Douglas MacLean, Harrison Ford, and many others all essayed the cheerful all-American "boy" whose basic decency, good humor, and relentless physical drive enabled him to overcome all odds to win the girl, the job, the money, and the good life. Denny was as accomplished as any of them, and moreover brought a certain aura of classiness that was no doubt an attribute of his English upbringing. Born in Surrey, he spent his childhood and adolescence on the British stage; after ten years of comic stardom as the (presumed American) lead in silent features, he enjoyed another ten years of comic support as the clearly British twit in sound features and B-movies, including the "Bulldog Drummond" series, before fading out in supporting roles for quintessentially American comedians including Bob Hope (*My Favorite Brunette*, 1947), Danny Kaye (*The Secret Life of Walter Mitty*, 1947), Cary Grant (English born, it is true, but mythologically American; *Mr. Blandings Builds His Dream House*, 1948), Abbott and Costello *(Meet Dr. Jekyll and Mr. Hyde*, 1953), and, er, Adam West and Burt Ward (*Batman*, 1966).

Mary Astor's performance is somewhat forced, stiff, and uncomfortable; there are only a few scenes in which she relaxes or in which she can escape her self-consciousness and give a physical performance, such as the flagpole sequence. Still only 19 years old and in the full flush of her young beauty, she somehow wears a baggy nurse's uniform in a way that lets you know she has on absolutely nothing underneath it and that you would be welcome to join her inside it.

While Denny and Astor engage in the sophisticated repartee of light social comedy, the rest of the cast delivers the broad physical slapstick that keeps audiences happy. Each of the three insurance muggers indulges in obsessive behavior (Ricketts, for instance, delicately paces out a triangle on the floor, while Harlan compulsively shreds paper when rattled) and unsubtle facial contortions (Mong) while overreacting to each ebb and flow in "Rufus's" health. All of the medical personnel (Astor, Geldart, Mattox, Payson) play it straight but, other than Astor, have parts that are written as caricatures and that play off against the insurance men. Helen Lynch plays the maid as a flirtatious good-time gal; modern audiences may hoot at her "hot" jazz-dance demonstration.

Bonus: Blanche Payson was a physically titanic comedian who provided scary-funny support to films from the middle of World War I to the middle of World War II. Allegedly 6'4" and weighing well over 200 pounds, she spent a brief period in her real life as a policewoman, which Mack Sennett's hyperbolic publicity machine exaggerated into a jailhouse reign of terror from which women's prison matron Payson emerged undefeated, unbloodied, and unbowed.

She doesn't look that imposing in *Oh! Doctor!*, possibly because several of the other performers were tall men (Mong, Denny, Geldart) and one (Ricketts) was as fat as a turnip. Payson plays an osteopath who wrestles Denny in a clearly painful version of Chaplin's to-do with masseuse Henry Bergman in *The Cure* (1917). She plays it, as she did most of her post-Sennett characters, grimly straight, which in this case may have been a mistake; some comic stretching on her part might have made the forced stretching of Denny's corpus a little more delicti to the wincing viewer.

ONE WET NIGHT

(1924, Universal)

Director: William Watson
Cast: Alice Howell, Bert Roach, Neely Edwards, Tiny Sandford
Running Time (Length): 11 minutes (one reel)
Availability: DVD (Classic Video Streams: *Anthology Series: Forgotten Comics*, vol. 2)

Background: Stan Laurel allegedly said Lucille Ball was the best female comedian of all time, but that Alice Howell was not far behind her—which provoked everyone else to wonder: "Who the hell is Alice Howell?"

Howell spent years in various live theatre circuits, including both vaudeville and burlesque (the latter being merely a venue for lowbrow humor at the time, not for stripteasing), before entering the movies at Keystone in 1914. This move was the result of relocating to California with her husband for the sake of his health; they both ended up in slapstick, although the husband, Dick Smith, soon narrowed his activities to offscreen responsibilities.

Mack Sennett was never particularly supportive of the concept of "funny women"; he let Howell drift away in search of greater stardom and more money, which she found at Universal (and, briefly, Reelcraft). During her 1924–1925 stint at Universal, she was teamed with a couple of nondescript comedians named Neely Edwards and Bert Roach. This threesome appeared in several one-reelers notable for being short, fast, funny, and frequently quite zany—the Sennett spirit would always define the Howell humor, even if she did imbue it with the un-Sennettesque conviction that a woman could be every bit as physically hilarious as a man.

Synopsis: It's a one-reeler, so there isn't time for any fancy-schmancy plot intricacies. Even at that, though, the first half of the short 11-minute running time is rather squandered: the idiot butler (Bert Roach) waters the lawn in the midst of a raging downpour, the carefree wife (Howell) phones her husband (Neely Edwards) at work to remind him to take his umbrella, Edwards gets mud-soaked on the homeward drive, and he arrives to find the stupid butler has hung all of his other suits to "air" in the rain, so he has to borrow one of the butler's own oversized set of dry clothes.

A couple of friends come over for "a sociable evening," and that's when the fun really starts. Tiny Sandford, the husband of the couple, contrives to blast a hole in the ceiling, which apparently also destroys a massive water pipe; how else to explain the consequent deluge? Everyone tries to "save the rug" from a soaking by catching the Niagara Falls of water in various containers, most of which they promptly empty onto the floor, and one of which is a grand piano, whose keys when pressed will now squirt a stream of water into the face of the nearest actor, much to their own hilarity.

With the room drenched from both the ceiling and the floor (where Sandford had drilled through to another water pipe), and everyone looking as sopping as if they had gone down with the *Titanic*, Sandford reluctantly takes his farewell with the explanation, "We'd better go before we get wet!"

Comment: It's really a pretty stupid film, but like so many, many, *many* a stupid film, it is stupidly uproarious. You can't help laughing yourself sick even while shrieking in disbelief at the sheer idiocy of what these people are doing. Really: rolling a *grand piano* under a spouting hole in a deliberate attempt to catch all the falling water, just to *save a rug*?! Shoving a movable bathtub under the downpour with the reasoning that when the tub is full, all you will have to do is pull the plug and all the water will disappear? These people are crazy! And you'll laugh like crazy!

Bonus: A few of Howell's films are slowly becoming more available to the public, and this is wonderful news. Her films have the old-time zip and bang of Keystone at its wildest, and unlike some of the other determinedly physical female slapstick artists such as Gale Henry, Howell isn't trying to beat the boys at their own shtick; she plays women's roles *as* a woman, finds the physical humor in them, and presents that humor as every bit as zany and funny as anything male slapstick artists have extracted from men's roles.

ON LOCATION

(1921, Hal Roach/Rolin)

Director: Charley Chase
Writer: Hal Roach (uncredited: Charley Chase)
Cast: Snub Pollard, Marie Mosquini, Noah Young, George Rowe, Tiny Ward, Mark Jones, Wallace Howe, William Gillespie
Running Time (Length): One reel

Background: If there was ever a person who proved timing was everything in the movies, it was Snub Pollard. Not that Pollard had great timing as a *comedian*. No, his great timing all took place offscreen. Born in Australia as Harry Frazer (so he clearly had no relation to the terrific silent comedy director who was legitimately named Harry Pollard, nor was he related to Daphne Pollard who was born Daphne Trott and was *not* his sister), he was luckily stranded near Los Angeles in 1915 when that city was experiencing its explosive growth into the movie capital of the world. He luckily washed up at the doorstep of Hal Roach just when that producer was looking for someone to play second banana to an emerging genius named Harold Lloyd. After four years of this work, Pollard was luckily engaged by Charley Chase to star in a new series of comedies to fill a niche in the Roach production lineup. Chase being one of the greatest and most versatile of silent comedy geniuses, he couldn't help but put his hand in to make sure this new set of films would be worthy of the brand name that had already eclipsed Mack Sennett's. Pollard's timing just couldn't have been luckier.

Synopsis: Dumbbell Pollard is hired as a gardener by a trusting elderly couple and is asked to house-watch for them while they go off to the gossip parlors. It's a beautiful house on a beautiful lot, born to be made the setting of a Civil War film, which is precisely what director Noah Young and cameraman George Rowe have been searching for. With idiot Pollard's vigorous support, or not, their filmmaking exploits destroy the house and grounds in short order.

Comment: Nearly all of the superb comedy in this hilarious short comes from Chase's fertile imagination and direction. A pure Chase-the-writer moment comes when Pollard breaks down the front door and we catch the quickest of glimpses of the film-within-the-film's leading man and Marie Mosquini making out on the couch inside. A pure Chase-the-director moment is the setup of Rowe's camera when the latter is having trouble constructing a long shot that will take in the whole of the house: Chase sets up *his* camera so that a single stationary shot includes the entire house, Rowe's equipment outlay, *and* the obstacle bedevilling Rowe's shot. This is brilliance at work, and it's all Chase's brilliance, not Pollard's. Pollard is just the *lucky* recipient of it.

Bonus: Noah Young was one of the great supporting villains of silent comedy. Son of a bare-knuckle boxer and coal miner, Young took this genetic inheritance of bulk and truculence a bit further by becoming an amateur body-building champion. Tall and prodigiously built, he added a natural glower and some rather venal false teeth to project the most menacing visage in comedy—even scarier than Eric Campbell, who relied heavily on false eyebrows and weeping-willow facial hair for a lot of his intimidation. Young worked almost entirely for Roach in the silent era—apparently his voice didn't come across well in the talkies—and in that capacity he shows up in seemingly every other film the studio churned out. He supported Harold Lloyd, Pollard, Stan Laurel solo, Laurel and Hardy, Chase, Glenn Tryon, Clyde Cook, Charlie Murray, Earl Mohan, Our Gang, Will Rogers, Eddie Boland, James Finlayson . . . you name 'em, and if they were a Roach comedian, they worked with Noah Young at some point in the Twenties.

In *On Location*, Young plays the director of the film-within-the-film. I was unable to recognize him until the fifth or sixth time I watched it. He wears padding to make himself look pear-shaped, and dons a prescient Groucho mask of round black eyeglasses, false nose, and moustache that completely disguises him. As chief director for the "Disastrous Film Company" (presumably a subsidiary of Irwin Allen Productions), Young really manhandles people in this movie, flinging them aside, shoving them backward, tossing them out of his way, pushing them with a violence that is quite hilarious. All in all, *On Location* is a wonderful showcase for an unforgettably comic bad guy.

P

A PAIR OF SILK STOCKINGS

(1918, Select Films)

Director: Walter Edwards
Writers: Edith Kennedy and Cyril Harcourt
Camera: James Van Trees
Cast: Constance Talmadge, Harrison Ford, Wanda Hawley, Vera Doria, Florence Carpenter, Thomas Persse, Louis Willoughby, Helen Haskell, Sylvia Ashton, Robert Gordon, L. W. Steers
Running Time (Length): 60 minutes (five reels)
Availability: DVD (Alpha Video)

Background: The Talmadges are one of the earliest examples of a parent, specifically the archetypal stage mother, pushing not just one or two offspring (as in the Pickford and Gish families) but every darned kid in the family into the movies.

Natalie, the middle sister, was an also-ran as an actress because she was easily the least attractive and the most unpleasant of the kids. The latter attribute was given full force offscreen in her catastrophic marriage to Buster Keaton, which came to consume her entire life with bitterness, hatred, and vindictiveness—entirely one-sidedly, incidentally.

Norma, the eldest sister, was immensely revered in the Twenties, consistently one of the year's top box-office draws as she played nobly in an endless string of weepers, potboilers, and "women's pictures." Men could hardly stand her, but women absolutely worshipped her.

The youngest sister, Constance, was almost as popular as Norma. Because she stuck to light comedy (at least, after making her mark in D. W. Griffith's portentous *Intolerance* [1916]), she wasn't taken as seriously as Norma. On the other hand, this had the salutary effect of making her a lot less self-important than Norma; she was a party girl, plain and simple, and that's all she cared to be. That came across in her performances just as much as it did in her life.

Synopsis: Connie Talmadge is "Mrs. Sam Thornhill"; Harrison Ford is, we are informed by intertitle, "The husband of Mrs. Sam Thornhill." If you enjoy that witticism, you're going to enjoy this film.

Constance Talmadge and Harrison Ford unveil the season's most beautiful stockings, albeit on the wrong set of legs. *A Pair of Silk Stockings* (1918). *Courtesy of Derek Boothroyd*

Ford's character, a British Twit of the Year contender for 1918 if Monty Python's Flying Circus had existed then, is prone to ideas of "colossal idiocy." One such—to make Connie think he is two-timing her—results in a prompt divorce. Since they both still love each other, circumstance must bring them together again with the opportunity to reconcile.

This opportunity comes when a dolorous Ford participates in a social house party that includes a collective reading of "this darling Ibsen play." That is surely, satire aside, the only time in history that any Ibsen play has been described as "darling," and it is typical of the jaunty humor of the intertitles. Ford is ordered to get into makeup as an unrecognizably bearded, hairy, poverty-stricken Norwegian so as to improve his performance (his performance in the reading, that is, although it also improves his performance in the film itself). While he does so, Talmadge arrives unexpectedly and must be put up for the night in a bedroom belonging to the absentee adult son of the hostess.

Through another of Ford's colossally idiotic ideas, he gets mistaken for a burglar and tied up by Talmadge and the (returned) son with her silk stockings. (They had amazing, lovely, intricately embroidered patterns on the *front* of stockings in those days; it's a treat to see them.) The usual complications ensue and lead to the usual happy ending.

Comment: A Pair of Silk Stockings is a silly trifle that defiantly mocks its own silly triviality before you can do so. It does this mostly through intertitles that are often funny, usually jocose, and only occasionally smart-alecky. I especially enjoyed the one in which the society hostess informs Talmadge, deceitfully, that the post-divorce Ford is drinking himself to death, and that the hostess would stop him were it not for the fact her husband gets most of his income from a distillery.

Constance Talmadge laughs gaily at everything to let us know she is playing a character who laughs gaily at everything. She really does give the impression of being an actress who couldn't care less about her career because all she wants to do in her real life is have fun and go her own way in her own sweet time—an empty woman with so much money that she will never have to worry about her reputation, let alone her survival. This lack of artifice is what makes her so charming onscreen.

Harrison Ford is his usual muddled-twit self, only much more so because here he has the additional twittiness that comes with playing a brainless English fuddy-duddy (which is quite an artistic stretch for a boy from Kansas City, Missouri). Although extremely popular and prolific, Ford was never anything more than a dinner-theatre ham actor. His style is therefore a nice contrast to Talmadge's. The film, knowing this, takes a detour in one scene to show how Ford expected Talmadge to react to his biggest dumbbell idea, and then shows how Talmadge actually reacted to it; the juxtapositions neatly demonstrate his life-as-it-should-be bombast to her life-as-it-is realism. They play well together even if you can't believe she would marry such an idiot, or at least marry him for anything other than his money and title. (As yet another intertitle says, a title "makes all the difference in the world!")

It's all a lot of amiable nonsense and inconsequential fun.

Bonus: Excluding *Intolerance* (1916), which is an ultra-serious Great Film, and *The Matrimaniac* (1916), in which she gives Douglas Fairbanks the most spirited onscreen girlfriend he ever had, any Constance Talmadge film is interchangeable with any other Constance Talmadge film. If not *A Pair of Silk Stockings*, then *The Duchess of Buffalo* (1926) or *The Primitive Lover* (1922) or *Her Night of Romance* (1924) or *Her Sister from Paris* (1925) or . . . They're all the same film, they're all pleasantly entertaining, they're all instantly forgettable.

And yet, she was a really significant figure in long-form silent comedy in terms of being popular, dependable, likable, and as good an actress as she had to be. Any book on silent comedy films that ignores her in the historical record lacks credibility. It matters not that her films were never anything more than time wasters.

The post-*Intolerance* Connie Talmadge ranks in much the same level as the post-*E.T.: The Extra-Terrestrial* (1982) Drew Barrymore. Both are adorable, winning, pretty blondes with adequate acting and comedy chops, who starred in a slew of romantic comedies that did better than breaking even at the box office (which is why they were kept busy drumming out these homogenous films) but which sank instantly from consciousness the moment you got out of the theatre or took the disc out of the video player.

One caution: in *The Duchess of Buffalo*, Talmadge is disconcertingly similar in appearance to Jack Lemmon's drag character in *Some Like It Hot* (1959). The same short curly blonde hairstyle, the same bluish eye shadow, the same long nose and long chin, the same white-toothy smile, and . . . the same clothes, too!

It has got to be one of the greatest ironies of their lives that in the end, the only Talmadge to achieve cinematic immortality was the least-interested one, Natalie—and only because her virulently despised husband, Buster Keaton, had the chivalry to star her in *Our Hospitality* (1923), one of his great feature comedies.

A PAIR OF TIGHTS

(1929, Hal Roach Studio)

Director: Hal Yates
Writer: Leo McCarey
Titles: H. M. "Beanie" Walker
Camera: Art Lloyd
Editor: William Terhune
Cast: Anita Garvin, Marion Byron, Edgar Kennedy, Stuart Erwin, Spec O'Donnell, Edgar Dearing, Charlie Hall, Ellinor Vanderveer
Running Time (Length): About 23 minutes (two reels)

Background: Under the direction of Leo McCarey and Charley Chase, Hal Roach's comedy division was perpetually awash in brilliant comedy scenarios—more than could be filmed even by his large stable of fantastic comedians. McCarey and Chase and the other writers were so prolific, sometimes a juicy script had to be assigned to supporting performers instead of the stars for whom it had been intended.

So it was that *A Pair of Tights* was written with Laurel and Hardy in mind, but because they were already on fire with productions, it ended up being assigned to a quartet of perpetual second bananas. These were no lemons. Edgar Kennedy was already acknowledged as the best supporting comic not named Oliver Hardy or Vernon Dent, and he had been working steadily since 1911. Anita Garvin was the scintillating female who incinerated silent shorts as one of the three greatest nonleading ladies of slapstick (along with Jobyna Ralston and Bebe Daniels). Stuart Erwin was one of those forgettable but indispensable boyfriends-of-the-second-leading-lady who kept on filling small but important roles in films, in his case all the way to 1964. Marion Byron was a tiny cutie who is much overlooked even by comedy historians but who displays in *A Pair of Tights* a quite impeccable comic timing and expressions. And, of course, there is also a fifth wheel in the person of the immortal Spec O'Donnell, here looking incredibly skinny and, somehow, younger than he had two years earlier in *Call of the Cuckoo*.

Synopsis: Gal pals Marion Byron and Anita Garvin are penniless and starving. They are depending on Byron's boyfriend, Stu Erwin, and his boss Edgar Kennedy (who is about to blind-date Garvin as a favor to Erwin), to relieve their hunger pangs by treating them to dinner at a restaurant. Unfortunately, the men are equally penniless, save for a dollar bill that Kennedy secretes in his blazer pocket. Garvin, having seen them glumly turn their pockets inside out before they ventured into the lionesses' den, is quite a bit less than impressed by her date. Erwin

Anita Garvin, star of *A Pair of Tights* (1929), pretends to have been beaten to the punch by Our Gang's "Wheezer" in this publicity still. *Author's collection*

unwisely introduces Kennedy to her as "a bear with the women," an evaluation Kennedy bashfully acknowledges as no more than the truth. Garvin proceeds to peel the fur, the hide, the epidermis, and the flesh off Kennedy with a relentless stare of ice-cold disdain that lasts two and a half minutes. In fact, the entire scene of these two non-lovebirds sitting on a piano bench lasts a riotously uncomfortable five full minutes. See this scene, and you will never again call any date of your own "the date from hell."

Somehow the ladies force the gentlemen into agreeing to take them out for dinner. In the front seat of the open-air car, Erwin and Byron cuddle as closely as possible; in the backseat, Kennedy and Garvin put as much as distance between themselves as possible. When Byron spots an ice cream store, the men, with the crafty imbecility of all males (seeded by a cynical hint from Garvin, who knows exactly what she's doing), figure they can get out of paying for an expensive dinner by spoiling the women's appetites with ice cream cones.

The entire second reel of this film is taken up with first Byron's and later Garvin's attempts to bring four cones out of the store without spilling them on account of swinging doors, excited dogs, excited Spec O'Donnell, or other obstacles. Meanwhile, cop Edgar Dearing matches them mishap for mishap in trying to nail Erwin for double-parking in front of the store. Eventually, the sidewalk in front of the store becomes a battleground of men (and only one or two women other than

Garvin and Byron) chopping each other's legs out from under them, until at least twenty dazed victims are sitting on the pavement in a too-obvious rip on Laurel and Hardy's fondness for mass mad mayhem.

Comment: Do not make the mistake of assuming from the title that this is a comedy about women's hosiery. If the writers had had a less sly sense of humor, they might have given it the more precise title of *A Pair of Tightwads.* That's right: the "tights" are not stockings, they're Erwin and Kennedy being penny-pinchers.

If you go into this film with your eyes wide open about the title, you will find it an engaging and very funny short. It makes amazing use of only two settings: the girls' apartment (and the sidewalk outside it), and the street/sidewalk in front of the ice cream parlor.

The number of variations these adroit comedians can come up with for destroying ice cream cones is mind-blowing, and almost all of them are truly hilarious. Likewise, it is really impressive how many different ways they invent to foil Dearing's efforts to waylay Erwin in his car.

Unfortunately the ending drops off the cliff into mere silliness; it sorely misses the dumb dignity and affronted self-respect Laurel and Hardy would have brought to it. In the lead-up to it, it is impossible not to see the direct reflection of Hardy (in this case, Kennedy) tugging up on his heft as he steps out of the car to come to the aid of his pummeled pal (in this case, Garvin), just as in *Two Tars* (1928), followed by the free-for-all on the sidewalk that imitates the shin-kicking in *You're Darn Tootin'* (1928). Up to that point, though, the quartet has made the film their own, and a great job they did of it.

Bonus: Roach quite deliberately strove to create comics that filled definite niches. Most obvious was his creation of Our Gang to fill the niche of "kid comedians." He had a "light comedian" with Charley Chase, and a "slapstick comedian" (as well as a "male and female comedy team") with Snub Pollard supported by Marie Mosquini. He had an "ethnic comedian" with Max Davidson. He even had an "animal comedians" series with the Dippy Doo-Dads. And when he hit pay dirt (again) with Laurel and Hardy as "buddy comedians," it made him realize there was also a niche for a team of "lady buddy comedians."

In the talkie era, this team was the highly enjoyable pairing of Thelma Todd with, first, ZaSu Pitts, and then Patsy Kelly. Prior to them, however, there was the silent-era teaming of Anita Garvin and Marion Byron.

As noted above, the ladies were quite blatantly patterned on Laurel and Hardy and were given scripts The Boys were too busy to take on. The team lasted only three films. That was not a reflection on the quality of the films. *A Pair of Tights* is very often cited as one of the best silent short comedies ever made. Aficionados who have been able to see the incomplete surviving reels of *Feed 'em and Weep* (1928) suggest it might have been even better than *A Pair of Tights.* I have not been able to find much information about the middle of this trio of films, *Going Ga-ga* (1929), other than the cast list.

Byron, who made her debut as Buster Keaton's girlfriend in *Steamboat Bill, Jr.* (1928), was so tiny—not more than five feet tall even in heels, and probably weighing not more than 80 pounds soaking wet—and so pubescent in face, body, and energy level that she has a hard time posing as a credible girlfriend to anyone too old to be a member of Our Gang. The requisite contrasting physique was supposed to be Garvin's alleged six feet in height (she was probably 5'10": in one scene, she is *almost* able to look six-foot-one Edgar Kennedy straight in the eye while wearing two-inch heels), very svelte without an inch of fat on her, and very definitely a grown-up woman of the world.

Although they play well together, they don't make for a charismatic team. Byron looks too much like Garvin's daughter rather than her best friend. As well, a key element to the brilliant interplay of Laurel and Hardy and of their comedy is Hardy's assumption that he is the brains, the sophisticate, the worldly member of the pair, when in fact he is at least as idiotic and inexperienced as the less-pretentious Laurel; Garvin actually *is* the brains, the sophisticate, the worldly member of her pairing with Byron, and Byron is far from being Laurel's complete blockhead; the contrast in self-perception *and* the similarity in cluelessness just aren't there for the ladies. Still, they are both excellent comedians, and this is an excellent comedy.

PATHS TO PARADISE

(1925, Paramount)

Director: Clarence Badger
Writers: Keene Thompson and Paul Armstrong
Camera: H. Kinley Martin
Cast: Raymond Griffith, Betty Compson, Bert Woodruff, Tom Santschi, Fred Kelsey
Running Time (Length): Seven reels
Availability: DVD (Televista)

Background: Raymond Griffith was born into a show-biz family and went through the usual steps of live theatre training—vaudeville, circus, stage, etc.—before heading into films in 1914, just 19 years old. At least, that's the story he allowed to spread; there is some controversy over how much of it was the truth. Similarly, there are conflicting stories about how he lost most of his voice: he claimed it was from screaming onstage every night as a child in part of his parents' act, others assert it was damaged by childhood disease, and still others assert he lost it as an adult from being gassed in World War I.

Are these a publicist's fantasies spooned up for fan consumption, as was standard practice in the first half century or so of Hollywood's promotional machines? Or were they the fabrications and evasions of a con man? The question isn't irrelevant when one considers that Griffith's best starring features all cast him in con-man characterizations.

To be a successful con man, you need an all-encompassing self-confidence, an ingrained arrogance, even if your con involves presenting yourself as a meek milquetoast. Griffith's onscreen characters have so much self-assurance that they never see any need to contemplate possible failure in anything they might undertake. This is as much a weakness in his movies as it is a strength: he never seems vulnerable onscreen.

He seems to have exuded that same lofty opinion of his own talents in real life. He expected to be a quick success when he entered the movies; the film industry, however, doesn't always respect a newcomer's generous self-evaluation. Griffith was forced to drum his fingers impatiently through seven or eight years of unobtrusive roles, including several at Sennett. If the industry was going to be leisurely in recognizing his acting skills, though, he wasn't going to spin his wheels: he expanded his portfolio of talents to become an accomplished scriptwriter and gagman. In fact, he proved so valuable as a writer, script editor, and eventually director that his acting credits petered down to almost nothing for a couple of years. The bug bit him again in 1922 and he resurfaced in a handful of feature films. In 1924, he perfected the character that established him as one of the most admired comedians of the late silent era: a suave upper-class gentleman quite clearly borrowed from Max Linder (who by now was gone from America, almost finished with movies, and only a year away from suicide).

Griffith's heyday did not last long—he was physically unable to speak audibly enough for the talkies—and he moved back into behind-the-scenes roles as a production manager and producer. His enormous reputation rests on a very small body of work made in a very small window of time and opportunity, specifically 1924–1927.

Raymond Griffith and Betty Compson agree to join forces in the service of jewel thievery in *Paths to Paradise* (1925). *Courtesy of Bruce Calvert*

Synopsis: The concept of "slumming," which we generally use nowadays to disparage someone's doing something that should be beneath him or her or that constitutes an act of patronization toward one's inferiors, was a genuine "recreational activity" in the 19th century that lasted well into the 20th century. Tourists and upper-class thrill-seekers wrapped themselves in their furs and tuxedos and put themselves into the hands of hired guides to the "underworld" for a couple of hours; this could mean a visit to "a Negro nightclub," a gambling den, a workhouse/poorhouse, an orphanage (where the children would be forced to "perform" for them), or even an insane asylum.

Naturally enough, the underclasses quickly realized there was money to be made in faking these establishments. And that's where we enter *Paths to Paradise*: guided tours for titillated snobs and gullible tourists to a den of criminality, which quickly morphs into a den of opium addiction for the next troupe of suckers. Queen of this cynical rip-off, and an accomplished thief in her own right, is Betty Compson. It takes a con to catch a con, and Compson finds herself conned and ripped off by a con man. They'll meet again: a con must con the con who conned her.

And so they do: Compson in disguise meets up with the con man in disguise at the house of a wealthy couple whom both are targeting for a jewel robbery. They are competitors, but he's the charming Raymond Griffith and she's the charming Betty Compson; thus charmed by each other, they quickly become wary collaborators.

After a series of riotous plans, attempts, distractions, and disruptions, they actually do manage to swipe the jewels and make their getaway together. Pursued by what appears to be several thousand agents of law enforcement, they screech through one of the best car chases ever filmed and make it to Mexico. The very last reel of this movie is lost, and it appears to have been every bit as tremendously funny and exciting as the first six reels; but the ending as we now have it is perfect in itself.

Comment: A lot of people will probably wonder why I chose to include *Paths to Paradise* instead of Griffith's better-known and more-revered *Hands Up!* (1926). The latter is certainly a wonderful film. *Paths*, however, is actually funnier and its script is more accomplished. Despite being about a jewel thief, its morals and ethics are more empathetic than those of the amoral, patronizing spy/thief/traitor/bigamist/fop Griffith plays in *Hands Up!* The latter is more like the flip side of a Douglas Fairbanks hero than he is a suave and sophisticated version of Buster Keaton's dogged, sincere, unpretentious engineer in *The General* (1927). Griffith in *Paths* is clever, but not overly clever; he screws up, and has to go through some really tense yet funny situations in order to rectify the screw-ups. When Griffith in *Hands Up!* gets into a situation, he's so smooth and preternaturally competent that you feel no concern or sympathy, you just sit passively and watch as he cheats his way to escape. I think *Hands Up!* is an excellent comedy, but *Paths to Paradise* is both better and more provoking of laughter.

Bonus: Also recommended:

You'd Be Surprised (1926): A really fun kidding of the already-hoary old-dark-house and Ten-Little-Indians plotlines. The nonsense starts with a fake Aesop quote and the setting of a supposed houseboat that is quite clearly a full-blown, multilevel grand mansion on the shore. As it runs through its breezy one-hour length, the film throws up a startling number of prescient Marx Brothers riffs, including one fellow on the jury who is a ringer for Chico right down to the hat and hairdo. Even a modern-day audience, able to anticipate the development of the running gags, will get lots of genuine laughs.

Quite deliberately, the plot developments don't always hang together; the way the murders (and fake murders) were pulled off is never explained (or plausible, based on the few clues we're given); and Griffith brushes aside the killer's plea, "Don't you want to know why I killed him?" It's a joke, and a good one.

THE PAWN SHOP

(1918, Mutual)

Director: Charles Chaplin
Writer: Charles Chaplin
Camera: Roland Totheroh and W. C. Foster
Editor: Charles Chaplin
Cast: Charlie Chaplin, Edna Purviance, Albert Austin, Henry Bergman, Eric Campbell, Frank J. Coleman, John Rand, James T. Kelly
Running Time (Length): Two reels
Availability: DVD (*The Essential Charlie Chaplin*, vol. 8)

Background: Charlie Chaplin is on record as identifying his years at the Mutual Film Corporation as the happiest period of his life. It is certainly reflected in the quality of the 12 short comedies he made there: every one of them is excellent, and most of them rank among the very best slapstick two-reelers ever made.

The contract with Mutual included the creation of the Lone Star Corporation as a production company. This effectively gave Chaplin complete artistic freedom without any responsibility for the financial side of the business; in other words, he was free to do whatever the hell he wanted to do and never have to pay for it. Any artist would kill for such an arrangement. Not only was it a guarantee that no one would interfere with his personal artistic expression, it also meant he could sock away every penny of the gargantuan salary he was being paid. This is how Chaplin began accumulating the fortune that enabled him, alone among comedians except for Harold Lloyd, to finance his own later feature films and not have to suffer the intrusion of any outside partner, producer, or meddlers.

At Mutual, he also constructed the stable of actors who would support him faithfully for years: Henry Bergman, Albert Austin, John Rand, Edna Purviance, Eric Campbell, Leo White, James T. Kelley, Lloyd Bacon, and others. Moreover, Purviance brought a motherly stability to his private life as well, an unquestioning lover, a maternal confidante, a beautiful muse. Life was good, and this feeling permeates the films he made at this point in his life.

Synopsis: In one of his rare bouts of full employment, the Tramp works in a pawn shop run by a stereotypical Jew. As the dogsbody of the staff, Charlie does the cleaning, which leads directly to repeated, extended altercations with his co-worker (John Rand). Sent to polish the three balls that are the timeless exterior symbol of a pawn shop, he and Rand proceed to engage in by far the greatest take on that age-old slapstick trope, the man who knocks over everybody with the ladder he is carrying. Chaplin lets it run for some five minutes, and every second of it is tremendous comedy. He and Rand are in perfect synch, and any other player who happens to enter the game (Frank Coleman as a policeman; a boy played by an unknown lad; Henry Bergman) fits into their rhythm quite deftly. You can hardly imagine they are going to be able to poke genuine belly laughs out of every swing of the ladder because you know what's coming and you've seen the same stuff pulled by everybody from Billy Bevan to Bugs Bunny; yet every bit manages to be fresh and funny. One of the best "new" variations is when Rand's arms are pinned inside the ladder and Chaplin proceeds to box him with impressive skill.

The unending battles between Chaplin and Rand eventually result in Chaplin getting fired. He wins back his job by claiming to have six children of varying heights, and promptly imperils his restored position by flirting with the inevitable Beautiful Daughter (Edna Purviance), who makes doughnuts heavy enough to anchor the *Titanic*.

Chased out of the back room to do duty at the front desk, where he surely won't get into any trouble, Charlie's first customer is a heartbreaking old soul, whose tale of woe rends a Niagara of weeping from Charlie as well as a ten-dollar bill, the latter of which the broken-down old sod adds to his softball-sized wad of money with an actor's glee as he walks boldly out of the store.

Albert Austin enters, looking to make a fast buck on a large, cheap alarm clock. Charlie performs another of the all-time great silent routines, examining and dissecting the clock like a cardiac surgeon, ultimately shoveling the pieces into Austin's hat and regretfully sending him on his way in disappointment.

The film ends with a bit of nonsense about a would-be crook whose attempt at robbery is foiled by Charlie, who wins Purviance's hand as a reward.

Comments: The Pawn Shop (commonly spelled incorrectly as *The Pawnshop*) is one of those films that are apparently the apex of Chaplin's comedy in the minds of those who don't really like him for political reasons. It's what they have in mind (though in fact they seldom remember its title) when they complain that "the later Chaplin" of *The Kid, City Lights, The Great Dictator*, and *Limelight* became pretentious and self-admiring—that is, they think he did nothing of merit after making gems like *The Pawn Shop*. What we should take from this myopic and politically motivated whining is the fact that even his enemies conceded *The Pawn Shop* is a diamond, shining incandescently at the peak of countless film comedies before and since.

Bonus: This film introduces us to Henry Bergman. A member of Chaplin's off-screen supporting staff (today we would recognize it as his "entourage"), Bergman ended up playing multiple roles in nearly every Chaplin film for 30 years. As a fat but mobile man with feminine features, he easily slipped into a confounding variety of secondary roles: fat man, pompous stuffed shirt, fat woman, flirtatious ugly woman, military hero of countless dining tables, Jewish shop proprietor, ersatz film director, overly aggressive masseuse, unfunny circus clown—Bergman played them all.

Offscreen, Bergman poured his money into a restaurant—what else did you expect a fat man to pour his money into?—which for a while was the hip place to eat in Hollywood. Fellow movie personnel patronized it, apparently, out of loyalty to its owner rather than any affection for its reportedly pedestrian fare. Chaplin was the financial backer. This is a good illustration of the two-way loyalty between Chaplin and his entourage (including actor/mistress Edna Purviance) that explains why so many of them stuck with him for decades and why he in turn loved them enough to support them until their deaths (he outlived all of them).

THE PRIDE OF PIKEVILLE

(1927, Sennett)

Director: Alf Goulding
Writers: Earle Rodney, Jefferson Moffitt, Clarence Henneck, Phil Whitman, Harry
   McCoy, Randall Faye, Grover Jones, and Lex Neal
Titles: A. H. Giebler
Camera: St. Elmo Boyce and K. G. MacLean
Editor: William Hornbeck
Cast: Ben Turpin, Thelma Hill, Ruth Taylor, Andy Clyde, William McCall, Stanley
   Blystone, Vernon Dent, Patsy O'Byrne, Joy Winthrop
Running Time (Length): Two reels
Availability: DVD (Alpha Video: *Sennett Classics*, vol. 3)

Background: Ben Turpin is celebrating 20 years in comedy movies in 1927. He's been through a lot, good and bad, onscreen and off , including retirement and return, and his wife's long illness and death, followed with slightly unseemly haste by remarriage. What has he got to show for the years?

Well, first of all, a lot of money, as he truculently reminds everyone with wearying regularity and boastfulness—he even stops traffic at intersections to yell, "I'm Ben Turpin! I get paid $3,000 a week!" Secondly, he's world famous because of his crossed eyes, which make him instantly recognizable anywhere silent movies are shown, which is to say everywhere. And third, he's reached an age where he can still turn massive falls without injury but prefers to do slightly more cerebral comedy instead—but only slightly more cerebral.

Synopsis: "The Man You Love to Hate" was Erich von Stroheim, evil-eyed *faux* Prussian (he was actually Jewish Austrian), *faux* aristocrat (he was a hatter's son), *faux* cavalry officer (he made straw hats for his dad instead of riding army horses), *vrai* crazed film director-writer-auteur, who made a fetish out of—well, an awful lot of things, actually, including 19th-century military underwear and the panties of convent schoolgirls, but mostly out of *faux* cruelty. Among the many indelible marks he left upon movie history was his performance as a Great War German officer who throws an annoying baby out a window (*The Heart of Humanity*, 1918). Stroheim seemed to believe this behavior made him irresistible to women, or any rate decadent European women, so his characters were also ladykillers, both metaphorically and literally.

Ben Turpin demonstrates why he makes a more dashing Erich von
Stroheim than Erich von Stroheim does. *The Pride of Pikeville* (1927).
Author's collection

To Mack Sennett, Stroheim was a totally ridiculous phony whose films were
unwatchable. How better to devastate this pretentious blowhard than by casting
Ben Turpin as him in a farce comedy! Not wasting any time in driving home his
intentions, the opening shots of *The Pride of Pikeville* have Turpin riding a hobby-
horse and then eating an ice cream cone ("an American bracer"). He's in full
Stroheim regalia: white cavalry uniform and cap, monocle, Stroheim haircut, and
presumably proper 19th-century silk underwear. Seeing the withered, impossibly scrawny body and crossed eyes of this chinless wonder pretending to be the
physically magnificent (in his own mind) and sneeringly dignified Stroheim is an
instant flick of the switch to capacious laughter.

He's taking up a whole car of a train coasting across America, on the run from
European husbands tired of him seducing their wives. When he condescends to
reveal his superior presence to the plebes riding in the economy car, his crossed
eyes allow him to flirt with two women simultaneously. They both welcome it.
However, the spoilsport father of one of them, "Pearl Pepper," advises "Baron
Bonamo" that in this country, "We shoot men who look cross-eyed at our
women!" The "Baron" decides that in the light of this explanation, he had best
retire back to his own car.

"Pearl," notwithstanding Daddy and his guns, is not one to be discouraged. She ends up in the "Baron's" arms when the train goes through a tunnel, and Daddy is there quickly to ordain a shotgun wedding as a consequence.

The train, with its prospective wedding party, arrives in Pikeville. This was the "Baron's" apparent destination of choice anyway, for he has arranged in advance to seduce a willing bride-to-be in that town, "Ruth." The fiancé to whom "Ruth" is bride-to-be, a man named "Walter," is the choice of her dad, who quickly changes his mind when he sees the opportunity to marry her off to European aristocracy instead.

With two fathers both trying to shotgun-wed their daughter to the "Baron," he takes a powder and runs furiously enough to catch his train back east, only to find one of the compromised young ladies has refused to take "no" for an answer.

Comment: Sennett too was almost marking his twentieth year in movies: he had joined Biograph in 1908. *The Pride of Pikeville* indicates that it was his belief not much had changed over the years in the way of stories or scenarios. Sennett and his writers, as great as the latter often were, had only a handful of story ideas, and parlayed them into hundreds of films—which is to say, there isn't anything new or particularly interesting in the basic storyline of *Pikeville*; all of its virtues come from the execution.

The success of that execution starts with the casting of Turpin as Stroheim. Turpin plays it almost straight, which is the ideal way in which to satirize his target. Turpin had learned he didn't need to do anything to make the world laugh at him pretending to be people like Stroheim; Turpin himself was a walking mockery of such individuals by the nature of his own physical appearance.

The rest of the cast do their jobs efficiently. Ruth Taylor is just right as the self-interested blonde, "Ruth," whose prettiness means she has never in her life had to actually think about anything; she knows if she just tells a man she wants him, she'll have him . . . which "Baron Bonamo" has proven at long distance. Thelma Hill is too attractive to be believably "ugly" as "Pearl"; we need to remember that in this era freckles were considered scarring to a girl's beauty. Hill plays "Pearl" as someone who may have been disappointed in love countless times already but who remains enthusiastic about each new possible suitor, and not shy to chase him, either; if she's ugly, as other people keep telling her, she doesn't believe it, and rightfully so, and she won't let it stop her. As her father, Andy Clyde's performance is much stronger than his silly moustache. Patsy O'Byrne and Joy Winthrop are perfect in their tiny roles as clucking gossips sitting on a sofa at "Ruth's" wedding party. This film is impeccably cast.

The crew chips in with some really good stuff of their own. Title writer A. H. Giebler gets off a great terrible pun when the "Baron" is disgusted by the quality of American coffee: "This coffee tastes like mud, it must have been ground this morning!" And when the "Baron" blows cigar smoke, the artists get involved by arranging the smoke into shapes that reflect the "Baron's" thoughts: first a pretty girl, then a jackass sticking its tongue out at him.

Bonus: Turpin's career at Sennett's studios involved a lot of parodies of then-current movies and celebrities. My choice for a representative film came down to either *The Pride of Pikeville* or *The Shriek of Araby* (1923), both excellent examples of the genre. *Pikeville* was selected because it better demonstrates the little bit of growth Turpin had managed as a comedian. In *The Shriek of Araby*. made four years earlier, he is still entirely dependent upon the hilarity of his appearance for all of the laughs; he slavers in strabismic ecstasy at having a beautiful girl at his mercy. In *The Pride of Pikeville*, Turpin knows we already think it's side-splitting that this little stringbean is supposed to be a heartless heartbreaker, so he has the confidence to *not* belabor the point; he, as Stroheim would, takes it as merely rightful that all women should be throwing themselves at his feet. We laugh in both cases, but the *Pikeville* case is more satisfying because of the comedian's self-restraint and economy of performance—terms not often used to describe Turpin's shtick.

R

RENO OR BUST

(1924, Christie/Educational)

Director: Archie Mayo
Writer: Frank Conklin
Camera: Anton Nagy, Alex Phillips
Cast: Bobby Vernon, Duane Thompson, Lila Leslie, Victor Rodman, Blanche Payson,
    Billy Bletcher, Budd Fine
Running Time (Length): 25 minutes (two reels)

Background: As the shortest and best-dressed male in the room—any room—
Bobby Vernon never looked more than about 14 years old, and he resented the
hell out of it. Don't call it a Napoleon complex, but he was hell-bent on proving
he could do anything a bigger man could during his film career, and do it at twice
the speed even without the aid of undercranking. It was a pretty impressive career
too, particularly for someone who wasn't anything close to being a top-notch comedian (I ranked him #47 in *The 100 Greatest Silent Film Comedians*).

He started out with the legendary vaudeville comics, Kolb and Dill, and shifted
into films in 1913 just as comedy was really taking off with the Keystone Studio
products and Vitagraph's John Bunny and Mr. and Mrs. Sidney Drew. He pushed
Harry McCoy out of the latter's duo act with Max Asher the following year; another
year later, he was at Sennett, playing with Gloria Swanson as the world's shortest
romantic couple (and even at that, the teeny tiny Swanson was taller than Vernon).
This time he endured two years, not one, before moseying on over to Al Christie's
production house. Christie treated him like a star, giving him all the resources at his
disposal, publicizing his films as if they were the second coming of Buster Keaton,
and basically letting him have his head, which Vernon appreciated enough to stick
around for a dozen years—by far his longest stint anywhere. When the talkies came
in, he became comedy production boss at Paramount and died in that saddle in 1939.

Synopsis: Reno or Bust opens right in the middle of a chase scene and never shifts
gear: it is one nonstop chase film. Vernon and Duane Thompson (a woman, despite
the first name) are determined to get married; her parents, fiancé, and hangers-on
(including, oddly, the maid) are just as determined to prevent the marriage and get

her hitched to oily Victor Rodman instead. Although Vernon and Thompson succeed, she gets heisted away by her folks between the moment the minister finishes saying "Amen" and the moment he reminds Bobby to pay him his fee. The anti-Vernon faction is now in a mad dash for Reno so they can force Thompson to divorce Vernon and instantly marry Rodman. Naturally, Vernon is now chasing them.

In Reno, seemingly the entire city police force is ordered by the imperious mother to run Vernon out of town. They do so, dumping him in the desert, but he turns the tables on them, and they will end up like extras from the final scene of Erich von Stroheim's *Greed* (made the same year, 1924), staggering in their disintegrating uniform rags across Death Valley in torturous slow motion. Meanwhile, through various disguises and machinations, Vernon more or less kidnaps Thompson from under the noses of her parents and remarries her, which *this* time around endears him to her parents.

Comment: As the climax demonstrates with crystal clarity, none of the story points either make sense or have any connection with reality, particularly the reality of the law. So what? This is slapstick comedy, which has its own laws and its own reality. Vernon loves chases, loves speed, loves physical action, and this film is the acme of those loves. It's unbelievably fast for something made in 1924, and it's packed with good guffaws, even if the gags are devoid of originality. Vernon puts them over through sheer determination—and did I mention speed?

Bonus: Vernon's highly improbable real name was Silvion de Jardins. He actually used it in a few of his earliest films, before sanity prevailed. Like Leslie Hope, he chose to rechristen himself "Bob" because it was more folksy (and more American). The "Vernon" he took from his mother, actress Dorothy Vernon, who had nothing to do with Mary Pickford's bomb, *Dorothy Vernon of Haddon Hall* (1924). You will find Dorothy Vernon among the casts of a few films in this book; she was a well-respected veteran supporting actress whose comedy chops Bobby inherited.

ROBINET BOXEUR (ROBINET THE BOXER)

(1913, Societa Anonima Ambrosio [Italy])

Creator: Marcel Perez
Cast: Marcel Perez
Running Time (Length): 5 minutes

Background: Possibly—quite possibly—the greatest-ever silent comedian to ever disappear totally from the face of history is Marcel Perez. We owe an enormous debt of gratitude to musician-archivist (I'm not sure exactly how to describe his prodigious role in film preservation) Ben Model for resurrecting Perez in 2014 with his DVD, *The Marcel Perez Collection.* (Disclosure: I chipped in modestly on the Kickstarter campaign to produce the collection.) Kudos also to Ben's sidekick, Steve Massa, an indomitable researcher who has worked for decades to track down Perez's career and filmography.

Born in Spain as far as we can tell, Perez began his film career in France around 1907 for Pathé Frères, filming extremely short comedies under the name "Robinet" (various spellings, including the feminine form, which then confusingly enough was applied to his wife when she joined his cast). He ripped out something like 150 of these films in France and Italy before World War I broke out. In addition, he used a pantheon of pseudonyms for himself, which makes it even harder to track down these earliest films and give him proper credit for them.

These European films preceded the violence and surrealism of Mack Sennett's Keystone films, so those attributes can't be blamed on (or credited to) Sennett's influence. Prewar European silent comedies, from Russia to Spain, were extraordinarily brutal and fond of grotesque forms of destruction, both personal and environmental. *Robinet Boxeur* is an excellent representation of these films.

Synopsis: A black boxer destroys a rather effete white boxer. An outraged "Robinet" immediately challenges "Mr. Negro" to a match in order to avenge the honor of the white race. As a gentleman (of sorts), "Robinet" slaps the boxer across the face, twice, and both times the boxer responds with a casual blow that almost crushes him. When they shake hands on the challenge, "Robinet" is floored. Things don't look so promising, do they?

"Robinet" goes into training. He punches the speed bag so hard it tears holes in the floor and ceiling. He punches through walls, knocking people into bathtubs in the next room. Going out into the street, he punches a passerby so hard the man does more than 18 backward somersaults (I lost count after that many). Happening upon a vendor selling foot-high plaster copies of Venus de Milo, "Robinet" punches each statue to smithereens, and follows up by punching the vendor so hard in his fat stomach that the man literally blows up.

He stands in the front right corner of the frame as a trolley approaches from the back left corner. Repeatedly, he glances over his shoulder at the camera to build up our anticipation as the trolley comes nearer and nearer. Sure enough, he punches it so hard it reverses course (and changes its route number, incidentally).

Then he punches a lamplighter with an uppercut that hangs the poor man from the top of the streetlight. He's ready for the match!

Unfortunately the rest of the film is unavailable; we only know that once "Robinet" steps into the ring, "Mr. Negro" is easily disposed of.

Comment: The racism was typical of the time and of the place. Guardians of political correctness conveniently forget that Europe at that time was every bit as casually racist as the United States, as this film demonstrates in, er, spades. Putting that aside, Perez displays tremendous comic imagination in the fast flurry of punching

" TWEEDLEDUM AS A BOXER." (*Ambrosio.*)

Tweedledum is witness of a boxing bout between a white man and a negro, in which the latter is successful, and, full of anger at the indignity to his own race, the comedian challenges the black to a fight to a finish, and straightwa-

goes into training. His work with the ball is so heavy that he shatters the walls of his gymnasium, punches off the head of inoffensive pedestrians, causes others to explode by a terrific body blow, sends a tram hustling back the way it has come by a sturdy thump, and when he gets into the ring causes the negro to shrink with fear, and easily puts him out.

Released, April 13th.   Length 475 feet.

Marcel Perez, *Robinet Boxeur* (1913). *Courtesy of MDHI / Undercrank Productions* gags that constitute "Robinet's" training. Only once is a special effect incorporated, in the explosion of the fat vendor; everything else is done without mechanical or technological aid.

It's a wild comedy, all right. Five minutes of mayhem and rampant destruction. The rationales for the gags are, at bottom, quite stupid; the gags themselves are quite funny.

Bonus: In a very similar vein is *Robinet Jockey* (1910) (also known as *Robinet vuol fare il jockey*): he needs to lose weight quickly to qualify as a jockey, so he undergoes incredibly violent gyrations in other sports to burn off the pounds. The same levels of carnage and comedy permeate *Robinet Aviatore* (1911), which shows off a most dazzling fish-shaped airplane and then pulverizes an entire multi-story building floor by floor.

There are dozens of these European Perez films available on the Internet. It's quite a feast for those who enjoy both annihilation and hilarity.

ROWDY ANN

(1919, Christie)

Director: Al Christie
Cast: Fay Tincher, Eddie Barry, Katherine Lewis, Margaret Gibson, Al Haynes, Harry
    Depp, Edgar Blue
Running Time (Length): 21 minutes (two reels)
Availability: DVD (Grapevine Video: *Scarlet Days*; includes *Rowdy Ann*)

Background: Fay Tincher is one of the most intriguing of the lost silent comedians, and certainly that of the lost silent comediennes. How someone with her track record managed to fall out of the silent film legacy is one of the great puzzles of movie history.

She was there in the launching years of American slapstick comedy films, 1912–1914. Although originally cast in a mere supporting role as an office secretary named "Ethel" in an ongoing group of comedies about "Bill the Office Boy," she instantly took over the series and shot to tremendous fame and repute, a greatly admired comedian already. Well, "already" is a bit of a stretch; she was 30 years old when she started the "Ethel" series, a veteran of musicals and vaudeville, so she was more than prepared for "instant" success. And she was *hungry* for it: all of her performances are full of the kind of intensity and focus that can only come from someone who wants it so hard, she can taste it.

From the "Ethel" series, she moved on to make splashes in other genres of comedy, including several of the Western comedies of which *Rowdy Ann* is a sample. Then, in the 1920s, she scored another massive success as the wife in a long-running series about the "Gump Family." She rode that wave for five years, then disappeared with the coming of the talkies.

Synopsis: Al Haynes and Harry Depp are a couple of cowboys in love with tomboy-cowgirl "Ann," and not just because she's the heiress to one of the largest

Tough gal Fay Tincher distances herself from the delicate Grecian femmes of *Rowdy Ann* (1919). *Courtesy of Steve Massa*

and wealthiest landowners in the Wild West: she can ride horses, lasso anything, run the ranch, shoot holes through hats and not heads, and in general do everything a real *cowboy* can do better than a real cowboy. When bad-guy Al knocks down good-guy Harry, "Ann" takes over for the good wimp and pounds Al in a boxing match, mainly by stomping on his corns.

Her irate father decides it's time to send her to university "for to larn to be a lady." On the train, she exposes a card cheat and punches the hell out of him, then she chases the porter over the train top in her long johns and cowboy boots because he whispered sweet nothings to her in the mistaken belief she was his new wife.

Her first class at university is classical Greek dancing under the tutelage of a (stereotypically) effeminate male professor. Visibly hating the filmy, feminine gown she must wear for this class, she accessorizes it in the masculine manner with ten-gallon hat, gun and holster, and cowboy boots. Over time, however, she is (forcibly?) feminized to the extent of wearing a girly dress and ladylike shoes; we assume this is due at least in part to the influence of her properly womanlike roommates. One of them is a very rich girl about to elope with a much older man. "Ann" recognizes this man as the card cheat from the train, and prevents marital and financial disaster by lassoing him and giving him a solid punch in the face before turning him over to the police.

Comment: Tincher takes over the screen regardless of who else or how many other people are also in it: she's got that much presence. She's a forceful actress and one who doesn't suffer fools patiently. Very few actresses of the era would agree to a boxing scene, and fewer still would actually permit themselves to be filmed hitting and being hit (they would use a double for all but the close-ups). Tincher, in contrast, wastes no time in stripping to a tank top and laying into Al Haynes with real punches; he, in turn, goes through the necessary "I ain't hittin' no woman!" protest until he realizes she's delivering the real thing to his chin, then he starts tossing haymakers right back at her. This is just typical of Tincher: she goes into things wholeheartedly and unhesitantly, and woe betide anyone who gets in her way.

Her contempt for restraint must have made her an extreme right-wing nut-job politically in her personal life—I think it comes out somewhat in "Ann's" excessive fondness for firing her guns and in her Charlton Heston–like refusal to let anybody pry them out of her warm, live hands—but it certainly makes her a fascinatingly uninhibited comedian. I can't imagine how shocking the tank-top boxing scene must have been to an audience in 1919, only three or four years after women had been freed from whalebone corsets and floor-sweeping skirts.

Bonus: There aren't many of the "Ethel" films still available these days, and they aren't really all that great to our modern sense of humor. Nevertheless, they are all worth seeking out and watching at least once. Not only do they feature Tincher at her most aggressive and eye-catching (and not just because she wears mesmerizing striped outfits all the time), they also include some other surprising performers, such as a ridiculously youthful Max Davidson, Tammany Young long before he ended up as W. C. Fields's drinking buddy, and the future master writer-director of creepy, fetish-driven shock films, Tod Browning.

S

SAFETY LAST!

(1923, Roach)

Directors: Fred Newmeyer, Sam Taylor
Writers: Hal Roach, Sam Taylor, and Tim Shelan
Titles: H. M. Walker
Camera: Walter Lundin
Editor: T. J. Crizer
Cast: Harold Lloyd, Mildred Davis, Bill Strother, Noah Young, Anna Townshend,
  Westcott Clarke, Mickey Daniels, Charles Stevenson, Gus Leonard, Helen Gilmore,
  Mae Wallace, Earl Mohan, Roy Brooks, William Gillespie
Running Time (Length): 72 minutes (seven reels)
Availability: DVD (Criterion Collection)

Background: He's always described as the archetype of the all-American boy: clean-cut, super-energetic, super-optimistic, of sunny disposition, very handsome, a winning personality, athletic, indomitable, impossible to discourage or to keep down even when beaten bloody by a terrible killer-criminal, brightly tailored in neatly fitted sporty suits and a straw boater, unfazed by the (fake) eyeglasses that are supposed to indicate he has brains to match his charm. The negative side of that image is also always mentioned: his goals are always purely materialistic, his aggressiveness (especially with women) exceeds justification by his ambitions, he's jingoistic and corny in that milk-fed Nebraska patriotism, and he epitomizes the viciousness and greed that drive much of the American dream.

His name is Harold Lloyd. And he is funny as hell.

In real life, Lloyd was a driven man who actually did pull himself up by his bootstraps. From acting in various versions of live theatre, he plunged quickly into film comedy, and just as quickly discovered he had dived headfirst into a shallow trough or two. He made friends with Hal Roach, who starred him in Roach's first attempts at a comedy empire, which collapsed rapidly due to lack of experience, lack of resources, and lack of acumen. Lloyd put in time at Mack Sennett's studio until Roach was ready to launch his second attempt at becoming a genius producer. This time things clicked better, but it was still slow going as

Roach built up his studio and was testily reluctant to take any chances that might imperil his endeavors.

This meant Lloyd had to serve an onscreen apprenticeship as fail-safe (at the box office) Chaplin clones, the first called "Willie Work" and the second called "Lonesome Luke." Though the latter proved popular, Lloyd couldn't stand to shadow anyone else's genius when he had so much of his own. It took a long time and a lot of persistence (persistence being Lloyd's stock in trade both on and off the screen) to get Roach's permission to cast aside those characters and create something new, an ostensibly average young guy, usually named "Harold," whose distinguishing physical mark was his round-eyed glasses.

Most of the silent comedians of the day were considered grotesques, with moustaches the size and ornateness of antique newel posts, dopey hats, and clothes that fitted like both dirigibles and pipe cleaners and that were so loud in hue the film didn't need either a sound track or Technicolor to both deafen and blind the audience. But contrary to the myth, Harold Lloyd's "glass character" (*not* "glas*ses* character"; he was adamant on that point) was not the first to adopt a "normal" look. Roscoe Arbuckle never wore facial hair, lunatic outfits (he was fond of farmer clothes, but he was playing a hick on the farm, so how could that be called "grotesque"?), or crazy hats. Mabel Normand and all other female comedians except Louise Fazenda and Polly Moran looked normal; Gale Henry and Alice Howell affected certain idiosyncrasies that nevertheless did not disguise their regular appearances. Fred Mace, Charley Chase, Raymond Griffith, Sidney Drew, John Bunny, Max Linder, Douglas Fairbanks—they all looked normal, with Chase and Griffith and Linder even sporting normal moustaches. And, yes, all of these comedians were doing the look prior to 1917, the year the "glass character" took shape.

What made Harold's "Harold" different was the eyeglasses, a prop that no one else utilized; they made him incalculably less of a movie-star-pretending-to-be-an-average-Joe. Plus, his ebullience and youth put him squarely in the zeitgeist of the happy, progressive, zesty, dynamic America emerging from the Great War to take over the world; only his female counterpart, Clara Bow, could match him in that regard. And finally, let's not forget: the man made fast-moving, wildly entertaining, and exuberantly hilarious comedy films.

Synopsis: As so often in his films, Lloyd plays a hyperkinetic young man whose driving—no, make that *pile-driving*—ambition verges on the deranged, or at least the obsessive. His aim to become a successful department store manager pushes him to build a structure of desperate lies to delude his girlfriend back in the boondocks. When the fluttery fiancée (Mildred Davis) arrives in town to make sure her small-town hooks are still firmly embedded in her boyfriend's back, he of course won't give up the ruse: instead, he bullies and browbeats his fellow staffers in the pretense that he is their boss, thereby impressing the adoring simpleton from the sticks.

The next step in the delusion, however, puts "Harold" in the unenviable position of having to climb the exterior of the same department store he allegedly runs. It's the ultimate publicity-stunt-gone-wrong: pull it off, and he wins the girl plus $1,000 (equivalent probably to $1 million today); fail, and he loses not only the girl and the money but his life as well.

Comment: The climb up the exterior of the building is so justly famous, so brilliantly crafted in both structure and execution, so iconic in producing the best-known still picture of the silent comedy era—Harold dangling loose-leggedly from the bending arm of a giant clock—and so flat-out screamingly funny, no one ever remembers the first half of the movie.

That first half is some of the ugliest stuff Lloyd ever put on film. It's all about lying for selfish ends. He lies about being injured so he can divert an ambulance from real emergencies and use it as his personal unpaid taxi. He lies to his roommate, steals the latter's most cherished possession, and hocks it for his own monetary benefit. He lies to his fiancée about his status at his workplace, and then piles lies upon lies to maintain the façade when she shows up unexpectedly.

You can build a terrific comedy on the premise of lying, and plenty of great comedians (and even more lousy ones) have done so, from Molière to Jim Carrey; but your liar must always get his comeuppance, and do penitence even as he wins out in the end, else the lies trump the truth and make fools of the audience. And Harold Lloyd never gets his comeuppance, never does penitence, yet always wins. This is reprehensible ethics.

Bonus: One of the publicity stunts for *Safety Last!* that was urged upon film exhibitors (i.e., theatre owners) was to hire a real "human fly" to climb a local department store building, just like Harold. It backfired in one case, when a professional climber fell to his death. He was being paid a mere $50, which hopefully went to his widow and her two very young fatherless boys.

SATURDAY AFTERNOON

(1926, Mack Sennett)

Director: Harry Edwards
Writers: Arthur Ripley, Frank Capra
Titles: A. H. Giebler
Camera: Billy Williams
Editor: William Hornbeck
Cast: Harry Langdon, Vernon Dent, Ruth Hiatt, Peggy Montgomery, Alice Ward, Anna Hernandez, Leo Willis, Joe Young, Tiny Ward
Running Time (Length): Three reels

Background: Saturday Afternoon was Harry Langdon's twenty-second comedy in exactly two years since signing up with Mack Sennett. This was not an unusual pace; indeed, it was Sennett's normal pace for producing shorts. But keep in mind Langdon was forty years old when he started making movies; it is a bit surprising he had the energy at that advanced age to churn 'em out at a much younger comedian's rate. On the other hand, he didn't need to waste time: he had spent two decades polishing his act in vaudeville. He had his shtick down pat, even if Sennett and some of his crew couldn't figure it out. Langdon was able to work quickly by essentially ignoring the crew and doing what he wanted to do, what twenty years of grinding live tours had told him would work with his audience (not with "an" audience, but with *his* audience; critics consistently underestimate Langdon's sensitivity to the selectiveness of his own appeal).

In terms of Langdon-brand quality, he hit the mark with his first Sennett film (*Picking Peaches*, 1924) and polished that proven quality through another twenty-plus films—roughly the equivalent of twenty-plus years on the theatrical boards. With *Saturday Afternoon*, he achieved such a peak, proved himself so absolutely ready for the big move to feature films, that two other shorts made the same year (*Fiddlesticks* and *Soldier Man*) were shelved for a couple of years as being superfluous.

Synopsis: In the 1920s, the workweek still consisted of Monday through Friday *plus* Saturday morning. Add the fact that everybody was expected to spend Sunday morning in church and Sunday afternoon with the family (a lot of places in North America still banned Sunday sports) and everything was shut down tight Sunday evening, and you can imagine how fervidly all middle-class working people looked forward to the freedom of their Saturday afternoons.

"Harry Higgins" (Langdon) and "Steve Smith" (Vernon Dent) are living the dream. That is, they're dreaming if they think they're going to live it up on this or any other Saturday afternoon. "Steve" may or may not be married; he's just determined to chase girls regardless of his or their marital status, because it's the only way he has of blowing off steam. He sets up a date with two hot-to-trot (or so he hopes) pickups and sends his pal "Harry" home to get ready for a stompin' Sat'd'y 'noon.

If "Harry" wears the pants at home, they are rompers. His over-bearing wife and her only slightly more compassionate mother bully him into a subinfantile status. Spineless he may be, but he still has a tiny bit of cunning: after his wife takes all his pay *and* all the money he's been hiding under the rug, he slips out for his date with the money he's been hiding in a *second* spot under the rug.

Once the boys meet up with the girls, the girls meet up with other boys, and the result is an extremely brutal fight, highlighted by Langdon's superbly funny and varying "participation," which swings from concussed victim to grandstand cheerleader to gassed-up obliterator to simply obliterated. When a cop breaks up the fight and the fisticuff enthusiasts zoom away side by side in their cars, the still-dazed "Harry" ends up literally wrapped around a telephone pole, from which his wife extricates him and carts him off to life as a submissive little child burping on Mama's shoulder.

Comment: This is truly a showcase for Harry Langdon. The plot is nothing more elaborate than the stuff Mack Sennett scribbled on the back of an envelope in 1914—"brash guy and wimp pal pick up two gals and get into a fight with their real boyfriends"—and it could have been played by any two guys on the lot, or even any two gals in a role reversal. Like a jazz standard, it's a skeleton upon which every performer in the genre can emphatically lay his personal stamp.

And just as you can't imagine anybody but John Coltrane playing "My Favorite Things" once you've heard him do it (and do it, and do it, and do it, and do it), so you can't imagine anybody else playing *Saturday Afternoon* the same way Harry Langdon does. It's his picture. Buster Keaton or James Finlayson might have tried the hiding-money-under-the-rug gag and done it well enough, but Langdon's character of spineless, emasculated, unresisting victim who still manages a tiny rebellion—tiny yet not completely ineffectual—works against Ruth Hiatt's uncompromising nutcracker of a wife with a comic impact that, no, not even Keaton might have been able to match, because we know Keaton is resourceful and competent and is never browbeaten to the point of being satisfied with just a tiny rebellion; Keaton is going to *win* the war. Other comedians, such as Charley Chase or Roscoe Arbuckle or Larry Semon, just are not the whipped eunuchs that Langdon is; they never could have pulled off the same degree of puniness that makes it so funny when he manages to enact his minuscule cheats.

His interplay with Dent in the street scenes, whether it be watching him intently as Dent kisses his girl, or trying to match Dent's manly stride, or holding up his end of the ladykillers-at-large image by picking up streetwalkers, could have been handled by Laurel and Hardy. The small differences elicit much different audience responses. Laurel might have watched Hardy kiss a girl with puzzled interest, or perhaps with shock, and would have gotten laughs either way. Langdon watches Dent kiss like a kid on a Little League baseball team bending over with his hands on his knees as the coach shows him how to lay down a bunt; he's not just curious, or emotional or reacting, he's *learning* . . . and this is a married man!

The fight, likewise, could be played by any comedian for genuine belly laughs, and indeed fight scenes are endemic in silent comedy: *everybody* did them, so what matters is how they personalized them, and what the results display about their true level of comic ingenuity. Snub Pollard's total lack of creativity is laid bare mercilessly, during the boxing scene in *Looking for Trouble* (1919), whereas Hank Mann's exceptional subtlety as a foil shines quietly when he gets into the ring with Charlie Chaplin in *City Lights* (1931).

Once again, the gags Langdon inserts into his fight scene are genre standards: being "helpful" from the sidelines, getting clonked and rendered *hors de combat*, accidentally sipping a fluid that momentarily turns him into Jack Dempsey. He commands these gags and twists them to suit his character: making a tentative fist and speculating on the possibility of its being a lethal weapon, watching the other fist-swingers with all the empty-headed studiousness of a watermelon sitting on the teacher's desk, taking a punch and gently easing his body into a comatose state.

To borrow from Douglas Wolk's entry on John Coltrane's *Giant Steps* in *The New Rolling Stone Album Guide* (2004, edited by Nathan Brackett with Christian Hoard), these gags are where Harry Langdon declared that everyone had to sit up and pay attention to him.

Bonus: The despicable myth created by Frank Capra that he, Capra, was almost solely responsible for the greatness of Harry Langdon has been thoroughly disproved by researchers and critics such as Joyce Rheuban (*Harry Langdon: The Comedian as Metteur-en-Scene*, 1983), William Schelly (*Harry Langdon*, 1982), Joseph McBride (*Frank Capra: The Catastrophe of Success*, 1992), and Chuck Harter and Michael Hayde (*Little Elf: A Celebration of Harry Langdon*, 2012). But to give some credit to a rat fink who wanted far more than his share, it is true that the very best Langdon films were not coincidentally produced by a team consisting of Langdon, writer/director Capra, writer Arthur Ripley, and director Harry Edwards.

Edwards first directed Langdon in *The Luck o' the Foolish* in 1924, the comedian's ninth Sennett film. He directed the next twelve films (Langdon's three Sol Lesser films were made earlier but anachronistically released in the midst of the Edwards productions), including *Tramp Tramp Tramp* (1926), and the three films made in 1926 but not released until one or two years later. That's fifteen films in total, so to dismiss Edwards as an insignificant member of the team the way Capra does is quite obviously nonsense. Edwards helmed nearly *all* of Langdon's best films. Capra, for comparison, is credited as director only for *The Strong Man* (1926), an excellent movie, and *Long Pants* (1927), the film that started Langdon on his downward spiral.

As for Ripley, he is rightly credited by Harter and Hayde for injecting the extremely black thread of humor that eventually proved Langdon's undoing, but which was one of the absolutely vital elements of distinguishing him from all other silent comedians. Ripley's scripts and gags were downright evil at times, and as bizarre in their way as anything Tod Browning invented for the drama genre.

Ripley's contributions—as least as credited onscreen—began with *Boobs in the Wood* (1925) and then immediately steered Langdon down the streets of noir giggles with *His Marriage Wow* (1925). Ripley wrote all of Langdon's subsequent silent films (excluding only those made for Principal Pictures). It was almost certainly Ripley's weird, twisted sense of humor that was responsible for Langdon's drift into asexual characterization and sexually subversive material, which led directly to disaster both critically and at the box office. Capra's autobiography hints darkly at his objections to Ripley's leanings in the films they wrote together or that Ripley wrote and Capra directed; this complaint actually serves to undercut Capra's claims to have been the genius behind Langdon's fleeting success, since it establishes Ripley as the dominant influence and Capra as the weakling of the team.

Ultimately, Langdon had control of his pictures, and neither Ripley nor Capra (nor Edwards, for that matter) had the final say in the direction in which he took the "Harry" character. Langdon may not have been able to foresee the consequences of pursuing the path he chose; but he knew his audience, and he made the choices whenever the visions of Ripley and Capra could not be reconciled. Both for better and for worse, Harry Langdon decided on Harry Langdon, and nobody else had the final say.

THE SAWMILL

(1922, Vitagraph)

Directors: Larry Semon and Norman Taurog
Writers: Larry Semon and Norman Taurog
Cast: Larry Semon, Kathleen O'Connor, Oliver Hardy, Frank Alexander, Al Thompson, Ann Hastings, Bill Hauber, Rose Code, Peter Ormonds
Running Time (Length): Two reels
Availability: DVD (Kino Video: *The Oliver Hardy Collection*)

Background: Consistent in all accounts of Larry Semon's fall from grace are fingers pointing at the extravagance of his sets and stunts. Vitagraph Studios had a long and distinguished existence as the home of many silent comedy giants, beginning with arguably the very first great American film comedian, John Bunny, and one of the greatest-ever social comedy teams, Mr. and Mrs. Sidney Drew. But Vitagraph, though prosperous, was not reaping such revenues that it could afford Semon's production expenses for all eternity.

Prime exemplar of his wanton disregard for budgets, and often cited as the straw that broke the backs of Vitagraph bookkeepers, is the lumbering camp he constructed for *The Sawmill*. Five hundred miles from Hollywood, in the Sequoia National Forest, more than 100 workmen built "Semonville." Not only did this set include every possible kind of building, structure, and by-product that might conceivably be found in a remote lumber camp (there are thousands of freshly cut planks, beams, and boards piled everywhere in nearly every shot of the film), it also included a virtual town erected on the spot for the film's 75-person production crew; after all, being that far away from civilization, they had need of places to sleep, places to eat, and places to hang out. Fancy cooks were hired away from top restaurants, authentic workers' clothing was created with Erich von Stroheim historical precision, and special slots and tracks for advantageous camera shots were designed and gouged into the land by top technological talents, if not by prize-winning architects.

And then on or around the first day of shooting, one of the worst forest fires in California history erupted practically next door. Production was immediately halted and Semon's crew was recruited (a law forced all people in the vicinity of the fire to participate) to assist in fighting it for several days, after which filming was impossible for two weeks because of the smoke hanging in the air. At least that expense couldn't be laid at Semon's feet, but it did nothing to make Vitagraph forgiving about his spendthrift ways. In fact, for a year preceding and a year following *The Sawmill*, Vitagraph and Semon sparred with countering lawsuits over the legal justifiability of the latter's running up excessive production costs with, allegedly, malice aforethought (because he supposedly wanted Vitagraph to fire him so he could sign a more lucrative contract with a rival studio).

At the end of production, most of Semonville was destroyed for the climactic scenes; whatever was left over was ripped down afterward—just one more bitterly expensive pill for Vitagraph to swallow, and pay for.

Synopsis: Easygoing Larry is a leisurely employee at the sawmill owned by Frank Alexander and terrorized by foreman Oliver Hardy. Hardy has a couple of full-grown blackbirds for eyebrows and a moustache that could scrub bathtubs, so you can tell he's the bad guy; and if you have any lingering doubts, he quickly erases them by his actions: he is truly *brutal*, punching men ass over teakettle and flinging them around with the same vicious intent with which he flings yard-long tree stumps.

There's some kind of semi-romantic subplot involving Semon and Hardy competing for the hand of a wholesome brunette beauty in gingham and hair ribbons (Kathleen O'Connor), but they are apparently also competing for the hand of the owner's sleek, jodhpur-clad, blonde daughter (Ann Hastings). The unimportance of these romance threads is demonstrated by the fact that nobody makes anything of the fact that the men are both two-timing poor Kathleen, who disappears altogether about halfway through the film. At any rate, it's Ann that Larry ends up with in the river. We're not told if Hardy ends up with O'Connor, but it seems unlikely.

Comment: The above synopsis really doesn't convey much in the way of a storyline. That's because *The Sawmill* doesn't have a storyline, and I'm not being sarcastic. This is a film about its setting, not about its characters or story.

And what takes place in that setting? Just spectacular destruction. A thirty-foot-high, massive structure (all wood, of course) similar to a water tower was built to house tons of whitewash, and then destroyed so we could laugh at the whitewash soaking Alexander and Hardy. Another tower was built and filled with tons of sand, and then destroyed so we could laugh at the sand burying Alexander and Hardy. In one sequence, Semon tries to exchange his ripped overalls for new ones with due modesty by running into a fully functional log cabin; a huge tree is chopped down and falls on the cabin, leveling it entirely. Semon staggers out of the wreckage, starts putting on his new pants in the open, and a second massive tree is felled right behind him. Moving to a more open space, he stretches his arms and luxuriates in the pleasure of his new overalls, and a third gigantic tree crashes around him. A few minutes later, Hardy blows up an entire house in his attempt to open the owner's safe. That's not enough devastation for Semon, though, so he and Hastings climb up what looks like a 50-foot tree, Hardy's henchmen start chopping it down, and Semon and Hastings swing away from it on a rope as it goes smashing down. It's a wonder there was any forest left standing at the end of this film.

It's awesome. You can't take your eyes off the screen. It's not only an overwhelming comedy, it's a visually fascinating one precisely because of its meticulous depiction of a genuine lumbering operation, which few of us have ever seen either in real life or in the movies.

Bonus: The Sawmill may well be the last high-water mark among Semon's oeuvre. His financial, production, romantic, and health concerns, sometimes separately, sometimes concurrently, now reached the point where his work was obviously impacted. Too, public tastes were changing: Hal Roach's comparatively elegant and leisurely slapstick (two adjectives that hitherto had no business coming anywhere close to that noun), the rise of non-grotesque comics such as Harold Lloyd, Buster Keaton, Douglas Fairbanks, and arguably Harry Langdon, and an explosion in the number and popularity of feature-length social comedies such as those of Gloria Swanson and Constance Talmadge were forcing even the flamboyant Ford Sterling to turn genteel if he wanted to extend his career. Larry Semon struggled to adjust. The public was not sympathetic: they perceived him as rinsing and repeating the same old gags, and the fact that he was now using blue rinse didn't make the gags more sophisticated or mature.

Semon's post-*Sawmill* work includes two of the worst feature comedies—no, two of the worst feature *films*—ever made: *The Wizard of Oz* and *The Perfect Clown*, both in 1925, and both enough to destroy any comedian's career except maybe the regrettably indestructible Adam Sandler. Both deservedly bombed at the box office and devastated Semon personally and financially.

In the midst of all these midlife crises, it was given out that he had suffered a complete nervous and physical breakdown and was hustled away to a desert sanitarium for therapy in August of 1928. The remaining two months of his life are shrouded in mystery. Officially he died of pneumonia exacerbated by tuberculosis, but no autopsy was performed, and the body was ostensibly cremated *without its ever being viewed by anyone but the doctor who owned the sanitarium.* Even his soon-to-be widow, Dorothy Dwan, when allowed to enter the bedroom that was at all other times off limits to everyone, was not permitted to actually *see* Larry in his declining condition: she had to squint from the doorway into a darkened room where a figure that *might* have been Semon assured her in an unclear voice that he would soon be fine.

The historians who have done the most to research Semon's death—Richard M. Roberts and Claudia Sassen—are remarkably circumspect in reporting their findings, correctly wary of committing themselves to any speculation unsupported by concrete evidence. Neither of them, in reciting the pains taken by the sanitarium doctor to hide Semon from scrutiny both in life and in death, expresses overt suspicions as to whether the body was Semon's or someone else's or, indeed, not a human corpse at all. They are rightfully scrupulous because there can be no conclusive answer ninety years on.

Roberts interviewed Dwan in her final years and her bewilderment was still palpable. "I can hardly make him out and they won't let me get near him," she complained of what turned out to be her visit to his deathbed. Could she see enough of him to be certain it actually was Larry? After all, she was stunned by the news, two days after the visit, that Semon had died; this suggests she couldn't have seen him clearly enough to have gauged his condition as critical. To have pneumonia *and* tuberculosis, both long-term illnesses and both in their terminal stages, would have rendered Semon's near-death state all too obvious to the naked eye even in a darkened room—*if* the doctor had let her get a close enough look. The possibility has to be strong that either an imposter was in the bed, or else it was Semon and he wasn't particularly ill but had reasons to wish to create that impression. Let's not forget Semon was a big fan of using clown-white makeup, which with dim lighting could make him look like a ghost, so it would have been child's play for the *real* Semon to have made himself up to look like death warmed over for the sake of deceiving Dwan—*if* he had wanted to, and if the doctor had allowed her to see him close up, which didn't happen!

Sassen found extant telegrams allegedly from Dwan in which she waves red flags about Semon's condition, and Sassen works out a timeline that indicates Dwan couldn't have sent these telegrams. To me, this raises the obvious possibility that the resort faked the telegrams.

And why would the death be a hoax? Because death was the only way Semon could escape his untenable situation in life and work. He could have arranged to fake his death so he could start anew; he was only somewhere around 45 years old or younger (his birth year is disputable; 45 is thought to be the oldest possible age he could have been in 1928), and that is certainly young enough to begin a second life under a new identity. The sanitarium doctor specialized in plastic surgery; Larry with a pert little button of a nose would have been completely unrecognizable.

Or—yet more possibilities—he could have been the victim of the doctor, either by murder for whatever unknown motive; or by the doctor's sheer medical incompetence; or by what we now compassionately call "assisted suicide." The latter scenario would explain all the skullduggery, because at that time a doctor assisting a patient to commit suicide could have been charged with murder and given his own death sentence if found guilty.

Larry Semon's films invariably featured death-defying and preposterous stunts that he pulled off with the assistance of imposters (i.e., stuntmen) who were kept distant from the public view. In October of 1928, with the help of imposters kept distant from the public view, he may have pulled off the most death-defying and preposterous stunt of his life.

SEVEN YEARS BAD LUCK

(1921, Max Linder Productions)

Director: Max Linder
Writer: Max Linder
Camera: Charles van Enger
Cast: Max Linder, Thelma Percy, Alta Allen, Betty Peterson, Ralph McCullough, F. B.
   Crayne, Chance Ward, Hugh Saxon, Cap Anderson, Harry Mann
Running Time (Length): 48 minutes or 62 minutes (five reels)
Availability: DVD (Kino Lorber: *The Max Linder Collection*)

Background: Max Linder hit his peak as a France-based world comedy superstar in the years leading up to the First World War. The war hit him very hard—fatally hard. His film career was put on hold; an emotional, patriotic Frenchman, he had to get involved in it militarily. And like so many other men of his generation, the experience psychologically damaged him to a permanent extent.

He didn't exactly return to French filmmaking after being invalided out of the army, for his country was still in the depths of the conflagration when he signed a contract to make films for the Essanay company in America in 1916. The three films he made in the United States were failures, and Essanay tore up the contract and sent him back to Europe, thoroughly humiliated and depressed. Life was no better in France; indeed, it was worse, because the war still had another year to go, it was impossible to make movies, and Linder's depression (identifiable today as posttraumatic stress disorder) kept him in despair and inertia.

When the war finally ended in 1918, Linder made one reasonably successful film in France; thus reassured he still had something left to give, he returned to America and made three feature comedies in a heroic, guns-blazing, final assault upon the bastions of American success: *Seven Years Bad Luck* (1921), *Be My Wife* (1921), and *The Three Must-Get-Theres* (1922). Once again, American audiences proved impervious to Gallic charm; once again, Gallic charm was forced to retreat back overseas, tail between its legs; once again, sadly, depression prostrated the movies' first universal comedy superstar. He would not recover, only ending the pain with his wife in a suicide pact in 1925.

Synopsis: Having enjoyed his bachelor party with all the enthusiasm husbands-to-be around the world enjoy theirs, Max is now too hungover to notice his full-length mirror has been accidentally broken by his servants, and that a look-alike is impersonating his reflection in one of the earliest and best film versions of an old stage gag (which will be done most sublimely by the Marx Brothers a dozen years later in *Duck Soup* [1933]). By the time he catches on, the servants have taken delivery of and installed the new mirror; thinking he's about to wallop his imposter reflection, he instead smashes the mirror and condemns himself to seven years of bad luck.

There follows a series of loosely connected episodes and gag scenes, ostensibly linked by his attempts to run away from the bad luck. Except for the first in this series, however, there is almost no effort to stick to the premise. Several sequences are set in and around a train, one of which is a tad distasteful to modern politically correct audiences (yet they will have no problem enjoying the ageist humor in the next sequence, set in the railroad station). Max is on the run, as it seems there are a couple of dozen policemen with nothing better to do than chase a scofflaw who failed to pay for a train ticket. (He did pay for it, actually, but had the ticket and his wallet stolen by a clever trio of con men.) He's also trying to get his fiancée to forgive him for attempting to eliminate her annoying Shih Tzu doggie; the fellow he asks to speak to her on his behalf turns out to have been his rival, who promptly takes the opening to march the girl before a judge and try to marry her himself. Luckily, Max has been captured by the police and frog-marched (ethnically insulting pun intended) before that same judge, who agrees to marry the correct fiancé to the correct fiancée.

Seven years later . . . apparently the prophecy came true, for Max and his wife now have seven little brats and seven little doggies (not Shih Tzus, puzzlingly, although we catch a glimpse of their supposed mother in the doorway keeping an eye on her pups).

Comment: Virtually every comedian in any medium has a shelf life. Freshness and inventiveness are finite qualities everywhere; their passing is often blindingly, devastatingly, soul-crushingly obvious in an art whose goal is to make you laugh, laugh hard, and laugh often. But in other cases, the overnight plummeting of a comedian's popularity remains mysterious and mystifying.

Max Linder still had every quality in 1921 that he had had in 1912, in spite of the years, the intervening war, the debilitating and permanent psychological scars, the changes of taste and of fashion, and the stupendous maturation of film comedy—the year 1921 was when, symbolically enough, Roscoe Arbuckle's career was effectively murdered and the year when Charlie Chaplin took slapstick from the level of Arbuckle's crudities to a brand new level of sophistication and artistry with *The Kid*.

Linder's transition across the decade (and the ocean) looks effortless. The long opening sequence highlighted by the mirror gag is beautifully done, technically sophisticated, cleverly engineered, and displays sharp adaptation of tropes. The first shot is a close-up of Linder at first refusing, then shrugging and accepting a refill of his champagne glass, then repeating it again and again, each time a couple of frames of film shorter, the gesture of refusal disappearing slowly, the shrug disappearing slowly, the salutation disappearing slowly . . . it is a marvelous and amusing spin on a well-known device of narrative compression.

Linder really shows off his range. He does an extended chase sequence. He does a dream sequence. He does a Chaplinesque escape/avoidance train-hopping sequence. He does a transformation-of-appearance sequence, twice actually, most skillfully when he morphs himself into a doddering, gruff old man handling the mail in a railroad station. He does a "dramatic courtroom revelation" sequence. He does a social comedy sequence, trying to rid himself of his fiancée's dog. He does slapstick sequences. There is nothing, no version of silent comedy, that he does not do in this film, and he's funny doing all of them.

Why was *Seven Years Bad Luck* not a resounding success upon its release? Slapstick comedy of feature length was, if not still a novelty in 1921, still something of an experiment, and slightly disreputable, or at least disrespected; Harold Lloyd, Buster Keaton, and Harry Langdon were all still making short films, Arbuckle and Chaplin were each making their feature debuts, and Mabel Normand's move to features was sputtering due in part to her offscreen troubles. To audiences, Linder may have appeared to be trying to have it both ways: slapstick disreputability married to social-comedy respectability, and they didn't like (or morally approve of) the match, or perhaps just didn't know what to make of it. Perhaps they saw the film as old-fashioned. Perhaps they just couldn't get over their knee-jerk xenophobic rejection of Old World smarty-pants artists, although in this particular film the only thing vaguely foreign about Linder is his aristocratic dress and living arrangements, and even those last only for the first third of the movie before he becomes an ordinarily dressed grifter on the lam from the cops. Perhaps it was the somewhat choppy, yoked-together, episodic nature of the film; but again, this was nothing unusual for American comedy films in 1921. Perhaps American audiences remembered Linder's previous attempt to conquer their film screens and they were not willing to give this "old guy" another chance.

Or perhaps Linder's shelf life had simply expired.

Bonus: It was tempting to choose *The Three Must-Get-Theres* (1922) over *Seven Years Bad Luck*. The former was Linder's last self-produced effort (he made two later films for other producers in France before his death), so it is really his last testament, and a very funny film indeed.

The deciding factor was that *Seven Years Bad Luck* is closer to the traditional Linder comedy: totally his own creation and tailored to his character. *The Three Must-Get-Theres*, as its title suggests, takes Linder out of his character and borrows/builds upon the creations of others. This doesn't mean merely the Dumas story; it means also using the kinds of gags and jokes and puns that other American comedians were using. Musketeers = Must-Get-Theres; D'Artagnan = Dart-in-Again; Porthos, Athos, and Aramis = Octopus, Porpoise, and Walrus—these are bad puns that the classic Linder would never have condescended to use.

It goes without saying that Linder was satirizing Douglas Fairbanks's *The Three Musketeers*, an enormous hit in 1921. An essential running gag is the anachronistic placement of modern conveniences—the use of telephones, the Ford flivver being carried bodily by runners in place of a travel-coach, guns being used as often as swords, a straw boater atop the traditional musketeer uniform, etc. These are *really* funny—almost every one of them made me burst out laughing—but they're also a staple of American comedy; heck, Mack Sennett was using them nearly a decade earlier.

The Three Must-Get-Theres is highly recommended; just remember, please, that it isn't really a Linder-controlled Linder film, but rather a Linder film trying to be an American film.

SHOOT STRAIGHT

(1923, Roach)

Director: Jay A. Howe
Writer: Uncredited, probably both James and Charles Parrott
Cast: Paul Parrott (James Parrott), Jobyna Ralston, George Rowe, Eddie Baker
Running Time (Length): 10 minutes (one reel)
Availability: DVD (Undercrank Productions: *Accidentally Preserved*, vol. 1)

Background: Charley Chase, one of the truly *great* greats of silent comedy, was born Charles Parrott. His father died when Charles was very young. At age ten, he was performing in the streets of Baltimore. He had to, because his mother couldn't support the family. And man-of-the-family Charles felt the additional pressure of being "father" to his younger brother, Jimmy.

This set the pattern of Charley's life: the obligation to support an entire family, and the obligation to look out for Jimmy. So when Charley became a successful comic force called Charley Chase, it was only natural that he brought along Jimmy to become a less-successful comic force called Paul Parrott.

Jimmy shared something else with Charley: alcoholism. Jimmy had a series of ongoing health problems as well, which contributed both to his drinking and to the lesser level of his accomplishments. Unlike his older brother, Jimmy couldn't work whenever the booze got to him. And unlike Charley, Jimmy just couldn't ever come up with an onscreen character that had any discernible personality, let alone one that was consistent over the course of his output. It's impossible to identify a single trait of the Paul Parrott character. Physically, he resembled Chase and he sported a debonair French curlicue of a moustache; beyond that, he was a cipher.

Paul Parrott poured out a huge number of short comedies in the early 1920s. When these didn't catch fire at the box office, Roach paired him up with Snub Pollard in a brief series that likewise didn't catch fire. Where Parrott started to have real success was behind the camera: he was the director of many of Laurel and Hardy's classic films (where he was listed as James Parrott), and he had always been regarded as a good gagman. When the talkies came along, he retired from the screen and worked—when he was capable of work—behind it until his early death at 42.

Synopsis: Master hunter—actually identified as "the Amateur Hunter," but who's going to believe that?—Paul Parrott uses an ingenious weapon in his pursuit of small game: a rifle fitted out with a fishing rod, with a walnut on the line as bait for squirrels. The squirrels prove themselves a lot smarter than Paul. Forced to cut bait when a skunk takes it, Paul gets the rifle barrel twisted around in a tree hole and accidentally blows his own brains out. Unperturbed by this loss, he puts the rifle aside and uses socks to trap rabbits when they scurry into their warrens.

Even more masterful hunter George Rowe—with those crossed eyes, how could he be anything else?—accompanied by the delicious Jobyna Ralston, is leading a duck-hunting party when Paul stumbles into their midst and starts

Not-so-big-game hunter Paul Parrott tries in vain to outwit a squirrel in *Shoot Straight* (1923). *Courtesy of Undercrank Productions*

shooting up their decoys. The outraged fowlists send him off to get his own blind, complete with window frame and pull-down shade. Even a bird brain can outwit the brain-deficient Paul: he goes underwater shooting and fails repeatedly, he tries shooting them out of the air and gets a blizzard of feathers even though his shots missed them, and to add insult to injury one duck flies off with his rifle as a prize. Darn! And just when he needed it to shoot the baby bear that has chased him into a tree that has more large tunnels in it than the New York City subway.

Comment: For all purposes, this is a one-man show. Rowe, Ralston, and their hunting party make only a couple of brief and inconsequential appearances, although it's enjoyable to watch them totter across a hill at the top of the screen with the bear in pursuit in a surprising anticipation of one of Ingmar Bergman's most iconic images.

For his part, Parrott only has to mug his way through the hunting gags, which is something almost any silent comedian could have done in his sleep. That's fine, though, because the gags are just great. Parrott (and presumably his brother) came up with a textbook's worth of superb bits: there really isn't a lame one among them.

Bonus: It's impossible not to think about Elmer Fudd and Bugs Bunny while watching *Shoot Straight*. The crazy gang at Warner Brothers' cartoon empire must have all been lifelong fans of this little gem: it informs all the timeless toons they made twenty years later in which Fudd hunts that wascally wabbit.

SHOULDER ARMS

(1918, First National)

Director: Charles Chaplin
Writer: Charles Chaplin
Camera: Roland Totheroh
Editor: Charles Chaplin
Cast: Charlie Chaplin, Edna Purviance, Albert Austin, Henry Bergman, Sydney
  Chaplin, Loyal Underwood, Tom Wilson, Jack Wilson, Mark Jones
Running Time (Length): Three reels
Availability: DVD (Cobra Entertainment: *The Essential Charlie Chaplin*, vol. 10)

Background: Despite what his haters believe, Charlie Chaplin never evaded military service in the Great War. He fretted about it, really agonized over it: his British patriotism and detestation of the robotic despotism of the German political-military oligarchy urged him to at least inquire into his own suitability for soldiering in spite of his resolute principles against all war. Undeniably relieved when told he was too small for service and that the Allied military would much prefer him to contribute laughter to the war effort, he joined with his dearest friends, Douglas Fairbanks and Mary Pickford, to raise millions of dollars by selling war bonds through free public entertainment and through a short propaganda film, *The Bond.* That took care of contributing to the war effort financially; when he considered contributing laughter, he worked out the ideas for *Shoulder Arms.*

As always with Chaplin, developing the story and putting it before the camera was a prolonged struggle with anxiety and perfectionism. He wasn't utterly incapable of just tossing off a quickie, as *The Bond* proved; but that wasn't a Chaplin film, it was a government propaganda film featuring Chaplin. *Shoulder Arms* was going to be "a Chaplin film," and that meant he compulsively spent weeks of time and barrels of money getting everything just right, and then throwing out nearly everything he had just approved and starting all over again.

What was supposed to have been a five-reel epic following the "Charlie" character from the slums of the city and the manacles of family life to military glory and back again ended up being a three-reel tour de force focused entirely on army life and the terrors, triumphs, and laughs of war.

Synopsis: Exactly as smooth and efficient a recruit as we would expect "Charlie" to be in the army, he nevertheless dreams of military heroism and derring-do, beginning with sharpshooting, proceeding to survival in a swimming-pool of a trench, morphing into an exquisitely done camouflaged spy (you really can't spot him in his tree disguise even when you're looking for him), then into a skillful imposter of a German leader, and finally into the man who single-handedly delivers the Kaiser, the Crown Prince, and General von Hindenberg to captivity and ends the war—and let's not forget that he successfully woos and rescues the most beautiful girl in France.

Comments: If you can forgive this film's "It's only a dream" bookends—and personally there isn't a film cliché I loathe more—*Shoulder Arms* is as nearly perfect as any silent comedy film ever made. Certainly it remains the best comedy film—silent or talkie—about war ever made. That Chaplin could make it, and make it this funny, *during* the war is staggering.

It was released just barely ahead of the armistice, just barely in time for the real soldiers to watch it on their breaks from battle. And they loved it, even more emphatically than the home front loved it. They were stunned at Chaplin's success in capturing all the realities of trench warfare and exaggerating them only enough to make them incredibly funny. Truly, he had made one of the best and most thorough contributions of anybody toward the Allied war effort.

Bonus: In the silent film era, or at least up until the middle-to-late Twenties, making films was almost like running a junior high school play. Everybody pitched in at every kind of job: actors built sets, directors cranked cameras and cut film, writers played onscreen roles, prop men helped with lighting, everybody did their own makeup, and actors could end up onscreen in two or three different roles in the same film.

In *Shoulder Arms*, Henry Bergman plays at least three roles. Sydney Chaplin, Charlie's big brother, plays at least two roles. Albert Austin may be in as many as six roles, although we know two of them were edited out of the final print. The amazing thing is that you never notice them doing double/triple/quintuple duty unless you deliberately look for them; each of them was a skilled makeup man, each wore different outfits for each character, and Austin's versatility was aided by our being accustomed to his "always" wearing a moustache that looked like a sheaf of wheat onscreen, so all he had to do was take off the fake hair and we're at a loss to recognize him. The tight curls of his red hair and his tallness are the only clues to spot him.

SHOW PEOPLE

(1928, MGM)

Director: King Vidor
Writers: Agnes Christine Johnson and Laurence Stallings
Titles: Ralph Spence
Camera: John Arnold
Editor: Hugh Wynn
Cast: Marion Davies, William Haines, Paul Ralli, Dell Henderson, Harry Gribbon, Tenen Holtz, Sidney Bracey, Albert Conti, Polly Moran, Charles Chaplin, Douglas Fairbanks, William Hart, Kalla Pasha, Coy Watson, King Vidor (many other stars of the day in cameos or group pans)
Running Time: 81 minutes
Availability: DVD (Warner Archive Collection)

Background: The very term "mistress" is unknown to anybody born after 1960. The reasons why, in the past, it was a term packed with scandal and "ruined reputations" seem downright bizarre nowadays. Really, a young and pretty showgirl living unmarried with a rich old sugar daddy? What's scandalous about that? She's a corporate tycoon's trophy wife without the ring on her finger—so what?

Well, it really was scandalous back in the 1920s and '30s and even on up to the early 1960s, not to mention the preceding centuries. It was what Marion Davies had to endure when she accepted the proposition of an extremely rich, fat, old, ugly, and powerful newspaper tycoon, William Randolph Hearst. Publicly ensconced as his mistress in their castle outside Los Angeles, Davies fought against the moral opprobrium by ignoring it and doing all the right things that a trophy "wife" should do: she used her natural charm, good nature, friendliness, and talent to become the most admired hostess with the flashiest guest lists in the country, and a movie star for whom nearly everyone rooted to be successful. All of these genial and impressive attributes are on display in *Show People*.

Synopsis: Make way, Hollywood, for the next great idol of the dramatic movies! It's "Peggy Pepper" from Savannah, escorted by her daddy who, like all males from the post–Reconstruction Deep South, is supposedly a colonel. "Peggy's" grand manner and junior high school acting chops convince an indulgent casting agent to put her to work immediately. Contrary to her own expectations, though, it is not high drama but low comedy to which he assigns her.

Traumatized by the seltzer shower inflicted upon her in her first scene, "Peggy" is consoled by "Billy Boone," star comedian, and in no time they are not only boy/girlfriend offscreen but are also a popular slapstick comedy team. To "Peggy," though, this is a fate about as bad as death, and she jumps at the chance to sign with "High Art Pictures" to make costume dramas. The transformation is accompanied by a transformation in her personality and even in her name, as she becomes "Patricia Pepoire" and an affected, pretentious, effete snob along with it. No more "lowness, cheapness, and vulgarity" for her!

Her redirected career deservedly tanks. Looking for either a publicity boost or an escape to a life of ease, she decides that marrying what she thinks is a rich aristocrat is the ticket out of impending oblivion. "Billy" arrives moments before the wedding, spritzes her with seltzer, and it washes all those affectations right out of her.

Comment: As everyone knows—and not just with the benefit of hindsight from a less moralistic era—Marion Davies was an excellent comedian. She would have been immensely successful in that genre, probably even more so than Constance Talmadge. Hearst's infatuation with the costume dramas that he insisted she do at the expense of her comic strengths is lethally satirized in *Show People*; unfortunately, he never got the point, or else chose to ignore it.

Fans who belabor this lesson from *Show People*, however, are doing Davies a disservice almost as regrettable as that done to her by Hearst. *Show People* demonstrates that she was equally as wonderful in drama as in comedy: she was truly a complete actress. Her crying scenes are all profoundly moving and believable, especially her breakdown after doing her first comedy scene: these aren't Hollywood tears, she is genuinely heartbroken and not the least bit inhibited about showing it on the big screen, knowing full well it will make her look physically unattractive. She has undeniable truthfulness in her expressions of despair and disappointment. What makes her crying even more striking is that it comes not so long after one of the funniest scenes: her complete inability to cry on cue for her screen test.

In addition to trying to illustrate to Hearst why she prefers to do comedy, Davies pokes unmalicious (in my opinion) fun at Gloria Swanson and Mae Murray for their artificial *moués* and posings. I love it when a film director gets overfriendly enough to give "Patricia" a one-armed hug and she responds by haughtily waving away his plebian stench: he then discreetly slips a stick of gum in his mouth to make himself more fragrantly pleasing.

A lot of people seem to enjoy Harry Gribbon's deliberately over-the-top hamminess as the comedy director. I enjoy it too, up until he overdoes the overdoing as a rambunctious member of the audience in a theatre watching his own slapstick movie. Even the Three Stooges would be telling him to put a sock in it, as he wildly punches the air (it's a chase scene, *not* a fight scene, so what's provoking those punches?) and screams his jaw off its hinges with blatantly fake laughter.

William Haines, one of the most popular leading men in silent comedy features, is quite good as "Billy," although he follows Gribbon's unfortunate example in overexaggerating his own hilarity. Dell Henderson, a longtime reliable supporting comedian and director, gets less credit than he deserves for playing the "Colonel" with a pleasing balance of satire and genuine courtesy, pride, and confidence in his daughter. As for Polly Moran's imbecilic maid, though, the less said the better.

Show People is an unabashed Valentine to the Hollywood film industry. Every person in it is nice, kind, and understanding. In real life, the studio gate man would have thrown the "Pepper" duo out on their ears instead of directing them to the casting office; all the other stars (playing themselves) would have cut this newbie dead and done all they could to sabotage her career before it even got started, instead of smiling and waving at her as if they have all the time in the world for a silly girl dressed as if it were still 1865; most of the crews making films would have screamed for security to pitch the interloper out on her ear, instead of indulging her presence and providing friendly advice. Davies clearly had genuine love for Hollywood and was genuinely grateful that its denizens accepted her at a time when the moralists outside of the industry were intent on smearing her as a rich man's whore.

Bonus: Giving defiantly onscreen demonstrations of their acceptance of and affection for Marion Davies, more than a dozen movie stars put in cameos in *Show People*. That's not to overlook the people behind the scenes: directors, including King Vidor (director of *Show People* itself) are there onscreen too, and I'll bet the crews hanging around the cameras are all doing their actual jobs in lighting, continuity, photography, musical accompaniment, and so on.

Other than Charlie Chaplin—and even he might not be recognizable because he appears as his real gray-haired, clean-shaven, well-tailored self instead of as the Tramp—almost none of the stars seen briefly will be easily identified by anyone today except the most rabid of silent film fans. Doug Fairbanks and William Hart should be picked out by casual fans of the silents: Hart is smart enough to wear his entire Western regalia including the hat, and he and Doug share a skit with Davies that lasts long enough for the viewer to line them up with the right cards in the ol' memory box.

SKINNER'S DRESS SUIT

(1926, Universal)

Director: William Seiter
Writers: Henry Irving Dodge and Rex Taylor
Titles: Walter Anthony
Camera: Arthur Todd
Editor: J. R. Rawlins
Cast: Reginald Denny, Laura La Plante, Ben Hendricks Jr., Arthur Lake, Hedda Hopper,
   Lionel Braham, Lila Leslie, E. J. Ratcliffe, Henry Barrows, Frona Hale, William
   Strauss, Betty Morrisey, Lucille De Nevers, Lucille Ward, Broderick O'Farrell
Running Time: 89 minutes
Availability: DVD (Grapevine Video)

Background: A long-running stage hit, *Skinner's Dress Suit* was filmed in 1917 as a fairly straightforward record of the play. Nearly ten years later, the times had changed drastically: the Victorian era was long dead, the world was no longer on a war footing (with, as always, a few minor far-off exceptions), the Jazz Age was in full swing, and American cities were expanding into the first true modern suburbs. It was a perfect time to brush off the old hit and give it a smacking good updating.

Synopsis: "Mr. Skinner" is a highly successful, immensely valued senior employee at the firm of McLaughlin and Perkins. At least, that's what his bubble-brained, apron-wearing blonde wife has convinced herself, and half convinced him. Determined to keep pace with the neighbors in their manicured-lawn suburb, she not only assumes he has gotten the "well-deserved" raise she's been nagging him about, she goes right ahead and spends it into the next two years.

"Skinner" is somewhat perturbed by this behavior, not to say panicky, because he most definitely did *not* get the raise. Reluctantly playing into his wife's delusions, he signs up for an installment payment plan in order to acquire the dress suit that is de rigueur for the swanky parties that wifey wants to attend as part of her social-climbing scheme. When they use the latest hip dance craze to make a hit on this unhip social circuit, "Skinner" gains enough self-confidence to actually demand the contentious raise.

Far from getting it, he gets the heave-ho. Fortunately, at the *next* swanky party, he pals up to the nuts-and-bolts magnate whose $500,000 contract ends up in "Skinner's" hands; he uses it as leverage to not only get an enormous salary increase from his ex-employers but to make them his new *co-*employers—he becomes a junior partner in the firm.

Comment: From the moment it was released, *Skinner's Dress Suit* has been widely and rightly regarded as one of the best domestic comedy features of the silent era. Although it is a charming film and is frequently quite amusing, I suspect the major yet unrecognized reason for its reputation is its unexpected landmarking of a turn in American society.

Reginald Denny in a revealing moment with Laura La Plante in *Skinner's Dress Suit* (1926). *Courtesy of Derek Boothroyd*

This is the first film that looks like it was actually filmed inside and around a *modern* American house. The neighborhood is a perfect foreshadowing of the suburban neighborhoods of all the American TV family sitcoms of the 1950s and early '60s: bright, clean split-level and bungalow houses with lovely long front lawns and asphalt walkways that go straight down to the sidewalks, which in turn run in perfect parallels to the paved streets. Inside, every room in the house is spacious, not in the manner of the cavernous, ceilingless cathedrals that the movies had hitherto presented as the "typical" white-collar employee's house, nor the cozy-cramped English style that had been presented as the "typical" working-man's house; instead, they look comfortable and have elbow space just like the real split-levels in American suburbs. This is the first film whose house interiors—and exterior house architecture, too—don't resemble the 19th-century houses that all films had portrayed up to now, whether rich or poor. Not even quintessential "modern" comedians such as Harold Lloyd or Charley Chase had used anything but Victorian interiors.

Equally modern, shockingly so, are the social attitudes. Social climbing was not exactly new or unique to the Jazz Age, but conspicuous consumption to keep up with the Joneses (rather than merely to flaunt one's wealth for one's own personal satisfaction) suddenly becomes a suburban norm in this movie. Paying on instalments, buying on credit—these things were not new but the *attitude* toward them is new: the United States of Commodification is being born wearing *Skinner's Dress Suit*.

And so was the peculiarly American conceit that pure entertainment was a value tied to money. The only reason the Skinners succeed both as fake monied people and as real monied people is because they use the vacuous entertainment medium of nightclub dancing as both the means to and the ends of their financial success. This, too, was a fairly new phenomenon that took firm root and became a "normal" part of the American economic landscape beginning in the 1920s. There had always been "entertainers" who marketed their dancing skills to make a living (Vernon and Irene Castle are the first American couple to come to mind, of course), but that was their professional occupation. *Skinner's Dress Suit* nor-malized the idea of *non*-entertainers using dance or other artistic talents/skills to advance their economic interests in businesses outside the entertainment business itself. Put it this way: Mickey and Judy wouldn't have shouted "Let's put on a show!" in the 1930s if it hadn't been for *Skinner's Dress Suit* in 1926.

Watch *Skinner's Dress Suit* and you are watching the America of the 1950s being born.

Bonus: Laura La Plante is a close-enough ancestor of Barbara Billingsley's wife in TV's *Leave It to Beaver*: short feminine blonde hair, stylish but nicely (conserva-tively) dressed, constantly aproned, living her fulfilment through her husband's job. She's far more of an airhead than Billingsley's "Mom" ever was, but she is establishing a new type of American housewife, not modifying an old one as Billingsley did.

La Plante had been in pictures for nearly five years, without any great impact, when she was chosen one of 1923's WAMPAS Baby Stars. (The so-called Western Association of Motion Picture Advertisers would pick 13 young women they thought were headed for stardom each year from 1922 to 1934.) Although this "competition" gave a boost to many actresses over the years, including Joan Crawford, Clara Bow, and Ginger Rogers, the help it gave La Plante was a little slow in coming. She got more jobs in the immediate aftermath, but they were usu-ally Westerns, where the ladies weren't exactly taken seriously as great dramatic (or even comedic) performers.

By 1925, though, La Plante was a major star and remained so for the rest of the silent era. Her peak, most likely, was 1927's *The Cat and the Canary*, a grand old ripping yarn, one of the best of the old-dark-house comedy-mysteries; Bob Hope's 1939 version of the same film remains the funniest of its many remakes and is certainly among the three or four best films Hope ever made. La Plante made a dozen films in the 1930s, but the impression remains that her career flamed out quickly when the talkies came in.

La Plante was an undeniable charmer onscreen. She was wholesome and scrubbed and perky if a little colorless, the kind of sweet little good girl who made Clara Bow look loose, exotic, and dangerous in comparison. Some people find her aren't-I-adorable radiance off-putting; others fall in love (not in lust) with her at first sight and never cease sighing for her.

A SMALL TOWN IDOL

(1921, Sennett)

Director: Erle Kenton
Writers: Mack Sennett, Raymond Griffith, and John Grey
Camera: J. R. Lockwood, Perry Evans, Ernie Crockett, and Fred Jackman
Editor: Allen McNeil
Cast: Ben Turpin, Phyllis Haver, James Finlayson, Marie Prevost, Charlie Murray, Dot Farley, Al Cooke, Bert Roach, Billy Bevan, George O'Hara, Ramon Novarro, Derelys Perdue, Eddie Gribbon, Kalla Pasha, Jack Richardson, Louise Fazenda, Andy Clyde, Lige Conley, Gordon Lewis
Running Time (Length): Seven reels

Background: By 1921, Mack Sennett knew he had to produce feature-length comedies on a fairly regular basis if he wanted to continue to be regarded as the King of Comedy. He was rapidly losing ground to Hal Roach in the field of two-reelers, but Sennett's distribution deals had trapped him into pouring most of his time, money, cast, crews, and attention into the shorts. Others were also nipping at his two heels by now, such as Educational Pictures (which were anything but). The greatest comedians—Chaplin, Keaton, Langdon, Lloyd—were only a year or two away from abandoning the short form; Mabel Normand, Roscoe Arbuckle, and Douglas Fairbanks had already graduated. It was clear that comedy was undergoing a seismic evolution in form, and Sennett had to make some moves despite his hands being cuffed by his distribution deals.

He threw almost everything the Fun Factory had left into a giant stew-pot called *A Small Town Idol*. The cast list above is only about half of the total number of comedians (if you're willing to concede Ramon Novarro was a comedian) who appear in this film. I was tempted to add, "… however briefly," but those whose appearance in it is brief are usually in it *twice*, playing *two* brief roles. There are three writers, reportedly two directors, and reportedly five cameramen (I've listed four because the fifth is unconfirmed), which is another hint at Sennett's desperation. If he wasn't going to stay on top with quality, he would do his damnedest to stay there with quantity.

Synopsis: Ben Turpin, cross-eyed son of a cross-eyed mom, is on the verge of marrying his sweetheart (Phyllis Haver) when the dastardly, conniving villain (James Finlayson, who else?) accuses him of being already married, and to a big-time movie-star hottie at that (Marie Prevost). This being small-town America, the crowd of well-wishers turns instantly into a crowd of ill-wishers, and Turpin is driven out of town, vowing to return in triumph to vindicate himself.

And guess what? He does exactly that! "Super Art Films" turns him into a major Western movie star, and Ben returns to "Edendale" ready to clear his name and marry his patient sweetheart. Regrettably, nasty Fin retains contrary ideas. While the townsfolk are all clustered into the local theatre to watch Ben's latest "super art film," Haver's dad manages to shoot himself by accident, and Fin latches on to the evidence so he can accuse Ben of the dirty deed. Sheriff Charlie Murray has no choice, under frontier justice (Edendale is apparently still frontier), but to jail Turpin until a necktie party can be organized for him.

Fin, a would-be rapist and abductor in addition to his lesser non-virtues, exploits Turpin's situation to force himself upon Haver. Once the lynching jamboree begins, the plot complications get quickly wrapped up—calling in the marines does help—so we can move to the climactic showpiece of the film: one hell of a fistfight between Turpin and Finlayson.

Comment: Because it is feature length and people were still ambivalent about the feasibility of stretching out slapstick for seven reels, Sennett doesn't try to go for wall-to-wall laughter. Turpin in particular seems unclear as to which parts of the film are uproarious and which are pathetic (in the melodrama sense); he plays much of it straight. Finlayson, too, appears to believe his role is one that cannot be amusing: he is really a rotter of a character, through and through, and Fin declines to play him as a mere caricature of evil.

Fortunately there are enough pro comedians around these two who refuse to believe anything is off limits to fun. Onscreen or off, Charlie Murray was unable to ever resist turning the most solemn of occasions into an opportunity for buffoonery; he's a card, with wonderful comments about the lynching in particular. Marie Prevost has fun being a snotty movie beauty. Dot Farley manages to keep her eyes crossed long enough to be a credibly funny mother to Turpin, and she gets a great intertitle while watching the movie-in-the-movie: shocked to see Turpin's onscreen character jump off a high cliff, she turns to him in the audience and asks worriedly, "Were you killed?"

As always, the sublime Phyllis Haver beats everybody else for comic timing and expression. The hurt in her face when she watches Turpin's movie character kiss Prevost, and the nuance of changes of expression as she turns to Ben beside her in the audience, are an awe-inspiringly beautiful blend of humor, heartbreak, and bewilderment. Just minutes later, Haver will be punching Finlayson and getting shoved around with real manhandling; more than any other leading female comedian (including Gale Henry, no delicate violet), she could do the physical slapstick with the best of the boys and make it look real. She's got the pathos Turpin is looking for, and unlike Turpin, she doesn't sacrifice a single laugh to get it.

Bonus: It should be noted that the full seven-reel version of this film has been supplanted by a two-reel cutdown that eliminates a lot of Turpin's Hollywood episode. Reviews over the decades suggest that the shorter version is better, snappier, and funnier.

Obviously the epic fight between Turpin and Finlayson was inspired by the rousing brawl that electrified the blockbuster version of *The Spoilers* in 1914 (at least, it electrified the audiences of 1914; it's rather tame by today's standards). *Small Town Idol*'s battle is far better and uglier than that of *The Spoilers*, far more vicious, more than a little scary or disturbing, and the little bits of humor scattered throughout it add up to ensure its overall superiority.

However, Stan Laurel put an end to all efforts to top it for the next 20 years when he made his satire in 1923, *The Soilers*. (He was actually, very quickly, parodying the latest version of *The Spoilers*, which had been released only a few months earlier in 1923.) Laurel had the chutzpah to cast Finlayson in the same role of the bad guy in the fight, which was a bit of a nose-thumbing at Sennett.

Not only did Laurel and Fin proceed to bloody and obliterate each other for what seemed like hours on end, he had the guts to mock the entire machismo fakery of it all by having a blatantly gay cowboy swish around the fighters time and time again, culminating in his blowing a kiss at the victoriously staggering Laurel and cooing "My hero!" at him. Far from being offensive, the deliberately stereotyped "sissy" is killingly funny, *precisely* because he's showing up the silliness of manly-man brawls.

When John Wayne went at it with Randolph Scott in the next retelling of *The Spoilers*, in 1942, it was impossible for anyone who had seen Laurel's version to take the brawl seriously. Comedy trumps violence.

SOLD AT AUCTION

(1923, Roach)

Director: Charley Chase
Writer: Charley Chase
Titles: H. M. Walker
Camera: Robert Doran
Editor: T. J. Crizer
Cast: Snub Pollard, Marie Mosquini, James Finlayson, Jack Ackroyd, Wallace Howe, William Gillespie, Charles Stevenson, Noah Young
Running Time (Length): 21 minutes (two reels)

Background: Four years of hands-on guidance from Charley Chase had made Snub Pollard's films solid and reliable, if still only second-rate. In today's parlance, his brand was established in the market: dependably breezy and amusing and slightly eccentric, featuring a guy whose Fu Manchu hit the all-important audience recognition bell bang-on. His movies got good production values and strong supporting talent because they delivered at the box office, at least sufficiently to cover their costs with a bit of profit left over (Pollard was never a box-office smash, but he was never a box-office dud, either).

Ravishing a house of beauty had paid off in big laughs with *On Location* (1921), so Chase decided to take Snub back to the same well with *Sold at Auction* just two years later. To make up for lost time, *Sold at Auction* was twice as frenzied, twice as zany, and twice as funny as the earlier film.

Synopsis: One of the most personally violent slapstick films ever made, *Sold at Auction* opens with a deceptively demure gag: Pollard as a baby in a basket is left abandoned on a doorstep, and 25 years later, he's still there, waking from a Rip van Winkle sleep to find himself fully grown, fully clothed, and not fully shaven. A second deceptively gentle gag follows: he helps a little boy cross the street amid heavy traffic without even a close call. When he turns around and heads back the other way on his own, however, all hell breaks loose. He gets smashed by one car, run over by another, stuck in the middle of a two-car head-on collision that drives his skull through a windshield, and is otherwise knocked around over and over again before getting bulldozed for blocks on the seat of his pants. The bulldozing vehicle finally pitches him through the plate-glass window of a storefront auction house, wherein he bullets straight into a massive display case of thousands of items for sale, all of which cascade upon him. No worries, mate.

The auctioneer, obviously a man quick on his feet, instantly uses Pollard's battered appearance to clear out his inventory of first-aid kits, selling them at premium prices to his audience of hitherto lethargic buyers. Ecstatic at the marketing gift presented to him by the gods, or at least by Charley Chase, he hires Pollard on the spot to undergo staged beatings by Noah Young with a variety

Snub Pollard, *Sold at Auction* (1923). *Author's collection*

of weapons, which weapons he then sells out on the strength of this personal marketing approach.

Meanwhile, James Finlayson's neighbor, poverty stricken and looking to auction off his household goods to stave off starvation, is handed the key to Fin's house as the latter takes his family off on what will turn out to be a very short vacation. (They travel in a motorcycle with two sidecars and two baby carriages spread out to either side like airplane wings.) The neighbor accepts this bounty and hires Pollard to sell Fin's household goods instead of his own.

Pollard is so successful he even sells off "Grandpa's" false teeth. But Fin arrives home just as Snub is wrapping things up; understandably disturbed to find his house emptied of goods, an apoplectic Fin orders Pollard to buy back every item. He does so . . . somehow.

Comment: Once again, we are treated to Charley Chase's near-mystical ability to conjure uproarious laughter even when a dismal substitute comedian is fronting the action for him. Almost any other comedian could have done the job as well as or better than Pollard. What drives this film is not the lead performer but the gags, which Chase conceived and directed. The hardworking, hard-luck guy trying to do a good thing by his neighbor/friend/co-worker and having everything backfire on him is a classic Chase setup. With *Sold at Auction*, he wanted to do something more cartoonish, more surrealistic than his own onscreen character would credibly undertake; it fits a performer like Pollard, who has never been a particularly credible onscreen character (mainly because he's never *had* any kind of a character) but who is undeniably a hard, energetic worker willing to take orders.

Chase really unleashed his technical creativity, too. He appropriately supplements the cartoonish violence by having the actual film itself perform cartoonish effects. When Pollard's "light is going out" (i.e., he's losing consciousness), a candle is shown through time-lapse photography burning down to its wick and snuffing out. When he receives a concussion from Noah Young's blackjack, the film-frame melts, with thin smears of blood trickling down. There's a madcap scene in which Pollard literally drives a grand piano through the streets, using the pedals to brake, and finding the leisure to study the sheet music for a song called "Goodbye."

"Beanie" Walker, the Roach Studio's ever-dependable title writer, comes up with droll lines such as this explanation of Fin's plan for going away: "He expected to have a pleasant vacation, but his wife insisted on going along." And there's a sly in-joke: the false teeth are purchased by "F. Newmeyer," a dig at denture-wearing director Fred Newmeyer. (The film's "Newmeyer" is an avid flyer; I wonder if the real Newmeyer was notoriously afraid of flying?)

Without a doubt, this is one wild and wacky movie, roisterous, entertaining, and full of laughs.

Bonus: A frequent foil to Pollard, Marie Mosquini is another of the unjustly overlooked women of silent comedy. A brunette of quite unusual attractiveness, she was incredibly prolific even by the standards of the time, making more than *thirty* films *per year* in three different years and more than twenty-five per year in another two years. It wasn't just her prettiness that got her the work, either: she knew how to play with lead comedians, how to give them space and support them at the same time. She more or less retired simultaneously with the entrenchment of the talkies and her marriage to Lee de Forest, a famous engineer who invented the vacuum tube and the first really workable talking pictures. Her reminiscences, as reprinted in Steve Rydzewski's lamented *Slapstick!* magazine of the 1990s, reveal her to have had an effervescent personality off the screen, happy and a bit scatterbrained, or at least not well organized as a writer.

A SPANISH DILEMMA

(1912, Biograph)

Director: Mack Sennett
Writer: Uncredited, probably Sennett
Camera: Percy Higginson
Cast: Fred Mace, Mack Sennett, Mabel Normand, Dell Henderson, W. C. Robinson, J. Jiquel Lanoe
Running Time (Length): About 6 minutes (split reel)
Availability: DVD (Classic Video Streams: *The Directors, Rare Films of Mack Sennett,* vol. 1)

Background: Mack Sennett, the true father of American film comedy (despite being a Canadian of Irish descent), broke into the movies as a bit player with D. W. Griffith at the legendary Biograph Company around 1908. Besides setting the template for film comedy, Sennett also hammered out the template of the ambitious, driven, pesty, won't-take-no-for-an-answer movie hustler: he had scarcely notched up a few unimpressive acting credits before he was inviting himself to join Griffith on long walks in order to pump him about the filmmaking business and to pitch him on the idea of letting Sennett write and direct (of course, writing and directing was what the actor *really* wanted to do, as the cliché goes).

It took a long time to persuade the master to let him have his head. In 1909, the Biograph studio created a small comedy unit that might just as well have been called "the Canadian company." Under the direction of Frank Powell (b. Hamilton, Ontario), it included Sennett (b. Richmond, Quebec), Mary Pickford (b. Toronto, Ontario), and Dell Henderson (b. St. Thomas, Ontario). Two years later, Sennett succeeded Powell and began turning the focus onto the first great female film comedian, Mabel Normand, whose father was French Canadian.

The troupe churned out split-reel (six to eight minutes each) comedies at a tremendous pace. These were still the beginnings of the motion picture, at least in the United States: resources were more or less whatever you could dig up on your own, settings were whatever was outside your front door, wardrobe was whatever you pulled out of your own closet, scripts consisted of a one-sentence idea, and the actors doubled as most of the production crew. It was all totally seat-of-the-pants moviemaking, and our modern-day expectations need to be tempered accordingly.

What always come across most strongly in these Biograph comedies is the sheer *fun* these people were having. It was a real lark, a bunch of energetic overgrown kids playacting and unself-consciously enjoying themselves.

Synopsis: Señorita Mabel is the object of the affections of "Jose" and "Carlos," respectively played by Mace and Sennett. The two men are brothers, so their rivalry is almost friendlier than their feelings for Mabel. As she cannot decide between them, they agree to indulge in some tie-breaking games. It's not exactly a down'n'dirty grapple to the death, though. They cut cards, repeatedly matching draw for draw. They shoot cards out of each other's hands, matching each other for accuracy and dexterity. They duel with swords, but so evenly that Sennett almost falls asleep in mid-parry. Dell Henderson, meanwhile, has been chivalrously squiring Mabel to and from these pulled-punches skirmishes, and incidentally commiserating with her at the lack of resolution to the rivalry. His ministrations lead himself and Mabel all the way to an engagement and marriage. "Jose" and "Carlos," having finally drawn playing cards that didn't match, present Mabel with the winner, only to learn they are both losers.

Comment: A charming example of the simple humor of early comedy films, and that's not meant to be a condescending assessment. The viewer can hardly help but giggle as Mack and Fred struggle with their outsized, stereotype "Spanish" costumes, including the sombrero, or as they fake playing the guitar while singing under Mabel's balcony and end up wandering off in a duet that visibly entertains themselves far more than chasing the señorita does.

Bonus: Also recommended amongst Sennett's Biograph productions:

The Brave Hunter (1912): Mack is a phony big-game hunter chased up a tree by a real but very tame little bear that happens to be Mabel's pet.

Tomboy Bessie (1912): Mabel is an effervescent and annoying little brat sister, bent on driving hapless and inoffensive Mack away from the older sister whom he's trying to romance.

What the Doctor Ordered (1912): Hypochondriac Mack, his wife, their daughter Mabel and her suitor (Edward Dillon), and an adolescent Jack Pickford (Mary's real-life notorious wastrel of a younger brother) are ordered up into the snowy mountains for a health break. Pickford is obviously having the time of his young life throwing snowballs for probably the first time since his family deserted Toronto for New York City in 1907.

Helen's Marriage (1912): Mabel's father refuses to allow Edward Dillon to marry his daughter Mabel, but when Dillon spots a film crew, they hoodwink Dad into allowing them to star in a "movie marriage" scene that turns out to be all too true. Bonus points to this little sweetheart of a film for showing us how casual and spontaneous filmmaking was in those days (Sennett, who directed this film, directs the fake film-within-the-film too) and for treating us to the sight of the hulking, balding Fred Mace in bridal drag.

STEAMBOAT BILL, JR.

(1928, Buster Keaton Productions/United Artists)

Director: Charles Reisner
Writer: Carl Harbaugh
Camera: Dev Jennings and Bert Haines
Editor: J. Sherman Kell
Cast: Buster Keaton, Ernest Torrence, Marion Byron, Tom McGuire, Tom Lewis, J. J. King
Running Time (Length): Seven reels
Availability: DVD (Kino Lorber)

Background: In the mid-to-late 1920s, Buster Keaton's professional and personal lives were coming apart. His marriage to Natalie Talmadge was a humiliating, furious battleground, feeding his descent into adultery and alcoholism. While he was creating his greatest feature films, they were bombing at the box office; and when he grudgingly made lesser films for the sake of popularity, they bombed too.

Straddling these twin mountains of failure was his brother-in-law and business-manager/producer Joe Schenck, who had his own marital hypocrisies and movie-business failures to hide from Keaton. Although they genuinely liked each other, Keaton and Schenck clashed over the making of *Steamboat Bill, Jr.* Schenck brought in Harry Brand, a useless bean-counter, to ride the bucking bronco of Keaton's budget; Keaton essentially ignored him. Schenck refused to allow Keaton to implement the flood finale he wanted, because it was coming too closely on the heels of a real Mississippi flood; Keaton did get a wet climax to the film, but he did so by leading up to it with a stupendous—and stupendously expensive—cyclone instead.

In the end, the jaw-dropping destructiveness of the filmed cyclone proved the perfect metaphor for the filmmakers themselves.

Synopsis: "Steamboat Bill Canfield, Sr." is in trouble. He may be physically huge and intimidating with a temper and bitterness to match, but the much smaller, much older, and much richer "John King" has not only put his stamp on every business in town (including the bank), he has also introduced a "floating palace" that will put "Canfield's" dilapidated steamboat on the rocks, metaphorically and potentially literally. But help is coming in the form of "Canfield's" son, whom he hasn't seen since babyhood. (One of the unpursued questions of this film is exactly why the wife and son have spent two decades living far apart from the husband and father—Boston and somewhere along the Mississippi River, respectively—without permitting the father even one parental visit.)

Anticipating a hulking brute even more formidable than himself, "Canfield, Sr." is dumbfounded and humiliated to discover the boy is instead Buster Keaton at his most fey: a ukulele-plucking, beret-sporting, zoot-suit-wearing, Frenchman's-moustache-cultivating little wuss, half his dad's size and one-thousandth his manliness. Making things worse is that this scrawny wimp is the romantic partner of "King's" jaunty young daughter, "Mary." "King" himself is no happier about the romance; the two fathers clash repeatedly in their mutual efforts to squash this Montagues-and-Capulets love.

Although his efforts to remove his son's outward trappings of Eastern hipness eventually succeed, "Canfield, Sr." fails to crush the romance and he resolves to ship the boy back to Boston. Before that can happen, the father finds himself in jail thanks to "King." The son proves his external alterations have resulted in some internal alterations too, as he attempts to pry his old man out of the can. Alas, this effort is unsuccessful, and "Canfield, Jr." ends up in the hospital while his dad is still behind bars.

Then a cyclone hits town with much the same violence that "Canfield, Sr." had expected "Canfield, Jr." to do. Houses are ripped apart, trees are uprooted, the river is flooded, "King's" boat is capsized, the jailhouse is pushed off its moorings and into the river, where it is set to become "Canfield, Sr.'s" watery coffin. "Canfield, Jr." miraculously survives a series of astonishing disaster gags, including the eternally famous one in which the entire front of a two-story house crashes down upon him and he happens to be standing exactly where an open window lands. Good thing that window wasn't shuttered.

With the characteristic Keaton flourish of mechanical improvisation and unstoppable athleticism, spurred by love (both for "Mary" and for his father) and the simple will to survive, "Canfield, Jr." saves his father, his girlfriend, her father, and a convenient minister to bring everyone together in a happy finale.

Comment: From start to finish, *Steamboat Bill, Jr.* is a virtually perfect melding of story, comedy, and spectacle. Every scene has genuine laughs in it, even the quite serious one in which the father attacks "King" in the streets for having had his old steamboat condemned. Choosing a suitably macho hat has never been funnier. Attempting to sneak out for a midnight rendezvous has never elicited so many belly laughs. Natural disasters have never stimulated such gargantuan prop gags.

Marion Byron was only 16 years old when she played "Mary," and she looks even younger, maybe 13 or even 12: she hasn't even developed physically yet. While this makes her less than convincing material for marriage, it explains her character's bubble-headed perkiness and the attraction of her innocent flirtiness. You have no trouble understanding why a college kid like "Canfield, Jr." has fallen for her, and why a tough riverman like "Canfield, Sr." refuses to take her seriously as a prospective daughter-in-law.

At the opposite end of the spectrum is Ernest Torrence, who was three times Byron's age and four times her size. Torrence was a dominating supporting presence throughout the 1920s in both comic and villainous roles. Rivaling *Steamboat Bill, Jr.* as his most memorable performance was his absolutely terrifying work in *Tol'able David* (1921), the stuff of nightmares. His sheer size drew the eyes of viewers whenever he was onscreen; not being a camera hog, and believing himself to be strictly a supporting actor no matter where his name was located on the billing, Torrence never tried to steal a scene. Nevertheless Keaton still had to work hard to compete for the viewer's attention whenever they appeared together in the frame. The silent era produced extraordinary supporting actors—Oliver Hardy, Vernon Dent, Frank Alexander, Nils Asther, George K. Arthur, Noah Young, Theodore Roberts, Sunshine Hart, Tully Marshall, Josephine Crowell, Joseph Swickard—and Torrence was one of the very best of them.

Bonus: This film, great as it is, elicits a certain amount of sadness in retrospect, because it was the last time Keaton was free and easy in his production independence. Box-office failures and overspending put him so deeply in a financial hole that he had to look outward for help; his trusting nature and his aversion to the business side of business (so to speak) led him to blindly put his signature on an MGM contract when Joe Schenck put it in front of him.

As long as silent films were still the norm, MGM gave Keaton a loose leash. That lasted only two films, however: *The Cameraman* (also 1928) and *Spite Marriage* (1929), both of which are very good precisely because Keaton still had most of the artistic control. With the entrenching of the talkies, MGM yanked the leash extremely tight, and Keaton never again had the freedom to make a really good movie.

STRIKE

(1925, Goskino)

Director: Sergei Eisenstein
Writers: Sergei Eisenstein, Valery Pletnyov, and "the Proletkult collective"
Camera: Edward Tisse
Editor: Uncredited (probably Eisenstein with assistants)
Cast: Alexander Antonov, Mikhail Gomarov, Maxim Shtraukh, Grigory Alexandrov, Yudif Gliser, I. Ivanov, Boris Yurtsev, Ivan Klyukvin
Running Time: Roughly 90 minutes depending on version
Availability: DVD (Kino Blu-ray: *Battleship Potemkin* and *Strike*)

Background: Almost certainly the best-known and most highly regarded—and without question the most influential—Russian filmmaker ever, Sergei Eisenstein made his feature-length debut as a director and writer—as an auteur—with this movie about a factory strike under czarist oppression. It disseminated his theories about montage, which even today is a major part of the basic grammar of film.

Very famous even among people with barely a passing acquaintance with silent film, *Strike* is actually a still-frequently amateurish movie. Eisenstein's work became much smoother with its follow-ups, *The Battleship Potemkin* (1925), and *October* (1928). He had a bit of a hiccup with *Old and New/The General Line* (1929); then, after long periods of political "re-education" and state-imposed silence, he toiled for years to produce three titanic historical dramas: *Alexander Nevsky* (1938), *Ivan the Terrible Part I* (1944), and *Ivan the Terrible Part II* (1946). And that was pretty much it, unless you include the unfinished and not-very-interesting *Que Viva Mexico!* (1932, completed by others in 1979).

Synopsis: Discontent at a factory explodes when persecution by czarist puppets and spies leads to a worker's suicide. A strike is called, and everyone is excited and united. As it drags on, and as the puppets sow discord and factionalism among the workers, solidarity melts. Betrayal is facilitated. Basically, everyone on the side of good gets wiped out.

Comment: I know what you're thinking: "*Strike*, one of the world's greatest silent *comedies?!*" And I fearlessly respond, "You bet!" What's more, it doesn't matter at which end of the political spectrum you position yourself: *Strike* is hilarious, *intentionally* hilarious.

Strike is the Revolution as slapstick. One reason why I hated this film on first viewing was that I didn't realize it was supposed to be a comedy, and not even a satire but a flat-out knockabout farce. It's a Mack Sennett production of an Orson Welles picturization of a Clifford Odets screenplay, starring everybody who ever pulled on a Keystone Cops uniform.

Ten similarities between *Strike* and classic American slapstick:

1. A bad guy gets dumped headfirst into a vat of wet cement, much to the hilarity of every onlooker.

2. Two guys slug it out while balancing on top of a board that is teeter-tottering on the back of a prostrate mug.

3. After an extended sequence of people being attacked with water cannons, an intertitle immediately announces solemnly, "Part Six: Liquidation."

4. The main gang of goof-ups spends the first quarter of the film trying to get out of work, and the rest of the film trying to avoid going back to work. They fail.

5. The insurrection is ignited by somebody playing an accordion.

6. Editing is at breakneck speed, and full of visual non-sequiturs, just like Sennett films.

7. The three stockholders are played by Ton of Fun clones.

8. There is a snooty, sniffy butler who rolls his eyes disdainfully, albeit at the capitalist rich pigs instead of at the no-class, no-breeding, no-hope working-class losers.

9. Pratfalls and knockabout comedy abounds.

10. All the characters are caricatures.

There's no denying that *Strike* is also one hell of an ugly film. Cats and men alike are shown hanged, and (in the case of the cats) are allowed to remain visible in the background for ages. A child is thrown off a walkway to its death. A strike leader has his windpipe crushed in a doorway. A cow is bludgeoned and has its throat cut and its chest ripped wide open while it's still alive, all in full frontal close-up, without a flinch of the camera.

All that said, it's a heck of a gutsy film. Eisenstein threw in every damned trick he could think of, including double exposures, fancy wipes, overlapping/dissolving images, juxtaposition, parallel editing, reverse and upside-down photography, mirror photography, crazy camera angles, fish-eye lenses, everything, and damn the consequences.

For the most part, it's a mess, and for the most part, it's a mess that works. The energy driving this film is tremendous, the chaos reflects the chaos of an out-of-control strike, the caricatures help the viewer overcome the facelessness of the cast in order to identify the heroes and the villains, and nobody could control mob scenes like Eisenstein. He stinted on nothing—the water-cannon attacks, though overly long, are riveting precisely because they are obviously the real thing, not staged entirely through clever editing (though that's a part of it in some places). Certain ideas go no place, such as the elaborate introduction of the spies by their nicknames and animal counterparts, but they're left in there like stray wires in an elaborate lighting arrangement, usefully useless or uselessly useful, whatever you want, it's all part of the goulash of revolution.

For all that essential ugliness, it's a convulsively funny film. It's enjoyable to watch Eisenstein at a time when he was still having fun, before he began taking himself and his Soviet film genius responsibilities too seriously, and before the Stalinists decided to make him a public whipping boy to intimidate all the other brilliant Russian artists into toeing the line.

Bonus: One of the stranger silent comedy shorts to surface on YouTube in recent years is a Russian film whose title translates into something like *Baldy Is in Love with the Dancer*. Made in 1916, it stars and was directed by a significant comic in Russian film history, a transplanted Englishman known only as "Reynolds." Though there is some footage missing, the story is easily grasped: "Baldy" falls for a belly dancer and tries to meet her, or perhaps it's simply the dance itself that he falls in love with and tries to promote in various social settings.

The astounding thing about this film is "Baldy's" attempts to mimic the dance, which he does roughly every three seconds. (I do not exaggerate the frequency.) Each time, he essays a swivel of the hips from side to side, then quickly tacks on blatant pelvic thrusts, straight into the camera. The other actors react as if he has obscenely propositioned them, obviously "mistaking" his efforts to belly dance as a demand for sex. This is, truly, one of the oddest Russian comedies ever made; after the first gasp of shocked laughter, the viewer watches in stunned, giggling disbelief. (My thanks to David Denton for bringing it to the attention of www .nitrateville.com members in November of 2015.)

THE SUNDOWN LIMITED

(1924, Roach)

Director: Robert F. McGowan
Writer: Hal Roach
Titles: H. M. Walker
Cast: Mickey Daniels, Mary Kornman, Jackie Condon, Joe Cobb, Allen Hoskins, Andy Samuels
Running Time (Length): Two reels
Availability: DVD (Good Times Video: *Hook & Ladder* / *Hi Neighbor* / *Sundown Limited*)

Background: The filmography compiled by Leonard Maltin and Richard W. Bann in their flag-bearer book, *Our Gang: The Life and Times of the Little Rascals* (1977), lists 88 silent Our Gang comedies, plus another 133 talkies. Although there have been plenty of ensemble kiddie-comedy movies and TV shows over the past century, Our Gang's 23-year run still stands alone for the size and time span of its oeuvre—and for its quality.

Roach had long wanted to create an ongoing series of comedy films in which real kids would behave like real kids, rather than like a childless moviemaker's uninformed guesses as to how kids behave. Paradoxically, the first child he cast was Ernie Morrison, a precocious black lad who had already appeared in many Roach films (including some of Harold Lloyd's shorts) and even in his own brief series as "Sunshine Sammy"; despite this young lifetime in front of the cameras, Morrison's appeal was his absolute naturalism and total lack of self-consciousness or cuteness.

Although Morrison was the bedrock upon which Our Gang was founded, his lead was taken over by the time of the third film, which saw the introduction of Mickey Daniels. Was it racism? Not necessarily. Consider these facts: (1) Morrison continued to have major roles in the series until the talkie era; (2) he was replaced by another black fellow, Eugene "Pineapple" Jackson; (3) Allen "Farina"

Hoskins was a second black lead in almost all of the silent films even at age one; and (4) Hoskins's sister Jannie ("Mango") was sometimes a third black rascal in the troupe.

No, there was just something about Mickey Daniels—maybe the freckles so thick his face looked like cream of tomato soup—that drew the eye of the viewer; he was also usually the tallest and therefore the one to whom the other kids looked for leadership (and adults looked for accountability for the gang's mischief); and, as Maltin and Bann explained, "his wide range of wonderfully natural expressions . . . made Mickey easy to identify with and 'pull' for."

The other key members of Our Gang in the silent era were Mary Kornman and Peggy Cartwright as the dream girls, Jackie Condon as the troublesome but adorably tousle-haired little brother, Jack Davis as the rough tough kid, the aforementioned "Farina," and Joe Cobb as the sweet-tempered, sweets-loving fat boy (he didn't make his first appearance until the seventh film). Andy Samuels also appeared in several of these early films but seldom had a key role or a consistent character.

Synopsis: Boy, do those kids ever love trains! In fact, Mickey and Joe love them so much, they take off at the controls of a real one while the adult engineers are on lunch break. They run over Farina four times—Mickey's excuse is that "Us engineers got enough responsibility without looking after children"—but that's okay! What's not okay is that the adults punish them by kicking them out of the railyard. Moping outside the gates, they note that "Toughy" and his pal have built a dog-pulled locomotive that has attracted the ladies as passengers. What a great idea! And the Gang just happens to be sitting on top of an old boiler and sundry other remnants discarded from real trains, and there's a spur line right there in front of them; what's more natural for these rascals than to immediately build an insanely wonderful train, consisting of a locomotive and three cars? Stretching the limits of credulity, they complement the train with a ticket office, telegraph office, mail pickup, sleeper cars, and water tower to refresh the canine engine, all of this apparently slapped together in about fifteen minutes (with no visible adult help, either).

The fickle ladies desert "Toughy" for luxury berths in the Sundown Limited. This provokes "Toughy" and his sidekick to try several methods of sabotaging the superior railworks. Eventually they succeed in breaking up the tracks; but the indomitable Sundown Limited never hesitates as it careens through the gates and out into the streets. Dodging all over the roadway, smashing into vendor carts, blasting through buildings, dragging four cops for a mile on the seat of their pants, the train finally overturns while speeding down a hill, and the Gang scatters with even more speed.

Comment: Choosing just one Our Gang short is like choosing just one candy from a box of Smarties. You can hardly go wrong, whatever you pick. And like Smarties, the basic sweet chocolate doesn't vary much from candy to candy; it's just given a different coating. The plot of *The Sundown Limited* is pretty much the same as that of *The Big Show* (1923) and *Fire Fighters* (1922), to name but two. I picked *The Sundown Limited* mainly because it stretches the limits of the kids' imaginative repurposing of leftover junk parts about as far as they could ever go, whereas *The Big Show*'s repurposing is limited to putting different disguises on live animals. In addition, each Gangster has a slightly more distinctive character in this film.

Bonus: Those two other Our Gang silents with similar "transformation" themes, mentioned above, are well deserving of equal status as key, top-drawer entries in the series.

The Fire Fighters opens with a witty anthropomorphic parody in which a duck dressed in suit, tie, hat, and shoes goes all hubba-hubba over a provocatively dressed chicken, only to be run off by a police bulldog and then hen-pecked (what's the duck equivalent of hen-pecked?) by his wife-duck all the way back home, which turns out to be Sunshine Sammy's urban animal farm and laundry service. It's a fun opening, adroitly seguing into Sammy's efforts to outwit his mule and goat while helping to deliver the laundry washed by his mother and trundled off by his extremely aged father. Cue George Rowe and companion, who tap into a large tank by the barn for some suspicious liquid. Meanwhile, Sammy and Mickey are getting torn up by the tank's guard dog until they resort to the standard Our Gang ploy of setting a cat for the dog to chase. The dog blasts away after the cat at such speed that the tank-shed to which it was chained is ripped apart, and Sammy beholds the tank as the perfect fire engine. Then follows the usual brilliant translation of everyday materials into three fire engines, the barn into the fire station, etc. . . . the fantasies of an eight-year-old Mickey Rooney co-fathered by Rube Goldberg and Busby Berkeley. Lots of fun, as always.

The Big Show starts rather slowly, but once the Gang decides to put on their own circus, it becomes one of the iconic Gang films. Their transformation of dogs, ducks, cats, goats, and cows into cartoon versions of wild animals has all of the ingenuity with which they transformed refuse into a working railroad in *The Sundown Limited*; they even use the same trick of creating an "engine" by having a dog chase a caged cat to create the power that makes their gimcrack mechanisms mobile. Turning a dog into an elephant with a sock for a trunk, turning a cat into a giraffe by sticking a guinea pig at the top end of a long tube attached to the cat's body, making a dog into a zebra by adding black stripes to its white coat—just wonderful, imaginative stuff. Farina obviously enjoys playing the tiniest cop in history; and Jackie, who plays the vengeful "too little to play with us men" shunned villain, is given credible motivation for his destructive behavior. It is unsettling to see the many dogs of their circus end the movie with an enormous, fearsome dogfight that obviously was never scripted, but at least the kids have enough sense to keep away. The "movie within a movie" is brilliant; who knew a mere kid could do such a spot-on imitation of Chaplin in 1923, let alone imitations of Harold Lloyd, Douglas Fairbanks, and Ford Sterling? (The kid playing the cowboy isn't certain if he's Tom Mix or William Hart, and I'm not entirely sure who the girl is supposed to be: the curls suggest Mary Pickford, but she—if it's a she; I think it's a boy playing a girl—plays coy in a way Mary wouldn't have done.) The only disappointment is that there really aren't any girls in the Gang at this point; we barely see even the chick playing the snooty (Swanson? Negri?) society dame on "Sterling's" arm in the audience.

T

THREE OF A KIND

(1926, Standard/Joe Rock Productions)

Director: Harry Sweet
Cast: Frank Alexander, Hilliard Karr, Bill "Kewpie" Ross, Lois Boyd, Billy Franey
Running Time (Length): 23 minutes (two reels)

Background: Comedy has often—not always, but often—been the one exception to whatever political correctness happens to be in vogue throughout history. Comedy such as the commedia dell'arte was the only art that could make fun of the Catholic Church in the 16th and 17th centuries, when the Church was all powerful throughout Europe. Jesters were the only artists permitted to insult monarchs—as long as they could make him laugh, at any rate—from earliest monarchical times up until the position was "downsized" in the 18th century. Comedians like Lenny Bruce, Mort Sahl, and Godfrey Cambridge made their mark on American culture by being the only people allowed to mock Jews, blacks, current politicians (*bitterly satirize* the politicians, not lob affectionate joshings at them like Bob Hope did), and so on, albeit they did still get persecuted for it by the narrow foreheads of their era.

In silent films, anything was fair game for the comedians. All ethnic groups were caricatured. An exaggeratedly effeminate gay stole the show in Stan Laurel's *The Spoilers.* All disabilities were treated with rude humor, and fat people were easy targets because they were fat. Frank Alexander was visibly obese; Hilliard Karr and Kewpie Ross were merely big, heavy-set men. Together they were an imposing sight; put them inside fat suits and you had "Ton of Fun"—three guys, each of whom appeared to weigh more than 300 pounds and as a team were capable of stopping a runaway freight train merely by standing in front of it.

For three years, they made quick two-reelers for Joe Rock at one of the weaker studios. Rock had a good comic mind, and the films mostly stuck with a single set where all the mayhem took place, with outdoor shots utilizing freely available spaces that made the production values look better than they were; the results were a lot of very good comedies that have been lost from the culture, presumably because it is no longer acceptable to laugh at fat people.

Autographed greeting card of the *Ton of Fun*: "Fat" Karr, "Fatty" Alexander, "Kewpie" Ross. *Author's collection*

Synopsis: Welcome to yet another restaurant-bar called "Ye Bucket o' Blood"! Charley Chase wasn't the only comedian to be fond of this commercial name. One wonders what sort of clientele the owner expected his place to attract with that moniker. Well, in the case of *Three of a Kind*, he evidently expected a formally dressed class of patrons to show up for the advertised "refined entertainment." He got the formal dress, but he failed to provide the refined entertainment; his drunken Irish singer is not just booed from the stage, he is physically attacked and removed via stretcher.

This opens up an opportunity for Lois Boyd to call up her heavy friends as emergency replacements. Lois is the cigarette girl in the place, a job that was assigned to her when her skinflint uncle got thrown out for trying to cook his own meal with his own utensils at their table, and stuck her with the bill for her own meal. As a rube visiting town for the first time, of course, Lois had no money and was promptly put to work.

Her pals charge down the street like a snowplow, dominating the sidewalk and shoveling everyone else to the sidelines. The maître d' introduces them as "The Barrel Brothers," and they begin singing, dancing, juggling a piano, doing a Hawaiian act, and generally stinking up the place until the customers attack. It's war!

Comment: A well-paced film throughout, *Three of a Kind* builds to the most convulsively funny restaurant fight in silent cinema. The choreography of that fight is a thing of beauty. From the start of the movie, the laughs are strong even when the gags are old or predictable. One customer needs to brace himself to glance at his bill for the evening; Charlie Chaplin had done a wonderful "collapse" reaction to his restaurant bill in *The Immigrant* (1917), but in *Three of a Kind* the customer explodes with an apparent heart attack on the spot. When Lois's uncle is kicked out, he insists on a dignified stroll across the room to the exit, followed by the maître d', who is followed by the clenched-fists bouncer, who is immediately followed by a diminutive customer bearing a vase of mournful flowers for the anticipated funeral. When the war between entertainment and appetite is in preparation, the leader of the customers (Billy Franey) orders a massive crate of fruits and vegetables and proceeds to go around the room passing out this ammunition. Franey's first blow is a punch to Alexander's gut: it bounces back so fast and so hard, it knocks out the second-in-command, who was standing well back of Franey.

An unsung riot, *Three of a Kind* is best watched with a bunch of friends who are in the mood for broad—and broad-beamed—humor.

Bonus: Karr and Ross were basically unknown even in the 1920s—Karr had starred in a "fat" comedy series in the Teens that had only local success, and the local was Florida, where the series was filmed, so he wasn't a "name" by any stretch of the imagination. Alexander was a heroic supporting heavy, most commonly associated with Larry Semon; he was clearly expected to be the leader of Ton of Fun and is always found in the center of the trio, a space he made by being easily the fattest of them. In other words, Ton of Fun consisted of lifetime supporting actors, and the team concept wasn't designed to make stars out of any of them.

The three hefties were surrounded by help of a similar order. With the exception of guest appearances by Gale Henry, every person in their films is an actor who spent his or her career in the background. Lois Boyd, the female lead in most of their movies, was appallingly inept; she was the kind of "comedian" who spins her eyes every time she gets bonked on the head.

The lack of name comedians was probably one of the reasons why the Ton of Fun movies were allowed to fade from memory. This does not, however, mean that either the films or the performers (other than Boyd) were less than effective, or less than funny. They were both.

TIME FLIES

(1926, Educational)

Director: Jesse Robbins
Writer: Lupino Lane
Camera: Robert Doran
Cast: Lupino Lane, Wallace Lupino, Virginia Vance, Gwendolyn Lee, Otto Fries
Running Time (Length): 20 minutes (two reels)

Background: Generations of Lupinos went into the making of Lupino Lane as a stage performer in England: they were the first family of theatre entertainment (not acting) for so long, Lane could hardly be suited by genetic inheritance for any other kind of life. His name was actually Henry Lane George Lupino; it was changed at the demand of a rich aunt who vowed to make him her heir in return, but who then maliciously screwed the family by leaving them none of her fortune.

The family specialized in acrobatics, comedy, song, and dance. Lupino Lane had incredible physical flexibility and control; his composure while twisting, bending, and leaning his body gave absolutely no indication of the agony he was actually enduring as a consequence of broken bones, especially in his legs. These were comical contortions, too: he knew how to use them for funny effect.

Already a born king of the stage in England and having served an apprenticeship in a few British films, he headed west to conquer American movies in 1922. This coronation, like the inheritance, did not take place. His main onscreen character, that of a wealthy British twit who inexplicably could toss off Olympic-level gymnastic routines, never caught on. Even more importantly, and partially explaining the failure of the character too, was the fact that Lane never got a decent studio or script in the eight years he spent trying to crack the U.S. market. On this side of the ocean, he didn't have the clout of Chaplin, Keaton, or Lloyd to strike out on his own; he didn't have the support of Sennett or Roach; he didn't get a stable of great comic writers like Clyde Bruckman, Jean Havez, and Charley Chase; he didn't even get decent supporting comics, unless you consider Glen Cavender a decent supporting comic.

After a start with Fox, Lane got stuck at Educational Pictures. Worse, he got stuck at Educational Pictures just when Jules and Jack White were beginning the recycling-of-old-wheezes philosophy that applied not only to their gags but also to their stable of worn-out, lethally damaged, or otherwise unwanted comedians. It was a struggle for anyone, let alone an outsider like the foreigner Lane, to get their own decent material winched into the garbage scripts and productions foisted on everyone by the Whites. By the time the talkies had come in and Lane had gotten lost in a couple of them, he'd had enough of being a second-rater, and went back to being a first-rater on the English stage.

Synopsis: Lane plays three roles, although the first two are quite brief. Those roles comprise three generations of men who in chronological turn handle a fancy pocket watch. By the time the watch reaches the current generation, it is worth a million dollars. Lane falls prey to the thieving machinations of a forgettable Otto Fries and his unforgettable accomplice, the coruscating Gwendolyn Lee.

Comment: Gwen Lee has no shape to her body, not up front or in back or around the sides, but her dress and her performance make her sizzlingly sexy, possibly the only truly hot babe in any Lupino Lane film. Otto Fries and Lee's chasing of Lane, for once in a Jack White production, is very well done and structured to give maximum platform for Lane's outstanding acrobatics. His display of tumbles and falls and splits and slides in this film is the best on his available record, and that's why *Time Flies* represents Lupino Lane at his most entertaining. The only caveat is the extremely abrupt ending to existing prints; this may suggest missing sequences, but I don't think so—I think it is like the ending of *Only Me*, a last gag cut off too quickly.

Bonus: Because Lane never got a really solid script or production support in his American silent film career, his movies are all fairly mediocre and are saved only by his outstanding stage skills. But those skills are so prodigious, and can be so

Lupino Lane, publicity still. *Courtesy of Steve Rydzewski*

amusing in themselves, that he ranks as a significant silent comedian in spite of his woeful material.

A sampling of his other films:

Maid in Morocco (1925): A typical Educational Studios mix of future Three Stooges gags (bad), Jack White's disgustingly amateurish use of wires to make Lane leap superhumanly (bad), and White's blandly presented racism (bad), mashed up with Lane's occasional opportunities to show what a real superhuman acrobat and human flexboard he could be (good). One moment he's doing an astounding leg-split-and-pop-up, followed immediately by a total reverse spin and fall from a standing posture (good); the next minute, he's being forced by the degrading White to do one of those planted-foot turnaround runs that Curly Howard was to make his signature move (bad). Dressed in drag as a houri in the caliph's harem, he does a dance that goes from a Charleston to a vaudeville strut to a Rockettes line dance to a music hall Eddie Cantor shuffle to a can-can and finally plain old dance-floor acrobatics (good). And then White gets in a couple more racist gags to close the film on a grating note (bad).

Fighting Dude (1925): This film was written and directed by Roscoe Arbuckle under his "William Goodrich" pseudonym after scandal broke his own career. There are several Keaton rip-offs here, the most obvious being the effete aristocrat taking a chauffeured drive to the next house (*The Navigator*) followed by Lane tripping over the ropes when he enters a boxing ring (*Battling Butler*). And then there's the Chaplin rip-off of the masseuse torturing the undersized shrimp at the gym. The brothers Lupino Lane and Wallace Lupino do a synchronized comic boxing turn that probably slayed the audiences of the 1920s; we've seen so many variations on it, both before and after 1929, that it just doesn't impress anymore. Two small cameos make it a momentarily interesting film: one is an unbilled Dick Sutherland getting a toe-curling close-up as a scary boxer—he makes Rondo Hatten look like David Niven—and the other is George Davis playing the butler in a very gay manner.

Movieland (1926): Lane plays "Lester Limberlegs," a not exactly quotidian name that nevertheless nails Lane's greatest attribute. After wasting several minutes with a fancy-clothes problem that no one in the audience can identify with, he tries repeatedly to get into a movie studio facility in order to pursue his adoration of Kathryn McGuire, an "actress." This section of the film isn't bad, but it isn't inspired, either. The movie palpably perks up when circumstances lead him to pretend to be a dummy. This gives Lane the chance to display his truly impressive bodily control. For example, placed side by side with a "real" dummy, both sink slowly to the floor with amazing "soft bones" or "boneless" torpor that has to be seen to be believed.

And then, for some obscure reason, writer-director Norman Taurog and Lane completely waste the God-given prop device of a revolving room. Lane just braces himself against the varying walls as they roll over and over. It is incomprehensible why they didn't seize this vehicle to display his tumbling skills; they could hardly have received a more perfect device for that purpose.

Private Life (1926): Another William Goodrich (Roscoe Arbuckle) production. Arbuckle recycles several gags from his and Buster Keaton's *The Cook* (1918), a vastly superior film, which is recommended elsewhere in this book. Most blatantly, he uses the same horrifying gag of having a chef slam a huge chopping blade straight down on the comedian's neck, and it's not a rubber blade. Somehow it doesn't work as well in *Private Life*, and I can't quite figure out why. Possibly because the camera holds the joke this time, giving the audience time to recover from its shock; in *The Cook*, Arbuckle and Keaton practically threw away the gag, which made it all the more scary.

Hello Sailor (1927): A collection of tired gags and *ur*-Three Stooges destruction. The brothers Lane/Lupino perform as a full-fledged but unofficial team again, Wallace giving as good as he gets. There's *way* too much pushing and kicking each other in tit-for-tat fashion; it gets boring in a hurry. The only bright spot is the radiant Charlene Aber as the female lead (her sister Miniella, though a near-identical twin, is not as attractive in the second-girl role); beautiful Charlene resembles the young Lillian Roth of the Marx Brothers' *Animal Crackers* (1930).

Howdy Duke (1927): Lane plays a double role as a snotty, self-assured, athletic duke and the riffraff look-alike who impersonates him at a posh reception. It is impossibly lame. When director/writer Norman Taurog is bad, he's the absolute worst.

Naughty Boy (1927): Lane's father, looking to marry by faking his age, has told his bride-to-be that his adult son Lupino is just "a darling little boy," so of course Lane has to dress and act like a little boy when he's introduced to his future stepmother. But he falls for her daughter, Kathryn McGuire, in an adult way. Lane wears a Little Lord Fauntleroy suit and a curly red wig that looks exactly like what Harpo Marx was wearing on the New York stage at the same time. This film is a cut—a very small shaving-nick—above the usual Lupino Lane film because it makes a conscious effort to provide more comedy and less acrobatics.

Be My King (1928): Shipwreck survivors Lane and his brother Wallace Lupino wash ashore and straight into the cooking pot of stereotypical African tribesmen (and women: one of them is determined to marry Lane). Aside from a lovely bit of vaudeville synchronized soft-shoe-shuffling (in dirt, no less), this is a tired film full of the same gags that the Three Stooges would later, er, refine.

Only Me (1929): I did not choose this famous movie to be the representative Lupino Lane comedy because I find it a giant phony of a film. It is supposedly a one-man show, but in fact there are *many* unidentified supporting performers (only his brother, the inevitable Wallace Lupino, has ever been admitted to having appeared onscreen with Lane). They play with their backs to the camera, or with hair or other items obscuring their features, but there is no way the physical inter-action between Lane and the other characters could have been done artificially at that time; this isn't Mary Pickford kissing Mary Pickford in *Little Lord Fauntleroy* (1921), this is Lupino Lane interacting with actors pretending to be Lupino Lane in various disguises and costumes.

A second reason why I didn't pick it is because it steals much too blatantly from far better comedies starring far better comedians. The obvious influences are Chaplin's *Night in the Show* (1915) and Keaton's *The Playhouse* (1921), but Lane even steals from W. C. Fields (the "T'aint a fit night out for man nor beast" scene) and Harry Langdon (some of the facial reactions and physical mannerisms), plus Harold Lloyd, Stan Laurel, and others. There is, in fact, very, very little in *Only Me* that is shtick done by "only" Lupino Lane. The best thing about it is the wrap-up gag that closes the film. Even there, the scene is truncated and we barely have a second to laugh before "The End" pops up.

TRAMP TRAMP TRAMP

(1926, Harry Langdon Corporation/First National)

Director: Harry Edwards
Writers: Arthur Ripley, Frank Capra, Tim Whelan, Gerald Duffy, Hal Conklin, Murray Roth, and J. Frank Holliday
Camera: Elgin Lessley, George Spear
Editor: William Hornbeck
Cast: Harry Langdon, Joan Crawford, Tom Murray, Edward Davis, Alec Francis, Brooks Benedict, Carlton Griffith
Running Time (Length): 61 minutes (six reels)
Availability: DVD (Kino Video: *Harry Langdon: The Forgotten Clown*)

Background: The first official Harry Langdon feature film was not the first one he made; that honor belongs to *His First Flame*, made less than a year earlier than *Tramp Tramp Tramp* but not released until two years later as his fourth feature.

His First Flame is very good, yet it is a rather odd and uneasy sandwich of genre situations wrapped around one of Langdon's most freakish transgendering excursions. It makes eminent good sense to have shelved it temporarily and gone with *Tramp Tramp Tramp* as the film that would establish his marketability as a feature comedian.

The move to features fractured the team that had put Langdon there. Director Harry Edwards preferred to stick with short films and returned there quickly after *Tramp Tramp Tramp*. Head writers Arthur Ripley and Frank Capra openly tried to push Langdon in opposite directions. Langdon, because he now produced his films through his own corporation, became the employer instead of the co-worker; never having been a business boss, he did not know how to treat his employees. In the past, creative differences were usually settled by the expedient of Langdon simply ignoring the advice of other people and doing whatever he felt was right, without confrontation; now he became imperious and behaved as though differences of opinion had to be stamped out forcefully. That was not the way Capra was ever going to let himself be treated.

Synopsis: Who could possibly resist the unusual beauty of the 22-year-old Joan Crawford? Certainly not "Harry Logan," the witless but enthusiastic only child of beleaguered cobbler "Amos Logan." Old "Amos" is getting squeezed six ways

Brutal chain-gang criminals tenderly commiserate with Harry Langdon on the occasion of his nose getting bumped in *Tramp Tramp Tramp* (1926). *Courtesy of Bruce Calvert*

from Sunday, or at least two ways: his rival, "John Burton," is blanketing the countryside with his big-box shoe stores in pursuit of a national monopoly on footwear, and his landlord, "Nick Kargas," a champion long-distance walker (it is true long-distance walking competitions were huge in North America in the 1920s), will evict the old sole-heeler if he doesn't pay his back rent, and some forward rent would be helpful too.

"Amos" puts his faith in his son. Why? Well, family loyalty aside, it's not as though he has any other options. Besides, "Harry" is deliriously obsessed with "Betty" (Crawford), and she's going to present a $25,000 check to the winner of a walkathon; "Amos" prays the prospect of meeting the girl of his dreams to receive the check from her delicious hands will put wings, or maybe roller skates, on "Harry's" feet.

Oblivious to the fact—blared everywhere around him, including on his competition sweater and on the billboards featuring "Betty"—that the contest is sponsored by Burton Shoes for the greater glory of Burton Shoes and the destruction of his father's business, "Harry" makes a lifelong enemy of "Nick" just prior to the start of the race. This is most regrettable, since "Nick" got to be a champion by using dirty tricks as well as his impressive physique.

Three long gag sequences dominate the race, with terrific interstitial smaller gags linking them. The first, probably instigated by writer Tim Whelan who had served his apprenticeship on Harold Lloyd's thrill comedies, sees Langdon hanging literally by a thread from a high board fence over a sheer drop off a mountainside. At first he tries to extricate himself; then, upon realizing he will fall at least a mile if he frees his sweater from a nail, he frantically pounds every nail he can find through his sweater into the board. The nails he finds happen to be holding the boards of the fence together, so he ends up sit-surfing down the mountainside when the boards break off. There's a bit of a cheat here: the lead-up visuals clearly show an absolutely straight drop, but "Harry" sit-surfs down a rather gently sloping hillside. Notwithstanding that little bit of deception, the situation is delightfully realized.

A riotous short scene gets starving chicken-and-watermelon-thief "Harry" assigned to a chain gang to break rocks. This is another trope of silent slapstick, and again Langdon adroitly plays it as no one else possibly could, making it fresh and, more importantly, *funny*. After reducing pebbles to grains of sands while his fellow prisoners break rocks into boulders, "Harry" gets caught up and then abandoned in a breakout. His ball-and-chain—the literal thing, not a metaphorical wife—gets cut off without his knowing it; the process of discovering his release is replete with supremely skillfully done variations on the old theme of dropping heavy rocks on the toes of cops and bad guys.

The third and probably most famous long gag sequence is a filthy "Harry" attempting to clean himself up in a town beset by a cyclone. No, Langdon didn't steal this from Keaton's *Steamboat Bill, Jr.* (1928); Keaton picked up the idea from *Tramp Tramp Tramp*, and you can see why. Langdon's mental blindness and blank-faced confidence in the face of a natural disaster is a perfect inspiration for Keaton's mental blindness and blank-faced confidence in the face of *his* natural disaster. Keaton even replicates Langdon's throwing of a brick (a stick, in Buster's case) at the unearthly winds. The difference is that Langdon's brick actually succeeds in running the cyclone out of town.

The predictable conclusion is elbowed out of the norm by a coda, which could only have been created by Ripley, in which Langdon plays his own baby. It's one of those moments that creep out those who dislike Langdon for his infantilism and weird sexual ambiguity; those who like him will find it charming . . . and a little odd, even for him.

Comment: The transition from short comedies to feature comedies has really never been an easy one, then or now: one only needs think of the alumni of TV's *Saturday Night Live* and, for that matter, a lot of other half-hour TV sitcoms who couldn't stretch out to ninety minutes. In the silent era, Roscoe Arbuckle, Max Linder, (arguably) Mabel Normand, and even Buster Keaton either failed (Linder), had to radically change their shtick (Arbuckle, Normand), or needed a couple of features under their belts before fully conquering the longer format (Keaton).

Langdon didn't manage the move as smoothly as Harold Lloyd did, but *Tramp Tramp Tramp* is top-rank work. Remember, he already had *His First Flame* as his true debut in features; *that* is the film that shows the creases in going for the long form. Nowhere in *Tramp* is there evidence that three shorts are being stitched together; the three outstanding sequences described above are fully integrated into the same storyline, thanks to that marvelous interstitial material, so that the entire film holds together as one steadily progressing plot.

Bonus: The public was primed to expect some really good comedy from Langdon's first feature because he had built up a body of quality short work that was already getting him hailed as one of the three great comedians of the era (Keaton wasn't considered one of the three, but the other two are whom you would expect). Yet the film lost money at the box office, and reviews were mixed. Exhibitors, quoted extensively in Chuck Harter and Michael Hayde's brilliant book *Little Elf: A Celebration of Harry Langdon,* seem to have been less than impressed, yet most of them note that their audiences enjoyed the film.

This somewhat wobbly reception was followed by ecstatic reviews and popular opinion for Langdon's next film, *The Strong Man* (1926). Capra directed it, and pushed it so relentlessly in his determination to make his own reputation that his ego may have been the difference maker in the public perception of its quality. Certainly, even today, *The Strong Man* is considered Langdon's best film. It is an outstanding comedy from beginning to end.

Capra, as we know, had an extremely aggressive and self-assertive personality, with "clean" and "positive" values that flowered into what others derisively labeled "Capra-corn." (You can bet your bottom dollar he's the one who came up with the idea of making the girlfriend blind: instant sentimentality, instant perceived "virtue" and "purity" because, of course, in Capra's universe blind people are totally incapable of sinful thought, let alone sinful action.) His fallout with Ripley was largely fueled by the clash of that drive for sweetness and light against Ripley's propensity to wallow in dark weirdness. Langdon needed that dark weirdness—it added an idiosyncratic (to say the least) psychology to his outlandish character. Capra mostly banished it from *The Strong Man,* and that's why I consider *Tramp Tramp Tramp* a superior *Langdon* film.

TWO TARS

(1928, Roach)

Director: James Parrott
Writer: Leo McCarey
Titles: H. M. Walker
Camera: George Stevens
Editor: Richard Currier
Cast: Stan Laurel, Oliver Hardy, Thelma Hill, Ruby Blaine, Charlie Hall, Edgar Dearing, Edgar Kennedy, Charley Rogers, Clara Guiol, Jack Hill, Harry Bernard, Sam Lufkin, Baldwin Cooke, Charles McMurphy, Ham Kinsey, Lyle Tayo, Lon Poff, Letta Palmer, George Rowe, Chet Brandenberg, Dorothy Walbert, Helen Gilmore, Frank Ellis, Fred Holmes
Running Time (Length): Two reels

Background: Just one month earlier, *Early to Bed* (1928) had slightly discomfited Laurel and Hardy's massively swelling legions of fans: it had broken with formula by pitting them against each other, instead of pitting them together against the world. It was crucial to their chemistry that any conflict between them should be forgotten in their united front against wives, cops, villains Finlayson or Kennedy or Hall, Tin Lizzies, recalcitrant buildings or building materials, and whoever else might be passing by and take an interest in their shin-kicking or pants-ripping competitions. Wasting no time in paving over the breach in strategy, the Roach brain trust put The Boys back on the same side again and pitched them into battle side by side as *Two Tars*.

Synopsis: On shore leave, mighty seamen Laurel and Hardy are determined to have what they imagine is the standard navy "good time." This consists of renting a Ford, picking up girls, and . . . treating them to gumballs. The gumball machine outside Charlie Hall's store buckles beneath their trained assault and covers the sidewalk with a treacherous rolling carpet. The resulting mayhem puts the boys and their gal pals into a suitable mood for the massive traffic jam they subsequently find themselves driving into. Road rage, 1928 style, ensues. Cars are ripped apart, camping items and furniture are flung and smashed, lunches are eaten—metaphorically and literally—cops are outraged, hair is torn—from Hardy's chest, *ouch!*—and it all ends with, first, a side-splitting parade of the wounded vehicles, and last, Laurel and Hardy teetering out of a railroad tunnel in their disastrously compressed auto.

Comment: Utilizing the modus operandi of so many of their silent shorts, Laurel and Hardy give us an opening sequence that gets us in the mood for hilarity and establishes their teamwork without overshadowing the major sequence to follow. And as always, that major sequence is just one howl of laughter after another, right to the kicker of a final scene.

Bonus: When it comes to choosing the funniest and most perfectly Laurel and Hardy-ish of their silent short films, most fans pick *Big Business* (1929) by a hair or two over *Two Tars*. The films are similar in making the most of the standard

Edgar Kennedy struggles to think of a suitably apocalyptic revenge to bring down upon Laurel and Hardy in *Two Tars* (1928). *Courtesy of Bruce Calvert*

Laurel and Hardy trope, i.e., the tit-for-tat war of destruction pitting The Boys against one of their usual enemies (Finlayson, Kennedy, or Hall). The champions of *Big Business* sometimes cite it as being the purest expression of that trope: there is no extended preliminary sequence to distract or waste time from immediately plunging into catastrophe, and the engagement is solely between The Boys and their sworn enemy, Finlayson.

In those regards, yes, *Big Business* is purer than *Two Tars*, which has a mild initial sequence and expends its destructive energy over dozens of opponents who do not really personalize their antagonism toward The Boys.

The major advantage *Two Tars* has over the later film is the expansiveness of its setting. Since *Big Business* is restricted to the exterior of Fin's house and The Boys' car, there are limitations to the violence that can be inflicted. *Two Tars* has dozens of cars that can be assaulted and wounded in a broad variety of ways. Some of the cars are hauling more utensils and gimcracks than Fin has in his entire house, all of which can be destroyed or used as weapons of mass destruction. Food, especially juicy fat tomatoes, is readily at hand for flinging. The hundreds of people in those cars are all ripe for their own variations of comic battering. There are simply more resources to fuel more creative acts of chaos, and to thereby instigate more hysterical laughter among viewers.

U

UNCOVERED WAGONS

(1923, Roach)

Director: Jay A. Howe
Writer: Uncredited, probably Charles and James Parrott
Cast: Paul Parrott (James Parrott), Katherine Grant, Noah Young, George Rowe, Mark Jones
Running Time (Length): 10 minutes (one reel)

Background: One of the mightiest hits of 1923 was *The Covered Wagon*, James Cruze's epic picture of the pioneers who crossed America westbound in prairie schooners. Although rooted in the basic reality of the excursion, the film was a compendium of Western hokum dangling from the palsied branches of the most tepid of cliché romances. Beautiful to look it, enervating to actually watch, its relentless march of banalities and tedium proved catnip both for the box office and for the comedians. Tens of thousands of Americans were drawn to its patriotic porridge. At least two comedians were drawn to its banal silliness. Will Rogers mocked it in *Two Wagons, Both Covered* the next year; Paul Parrott was even faster, whipping off *Uncovered Wagons* within weeks of the original hitting the screen.

Synopsis: In the days when the West was wild and untamed, pioneering souls braved the arduous trek from Ogden to Los Angeles in simple Ford Tin Lizzies. Led by intrepid explorer Paul Parrott, they let no obstacle stay their progress. Faced with deep waters with no bridge in sight, they—what else?—*Forded* the river to the other side. On that shore, they found themselves terrorized by Indians rampaging on bicycles. And not just any bicycles, either: they had two-seaters, three-seaters, even four-seaters, plus tricycles and an era-appropriate penny-farthing. Running out of ammunition for his rifle, Parrott rips off a fender, bends it into the shape of a bow, and starts firing the Indians' arrows back at them. Various other Wild West myths get kidded before Parrott and Katherine Grant traipse off to, presumably, get married, buy a homestead, and begin farming in downtown Burbank.

Comment: This is straightforward parody. Taking it that way, it's great fun, almost all of its gags still lively (if a tad drawn out) 95 years after it was made, political incorrectness and all. Parrott is onscreen most of the time, but he doesn't dominate: he's part of a full cast of travelers. As if to emphasize the point, Noah Young as the rebellious member of the troupe frequently challenges Parrott, and usually gets the best of it, yet always ends up losing somehow.

Bonus: It's a toss-up as to which Paul Parrott film is his best of 1923: this one, *Shoot Straight*, or *Post No Bills*. *Shoot Straight* is pure laughter, with gag after gag moving briskly. *Uncovered Wagons* has only three main gag sequences, each running about three minutes, which is about a half minute too long for each; the laughter starts to peter out before we get passed on to the next gag. *Post No Bills*, for a long time my favorite Parrott film, is weakened by a mediocre opening sequence in which Parrott does battle with Jack Ackroyd while trying to flirt with Marie Mosquini in front of the movie theatre where they all work. Once Parrott starts wandering around town pasting promotional flyers to people's derrieres and nailing them into glass shop-windows, it becomes a nonstop riot. Although those disappointing opening minutes cost *Post No Bills* its own page in this book, it is still **very** much worth seeing.

W

WHY CHANGE YOUR WIFE?

(1920, Paramount)

Director: Cecil B. De Mille
Writers: William de Mille, Olga Printzlau, and Sada Cowan
Camera: Alvin Wyckoff
Editor: Anne Bauchens
Cast: Gloria Swanson, Bebe Daniels, Thomas Meighan, Theodore Kosloff, Sylvia Ashton, Clarence Geldart, Maym Kelso, Lucien Littlefield, Edna Mae Cooper, Jane Wolfe
Running Time (Length): 91 minutes (eight reels)
Availability: DVD (Video Cellar)

Background: In 1918, Cecil B. De Mille released *Old Wives for New*. It was enough of a hit that he remade it the very next year as *Don't Change Your Husband* (1919). And when that proved just as big a hit, he remade the remake the following year as *Why Change Your Wife?* The modus operandi of modern-day franchise films like *Spider-Man* and *Rocky* could be said to owe everything to De Mille.

In fact, he remade the basic premise of this "marital trilogy" several other times in the late Teens and early Twenties, such as *Male and Female* (1919), *For Better for Worse* (1919), *Saturday Night* (1922), and so on. After that, he moved his peculiarly cynical moral goalposts a lot closer to self-sainthood by developing the biblical and pseudo-historical epics for which he is best known today.

Synopsis: Gloria Swanson and Thomas Meighan are happily married. At least, she is, because, as old wives know, being married means you never have to have sex again. Tom, like all husbands, thought being married meant getting free sex morning, noon, and night. He's having trouble adjusting to the reality that Gloria has imposed upon him, although she's not having any problems. Well, just one little problem, which is Tom's occasional but tiresome (to her) attempts to be amorous.

Gloria's solution is to wear specs and frumpy dresses with as much protective, practical underwear as she can stuff under her sackcloth and ashes. Her postmarital philosophy is (uttered in a deeply offended and scandalized tone of voice): "Do you want your wife to lure you?" The answer she assumes is an emphatic "No!"

Which proves to be incorrect, as Tom is easily seduced by the outrageously overdressed and sexually aggressive Bebe Daniels. "Merciless virtue is stronger than love—and wrecks a home!" dramatically announces one of De Mille's many, many, *many* D. W. Griffith–like pompous and verbose intertitles, as Gloria divorces Tom and he rebounds into Bebe's rapacious arms.

Learning her lesson too late, Gloria throws away her granny glasses and her granny gowns and her granny morals and reverts to being the hedonistic clothes horse that her publicity claimed she was in real life. She takes a holiday (from what? She does no work) at the same hotel where Tom and Bebe just happen to check in. Naturally Gloria and Tom fall in love all over again. By another coincidence (De Mille crams about thirty words into another intertitle to inform us we are "fools" for calling it that), Tom and Gloria end up taking the same train home.

De Mille is really having us on now. When the non-couple arrive in the city, he has Tom *slip on a banana peel* and knock himself out. Tom ends up recuperating in Gloria's home, which brings Bebe running to reclaim him. What ensues is a hell of a catfight, brought to a screeching (silent) halt by Gloria threatening Bebe with . . . *eyewash*. As in, "This nonsense is just a whole lot of—"

In a coda, Gloria demonstrates to us the proper attire and attitude of a wife. Dressed to the triple nines, she trots around like "Edith Bunker" (of TV's *All in the Family*), trimming Tom's cigars and serving his drinks, while Tom relaxes in his wing chair exactly like "Archie Bunker" in *his* wing chair. Unable to resist his compulsion to emphasize the obvious in yet another epic-length intertitle, De Mille haughtily informs women viewers of the moral of the film: "Wives should be sweethearts."

Comment: For all its lighthearted silliness, this film nails masculine complaints about wives with a guffaw-inducing accuracy. Yep, the hot babes we marry *do* think marriage is a justification for putting away the sexy negligees and dressing like an aunt instead of a sweetheart, at least after the first couple of years of rambunctious bunny-hopping. And yep, they *do* tend to hog the bathroom and disrupt our attempts to shave every morning. Not that the men are all that much better; see De Mille's earlier *Don't Change Your Husband*, and note that Meighan's character in *Why Change Your Wife?* is not only all too easily seduced by Bebe's obvious gold digger but is also stupid enough to commit the same marital error twice . . . or thrice, if you think he's wrong to remarry Gloria.

The clothes, supposed to be a recurring highlight, are disappointing: badly dated, but more to the point, poorly photographed. And the swimwear! Time has rendered it absolutely hilarious: women sporting voluminous layered dresses with eight-foot-long wraps, enormous gymnasium shorts underneath, elaborately embroidered silk knee stockings, feathery headdresses, parasols, and leather shoes with two-inch heels . . . to go swimming in! This was more than a dozen years after Annette Kellerman introduced the one-piece bathing suit, and a half dozen years after Mack Sennett firmly established the one-piece as the standard swimsuit by parading his Bathing Beauties in them in nearly every second film he produced. Making the watery overdressing even more anomalous was De Mille's defining excess of gratuitous lingerie and semi-nude shots on dry land. Whatever would he have made of the thong bikini?

Thomas Meighan is a likable fellow. He seems very natural and unactorly, prone to true-to-life eye-rolling at his wife's prissy behavior. If only he didn't glance inadvertently at the camera at least once in almost every scene; and Bebe Daniels does it, too . . . what was going on there? Was De Mille yelling at them so much they were losing confidence? Swanson never does anything so unprofessional. In fact, Swanson proves herself again to be a terrific actress, actually more convincing as a sobersides than as a flirty flapper (she tends to artificial hilarity too much when, in any film, she wants us to know her character is putting up a gay front to hide her heartbreak).

The fight between Bebe and Gloria doesn't use any doubles or cut any corners: Bebe really does bend Gloria over backward on the dressing table.

The ending is predictably pat, and you wonder how much longer they'll go on as a newly randy pair before Gloria gets tired of dressing sexily and waiting hand and foot on Tom, and Tom reacts by letting his eye roam again. But that's inconsequential, like the rest of the film. It's meant to be a lark, and that's exactly what it is.

Bonus: The first film in this series, *Old Wives for New*, is actually a serious melodrama. The second film, *Don't Change Your Husband*, is serious with a bit of levity in it, or call it a drama with comic overtones. By the time he made *Why Change Your Wife?*, De Mille had had enough of this eyewash and he played it for laughs. As always, comedy beats drama, especially melodrama: the third film is the one I would recommend to anyone interested in this phase of De Mille's career. It has tossed-off polish, proving De Mille was so talented—almost as talented as he considered himself to be—that he could turn out a completely satisfying entertainment while giving it less than half of his attention.

A WOMAN OF THE WORLD

(1925, Paramount)

Director: Malcolm St. Clair
Writer: Pierre Collings
Camera: Bert Glennon
Cast: Pola Negri, Charles Emmett Mack, Holmes Herbert, Blanche Mehaffey, Chester Conklin, Lucille Ward, Guy Oliver, Dot Farley, May Foster, Dorothea Wolbert
Running Time (Length): 70 minutes (seven reels)
Availability: DVD (Grapevine Video)

Background: The exotic and titillatingly peculiar European beauty has been a part of Hollywood since the town was invented as the center of the motion picture industry. It can be said to have started with Theda Bara in 1914; safely middle-American in real life (you can't get more middle-American than being born in Cincinnati), she was reinvented as the deadly vamp-woman from a mysterious place that seemed to be Arabia-in-Romania. That same mythical locale produced a string of similar vamps who were nevertheless true-blue Americans, like Nita Naldi (b. New York City), Evelyn Brent (b. Tampa), Valeska Suratt (b. Owensville, Indiana—apparently a vamp *can* get even more middle-American than being born in Cincinnati), and others.

In the 1920s, when the vamp craze was pretty much over, it finally occurred to Hollywood that maybe a European ought to be given the chance to play this quintessentially European femme fatale. For this purpose, they chose Pola Negri, a young Polish actress whose dangerously dark beauty made her visually ideal for a vamp.

Negri had built up film experience slowly and steadily, spending about three years in the Polish industry, which, being tiny and impoverished due to that country's difficult years during and after World War I, was easily conquered even by a teenaged girl. She then spent five years in Germany, mostly with Ernst Lubitsch. When the Americans came calling in 1923, she was ready to take on the biggest film market in the world.

Already she knew the value of reinventing herself (a practice she continued right up to and in to her 1970 autobiography, the humbly titled _Memoirs of a Star_), and of getting bad publicity whenever she could not get good publicity. She hit America with all the swanning and hysterics and adorably accented English of someone who was shrewd enough to practically invent the Grand Romantic European Film Star stereotype and milk it for all it was worth. Alleged affairs with everything in well-known pants, buffaloing a stunned Charlie Chaplin into a sensational engagement that she then even more sensationally broke off, flamboyant public grieving over the corpse of Rudolph Valentino (she infamously threw herself on his coffin after giving photographers a heads-up), more engagements to exiled royal playboys (and actually marrying one), studio-fabricated titanic "feuds" with the only female star who was still bigger than she was (the physically tiny Gloria Swanson)—Negri practically invented all of this baggage that every female European film star was expected to lug around over the next 40 or 50 years.

Her career in America was remarkably brief: her act on- and offscreen was old hat by 1926, just when Greta Garbo arrived to etch out the alternative stereotype of the mysterious, tragically beautiful, lonely sphinx of a European slinkster. _A Woman of the World_ captures Negri at the exact turning point of her American career: still the genuinely mesmerizing exotic, but sensitive enough to the growing titters and guffaws amid her shrinking audience to play the role for laughs as well as for glamour.

Synopsis: At home in the Italian Riviera, Pola Negri as the "Countess Natatorini" catches her latest boy-toy fooling around with another woman. He tells her that "as a _woman of the world_" (italics his), she should just laugh it off. Apparently, despite her world-weary demeanor and sophisticatedly sad half-smile, she isn't a true "woman of the world," because she takes it hard enough to decide on the spot that she will become a "woman of the other side of the world." And that's how she ends up in Maple Valley, a hick town somewhere in the midwestern United States, crashing with easygoing uncle Chester Conklin and his wife. So that we get the point about Conklin being poor but honest, he's given the fancy Italian (not!) name "Samuel Poore."

Negri is certainly exotic in this setting. In fact, not too subtly, she is constantly dressed in extravagantly profuse dresses and accoutrements (brought all the way from Italy in, apparently, a doctor's medicine bag, her only luggage from the train) of pure white and black, while all the townsfolk dress in various

Charlie Chaplin didn't appear in Pola Negri's *A Woman of the World* (1925) but the supposedly "engaged" couple posed for a publicity still together to keep the gossip columnists nattering. *Author's collection*

shades of grey. She's a brilliant white orchid among colorless wheatfields. Her hair is cut in a tight, slick bob with long curled sideburns, her eyebrows have been stenciled in with black highway paint after a complete plucking, she smokes—often with a cigarette holder, which somehow makes it even more scandalous—and most heinous of all, she has a small tattoo on her wrist.

She had told her Riviera plaything that while she might have been a woman of the world, she wasn't the world's woman. Maple Valley townsfolk would have it otherwise, mainly because of that tattoo. In that day and place, a tattooed woman was a trashy woman. And no one is both faster and slower to trash "the Countess" than "District Attorney Granger." In the timeless tradition of American politicians, he is the "stainless knight of Maple Valley" trying to impose his "lovely morals" (as the Madame Defarge town gossips call them with as much sarcasm as admiration), going so far as to jail male "escorts" who allow their girlfriends to smoke, which makes "the Countess" his Public Enemy Number One; at the same time, the two of them are of course in the grips of the most ill-matched passion since, I don't know, Sessue Hayakawa and Fanny Ward, maybe? (*The Cheat*, 1915).

Interestingly, everybody else in town seems to despise "Granger" even as they admire him and vote for him. He makes no friends and earns a lot of contempt with his efforts to get "the Countess" run out of town; she, on the other hand, appears to be well liked and retains the awed respect accorded an exotic sophisticate even as they go out of their minds with moral shock over the little tattoo.

The inevitable and completely unbelievable happy ending is provoked by "the Countess" horsewhipping "Granger" across the face in front of "the council" of old men who run the town. (Erich von Stroheim would approve.) It is a most satisfying inversion of the Hollywood old-men's convention that these uppity modern women all secretly love to be beaten half to death by their brainless hick goon of a husband/boyfriend.

Comment: A thoroughly enjoyable comedy, *A Woman of the World* is not great, not ambitious, certainly not a perfect film, but absolutely fun from start to finish. This is no surprise, given the cast. Three longtime Sennett veterans provide support: Blanche Mehaffey, Dot Farley, and Chester Conklin. (Conklin has a wonderful moment when he reveals *his* incredible tattoo.) Pola Negri can easily handle light comedy. Malcolm St. Clair was a reliable comedy director of great experience, to that point in his career mostly in the slapstick vein, but with this film he began making a big name for himself in light comedy features, too.

The opening scenes in the Riviera are played straight with a chaser of irony; they end up poking giggles out of the viewer, especially when Negri attempts to portray bitterly sardonic drunkenness. Once the film shifts to Maple Valley, though, St. Clair hits the right balance of tone for social farce. There's just no way in hell a real Italian countess would fall for the crusading Puritan district attorney—aside from his crusading, he's way older, not physically attractive, and totally deficient in charisma—and Holmes Herbert plays the role with the puzzled intensity that made him a fairly effective "Sherlock Holmes" in other films but which couldn't possibly arouse the sexual interest of the real Negri. From beginning to end, we never believe their mutual attraction for one second. St. Clair doesn't use this disbelief to ratchet up the farce or to milk cheap laughs, and it's debatable whether that makes the film stronger or weaker. Somebody like Richard Barthelmess in the "Granger" role would have given the concept both romantic and comedic credibility.

Negri has a delightful time playing the vamp. In addition to being completely credible as a sophisticated European woman-of-affairs, she has fun with her character's sense of mischief, which is never allowed to undermine her sense of self-worth. She really is a diamond out of place, dazzling the rubes without condescension or patronization; she seems to genuinely like them and avoids giving us any exposition as to why she does so, which makes it all the more sweet and sincere. As with any Negri performance, she's uneven in places (such as the drunken scene in Italy), but that's always a large part of her charm as an actress: it plays to her vulnerability, which makes the viewer like her.

In sum: a really pleasant vamp comedy, and a top number for Negri fans.

Bonus: In the European phase of her career, Pola Negri had been seen by everyone—herself, the filmmakers, the audiences, and the critics—as a serious actress of great potential and almost incidental great beauty. A genuinely talented performer, she needed a strong director to stabilize her presentation; left to herself, she tended toward overdramatization. Although mostly not comedies, her other work in silents can be recommended.

Gypsy Blood (1918): The "Carmen" story seems to work well in silent film, because the filmmakers go back to the original Merimee story instead of trying to find a way to replicate the Bizet opera in silence, and the story is so strong and colorful that it's almost impossible to do it wrong. Ernst Lubitsch has a few careless minutes in which he allows superfluous bits like the army attacks on the gypsies in the bluffs instead of ruthlessly excising extraneous material, but overall this film version is very strong. Negri is completely believable as Carmen, being very young and attractive, and also possessing the hard-hearted savagery and used-to-being-adored-no-matter-what-she-does quality of a young sexpot trading on her intrinsic and unshakable allure.

One Arabian Night (1918): This is one black-and-white silent film that would really benefit from color, or at least tinting: the settings and costumes must be gorgeously multihued. The plot is typical non-Arabian fanciful suppositions about the nature of true Arabian love stories, but since this is a German silent film, everybody goes mad and dies in the end instead of living happily ever after. God, I love German silent films—they give fatalism a good name. Pola Negri's attempts at being seductive and alluring look like a prepubescent virgin's first attempts at vamping her own four-year-old brother (or worse, her own mother), and a few other scenes expose her as a technically uncertain performer at this point in her career; but when she hits the mark, even if only for a fleeting second, she's so right that she makes you believe she's a truly great actress.

Eyes of the Mummy Ma (1918): She seems rather unsure of herself in this film, perhaps because the film is unsure about itself, too. As horror, it's pretty thin; as a melodrama about transplanting a foreigner into "civilized" society, only to have her killed by a past lover/owner, it's still pretty thin. All illusions about her character's Middle Eastern background are vanquished when Negri does her silly little dance, consisting of a faint shake of her hips evidently meant to simulate belly dancing. It drives the Western men wild with passion anyway, which further destroys the credibility of the whole enterprise. And then that nutty murder scene! Sure, it's undoubtedly happened in real life that someone has been killed by a fall down a mere three steps, but that's not a reality you can put across convincingly in a film.

Passion (a.k.a. *Madame Dubarry*) (1919): Legendary for many reasons, all of them right (i.e., deserved): spectacle, crowd scenes, sets, strong directing, and superb acting. It's very long, but Lubitsch keeps it moving, so much so that we end up feeling we got little more than a taste of the full story. Negri is completely natural in this film, and fully believable. It may be the only film in which her performance is consistent throughout.

The Spanish Dancer (1923): Pola was born to wear Gypsy clothes (possibly because her father was a Gypsy, although she always claimed he was a Slovak tin-smith). This film has much the same elements as *Passion*: spectacular sets, crowd scenes, a director who can frame wonderful shots and guide his actors to strong and consistent performances, and an unfortunate melodramatic and silly plot.

Hotel Imperial (1927): Mauritz Stiller is one of those directors whose camera placement and lighting instantly mark him as one born to the role. It's his natural medium. Fascinating angles, overhead shots, dollying and tracking shots, chiaroscuro, and framing all mark him as an instinctive master. But he is also skilled at gauging just the right amount of artifice in his actors' performances. Max Davidson offers a very restrained version of his *oy-vey-iz-mir* slapstick character for the lightest of comic relief; James Hall doesn't overdo the heroics, and neither does George Siegmann overdo the villainy. Pola Negri is deglamorized, frequently photographed in rather unflattering ways, with minimal makeup; both she and Stiller are obviously far more interested in extracting a serious dramatic portrayal than in showcasing her as a Beautiful and Famous Movie Star Proving She Can Act—and she really can. Especially good is her revulsion at the gross Siegmann even as she gamely leads him on carnally. This film is so well done, it takes a real effort to remember it is portraying *our* enemies (the Austro-Hungarian imperial army) as the heroes, and *our* allies (the Russians) as the evil villains.

The Woman He Scorned (1930): When Pola Negri sashays through the doorway of a den of iniquity known as the Blue Paradise bar, we're on our way through a stylishly done, noir-ish sequence among card cheats, whores, and brutal pimps. Then it transitions to her startling marriage to . . . a lighthouse keeper. We see this mismatched couple feeling their way through life together, and the story leads moodily to a tense climax that really sticks it to the anticipated Hollywood happy ending.

Negri has a few weak spots, as usual, but in general is truly excellent. And we get to really see both sides of her; she is strikingly beautiful, yet can also look flabbily dreary and isn't afraid to show off her too-broad Polish peasant's hips. She has real screen presence, and unlike in some of her other silent films, in this one she draws the light toward herself.

The film does have a problem with the intertitles, which interestingly enough are used strictly to convey dialogue (not narrative). Unfortunately, that dialogue is in hopelessly stilted English, totally unsuited to the petty sleaze of the characters and settings.

Y

YOU'RE NEXT

(1919, Jester)

Creator: Marcel Perez
Cast: Marcel Perez, Dorothy Earle, William Slade, Pierre Collosse
Running Time (Length): 21 minutes survive from two reels
Availability: DVD (Undercrank Productions: *The Marcel Perez Collection*)

Background: With the Great War over and a lot of great talent returning to the movies (e.g., Buster Keaton, about to hit his true greatness), Marcel Perez found himself competing with ever more comic product of intimidating quality. On the one hand, he was now more comfortable in American movies and had the self-confidence to let his wonderful comic imagination run more freely. On the other hand, he was still insecure as to what made Americans laugh, and continued to feel a nervous need to do what others were doing that seemed to be successful.

Notably, he was still working for lesser studios such as Vim, Eagle, Jester, and Reelcraft, which meant he wasn't able to access performers and crews that were up to his own level of skill and creativity. The jaw drops and the eyes pop at what might have resulted from the anarchic, cartoon-violence-loving Perez working with Larry Semon, Frank Alexander, and Oliver Hardy at Vitagraph.

Synopsis: In the Roscoe Arbuckle Comique tradition, Perez clearly made *You're Next* as two one-reelers, tenuously linked so that they could be split up and marketed separately if they didn't succeed as a glued-together two-reeler.

The first reel announces a sweep of "pirate landlords" in Harlem that results in "Twede-Dan" waking up to find himself, and sections of his former apartment, now established in the middle of a busy New York street. Maintaining equanimity, he invites the police department to join him in a game of checkers before they courteously assist him in relocating his premises into one of their jail cells—the one with eight prostitutes on one side of it and three drunken thieves on the other side of it. After a sweet night's sleep for all of them, especially the police—apparently no real crime ever happens in New York City at night—"Twede-Dan" entertains all in the morning with some ragtime piano. Everyone is released from their cells for a lovely dance. The thieves and prosties ungratefully take the opportunity to escape, which so upsets the trusting police that they toss "Twede-Dan" outside on his ear. He rolls up against Dorothy Earle, who is sitting on the curbstone, similarly evicted from her apartment even after trying to pay the landlady $300 in rent (probably equivalent to $300,000 today; the apartment probably rented for $3 per week).

And now the second reel is launched. A film studio just happens to be across the street—wait, wasn't that where the police station was located?—and a director invites Dorothy to join the movies. To demonstrate that he, too, deserves to be in the movies, "Twede-Dan" does a quite lengthy and reasonably good Chaplin imitation, which gets him hired . . . as a property man. Well, no surprise there, because his imitation had included getting run over viciously by a truck and falling straight off the top of a five-story building. The director must think he did it with props. (The director is right; this isn't *A Busy Night*, after all.)

The rest of the movie is fairly standard behind-the-scenes gags, similar to Ben Turpin's *A Studio Stampede* (1917) and Chaplin's own *Behind the Screen* (1916), not to mention many others. The last few minutes of *You're Next* are lost.

Comment: There are very good laughs throughout *You're Next* and it ranks among the best films Perez ever made, especially in America.

The second reel tends to get denigrated because he has taken a warhorse storyline instead of inventing something new; yet it is really funny in spots, such as a sequence in which various props (including "Twede-Dan" himself, or at least a dummy of him) get thrown back and forth across not one, not two, but three different movie sets, each time alighting on something that results in a truly hilarious group pose.

The first reel is something else: a great laugh from start to finish. Lloyd Hamilton ripped off its opening scene in his later film, the fine *Move Along* (1926), and developed its basic premise into his own best-known sequence. Perez's version of "living in the street" is actually funnier than Hamilton's, because Hamilton was going for pathos more than for laughs, whereas Perez is going for laughs and nothing but.

The languor and the amiable cooperation of the quasi-Keystone Cops is uproarious: they have to be the most mellow flatfeet in movie history, cheerfully taking the time to move furniture, assisting "Twede-Dan" in installing curtains in his cell, and serving him breakfast in bed. Perez sustains the mirth throughout the entire reel—even Dorothy Earle's eviction gets a big laugh when she offers the landlady a massive amount of money (and pulls out her bankroll to prove it's not just an empty promise).

Bonus: By 1923, Perez was done as an onscreen performer. Cancer had cost him a leg, and other injuries suffered in his performances had accumulated to the point where health forced him to retire from the screen. But he continued to work as a gagman, writer, and director almost until his death in 1929.

Bibliography

Agee, James. "Comedy's Greatest Era." *Life*, 3 September 1949, repr. James Agee. *Agee on Film*. Boston: Beacon, 1958.

Anthony, Brian, and Andy Edmonds. *Smile When the Raindrops Fall*. London: Scarecrow Press, 1998.

Balducci, Anthony. *Lloyd Hamilton: Poor Boy Comedian of Silent Cinema*. Jefferson, NC: McFarland, 2009.

Ballin, Albert. *The Deaf Mute Howls*. Washington, DC: Gallaudet University Press, 1998, originally published in 1930.

Basinger, Jeanine. *Silent Stars*. New York: Knopf, 1999.

Birchard, Robert. *Cecil B. De Mille's Hollywood*. Louisville: University Press of Kentucky, 2004.

———. *King Cowboy: Tom Mix and the Movies*. Burbank, CA: Riverwood Press, 1993.

———. *Monty Banks: A Filmography 1920–1924*. Middletown, DE: Author, 2015.

Blesh, Rudi. *Keaton*. New York: Collier Books, 1974.

Brownlow, Kevin. *Mary Pickford Rediscovered*. New York: Harry Abrams and the Academy of Motion Picture Arts and Sciences, 1999.

Cahn, William. *Harold Lloyd's World of Comedy*. New York: Duell, Sloan and Pearce, 1964.

Cantor, Eddie. *My Life Is in Your Hands* and *Take My Life*. Repr. two books in one, New York: Cooper Square Press, 2000; originally published in 1928 and 1957 respectively.

Cassara, Bill. *Edgar Kennedy: Master of the Slow Burn*. Boalsburg, PA: Bear Manor, 2005.

Chaplin, Charlie. *My Autobiography*. Middlesex: Penguin, 1964, repr. 1974.

———. *My Life in Pictures*. Toronto, ON: Bodley Head, 1974.

Connelly, Robert. *The Silents: Silent Feature Films 1910–36*. Highland Park, IL: December Press, 1998.

Dardis, Tom. *Harold Lloyd: The Man on the Clock*. New York: Viking, 1983.

———. *Keaton: The Man Who Wouldn't Lie Down*. London: Penguin, 1979.

Everson, William K. *The Films of Hal Roach*. New York: Museum of Modern Art, 1971.

———. *The Films of Laurel and Hardy*. New York: Citadel, 1967.

Fields, Ronald J. *W. C. Fields: A Life on Film*. New York: St. Martin's Press, 1984.

Fields, W. C. *W. C. Fields by Himself*. New York: Warner, 1974.

Guiles, Fred Lawrence. *Stan: The Life of Stan Laurel*. New York: Stein and Day, 1980.

Harter, Chuck, and Michael Hayde. *Little Elf: A Celebration of Harry Langdon*. Duncan, OK: Bear Manor Press, 2012.

Katz, Ephraim. *The Film Encyclopedia*. New York: Harper, 1994.

Keaton, Buster. *My Wonderful World of Slapstick*. New York: Da Capo Press, 1960/1982.

Kerr, Walter. *The Silent Clowns*. New York: Knopf, 1975.

Klepper, Robert. *Silent Films, 1877–1996*. Jefferson, NC: McFarland, 1999.

Kline, Jim. *The Complete Films of Buster Keaton*. Secaucus, NJ: Citadel, 1993.

Lahue, Kalton C., with Sam Gill. *Clown Princes and Court Jesters*. Cranbury: A. S. Barnes, 1970.

——. *World of Laughter*. Norman: University of Oklahoma Press, 1966.

Louvish, Simon. *Man on the Flying Trapeze: The Life and Times of W. C. Fields*. New York: Norton, 1997.

——. *Stan and Ollie: The Roots of Comedy*. London: Faber & Faber, 2001.

Maltin, Leonard. *Classic Movie Guide*. New York: Plume, 2005, 2010, 2015.

Maltin, Leonard, and Richard Bann. *Our Gang: The Life and Times of the Little Rascals*. New York: Crown, 1977.

Massa, Steve. *Lame Brains & Lunatics: The Good, The Bad, and The Forgotten of Silent Comedy*. Albany, GA: Bear Manor Press, 2013.

——. *Marcel Perez: The International Mirth-Maker*. New York: Undercrank, 2015.

——. *The Mishaps of Musty Suffer*. DVD Companion Guide. New York: Undercrank, 2014.

Massa, Steve, and Ben Model. *Accidentally Preserved: Rare/Lost Silent Films from Vintage 16mm Prints*. DVD Companion Guide. New York: Undercrank, 2013.

McCabe, John. *Babe: The Life of Oliver Hardy*. London: Robson Books, 1989.

——. *The Comedy World of Stan Laurel*. Beverly Hills, CA: Moonstone, 1990.

——. *Mr. Laurel & Mr. Hardy*. New York: Signet, 1968.

McCabe, John, with Al Kilgore and Richard Bann. *Laurel & Hardy*. New York: Ballantine Books, 1976.

McDonald, Gerald, Michael Conway, and Mark Ricci. *The Complete Films of Charlie Chaplin*. Secaucus, NJ: Citadel, 1965/1988.

Miller, Blair. *American Silent Film Comedies: An Illustrated Encyclopedia of Persons, Studios, and Terminology*. Jefferson, NC: McFarland, 1995.

Milton, Joyce. *Tramp: The Life of Charlie Chaplin*. New York: HarperCollins, 1996.

Mitchell, Glenn. *A–Z of Silent Film Comedy*. London: B. T. Batsford, 1998.

——. *The Chaplin Encyclopedia*. London: B. T. Batsford, 1997.

——. *The Laurel and Hardy Encyclopedia*. London: B. T. Batsford, 1995.

Moore, Colleen. *Silent Star*. New York: Doubleday, 1968.

Negri, Pola. *Memoirs of a Star*. New York: Doubleday, 1970.

Oderman, Stuart. *Roscoe "Fatty" Arbuckle*. Jefferson, NC: McFarland, 1994.

Paris, Barry. *Louise Brooks*. Minneapolis: University of Minnesota Press, 1989.

Pauly, Thomas. *Murder Will Out! And It Did, in "Chicago."* DVD Companion Guide. Los Angeles: Flicker Alley, 2010.

Roberts, Richard M. *Smileage Guaranteed: Past Humor, Present Laughter. Musings on the Comedy Film Industry 1910–1945*. Vol. 1: *Hal Roach*. Phoenix, AZ: Practical Press, 2013.

Robinson, David. *Chaplin: The Mirror of Opinion*. London: Secker & Warburg, 1984.

——. *Charlie Chaplin: His Life and Art*. New York: McGraw-Hill, 1985.

——. *The Great Funnies: A History of Film Comedy*. London: Studio Vista/Dutton, 1969.

Rogers, Will. *The Autobiography of Will Rogers*. Edited by Donald Day. New York: Avon, 1975.

Roots, James. *The 100 Greatest Silent Film Comedians*. Lanham, MD: Rowman & Littlefield, 2014.

Rydzewski, Steve. *For Art's Sake: The Biography & Filmography of Ben Turpin*. Duncan, OK: Bear Manor Press, 2013.

Sassen, Claudia. *Larry Semon: Daredevil Comedian of the Silent Screen*. Jefferson, NC: McFarland, 2015.

Schelly, William. *Harry Langdon*. London: Scarecrow Press, 1982.

Schuchman, John. *Hollywood Speaks: Deafness and the Film Entertainment Industry*. Chicago: University of Illinois Press, 1998.

Sennett, Mack, as told to Cameron Shipp. *King of Comedy*. New York: Pinnacle, 1975.

Skretvedt, Randy. *Laurel and Hardy: The Magic behind the Movies*. Beverly Hills, CA: Moonstone, 1987.

Slide, Anthony. *She Could Be Chaplin! The Comedic Brilliance of Alice Howell*. Jackson: University Press of Mississippi, 2016.

Stein, Lisa K. *Syd Chaplin*. Jefferson, NC: McFarland, 2011.

Stenn, David. *Clara Bow: Runnin' Wild*. New York: Penguin, 1988.

Stone, Rob. *Laurel or Hardy: The Solo Films of Stan Laurel and Oliver "Babe" Hardy*. Temecula, CA: Split Reel, 1996.

Swanson, Gloria. *Swanson on Swanson*. New York: Random House, 1980.

Vance, Jeffrey. *Chaplin: Genius of the Cinema*. New York: Abrams, 2003.

———. *Douglas Fairbanks*. Berkeley: University of California Press, 2008.

Vance, Jeffrey, and Eleanor Keaton. *Buster Keaton Remembered*. New York: Abrams, 2001.

Vance, Jeffrey, and Suzanne Lloyd. *Harold Lloyd: Master Comedian*. New York: Abrams, 2002.

Walker, Brent E. *Mack Sennett's Fun Factory*. Jefferson, NC: McFarland, 2010.

White, James Dillon. *Born to Star: The Lupino Lane Story*. Toronto, ON: Heinemann, 1957.

White, Wendy Warwick. *Ford Sterling: The Life and Films*. Jefferson, NC: McFarland, 2007.

Whitfield, Eileen. *Pickford: The Woman Who Made Hollywood*. Toronto, ON: MacFarlane Walter and Ross, 1997.

Index

About the Author

James Roots is the author of *The 100 Greatest Silent Film Comedians*, which the *Literary Review of Canada* called "one of the finest books on . . . 20th century pop cultural history ever written" and which *Huffington Post* chose as one of the best film books of 2014. A widely respected book reviewer for more than 25 years, he has also been a leader in the disability rights community for more than three decades. He was born and raised in Toronto and currently lives in Ottawa, Ontario, Canada.